1823-1827

GRAHAM GLEN

1855

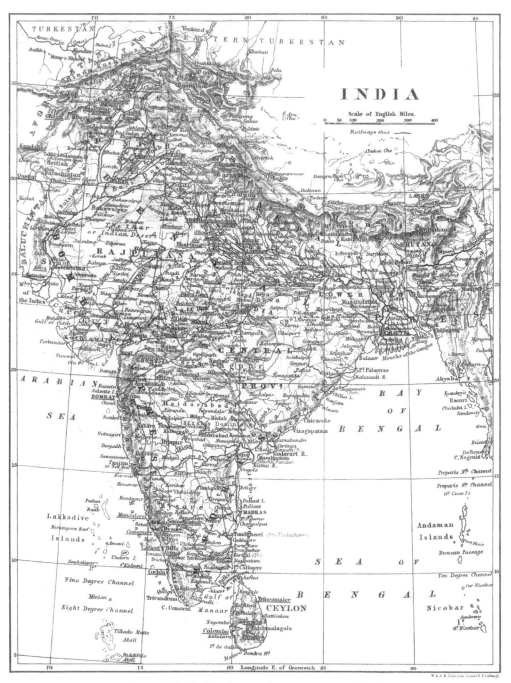

The places marked with red lines illustrate the movements mentioned in the text

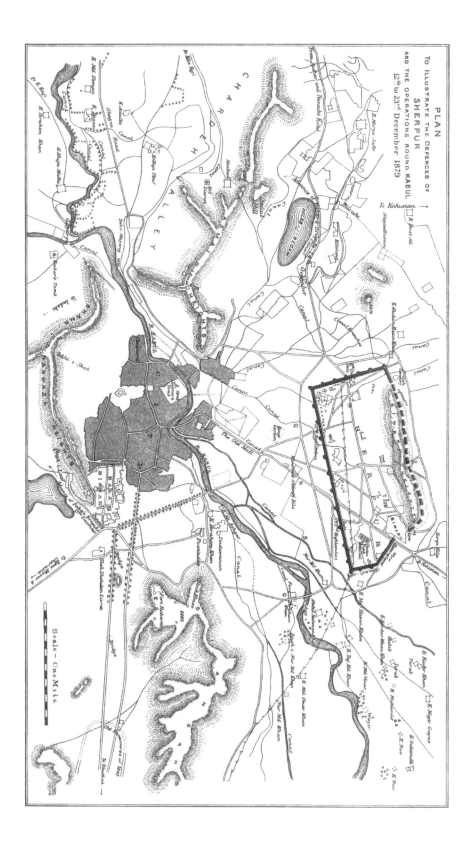

PLAN
TO ILLUSTRATE THE DEFENCES OF
SHERPUR
AND THE OPERATIONS ROUND KABUL
12th to 23rd December 1879

Scale—OneMile

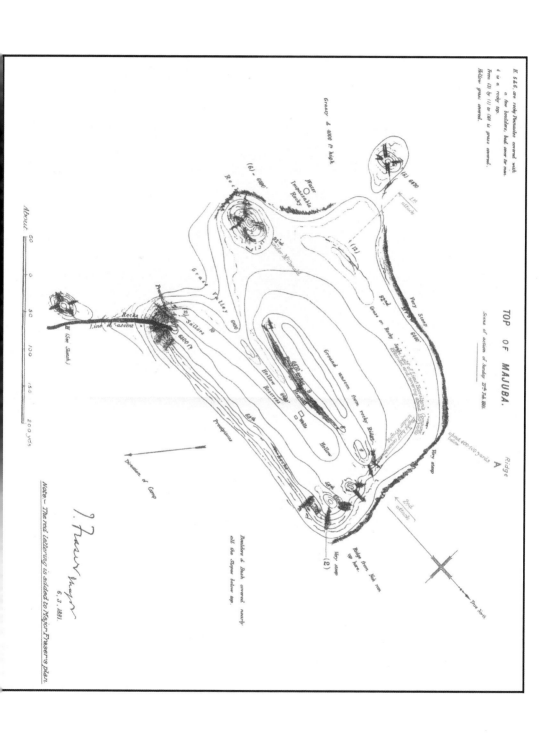

TOP OF MAJUBA.

Scene of action of Sunday 27th Feb. 1881.

A Ridge

Direction of Camp

Note.— The red lettering is added to Major Fraser's plan.

J. Fraser Major
6. 3. 1881.

About

50   0   50   100   150   200 yds

THE LIFE OF A REGIMENT
THE HISTORY *of the* GORDON HIGHLANDERS
VOLUME II

THE LIFE *of* A REGIMENT

THE
HISTORY OF THE GORDON HIGHLANDERS
FROM 1816 TO 1898

INCLUDING AN ACCOUNT OF THE 75TH REGIMENT
FROM 1787 TO 1881

BY

LT.-COLONEL C. GREENHILL GARDYNE

" I would therefore recommend you, as a last parting word of advice, to make yourselves intimately acquainted with the History of your Regiment."—*Extract from Farewell Order by Lieut.-Colonel A. W. Cameron, dated 5th September* 1876.

PREFACE TO FIRST EDITION

I HAVE been encouraged in my intention to continue this history, both by finding that the first volume had some interest for the general public, and by letters from the descendants of officers and soldiers who took part in the events narrated. But the period from 1816 to 1854 presents none of the picturesque and stirring incidents which crowded the preceding twenty years ; and the wars in which the Gordons afterwards took part, though they afforded opportunities for the same display of disciplined courage in the defence of the British Empire and commerce in the East, have not the overwhelming interest of the great Napoleonic wars, when the heart of the Empire itself and the freedom of every individual in the British Isles depended on the issue of a struggle in which our opponents were as well armed and organised as ourselves.

The account of the 75th Regiment (now First Battalion Gordon Highlanders) takes us back to the Indian wars of a hundred years ago, and to the terrible times of the Mutiny of 1857. In describing the later campaigns, I have received great assistance from the many distinguished officers, and from many n.c. officers and men, whose names are given as authority for statements in the text.

My thanks are due to S. M. Milne, Esq., author of " Colours and Standards of the British Army " ; to Malcolm MacFarlane, Esq., Elderslie ; to the Secretaries of the Gordon Highlanders' Associations. I received valuable information from the late Sir George Warrender, Bart. ; as also from gentlemen mentioned in connection with the account of the 75th Regiment, and others who have most kindly helped me.

I am also greatly indebted to the courtesy of those Authors and Publishers who are mentioned by name in the List of Illustrations.

It was my intention to have given a short history of the Royal Aberdeenshire Militia (now Third Battalion Gordon Highlanders) and of the Volunteer Battalions of the Regimental District ; but finding that space would not admit of justice being done to these subjects in the present volume, I can only hope that whoever continues the history of the regiment will include an account of the Third and Volunteer Battalions, of whom so many members bore their part with the First and Second during the late war in South Africa.

It has been suggested that the description of the retreat to Corunna in Volume I emphasises the sufferings and irregularities of individuals rather than the general good discipline for which the Gordons have always been remarkable. Many of the details were taken from a sergeant's journal and from the letters of a subaltern (lent to me by Dr C. A. Innes, late of the 52nd Light Infantry and 16th Lancers). They evidently took the character of their regiment for granted ; and I was not then aware that documents are preserved at the Record Office which would have enabled me to throw a broader light on the subject.   One of these was lately published in Oman's interesting and exhaustive " History of the Peninsular War."   It shows that, with the exception of two battalions of the 1st (now Grenadier) Guards, the 92nd had a smaller percentage of stragglers from their ranks during the campaign than any battalions which went through the whole retreat ; and no doubt the number of stragglers from a regiment is an indication of its discipline and of the stamina of its men.   An extract from the return is given in Appendix I, Volume I.

The sketch I have endeavoured to draw of the Life of the Regiment shows that a high standard of duty is set before its members. They may not always act up to that standard ; but it tends to produce the spirit of self-abnegation and *esprit de corps* which was so well illustrated, on the 4th of July 1901, by a survivor of Lieutenant Best's party near Naboom's Spruit, as told by the Boer Commandant, De Villars, to Lord Kitchener, and reported by him to the King.   When asked by the Boers why he and his comrades, when surrounded, did not save themselves by surrender, there was no thought of self in the reply, " Why, man, we are Gordon Highlanders ! " [1]

The self-respect which is accompanied by respect for others is promoted by the greater attention to personal cleanliness and appearance which is characteristic of the soldier ; but he does not cock his bonnet only for his own credit, but for the credit of his corps.   Soldiers are neither all heroes nor free from the failings common to humanity ; but those who have had much to do with both will agree that their manners and conduct compare very favourably with those of their fellows in civil life.   Some of the many critics of our army find fault with the youth of recruits ; but it has, at any rate, this advantage, that a lad enlisted at eighteen will adapt himself to the requirements of military life more thoroughly than if he entered his profession at twenty-two.   The impatience of discipline—even of parental discipline—which is a feature of our time, is more easily overcome at the former than at the latter age.

The story of the regiment seems to show that the martial spirit is not dead, and that it is easily roused in time of war, but can only be kept awake in ordinary times by advantages commensurate with the duties and foreign service required.   No doubt the number wanted affects the standard of recruits, but from a comparison of

---

[1] Lieutenant Best, one sergeant, and twenty rank and file were escort to a train which was attacked and surrounded. The officer and nine men were killed and seven wounded before the five survivors could be taken prisoners.

the rate of wages with the Size Roll at different times—say 1850 and 1890 [1]—it seems evident that when the soldiers' advantages were greater or even as great as those enjoyed by lads of the agricultural classes, who make the hardiest and best soldiers, the average height of the men was greater ; when the enormous rise in wages (which are higher in Scotland than in most parts of England or any part of Ireland) took place during the last thirty years, recruiting became more difficult and the standard was lowered. The spirit of enterprise and national sentiment influence young men in joining the army and in their choice of a regiment. Nothing is more unpractical than to ignore sentiment as a factor in human affairs, but there is a point when practical considerations come in. Many a young Highlander with a turn for soldiering has been prevented by the feeling that he could not afford to gratify his taste. When he finds the pay and position of a soldier is superior to that ordinarily attainable by young men of his age and station, he will be a soldier, and for much the same reasons that induced his great-grandfather to enlist ; but in estimating those reasons, it must be remembered that the Government pay and pension was in early times often supplemented by privileges on the land granted to the parents of the recruit, or promised to himself on his return.[2]

The terms in which the Duke of Wellington sometimes described the soldiers of his time were considered unjust by many general and regimental officers. He seems to have compared the soldier with his own high standard of military conduct, rather than with the behaviour of the sailor, the artisan, or the labourer of the day, with whose lives and characters he had indeed little opportunity of being acquainted. The Duke's words could not have been applied to the class of which Highland regiments of the period were principally composed, but they have been constantly reiterated in Parliament and in the Press in a manner very unfair and discouraging to the army.

It has been shown that so long as recruiting was in the hands of their Colonels, the Gordons were particular as to the class enlisted, and that with such exceptions as occur in all communities, the regiment was composed of an honourable body of men, not

---

[1] In 1850, 54·8 per cent. of n.c. officers and men of the 92nd were 5 feet 8 inches and upwards. In 1890, 24·2 per cent. of the same battalion (2nd Gordon Highlanders) were 5 feet 8 inches and upwards.

[2] There is preserved by Maclaine of Lochbuie a very complete list of men who joined the army with one of his family in the latter part of the 18th century. Opposite the name of each recruit is entered the extra grazing or arable land to be given to his parents during his absence, or the promise of a holding to himself on his return ; or in one or two cases an additional bounty in cash.

The kiss and the guinea with which the Duchess of Gordon undoubtedly favoured some individuals when the Gordon Highlanders were raised, was in addition to the Government bounty—not instead of it, as some seem to suppose.

without some of the faults of their contemporaries in other walks of life, but who constantly received special marks of confidence and esteem from the magistrates and inhabitants of the districts in which they were quartered. The number promoted from the ranks of the regiment of late years shows that the same character is preserved in the men who join under the present system.

C. G. GARDYNE.

Finavon, Forfar,
March 1903.

PREFACE TO SECOND EDITION

FOR some time the Officers, past and present, of the Gordon Highlanders have had under consideration the question of bringing up to date the History of their Regiment, which had been written up to the year 1898 in the original work on the subject : *The Life of a Regiment.*

In 1926 they appointed a committee of their number, under the presidency of General Sir Aylmer Haldane, G.C.M.G., K.C.B., etc., to formulate a scheme for a complete History ; and the original book having been out of print for many years, it seemed imperative that the first step should be to publish the new edition of it which is here presented.

The work is reproduced without more variation than the excision of a few errors, the incorporation in the text of the numerous notes, additions, and amendments collected by the late author in the years since 1903, and of a little material from other sources, new matter of over six lines being indicated by indentation of type on left side ; but it has been found possible to add to the original illustrations portraits of several illustrious officers and others connected with one or other battalion, while the print and paper have been improved.

The two volumes now published should be considered as the first portion of the complete History of the regular and other battalions of the Gordon Highlanders up to the reconstruction of the Army after the Great War.

A. D. G. GARDYNE.

Glenforsa, Isle of Mull,
September 1928.

CONTENTS

CHAPTER I. 1816-1828

CHAPTER II. 1828-1834

CHAPTER III. 1834-1844

CHAPTER IV. 1844-1846

CHAPTER V. 1847-1857

CHAPTER VI. 1858-1862

CHAPTER X.   1878-1879

CONTENTS

CONTENTS

CHAPTER XX.   1849-1857 (75TH REGIMENT)

CHAPTER XXI.   1857-1862 (75TH REGIMENT)

CHAPTER XXII.   1862-1881 (75TH REGIMENT)

CONTENTS

CHAPTER XXX

APPENDICES

LIST OF ILLUSTRATIONS

Without pretending to give all the various changes, the illustrations show the arms and uniforms of several periods, and being taken from contemporary authorities, they may be of use to future painters of military subjects. The rank and file had not in former times the elaborate wardrobe of the present day—only a red coat and white jacket; a kilt, which was worn out of barracks and always under arms, including musketry; and trousers for barracks and fatigue duty. The officers' uniform became more varied after Waterloo; it was often changed, and included details sanctioned apparently only by regimental authority, as the words "Gordon Highlanders" on epaulettes in 1815. The Highland articles were worn according to the fancy of the officer commanding for the time and, to a certain extent, of the individual.

Vol. I. Brussels, 1815, page 348. I took the drummer's jacket from that of an infantry drummer in the Museum of the Royal United Service Institution, which has red sleeves. Mr Milne afterwards sent me a drawing of a 92nd drummer of that period, copied from the original in the Windsor Castle Library, which shows that the 92nd had not red, but yellow sleeves.

VARIOUS REGIMENTAL SPORRANS

MAPS AND PLANS

CHAPTER I

1816–1828

AFTER the festivities which greeted the Gordon High-landers in Edinburgh, many took advantage of the opportunity to visit their homes in the north, the Waterloo medal on their breasts ensuring hospitality by the way. They gave, as they passed along, news of absent comrades to many an anxious parent, and, as I have heard old people relate, astonished their own families, who had last seen them as halflin' laddies, by their martial bearing as they stooped their tall bonnets at the cottage doors.

Up to this period I have been able to refer to Order-books, monthly returns, etc., which, though many are missing, have been of great assistance in my endeavour to describe the Life of the Regiment. It appears that, in 1823, an abridged record was called for by the Adjutant-General ; it was made by the officer commanding, who had not served with the regiment in the war, without consulting a single officer who had done so.[1] The original books had then been considered as waste paper. Colonel MacDonald afterwards saved such as remained, and they were lent to me by his son, but few later than 1816 have been kept.

On the 3rd of December the regiment was inspected by its Colonel, Lieut.-General the Earl of Hopetoun, and he expressed his satisfaction to Brevet Lieut.-Colonel Donald MacDonald, who commanded in the absence of Lieut.-Colonel Mitchell, C.B.

Among the distinguished visitors at that time in Edinburgh was the Grand Duke Nicholas of Russia, who expressed a desire to see the Gordon Highlanders. The regiment was paraded accordingly, and His Imperial Highness expressed his admiration of the corps.

In January 1817, an order was received for reducing the additional or recruiting company, and for placing the officers on half-pay.[2]

After a visit to Scotland of only seven months, the Gordons were ordered to Ireland. Before leaving, they were inspected by Major-General Hope, who bore witness to the good conduct of the regiment

during the period it has been under his command in North Britain, and he will not fail to report to H.R.H. the Commander-in-Chief on the very steady and orderly behaviour of the corps during their stay in the country. The Major-General has no doubt that the uniform good conduct for which the 92nd has always been conspicuous will be the same in whatever part of His Majesty's dominions the services of the regiment may be required.

---

[1] Memo. by Colonel J. MacDonald.

[2] Recruiting had been carried on at Glasgow, Forfar, Elgin, Inverness, Dingwall, and Inveraray.

On the 7th April 1817 the regiment commenced its march by divisions to Portpatrick, there to embark, and arrived at Belfast on the 24th. Detachments were sent to Carrickfergus, Downpatrick, Crumlin, Ballymoney, Newton Glens, Castle Dawson, Ballycastle, and Randalstown.

In October, Major-General Burnet complimented them on their appearance, drill, precision of firing, etc., and particularly remarks " the well-regulated system of interior economy which prevails in the corps," and that the detachments he visited were in the best order.

On the 28th April 1818 they were inspected by Major-General Sir Sydney Beckwith, who issued a very complimentary order, mentioning their " soldier-like and respectable appearance," and that he was equally gratified with that of the detachments, " but no less was to be looked for from a regiment who have always preserved their regular military habits under the most trying circumstances."

On the 23rd October 1818 the establishment was reduced to 620 privates.

On the 17th of June the regiment marched in two divisions to Castlebar, and arrived on the 28th. Here they were again broken up into no less than twenty detachments ; but notwithstanding this disadvantage, Major-General Buller, in October, expressed his approbation of their conduct and appearance. On the 4th November 1818, the regiment was held in readiness for embarkation at Cork for Jamaica. It marched, on the 8th January 1819, for Fermoy, where it remained till the 12th April, when it proceeded to Cork, and on the following day embarked at the Cove on board the transports *Chapman*, *Nautilus*, and *Ocean* ; having enjoyed less than two and a half years of home service, during which it had marched through England, Scotland, and Ireland.

Many of the veterans, both officers and soldiers, had retired at this period, fortunately for themselves, as events turned out ; for instead of being exposed to the risks of a West Indian climate, many lived the proverbially long lives of pensioners. Passengers by the Caledonian Canal in the early 'sixties, when at Fort-Augustus they remarked the light step and upright figure, in red kilt and tartan hose, of Captain Ewen Cameron Ross, could hardly believe that he had stood with the Gordons on the heights of Maya and charged at Waterloo. Others are mentioned in " Brave Men of Skye " ; among them Donald Campbell, who, though wounded in the arm, shot through the nose and also through the forehead, the ball going out at the back of his neck, enjoyed his pension for many years at Sleat. On the other hand, the Rev. W. Forsyth, minister of Dornoch in 1863, mentions David Ross, one of his elders, who had served with the Gordons throughout the war since 1794 without a scratch.

I remember another of these veterans in Inverness ; no man was better known (though possibly some may have been more highly respected) in the Highland capital than the " Saighdear dhu," " black soldier," as he was called. A keen sportsman, he followed his favourite pastime without perhaps much regard to legal rights. He was not, however, a " Piper of one tune," and varied his occupations by occasionally helping drovers with their cattle. One day while thus employed he was overtaken on the Fort-Augustus road by some Englishmen, who, with an assumption of superiority too common among a certain class of British tourist, began to chaff and interrogate the simple native they took him for. In reply to their questions he told them the cattle were going to Falkirk Tryst. " What will they be worth there ? " " They 'll no' do badly if they bring ten pund a-head." " Only ten pounds ! That 's nothing to English prices. If you take them to London, my good fellow, you 'll get twenty ! " " If you 'll tak' Loch Ness to H-ll," retorted Donald, " you 'll get a shilling the glass for the watter ! "

Among the names of regimental characters which disappear at this time is that of Piper Cameron (who acted as pipe-major). He is described as one of the ancient order of Highlanders ; proud of his position as a soldier, whose music inspired his comrades in the " Dance of Death," he rightly considered himself the superior of mere civilian pipers. Well versed in Highland lore and legend, the notes of his bagpipe suggested these more vividly than words. In the pibroch "Tarbh breac dearg,"[1] he told of Keppoch's feud with Lochiel ; " Mnathen na glinne so "[2] recalled the sad story of Glencoe ; or he tuned up the lively " Ochd fir Mhuidart," in memory of the seven men of Moidart who, while cutting peats, heard that Prince Charlie had landed, and danced a joyful reel, setting a spade in the ground to complete the set of eight. There is no doubt that musicians of his stamp had the best effect on the spirit of a Highland corps.

On the 14th April, Major-General Benjamin Gordon expressed

[1] The story of the pibroch " Tarbh breac dearg " (the red-spotted Bull) is this : Ronald MacAilean Og (a Macdonald of Traigh in Morar) was on his way to visit Cameron of Lochiel. Some Camerons took a vicious red bull from Loch Arkaig side and put him in front of Ronald at the river Sgaithail. Ronald proposed to avoid him, but his servant said it would be a pity to let the Camerons think they were afraid, so Ronald went on. The Bull attacked him, but Ronald killed him with his sword. He twisted off the horns and made his servant carry them. Ronald then composed the tune as he rested on Lochielside and played it as he approached Achnacarry Castle (Lochiel's house). On leaving Lochiel he visited Macdonald of Keppoch, who admired the tune so much that he asked to have it as his " Failte " or " Welcome."—Told in Gaelic to the author by Peter Macdonald, piper in Moidart.

[2] " O women of this glen." Another title makes it : " Ye men of this glen." It is said to have been played by a Campbell piper to warn the women of Glencoe of their danger. It is also said that it was played at Brussels to rouse the Highlanders for the march to Quatre-Bras.

" his marked approbation of the steadiness and very soldier-like appearance of the regiment, and the regularity with which its embarkation was conducted yesterday." [1]

The regiment disembarked on the 4th June at Kingston, Jamaica, the whole population crowding to see the novel sight of a Highland regiment as they marched to their quarters at Up-Park Camp.

Here the Gordon Highlanders entered on the most melancholy epoch of their history. Their arrival in the hot, unhealthy season was ill-timed, and the intrepidity which enabled them to defy the legions of France was of no avail against a more subtle foe. Shortly after their arrival they were attacked by yellow fever in its most virulent form. The regiment was dispersed, some to Stonyhill, others to the Apostles' Battery ; the guardship off Port Royal, H.M.S. *Serapis*, received the headquarters and a large number of convalescents under Brevet Major Wilkie, for Lieut.-Colonel Mitchell, C.B., after serving with the regiment since its formation, had retired to his native Lochaber ; and Brevet Lieut.-Colonel Blainey (who had exchanged from half-pay with Brevet Lieut.-Colonel Donald MacDonald) died in August, and Major Ferrier in September. Nothing can depict the state of the regiment better than the fact that Major Wilkie was obliged to write to the Assistant Adjutant-General that the returns could not be sent in at the time required, as he had lost during the month (September) " the adjutant and every one acquainted with the important duty of the orderly room."

On November 5th, Sergeant-major William Grant was promoted ensign and adjutant, and Sergeant John Anderson became sergeant-major.

The regiment re-assembled at Up-Park Camp in November ; those who had been at sea remained healthy, but those who were left on shore still suffered. The loss sustained by the regiment from the 25th June to the 24th December 1819 was ten officers, viz. Majors Archibald Ferrier and John Blainey (Brevet Lieut.-Colonel), Lieutenants Andrew Will, Thomas Gordon, Hector Innes (whose interesting letters from the wars I have so often quoted), George Logan, Richard MacDonell,[2] and George Mackie (adjutant), Ensign Francis Reynolds and Assistant-Surgeon David Thomas ;

---

[1] Embarked :—Field officers, 2 ; captains, 7 ; lieutenants, 10 ; ensigns, 5 ; staff, 4 ; sergeants, 31 ; drummers, 21 ; rank and file, 603 ; officers' wives, 5 ; officers' children, 5 ; soldiers' wives, 72 ; soldiers' children, 59. A small depôt was left, which went to Scotland.

About this period white gaiters replaced the black. The bonnets in marching order were covered with oilskin, a fashion copied from the Prussians and adopted also by our light cavalry. It prevented the protection from the sun given by the feathers, and the wet ran down it into the wearer's neck.

[2] Lieutenant MacDonell, who had been with the 92nd since 1808, was grandson of Alexander MacDonell of Keppoch, who was killed at Culloden, where he commanded Clan Donald.

13 sergeants, 8 drummers, and 254 rank and file, 2 officers' wives and 2 children, 32 soldiers' wives and 29 children.[1]

The feeling of despondency, even despair, occasioned by such a grievous mortality finds pathetic utterance in the words of a soldier who was seated by the wayside, his face buried in his hands. " My wife is dead," he said ; " my bairns are dead, and I wish I was dead." [2]

Lieut.-General John Hope was appointed Colonel of the 92nd on the 29th January 1820, in succession to General the Earl of Hopetoun, G.C.B., who was removed to the 42nd Royal Highland Regiment.

In February 1820, Major-General Conran inspected the regiment, and, notwithstanding the unhappy circumstances in which they had been placed, their appearance and steadiness under arms elicited his praise.

In March the regiment moved to Fort-Augusta and Port Royal, where they enjoyed comparatively good health ; and in May a draft of 55 rank and file joined from Scotland.

In October, Lieut.-Colonel Sir Frederick Stovin, K.C.B., who had been promoted from the 28th Regiment the previous September, joined and assumed the command of the 92nd. Sir Frederick had served in almost every campaign since 1800, was aide-de-camp to Picton at Ciudad Rodrigo and Badajos, and Assistant-Adjutant-General to the end of the Peninsular War, after which he was wounded at New Orleans. His record was indeed a splendid one, but he was quite unfitted for the command of a Highland regiment ; he did not understand, and had no sympathy with, the peculiar feelings and ideas of the men who composed it. He gave great offence by appearing at their head in a cocked hat instead of a bonnet, and generally went against all national and regimental customs. Soon the orders directed that white trousers should be worn on all parades and duties, and whatever the opinion of individual soldiers may have been as to the kilt, they were agreed in objecting to such a change being made by one whom they looked on as a stranger. Their sense of discipline was, however, too strong to allow their dissatisfaction to be loudly expressed ; but it evidently, after a time, became known to the General, who repre-

---

[1] Cannon's " Record."

[2] There is also the wail of a soldier in Jamaica longing for his Highland home :—

> " Tha mi fo ghruaim gar an dean mi innseadh
> Ged's tric do smuaintean a tighn a'm' chridh,
> Bearr leam *furlough* air ais gum' eolais
> Na làn mo phòca de dh'òr am Righ."
>
> I 'm sad at heart—how sad I dare not tell—
> Vain thoughts of you in my lone heart ever dwell ;
> And all the riches of this torrid land
> Would I barter for a furlough to my native strand.

sented to the Duke of York, in a confidential report, that the clothing and appointments had been changed by the commanding officer without authority. Sir Frederick received leave of absence, and shortly after was removed to the more congenial " grey breeks " of the gallant 90th. " The Highland garb, with every part of the original and proper dress of the corps, was immediately resumed."[1]

In January and February 1821, drafts, making a total of 214 men, joined from the depôt. On the 24th October, orders were received to reduce the regiment to an establishment of eight companies, consisting of 29 sergeants, 12 drummers, and 576 rank and file. In November a detachment of 2 subalterns, 10 sergeants, 1 drummer, 32 rank and file embarked for New Providence.

Though more healthy than immediately after their arrival, there was still a considerable loss of good soldiers, among them Ensign and Adjutant Grant, who had joined the 92nd as private in 1800, from the Clan Alpine Fencibles ; and they were replaced by recruits not always of the stamp of those who had hitherto filled the ranks of the Gordon Highlanders.

At this period the 58th and 61st Regiments being about to return to Europe, their men were permitted to volunteer to corps serving in Jamaica, which, notwithstanding yellow fever, seems not to have been an unpopular quarter with thirsty souls. " A fine country," said an old toper; " ye 're aye drinkin' an' aye dry."

Men who volunteer for active service are naturally the most spirited and best ; but when they leave their regiment for another, unless for some special reason, they are not always an acquisition. The 92nd was ordered to receive 33 men from the 58th and 47 from the 61st, and a note on the margin of the Description Roll describes them as " a total of 80 men of the worst character and description." None of them appear to have been Scots.

In March 1822, the headquarters were at Falmouth, with detachments at Port Antonio, Lucca, and Maroon Town. While at Falmouth, the Rev. W. Fraser, rector of Trelawney, was appointed to act as chaplain.[2] Major Peter Wilkie had commanded since Sir Frederick Stovin left.[3]

Meanwhile Lieut.-Colonel David Williamson, from half-pay, of the 4th Regiment, had been appointed Lieut.-Colonel of the

---

[1] Regimental Record.

[2] Till 1836 no provision was made for Presbyterian services out of Scotland, or for Roman Catholic services anywhere.—*Clode's Military Forces of the Crown*. The regiment attended the Episcopal or Presbyterian Church, as happened to be convenient. In 1858 nineteen Roman Catholic and five Presbyterian clergy were commissioned as army chaplains. The number is now (1902) largely increased.

[3] About this period all officers of the 92nd were ordered to wear silver wings instead of epaulettes, and the n.c. officers and men of battalion companies to have the same wings as the flank companies, in place of shoulder knots. Field officers to wear both epaulettes and wings.

92nd in the previous October. He joined at Falmouth, Jamaica, in April, when a draft of sixty-nine rank and file also arrived from the depôt.

On September 6th, 1823, Lieut.-General the Hon. Alexander Duff was appointed Colonel of the 92nd, in succession to Lieut.-General Sir John Hope, G.C.B., who was removed to the 72nd Highlanders.

In February 1824, a draft of thirty recruits joined—this time of excellent quality.

In April the regiment was removed to Fort-Augusta and Kingston Barracks. During the time they were stationed on the north side they had enjoyed good health, and when they left Falmouth, the magistrates and vestry of Trelawney, in a letter to Lieut.-Colonel Williamson, declared their "sense of the exemplary conduct of the officers and orderly demeanour of the men during the time they have been stationed among us"; and expressed their satisfaction at "the cordiality that prevailed between your regiment and the inhabitants of the district."

About the middle of April 1824, the recruits lately arrived were attacked by fever, which carried off about a third of their number.

At this time an improved system of drill was introduced by Sir Henry Torrens, K.C.B., Adjutant-General of the Forces ; and Sir John Keane, commanding the troops in Jamaica, complimented the regiment on the attention they had paid to it.[1]

In those days the West Indian sugar plantations were culti-vated by slave labour, and symptoms of insurrection having appeared among the slaves on the north side of the island, four companies of the 92nd embarked in June on H.M.S. *Hussar* ; two were landed at Savana la Mar, one at Black River, while the fourth remained on board the frigate on its cruise round the island. The detachments rejoined headquarters in August.

In January 1825, the regiment was united at Up-Park Camp. Lieut.-Colonel Williamson having gone to Europe, Major Andrew

---

[1] Sir David Dundas' "Eighteen Manœuvres," founded on the Prussian system, had been introduced in 1792. The pace was slow, seventy-five paces to the minute, and ranks three deep, but occasionally two deep, as in skirmishing ; steadiness was insisted on, and marching past was a test of this. The three-deep formation was abolished in 1808, and the drill-book slightly altered from time to time.

AUTHOR'S NOTE.—By Horse Guards circular, December 24th, 1825, it was ordered that the men are to be paid daily, " as an arrangement likely to secure the soldier from the temptations and irregularities and consequent punishment which have been found to result from allowing balances to accumulate."

Amount of soldier's weekly pay and beer-money,   £0 7 7

Amount of messing and washing, everything included,   0 4 9½

                   £0 2 9½

Remainder to each man not in debt to be equally divided and paid daily.

R. Charlton, who had been appointed the previous year, was left in command. In February a draft of twenty-four recruits arrived from the depôt, and were followed in June by two officers and sixteen recruits, whose general appearance was " most excellent." In July 1825, the establishment was raised to ten companies—six *service* and four *depôt* companies.

At this time the regiment was again attacked by fever, which in two months carried off Major Charlton, Captain Andrew Donaldson, Lieutenant and Adjutant James Deans, and sixty men. The command devolved upon Captain Robert Winchester, who was now promoted major ; and during the six months he commanded, the regiment appears to have been in excellent order. Among other things, the flourishing state of the regimental school was particularly noticed.

In February 1826, Lieut.-Colonel Williamson arrived with a draft of three officers and sixty recruits on board H.M.S. *Magnificent* ; recruits' appearance described as " promising." In August 1826, the regiment received orders to be ready to embark for England, and on the 19th February 1827, the headquarters division embarked at Kingston on the *Arab* transport, and sailed on the 24th February, arriving at Spithead on the 25th April. They were transhipped in Portsmouth Harbour, landed at Leith the 10th May, and marched to Edinburgh Castle, where the four depôt companies from Glasgow joined on the 23rd. The three remaining companies embarked at Kingston on the 30th March, and joined headquarters at Edinburgh Castle, May 31st, 1827. Thus ended a most painful episode in the life of the regiment. In eight years they had lost more by fever than were killed in action during all the war with France.[1] Had hygienic science been understood as it is now, no doubt the greater number of these valuable lives would have been saved. The testimony of the General Officer Commanding at Jamaica shows that they bore with exemplary fortitude an ordeal far more trying than the dangers of the battlefield ; but the regiment did not recover from the effects for many a day.

There being no longer a second battalion to keep up a supply of carefully selected and well-trained recruits, the ranks had to be filled at first with an inferior class ; and though afterwards greater care had been taken in the choice of reinforcements, the transfer from other regiments of dissolute characters, who, though they

[1] Total loss of the regiment in the island of Jamaica from June 1819 to May 1827 : Officers, 17 ; sergeants, 31 ; drummers, 9 ; rank and file, 645 ; women, 67 ; children, 91 ; total, 860.—*Regimental Record.*

AUTHOR'S NOTE.—H.R.H. the Duke of York, Commander-in-Chief, died in 1827. He was popular with the army, and was called " The Soldier's Friend." He was succeeded by the Duke of Wellington.

may have been smart soldiers, had none of the feelings of Gordon Highlanders for the character of the corps, contaminated the young men ; while the few remaining old warriors who had maintained its good name felt that the honour of their regiment and their own was tarnished by the introduction of such low-living companions. The situation was aggravated by the loss of so many of the officers and n.c. officers, who had been brought up in that system of strict but considerate discipline which had made the regiment a home, to which a majority of all ranks had come from the same Highland districts, knowing and respecting each other accordingly. Commanding officers had been appointed who were not to the manner born, and who were unequal to the occasion. The consequence was an increase of misdemeanours and crimes by the bad men, too great to be checked by the influence of the good ; punishments, which under different circumstances had been rare, now became common ; and a regiment which, when last in Edinburgh, was distinguished by its national characteristics, its " uniform good conduct " and " very steady behaviour," elicited no such compliments from Major-General Sir Robert O'Callaghan at his inspection on the 27th June, when its strength was : Sergeants, 37 ; drummers, 11 ; rank and file, 631.

I will now give a short account of the depôt companies, showing that, at any rate after the first difficulties of 1819-23, when great exertions were made to replace the loss at Jamaica, and less attention was paid to the nationality and character than to the number of recruits,[1] the fact was fully recognised that without good raw material you cannot have a good manufactured article, and that accordingly every effort was made to replenish the ranks with the same class of young men from the country districts as formerly filled them.

The depôt went to Edinburgh in 1819, but subsequently moved to the Albany Barracks, Isle of Wight, where it formed part of the West Indian depôt stationed there. For a time the company was commanded by Captain Winchester. Some of the correspondence which exists shows that he had at heart the interest of the regiment, and of all belonging to it. He writes to General Sir H. Hardinge, asking him to recommend to the Commander-in-Chief the petition of Private Alexander Cooper, who had been present as his servant with Sir Henry at the Battle of Ligny, which entitled him to the Waterloo medal, for which he had not been returned.

---

[1] It must not be supposed that the influx of these men had altogether changed the nationality of the 92nd. I find in a description book which goes down to men enlisted in 1823, that even after the great loss in Jamaica the clans were well represented—among them 46 MacDonalds, of whom 10 were Donald.

The description of a deserter is sent to the minister of Laggan to be posted on the church door. This custom continued for many years, and was considered in the Highlands a great disgrace to the deserter's family.

In June 1823, by desire of Sir John Hope (Colonel of the regiment), he applies to the Adjutant-General to have the recruiting party moved from Aberdeen, "where we have always been unsuccessful, and add it to the permanent party at Huntly," from whence it is his wish to have detached to Grantown in Strathspey, Sergeant Ross and Private Donald Skinner, and to send Privates John Beaton and John Campbell from Glasgow to Kingussie in Badenoch (from which they were to visit Lochaber), to be also under the officer of the permanent party at Huntly ; "the object of this arrangement is for the purpose of having men in the Highlands who can speak the language of the inhabitants."

An officer of the regiment had his headquarters at Huntly, whence he had charge of parties at Inverness, Dingwall, Grantown, Kingussie, Elgin, Banff, and Nairn, while apparently there were also recruiters of the regiment at Glasgow and Perth.

There are instances of soldiers in English regiments, Highlandmen, being transferred to the 92nd at their own request by permission of the Commander-in-Chief, getting a man from the 92nd to exchange. Whole families seem to have served in the regiment, as Donald MacLean of the 91st, having three brothers, two of them colour-sergeants, in the 92nd, and his father having also served in it, applies to be transferred, which is granted, a man going to the 91st in his place. There are applications from boys in the Highlands to be taken as " Boys," being sons of men who had served in the regiment during the war.

Great consideration seems to have been shown to married men when their wives could not be allowed to embark, by keeping them at home, bachelors going in their place.

There were constant inquiries as to the effects and prize-money from the heirs of men who had been killed in the war or died since.

The battalion of which the 92nd depôt company formed part was under the command of a lieut.-colonel on the Staff. The piper of the company was a quaint specimen of the old-fashioned Gordon Highlander, named Duncan Smith. The first time the battalion marched out for exercise, the drummers and fifers of all the depôts played together at the head of the column, but the Gordons, who were the rear company, were marching to the strains of Duncan's pipe. The colonel naturally thought the piper should also be at the head of the column, and ordered accordingly, desiring him to play up, but Duncan could not bear the idea of playing to soldiers in " chacos." " She 's nae mair wind," he replied, with a respectful

salute, but a twinkle in his cunning old eye.   Presently the notes
of " Gillian an' fheile " were heard from the rear ; again he was
ordered to the front.   With an innocent look he again excused
himself by, " She has nae mair wind."   The colonel gave it up,
and never asked the piper again to play away from the bonnets.
A portrait of Duncan by the late General Archibald Inglis Lockhart hangs in the room where I write.   Many stories have I heard
of him.   When asked how he felt at Waterloo—" Och ! shust
plaw awa', no gie a d—— whether she 'll be shot or no'."   On
another occasion he had to give evidence on some trial.   The
lawyer who was badgering him asked, among other questions, if
he had fought at Waterloo—" Hoo cud I be fechtin' when I was
plawing the pipes a' the time ?   It was mair wind than wark wi'
me, like a lawyer ! "   On no account would he wear the fatigue
trousers which formed part of his kit.   He was never known to
wear anything but the kilt except once, when, having been ill, a
lady presented him with a warm pair of trousers.   Out of compliment to her he put them on, but got so bothered by the unaccustomed buttons and braces, that he threw them away in a rage.   He
wore the shoe that was on his left foot one day on the right the next,
his hose alternately in the same fashion, and was altogether an
eccentric character, but a first-rate musician of the old Highland
school.   He became lance-sergeant and pipe-major, and served till
quite an elderly man ; he retired, in 1831, to his native place in the
Black Isle, with Waterloo medal, pension, gratuity, and good conduct medal.   The officers presented him with a set of bagpipes.

There were still men at the depôt suffering from the effects of
active service.   The authorities inquire why Private D. M'Donald
is unfit for further service, the answer being that he was wounded
in the left side by a shell at Vittoria, and in the right knee by a
musket ball at Waterloo.   There is also mention of Sergeant Ross
and others suffering from rheumatism contracted on the retreat to
Corunna and in the Peninsula.   At the same time the recruiting
officer applies to be allowed to enlist men who had been discharged
for wounds, but recovered, and were anxious to rejoin, and whom
the officer knows to be of good character, which is granted.

In March 1824, Captain Winchester informs the colonel that
in order to have a superior stamp of recruit he has received authority
from the Commander-in-Chief for the recruiting parties of the
92nd to confine their enlistments to men of 5 feet 8 inches and
upwards till further orders.[1]   In December " they are getting fine
young lads," but recruiting is affected by the increasing rate of

---

[1] The standard seems to have been reduced in 1820 to 5 feet 5 inches, and a great many
lads of 16 and 17 years taken at 5 feet 4¾ inches, so that the average height of the regiment
became reduced.

wages, and by the increase in the standard height.   After a time
the standard was reduced to 5 feet 6 inches and upwards.

On account of the " luxuriant harvest and consequent high
wages to shearers," recruiting in the autumn of 1825 is reported
not so good at Huntly, to which district many lads from the Highlands resorted at that season.[1]

In 1825, the four company depôt was formed, and in August
they were at Edinburgh Castle.[2]

The "full" colonel had a much more active interest in his
regiment than at the present day.   Power was vested in him to
reduce a n.c. officer summarily to the ranks.   He supplied the
clothing, orderly room stationery, store chests, etc.   It was the
lieut.-colonel's duty, on the one hand, to see that the men were well
supplied, and on the other, that the colonel did not suffer loss.[3]
Lieut.-General the Hon. Sir Alexander Duff, who became colonel
in September 1823, had to pay to Sir J. Hope, whom he succeeded,
the value of all clothing, etc., in store.   He had regular reports
from the officer commanding the depôt, and from Lieut. Campbell,
in charge of the recruiting in the north.   Sir Alexander corresponds
constantly about sons of tenants of his brother (Lord Fife) who
were in the regiment, as to recruiting on his brother's Highland
estates at Crathie and Braemar, and as to widows of 92nd men in
the Highlands.   There are curious letters about some of the
recruiters, in which Sir Alexander is informed that Sergeant
Fraser superintends his brother's farm, Private Thom works at his
trade as a weaver, Donald M'Donald as a shoemaker, Corporal
Renton keeps a shop in Elgin, and Private Cheyne drives a
carrier's cart from Elgin to Fochabers, and that they only wear
uniform on market days and Sundays.   Lieutenant Campbell
says the report is exaggerated, that the men are sober and steady,
and attend all the markets within twenty miles.   He considers
the working does not interfere with their duty as recruiters, as

---

[1] In 1825, workmen's wages in Caithness were 9d. to 1s. a day, or 4s. 6d. to 6s. weekly.—
Scotsman, June 24th, 1899.

[2] The loss of so many good sergeants made it necessary, for the first time since the formation of the regiment, to take a sergeant-major from outside, and on 25th June 1825, Sergeant
William Ross of the 72nd (a native of Dornoch) was transferred to the 92nd, and appointed
depôt sergeant-major.

[3] At this time the colonel paid for sergeants' tartan, 2s. 5d. a yard; privates' tartan, 1s. 6½d.;
sergeants' bonnets (humble), 2s. 1½d. each ; privates' bonnets, 1s. 7½d.

NOTE.—27th November 1826, Colour-sergeant Ronald M'Lean, native of Ardnamurchan,
was discharged.   He had been enlisted at Gibraltar, 1796, at the age of 7 years and 3 months ;
also Allan M'Lean, enlisted at Chelmsford, 1799, at the age of 6¾ years, evidently sons of an
Ardnamurchan man who had joined with wife and family in 1794.

NOTE.—In 1827, mounted officers were directed to wear shoulder belts with slings,
instead of waist belts.   A Horse Guards circular, of 12th September 1828, directed that
steel-mounted swords be adopted by officers of Highland regiments when those in use became
unserviceable.   (For some years brass-mounted ones had been worn.)

it promotes a good understanding with the country people. Sir Alexander, however, does not approve of their ever appearing out of uniform.

The changing habits of young men in Highland districts is noticed in a letter from Lieutenant Campbell, who asks that the party at Kingussie may be moved at once, before the road is blocked by snow, " as most of the young men of that country are generally flocking down to the lowlands for the purpose of obtaining work." He suggests Forres as a suitable place to meet them, numerous feeing markets being held in the neighbourhood in November, when " we shall be able to get some fine lads," and he states that " Forres is the only town on the Moray Firth at present unoccupied by a party of the regiment."

From Edinburgh the depôt was moved to Glasgow, where it was stationed till it joined the service companies at Edinburgh on their arrival from Jamaica in May 1827.

Soon after the death of the 4th Duke of Gordon, his remains arrived in Edinburgh. They were met at a distance by the officers of the 92nd in two mourning coaches and escorted by them to Holyrood House. On 12th July 1827 the remains were removed from Holyrood on their journey to Gordon Castle, being escorted by two companies of the 92nd with their band playing the Dead March in " Saul." In the procession through the streets of Edinburgh were two mourning coaches containing officers of the 92nd.

On February 25th, 1828, four companies, under Major Winchester, marched for Glasgow. The 3rd and 5th of April the headquarters were inspected by Sir R. O'Callaghan, and exercised on Bruntsfield Links. The regiment marched for Glasgow in four divisions, the last arriving on the 30th April.

On the 26th of May, Lieut.-Colonel Williamson having received leave of absence till further orders, the command devolved upon Major Winchester, and in June the General was pleased to observe an improvement in the state of the regiment.

On the 29th July and the two following days, the 92nd embarked on the *Eclipse, Sheffield,* and *Frolic* steamboats, arriving at Belfast on the 30th and following days, where they were billeted.

This is the first time that steam power, which was destined to exercise such enormous influence on the world, entered into the life of the regiment.

They embarked at Belfast, August 3rd, on two steamboats, and arrived the following day in Dublin, where they were billeted, and were inspected on the 5th in the Phœnix Park by Lieut.-

General Sir John Byng, commanding the forces in Ireland. On the 6th and 7th they marched for Fermoy, where they arrived on the 15th and 16th.

In October they were inspected (under Major Winchester) by Major-General Sir George Bingham, K.C.B., commanding the southern district, and on the following day by Sir John Byng.

CHAPTER II

1828-1834

IT will have been observed that of late the usual complimentary remarks by inspecting officers have not been made. The character of a good regiment or a good family may suffer for a time from the conduct of some of its members, and unfortunately this was the case with the 92nd ; the wrong men had been introduced into its ranks, the right men had not been appointed to command them, and a general slackness had been allowed to prevail. Lieut.-Colonel David Williamson seems to have been an amiable gentleman, but from the letters of the colonel (Sir Alexander Duff) it is evident that he was not satisfied with his lieutenant, to whom he alludes as " our friend Dainty Davie." He looked for a man to replace him, and found him in Lieut.-Colonel John MacDonald of Dalchosnie, half-pay, of the 91st Regiment, who was then at home in Rannoch, where he was known by the sobriquet of " Ian dhu nan cath,"[1] for he had seen many battles : at Buenos Ayres, and in the Peninsular War, where he had successfully commanded the 14th Portuguese Regiment in the same division as the 92nd, with which corps he was intimately connected. His uncle had joined the Gordons soon after they were raised, and commanded them at Waterloo ; one brother had died of wounds received with the regiment at Maya, and another was now a captain in it. Colonel MacDonald had been six times wounded,[2] and had had two horses shot under him. He was well known in the army as a gallant, firm, and experienced officer ; and to the old soldiers of the 92nd as a Highland gentleman thoroughly understanding the language and feelings of Highlanders. He was, in fact, a worthy successor to " Fassiefern."

Lieut.-Colonel MacDonald was appointed to the regiment on the 21st November 1828, and he joined at Fermoy on the 19th January 1829.

Well aware of the circumstances in which the regiment had been placed, he knew that a corps with such a history as the Gordon Highlanders could soon be brought back to a state of excellence worthy of that history ; and he took steps, at once firm and conciliatory, towards a return to the accustomed good conduct, regularity, and smartness.

R.O., Fermoy, 23rd January 1829.—Lieut.-Colonel MacDonald, on taking command of the 92nd Highlanders, feels that honourable pride which

---

[1] " Black John of the fights."

[2] A story is told of an incident in an Irish disturbance about 1831, when the populace became threatening. Colonel MacDonald drew his sword to use it against a ringleader, when Kenneth M'Kenzie said to him, " Remember your £300 a year," and he returned the weapon to its scabbard. He had that pension for a wounded arm which was always in a sling.

an old soldier must always be alive to when a mark of distinction is conferred upon him by his superiors ; and he is truly sensible of the honour which His Majesty has been graciously pleased to bestow on him, by entrusting to his charge one of the most distinguished of the very distinguished regiments of which his native country can boast.

The Lieut.-Colonel takes this opportunity of assuring every individual in the corps that they will be certain to meet the most strict and impartial justice at his hands ; that he will give his most full and determined support to the officers and n.c. officers in the execution of their duty, and exact that from them which they are bound as gentlemen and as soldiers to perform to their King and Country, and particularly to the regiment in which they have the honour to serve.   He begs leave to impress upon the minds of the officers that His Majesty would not have called them to the situation they now hold merely for the purpose of their own amusement, and that an attention to their duty is expected of them as men of honour ; and he is confident, from his own experience in the service, that by their attending closely to the interest and comfort, and watching the conduct of their men, they will ensure themselves the confidence and respect of the soldiers, and thereby prevent the commission of crimes, which at present are too frequent.   By pursuing the course thus pointed out, the officers will find in a short time that they will have but little trouble, and that the duties required of them will grow into a habit which will prove a source of pleasure in itself ; and by these means they will re-establish the good opinion of their superiors, and restore the 92nd Highlanders to that high and honourable post which they attained of old by their gallant conduct in the field, and their uniform orderly and becoming behaviour in quarters. The Lieut.-Colonel regrets to perceive the books of the regiment soiled with crimes almost unknown amongst Scotsmen, viz., desertion, drunkenness on duty, insubordination, and even robbery—crimes which he is determined to visit with the utmost rigour which the law will admit of.   At the same time, he trusts the soldiers will not force him to such an extremity by a continuance in a line of conduct so disgraceful, but on the contrary, feel an honest pride in having it in their power to say to each other, " I have never been in confinement, or brought under the Commanding Officer's notice for punishment." And what can be a more noble boast from a soldier of some standing in the service ?   In this hope, the Lieut-Colonel, with the determination to bury the past in oblivion, directs that the adjutant and commanding officers of companies will draw a score across the defaulters' books, in order that from this date no reference may be made to past conduct except in cases required by the rules of the service.   By adopting this measure, he sincerely and confidently hopes that the soldiers who may have been guilty of misconduct may reclaim and turn over a new leaf ; and they will find their military duties become comparatively easy to themselves and their well-disposed comrades, and that their officers will, in consequence, be enabled to grant many indulgences which their own conduct would otherwise deprive them of.

R.O., 12th February 1829.—In future the warning pipe will sound forty minutes before the formation of the battalion on parade.   Immediately on the pipe playing the men are to accoutre, and will form in squads at the sound of the gathering.

In *R.O.*, 15th February, he insists on uniformity of dress,[1] finds fault with the various ways in which the bonnets are worn and feathered—" undoubtedly the most becoming soldier's head-dress in Europe, and consequently requiring greater attention on the part of the wearers. What disfigures one man tends to disfigure his regiment." As to men slovenly on recruiting service—" How unlikely for a high-minded young man to enlist in a corps of which he sees such specimens." Drill was practised, discipline enforced, and excellence encouraged.

However satisfactory the return to the old régime may have been to the majority, it was by no means relished by the evil-doers, and some of them were foolish enough to show their discontent by refusing to turn out for parade. They did not yet know Mac-Donald. An armed party was sent for them ; they were tried by drum-head court-martial, and punished on the spot, whence they retired wiser, if not better men. Later the commanding officer alludes " with both shame and sorrow " to conduct " which will make the 92nd proverbial in the army for deeds of a very opposite character to those for which they were at one time famed," and he addresses himself to every individual soldier to exert himself to prevent the misconduct of a few. No neglect of duty was passed over, whether by officer, n.c. officer, or soldier.[2] The zealous found themselves supported, the lazy or dissipated reformed, or were got rid of.

On the 30th April 1829, Major-General Bingham made his half-yearly inspection, and recorded his pleasure in observing the change in the conduct of the men and the improved appearance of the regiment.

In May they moved to Kilkenny, where Major-General Dalbiac made a most particular inspection in September, both in quarters and in the field, and he desired the commanding officer to express how much he was gratified at everything he had seen connected with the regiment. And when Sir John Byng, commanding the forces in Ireland, reviewed the regiment on the 5th of October, the lieut.-colonel had the pleasure of being directed by him to make known to all ranks " the gratification which he felt at witnessing

---

[1] The following rules are laid down for " cocking and making-up of bonnets " :—The slit and ribbon tie shall be placed directly behind ; the cockade directly over the left ear ; the heckle perpendicular and at a right angle with the man's front ; the centre ostrich fox-tail feathers to hang over the right ear, two to the front and two to the rear of them, none to hang lower than the binding of the bonnet or more forward than the line of the right eye, so that the soldier can take aim without having his feathers burnt by the priming or his vision disturbed by their fluttering in his eyes, etc.

[2] The officers do not appear to have been all great tacticians. One of them having got his company clubbed, was heard to give the very practical, if not very military command—" Threes ; back again afore the Cornal sees ye !" *N.B.*—Movements were made either by " threes " or by " fours."

their soldier-like appearance and the correctness of their movements, as well as the excellent style and cleanliness in which their
barracks are kept.   That from their former services together, he
considers them to be old friends, and was therefore the more
pleased to find the 92nd greatly improved since he last saw them,
and that immediately on his return to Dublin he would make a
point of reporting the very high state of discipline in which he
found the regiment, and which, he was sure, would also afford to
General Lord Hill [1] a pleasure the most sincere."

The little cloud, which for a moment had dimmed the lustre
of their reputation, had passed, never to return so long as the ranks
of the Gordon Highlanders are filled by men of the class who made
the regiment famous, and they are commanded by capable officers
having at heart the true interest of the corps.

Meanwhile, Lieut.-Colonel MacDonald exerted himself to
obtain for his regiment the honours which were their due, and in
forwarding a copy of the revised records to the Adjutant-General's
Office, Horse Guards, he stated that, from his intimate acquaintance with many officers who had served with the 92nd during the
war, and his own knowledge of the conduct of that corps in several
battles, he was led to understand, previous to his joining it, that a
strong feeling of regret and disappointment existed among the
old officers and discharged soldiers as well as in the regiment itself,
because certain badges which were conferred on others similarly
situated had not been granted to their corps.   Major-General

---

[1] At this time Commander-in-Chief, the Duke of Wellington having resigned.

NOTE.—In 1829, a letter was received authorising the adoption of tartan trousers by
officers and soldiers for all occasions when the kilt was not worn.   Previously recruits had
grey or blue pantaloons served out, but as these were worn only on fatigues they were not
expected to be uniform, and the men seem sometimes to have used the tartan of their old kilts.
The officers had latterly French grey trousers with a double stripe of silver lace, with a centre
stripe of dark blue or black and silver mixed.   A forage cap with large flat top and Gordon
tartan band was, for the first time, authorised for officers, who seem previously to have worn,
when walking out at different periods, a hat and feather, a bonnet with one feather in front, or
the feathered bonnet ; the latter was still worn on all duties.   Officers of battalion companies
were directed in future to wear epaulettes, as in other infantry, in place of the wings adopted
in 1822 ; but officers of flank companies and the men of all companies continued to wear wings.
A plain blue frock coat was introduced for officers' undress, to which gold and crimson
shoulder cords were added in 1830.   Previously the undress was merely the dress jacket
buttoned across, blue-grey trousers with lace stripe, and dirk worn on the left side, as per
dress regulations, 1822.   The lace was only authorised in some regiments.

Extract from Monthly Return, 92nd (Highland) Regiment of Foot, Kilkenny,
25th January 1830.
NUMBER OF EACH COUNTRY.

	Sergeants.	Drummers.	Corporals.	Privates.	TOTAL.
English,	2	1	0	36	39
Scottish,	36	12	33	542	623
Irish,	3	1	3	60	67
Foreigners,	0	0	0	0	0
	41	14	36	638	729

Bingham, finding, at his inspection, that the names of general actions in which he knew the 92nd had been engaged were not on its colours, mentioned the circumstance in his confidential report, and a letter from the Adjutant-General of the Forces to Sir John Byng was forwarded to the lieut.-colonel. It stated that " the claim of the 92nd Regiment to certain distinctions is always open to representation and will be considered," etc. Colonel Mac-Donald, having discovered the remaining original records, with the aid of private journals compiled a revised record to replace that referred to on p. 1 of this volume. After giving particulars in a long letter to the Adjutant-General, dated 16th September 1829, he continues—" The 92nd cannot conceal from itself that the absence of these distinctions must hereafter lead to an impression that its conduct on the occasions in question was otherwise than what I am sure it is viewed at headquarters." The result was that, in February 1830, a letter was received by the colonel acquainting him that His Majesty was graciously pleased to approve of the 92nd being permitted to bear on its colours and appointments, in addition to any other badges heretofore granted, the words Corunna, Fuentes d'Onor, Vittoria, Pyrenees, Nive, Orthes, and Almaraz, in commemoration of the distinguished services of the regiment in these actions.

On the 26th May 1830, the regiment marched for Birr, arriving on the 29th, the detachments rejoining about the same period. The following letter was entered in the Order-books :—

MARYBOROUGH, *7th June* 1830.

SIR,—We, the undersigned, magistrates of Maryborough district, at Petty Sessions assembled, avail ourselves of this, the earliest opportunity of expressing our high approbation of the conduct of the different detachments of the Ninety-Second Highlanders, quartered in the town of Maryborough for the last twelve months. In justice to the excellent character of the men, we feel called upon to testify that not a single complaint was made by the inhabitants against any of them, and that their conduct was uniformly correct and exemplary.

The general zeal and intelligence of the officers, supported by the steadiness and discipline of the men, when co-operating with the civil power, particularly during the last winter (in suppressing outrages of a " whiteboy " nature, which, unhappily, extended to our hitherto peaceable county), demand our cordial thanks ; and we beg that you, Sir, will be pleased to make known to the officers and men these our sentiments, and to assure them that their services will long be gratefully remembered by every respectable inhabitant of this town and vicinity.—We have, etc.   (Signed)   W. PERCEVAL, J.P.
                                                                                   D. O'DONOUGHUE, J.P.
                                                                                   MATT. CASSAN, J.P.

Lieutenant-Colonel MacDonald,
Commanding Ninety-Second Highlanders, etc.

A letter was also received expressing thanks and approbation from the Lord-Lieutenant to Lieut.-General the Right Hon. Sir John Byng, K.C.B., and from him to the regiment, for the spontaneous interference of some soldiers of the Grenadier Company in saving the life of a police constable, and retaking a prisoner who had been rescued from him by a mob at Maryborough on the 20th May 1830.

On the 18th June, Waterloo Day, the garrison of Birr was reviewed by Major-General Sir Thomas Arbuthnot, K.C.B. The 92nd afterwards went through the sword exercise,[1] and the Major-General expressed his approbation of the splendid appearance made by the regiment.

On the 2nd July the regiment fired a *feu-de-joie* to celebrate the accession to the throne of His Majesty King William IV, and the regiment went into mourning for His Majesty King George IV, who died on the 26th June 1830.[2]

On the 8th and 9th October the regiment marched from Birr, arriving at Dublin on the 13th and 14th, and was quartered in the Royal Barracks.

On the 30th October the regiment was inspected by Major-General Sir Edward Blakeney. After a most minute scrutiny into the system of the interior arrangements and formation by squads, he expressed his entire and unqualified approbation, and particularly noticed the " respectable and comfortable footing on which the Sergeants' Mess is established." In the afternoon the regiment performed a variety of light-infantry movements in the Park, which drew forth the admiration of the Major-General and the numerous spectators.

On the 12th November the following was promulgated in regimental orders :—

The Bench of Magistrates assembled at Petty Sessions in the Court House, Nenagh, November 1830—Lord Dunalley in the chair.

The undersigned magistrates have observed with great satisfaction the

---

[1] All Gordon Highlanders were taught the sword exercise, and it was the custom to do it after inspections till the Crimean War. Officers, n.c. officers, and private soldiers in line at open order ; in Highland dress, with forage caps.

[2] In August 1830, His Majesty ordered that discharged soldiers receiving a gratuity for meritorious conduct shall be entitled to a silver medal with the words, " For long service and good conduct," and on the other side the king's arms, with the name and rank of the soldier, and the year ; to be delivered on parade, or, if circumstances prevent that, it shall be delivered through the Adjutant-General at the Board of Chelsea Commissioners. The grant to be recorded on the man's discharge certificate, in regimental orders, and in the register of soldiers' services.

At this period the uniforms of all officers of the regular forces were ordered to be laced with gold ; accordingly, the officers of the 92nd changed to gold from the silver hitherto worn (this change was no improvement to a regiment with yellow facings). The silver mounting of the dirks was, however, retained. The gorget was abolished. Sergeants were armed with fusils and bayonets instead of pikes ; an ammunition pouch and belt was added to their accoutrements ; their claymores were retained.

uniformly regular and soldier-like conduct of the detachment of His Majesty's 92nd Highland Regiment during the period they have been at Nenagh, under the command of Captain Bayly, a conduct which reflects great credit on the system, discipline, and interior economy established in that corps, and has merited not only the notice and approbation of the gentlemen of this part of the country, but also secured for the individuals of this detachment the admiration and cordial regard of all classes of the inhabitants of Nenagh, as strongly manifested on the departure of the troops for Dublin.   The magistrates, feeling it to be their pleasing duty to mark their approbation of such good conduct, request their chairman may be pleased to communicate these their sentiments to Lieut.-Colonel MacDonald, commanding the 92nd Regiment.

Signed by the chairman and nine other magistrates.

December 13*th*, 1830.—The regiment was formed in Palatine Square to receive His Excellency Lieut.-General Sir John Byng, commanding the forces in Ireland ; a new stand of colours (the gift of the officers), on which were emblazoned the seven additional badges of distinction conferred on the regiment, was escorted by the grenadier company from the lieut.-colonel's quarters.   His Excellency then made a most appropriate and flattering speech, in which he alluded to the battle of the Nive,[1] of which that day was the anniversary, and to the brilliant and distinguished conduct of the 92nd on that occasion, as well as on many others of which he himself was an eye-witness.   After receiving the colours from the officers of the grenadiers, and remarking how delighted he was to see the names of so many well-earned battles emblazoned on them, he placed them in the hands of the ensigns, and the regiment saluted.   Addressing the regiment, he observed " that he made no allusion to the necessity of defending those colours—any such remark would be out of place when addressing the 92nd ; however, he could not give the young officers and soldiers a better advice than to follow the steps of those who preceded them."   To which the lieut.-colonel replied, that if anything could enhance the value attached to those colours by the regiment, it was their being placed in the hands of the ensigns by one who had, that day seventeen years, shown himself so very conspicuous in placing the colour of a regiment on the enemy's redoubt,[2] and that he pledged himself in the name of his brother officers and soldiers for their honour and safety.

At a meeting of the officers during Colonel MacDonald's

---

[1] St Pierre.

[2] Sir John Byng, afterwards Field-Marshal the Earl of Strafford, Colonel of the Coldstream Guards, led his brigade at the battle of St Pierre to the assault of a strong height occupied in great force by the enemy, and having himself first ascended the hill with the colour of the 31st Regiment in his hands, planted it on the summit, and the enemy was driven down the ridge.

absence, it had been agreed, with his concurrence, that a new pair of colours should be ordered, and it was voted unanimously that the old ones should be presented to him—that " in consequence of your great exertions in revising the records of the regiment, and in obtaining the grant of these badges, you should be requested to accept of the old colours as a mark of respect for your indefatigable zeal in their cause. As the new ones have now been presented to us, I have been honoured with the commands of our brother officers to tender the former colours for your acceptance." [1]

In February 1831, the County Meath being in a very disturbed state, immense assemblages traversing the country, a company of the 92nd, under Captain James MacIntosh, proceeded in light marching order by forced marches to Drumcondra, and on its return on the 22nd March, a letter was received by the lieut.-colonel, which he was directed to communicate to the officers and men of the company, expressing the Lord-Lieutenant's approbation of the " exemplary patience, forbearance, and good temper which they had invariably displayed."

In February a letter was received which showed the interest taken in the regiment by the Commander-in-Chief, Lord Hill, under whom it had so long and actively served, and the pleasure he received from the reports of its high character.

At Sir E. Blakeney's inspection in May, in presence of the Lord-Lieutenant and a great concourse of spectators, the movements and appearance of the Gordon Highlanders elicited the admiration of their military superiors. In May the headquarters moved to Richmond Barracks, the companies at George Street remaining under Major Hugh H. Rose.[2] On July 7th, Sir Hussey Vivian (commanding the forces in Ireland for the time), after inspecting the regiment under Major Winchester, remarked the " high order of the barracks and hospital, which were a pattern and truly delightful to witness " ; the Sergeants' Mess " was the best he had ever seen."

On August 20th, Lieut.-General Sir John Hamilton Dalrymple, Bart. (afterwards Earl of Stair), was appointed Colonel of

---

[1] Letter from Major Winchester to Lieut.-Colonel MacDonald.

NOTE.—It would seem that these old colours had been in use since 1816, and were those of the late Second Battalion, as appears by the following extract from the report of the inspecting officer, preserved at the Record Office :—" Colours entirely shot away and worn out in service, but the regiment has now got those of the Second Battalion, which are perfectly new and good.—(Signed) JOHN HOPE, M.-General, Oct. 23rd, 1816."

Mr Milne, author of " Colours and Standards of the British Army," believes the Waterloo colours to be at Hopetoun. (See Appendix I.)

[2] Afterwards Field-Marshal Lord Strathnairn.

NOTE.—Circular Mem., Horse Guards, 5th March 1831.—" The coats of the drummers of regiments of infantry shall be red " (in place of the colour of the regimental facing, hitherto worn in some regiments).

the 92nd, in succession to Lieut.-General the Hon. Alexander Duff, removed to the 37th Regiment.

On the 10th September the regiment was again inspected by Sir Edward Blakeney in the Phœnix Park, who told officers and men " that they were all he could wish, and that their movements excelled everything he had ever seen."

In September, His Majesty conferred the honour of Companion of the Most Honourable Order of the Bath on Lieut.-Colonel MacDonald.

On 13th October 1831, the regiment proceeded by canal-boats to Killaloe, and on the 22nd headquarters were stationed at Clare Castle, having officers' detachments at sixteen places, besides four under sergeants at posts on the banks of the Shannon.

In February 1832, the regiment marched to Limerick, where Major-General Sir George Bingham, after inspecting in May, highly commended their interior economy, appearance, and movements, and stated that he was particularly delighted by the manner in which officers and men went through the whole sword and single-stick exercise, being the first time he had seen it performed by an entire regiment.

In May the headquarters marched to Fermoy, having nine detachments in the counties of Cork and Tipperary. At one of these villages, water had to be brought from a considerable distance by men detailed for that duty. One Sunday morning the cook found this had been neglected, and he had no water to make the porridge ; but observing a supply at the door of the R.C. chapel, and not considering that it was holy water, he took it. The priest complained of the sacrilege direct to the Commander-in-Chief in Dublin, and an order came for a court-martial on the offender ; but the colonel, having foreseen this, had brought the man into headquarters, and awarded a slight punishment, so that when the order came from Dublin the man, having been already dealt with, could not be tried ; but his company who had eaten the porridge was for many years called " The Holy Boys." In consequence of an outbreak of cholera at Bruff in July, the detachment there was withdrawn, and, for the same reason, that at Mitchelstown was withdrawn in August.[1]

During the latter part of 1832 and six months of 1833, the regiment and its detachments were frequently employed in aid of the civil power, in keeping the peace and enforcing the collection of tithes ; and in every instance the conduct and discipline of the Gordon Highlanders was approved by their superiors. Three

[1] 1832.—Shirt-frills were done away with. Field-officers to return to the use of waist-belts, only the adjutant to continue shoulder-belt with slings. The military year was from this period to commence 1st April, instead of 1st January.

letters of thanks from the Commander of the Forces were received for " the judicious dispositions made, for the excellent discipline and proper spirit" displayed, and expressing " regret that the service on which they were employed should have been of so harassing a nature."

When Major-General Sir Thomas Arbuthnot, commanding the district, inspected in June 1833, after intimating his satisfaction in every respect, he added, " It was most pleasing to him to find that the manner in which the regiment and its detachments are in the habit of comporting themselves towards the inhabitants of the country, and the very soldier-like manner in which they perform their duties has made them bodily and individually respected and looked up to by the magistrates and gentry residing in the vicinity of their quarters."

Colonel MacDonald told me the objection to pay tithe was so determined that on one occasion, when a priest's cow was ordered to be sold for payment of this tax, it took a squadron of cavalry, two guns of the Royal Artillery, and the Gordon Highlanders to enable the sale to take place—and then no one dare bid for the cow !

Among other incidents of the unpleasant duties of the time, the subaltern's detachment at Galbally was called on to protect two magistrates whose lives were in danger from the attack of a riotous mob. While escorting them towards Tipperary, at a place called Knockballimaloo Cross, a general assault was made on the party, to their imminent danger. The magistrates ordered the officer to fire, with the result that two of the mob were killed and several wounded. The situation of troops on such occasions was pretty much between the devil and the deep sea ; for if they failed in protecting those entrusted to their charge, they were liable to be tried by court-martial for neglect of duty ; while, if in the performance of that duty life was lost, they were tried by the civil power for murder, though of course—as in this instance—they were acquitted if circumstances had warranted their action. At the trial of this party, a lawyer, who was trying to make out a case against the military, endeavoured, in cross-examination, to extract from a young soldier an admission of undue violence and personal responsibility, but got no change out of the sturdy Scot.

" Now, sir, why did you fire on these innocent and defenceless people ? "

" Because I got the order."

" And why did you not sooner cease firing ? "

" Because I didna get the order."

" And how long would you have continued firing had you got no order ? "

" As long as I had a round in my pooch."

" How many rounds had you ? "

" Juist saxty ! "

In July, Lieut.-Colonel MacDonald was ordered to prepare the regiment for embarkation for Gibraltar, and the various detachments were withdrawn. The depôt was formed under Major Winchester. The six service and four depôt companies were inspected by Sir Thomas Arbuthnot, who expressed his regret at losing from his command a regiment " which had gained universal respect and esteem for the manner in which it had executed the numerous and trying duties which it had been called upon to perform."

At this time, complications in Spain, which resulted in the Carlist war of 1836, caused some apprehension ; and on the 8th of August a confidential communication was received, which caused the depôt companies to be blended with the others, and the whole regiment held in readiness to embark for service (supposed destination, Portugal) ; but these instructions being immediately cancelled, the depôt was re-formed, and on the 13th August marched to Cork, and embarked for Londonderry.[1]

The following address from the nobility and gentry of the county was presented to Lieut.-Colonel MacDonald, C.B., by Major-General Barry :—

FERMOY, *8th August* 1833.

The under-mentioned magistrates and other principal inhabitants of the town and neighbourhood of Fermoy, having heard with sincere regret that the highly distinguished regiment under your command has received orders to embark for foreign service, cannot permit them to depart without expressing the high sense they entertain of their uniform exemplary conduct during the protracted period of their being quartered in this garrison, which has been such as to create a very general feeling of admiration and attachment ; and they further beg you to accept this expression of their esteem for the regiment, and to add their best wishes for its future welfare.

Signed by   THE EARL OF ENNISMORE,
MAJOR-GENERAL H. G. BARRY,
and many others.

To Lieut.-Colonel MacDonald,
92nd Highlanders.

In December recruiting ceased for a time.

On the 19th and 20th February 1834, the regiment embarked at Ballinacurra, and was conveyed by steamboats to H.M. troopship *Jupiter.*[2]

---

[1] Major, 1 ; captains, 4 ; lieutenants, 4 ; ensigns, 4 ; staff, 1 ; sergeants, 12 ; drummers, 4 ; rank and file, 208.

[2] Embarked—Lieut.-Colonel, 1 ; major, 1 ; captains, 6 ; lieutenants, 8 ; ensigns, 4 ; staff, 5 ; sergeants, 31 ; drummers, 10 ; rank and file, 512. Four rank and file had been landed at Ship Island to be discharged, and one died on the voyage, so they disembarked 507 rank and file.

On the 21st a farewell and most complimentary letter was received, in which Major-General Sir T. Arbuthnot again expressed his " unqualified approbation of their good and soldier-like conduct," and his thanks to Lieut.-Colonel MacDonald for the manner in which he had at all times supported him.

Before following the fortunes of the Gordons to the Mediterranean, it will be well to mention an occurrence which took place during their tour of duty in Ireland, and in which their commander was a principal actor. It was so characteristic of the time that, though lamentable in its results, it cannot properly be passed unnoticed in the life of the regiment.

While the 92nd was at Fermoy, a regiment on the march was billeted in the town, and their officers dined at the barracks. One of them made a remark which seemed to Colonel MacDonald to be disparaging to his men, and with which he declined to agree. The retort was such that the colonel rose from table and left the room, accompanied by one of his officers. An apology was asked and refused. They met at dawn on the bank of the Blackwater. MacDonald fired in the air, when his adversary exclaimed, " I did not come here for child's play ! " and demanded another exchange of shots. This time the colonel fired with fatal effect, which was regretted by none more sincerely than by the surviving principal and his second. They obtained leave, and retired for a time to the wilds of Rannoch ; but as Colonel MacDonald soon returned to his command, it is evident that the result of the inquiry proved him to have acted according to what was then considered the code of honour.[1]

---

[1] The above account was given to me, with the expressions used by the officer at mess and on the ground, by an officer who was present with the regiment at the time, though not present at the duel. After this volume was published, the late Major-General Forbes Macbean brought to the notice of the author a detailed account of the duel written by the second of the officer who was killed. It entirely bears out the above.

CHAPTER III

1834–1844

ON the 10th March 1834, the regiment disembarked at the New Mole, Gibraltar, and occupied Rosea Barracks, moving on the 17th to the Town Range.

In June some cases of cholera appeared in the garrison, and all communication with Spain was stopped till September, when, to the joy of all, particularly to the inhabitants of St Roque, who depend greatly on the garrison of Gibraltar for subsistence, communication was resumed on the disappearance of the disease.[1]

The monotony of garrison duty was unpleasantly relieved in November by a fearful storm of rain, hail, and thunder, bringing down large masses of rock, stones, and sand ; many houses were destroyed, and some of the streets were filled with the *débris* as high as the second floors. Several lives were lost, and the detachment of the 92nd at Catalan Bay barely saved their lives, arms and accoutrements, escaping in a state of nudity from the barrack, which was instantly filled with rocks and rubbish.

The year 1835 passed uneventfully, and when the regiment sailed for Malta on the 20th January 1836, Sir Alexander Woodford, who had lately been appointed Lieut.-Governor, in his farewell order expressed " the high opinion which, even on short acquaintance, he has formed of its interior order, its conduct, and its discipline."

The regiment disembarked at Malta, the 8th February 1836, and was quartered at Fort Manoel, the island of Gozo, and Fort Tigné.

In June 1836, died George, fifth Duke of Gordon, who, as Marquis of Huntly, was the first Colonel of the Gordon Highlanders. Although long separated from the regiment officially, the connection was continued by many friendly ties, and it cannot be out of place, in the history of a Highland regiment, to notice the death of one whose position was so exceptional in the Highlands, particularly in the districts from which that regiment was principally recruited ; and where he is still remembered for his generous sympathy with the peasantry, and his friendly personal intercourse with all classes. His active charity and love of frolic are exemplified in the following anecdotes. He was in the habit of giving one of his agents a sum to be distributed in alms to the poor of the neigh-

---

[1] The 92nd lost 1 sergeant, 8 rank and file, 4 women.

AUTHOR'S NOTE.—1834. Officers' forage caps altered—blue cloth, red binding, diced band, gold embroidered thistle and Sphinx over it. (No number was ever worn on forage caps of officers or soldiers ; those of the latter had no badge except a grenade for grenadiers and bugle for light company.) The blue frock coat to have solid crescents fastened by shoulder straps of blue cloth laced round the edges, with thistles in the crescent, in place of the cords hitherto worn.

bourhood, but hearing that the money was not so applied, he one day appeared in beggar's rags at his almoner's door, and, with the trembling voice of age, solicited alms. A servant told him to be gone—" No beggars allowed here ! " In the well-feigned accent of the country he was pleading his necessity, when the master appeared and sternly ordered him to be gone, or he would set the dog at him ! When in the next annual accounts the usual charge for " incidental charities " appeared, the Marquis drew his pen through it, and reminded his agent with a severe rebuke of his conduct to the beggar.

One of a party, when his power of counterfeiting character was the topic of conversation, offered to bet that he could not be deceived. The wager was accepted, and in a few days a sturdy gaberlunzie, rigged out in rags and wallet, doffed his bonnet to the gentleman, whom he met in his avenue. After answering a few questions in the dialect of the district, he was sent to the hall, where he was served with an ample meal. On quitting the house he took care to cross the laird's path and make his bow.

" Well, old boy, how did you fare in the hall ? "

" Vara middlin'," replied the beggar ; " naething but cauld beef, soor bread, and stale ale ! "

Enraged at this impudence, the laird called some of his men and threatened to have him punished, when, like the " Gudeman of Ballengeich," Huntly

> Let a' his duddies fa',
> And stood the brawest gentleman that was amang them a'. [1]

The men of Lochaber were not, in the early part of the 19th century, the quiet, railway-riding, up-to-date people of to-day. Rent days, shinty matches (*camanachd*), weddings, fairs, and funerals were all festive occasions where liquor flowed, and outstanding quarrels were often settled by a free fight. The Rev. D. MacColl, Episcopal clergyman at Fort-William, was for some years factor on the Gordon estates in that neighbourhood, but in his absence the Duke sent a gentleman from his lowland property to collect the rents, telling him to be sure to have an ox killed and a cask of whisky broached with which to regale the tenants. The agent gave the entertainment *first*, with the result that the Highland blood was up ; he fled in terror of his life, and returned empty. His Grace, than whom no one better understood his Highland tenantry, laughed and said, " Never mind, I 'll go with you next time," which he accordingly did. The rents were willingly paid, *after* which another ox and cask of whisky were provided, and all went home happy and cheering their popular landlord.

[1] Kay's " Biographical Sketches."

HIS GRACE, GEORGE, FIFTH AND LAST DUKE OF GORDON, G.C.B., ETC.
From a portrait by Sanders at Gordon Castle

He was a keen deer-stalker, and those who visited him for that sport have described to me the simple life of those days at Glenfishie —box-beds, two in a room, the bill of fare composed of the produce of hill and stream, dinner announced by the sound of the piobreachd; in the evening, music from the ladies, or reels danced to the violin. The Duke and his Highland friends used the Highland dress on the hill and in the evening, and every guest was expected to sport at least a vest of Gordon tartan.

After the peace of 1815, all the best farms on the Gordon estates throughout the wide districts of Badenoch and Lochaber were occupied by retired officers,[1] among them Colonel Mitchell and others of the 92nd, and these gentlemen were constant guests both at Kinrara and Glenfishie, and at the more princely entertainments at Gordon Castle. Nor were the rank and file of the regiment forgotten. Sergeant MacKinnon, a Banavie man, who left a leg in Spain, was long postmaster at Kingussie, a situation obtained for him by the Duke, and his daughter, named Johanna Cameron, after " Fassiefern," still (1900) occupies the house built for her father, and relates how His Grace danced at the house-heating. To this day the sons of old 92nd soldiers occupy their fathers' holdings on what were once the Gordon estates ;[2] for the Duke's vast lands in Badenoch and Lochaber, with the exception of Kinrara, were sold, and it is not surprising to find that on his farewell visit to Badenoch a scene of the wildest enthusiasm took place, or that for years after his death " the memory of the fifth and last Duke of Gordon " was drunk in solemn silence at public dinners in the district.[3] The other estates went to his nephew, the Duke of Richmond.[4] The Dukedom of Gordon became extinct, but the title of Marquis of Huntly went to another branch of the family, the Earls of Aboyne.

In the " Highland Chieftain's Welcome," a poem written at the time of George IV's visit to Scotland, he is thus mentioned—

> And Huntly, at once the delight and the glory,
> The boast and the pride of the clans of the north,
> Renowned, not more in warrior's story
> Than in home's happy circle, for true manly worth.

. . . .

In March 1836, a detachment of 40 rank and file under Ensign

---

[1] Notes by the Rev. Thomas Sinton, Manse of Dores, and others. " History of Badenoch," by A. M'Pherson.

[2] Thirty years after the war there were well on to £2000 paid to pensioners at Kingussie on a single day. Many of these men had vests made of their regimental red jackets, on which they wore their medals on these occasions.—Rev. T. Sinton, on the authority of the late Mr Duncan M'Pherson, the bank agent who paid the money.

[3] Told by Cluny MacPherson in 1863.

[4] The Duke of Richmond was created Duke of Gordon, 1876.

Drake joined from the depôt in Scotland, and 17 n.c. officers and soldiers proceeded to Chatham to be discharged to pension as " worn out." [1]

His Majesty King William IV died at Windsor on the 20th June 1837.

On the 13th July the troops at Malta formed on their respective parades, and fired a *feu-de-joie* in honour of the accession of Her Majesty Queen Victoria to the throne.

A letter from Major Hugh Rose to Colonel MacDonald, who was on leave in Scotland, mentions by name several men, a woman and a child, who had died of cholera at this time, and that " no expense has been spared in attending to their wants. The men are in capital spirits, and it is quite a pleasure to see the way they attend to one another." One sergeant, 6 privates, 3 women, and a child died of cholera at Malta.

On the 28th November, His Excellency Major-General Sir H. F. Bouverie, K.C.B., G.C.M.G., inspected the regiment at Floriana, and directed Major Rose to express to them his approbation in any terms he pleased, as His Excellency " could not say enough of the singular intelligence and steadiness shown by all the officers and men, and that the field-day had the best effect of any he had ever seen."

In December, Colonel MacDonald rejoined, and Lieutenant James Cox, with a draft of one drummer and fifty-six rank and file, arrived from the depôt.

In March 1838, the regiment was ordered to resume recruiting to thirty men above establishment. During this year many men were discharged to pension, and a draft of one sergeant and thirty-one rank and file, under Lieutenant A. A. Campbell, joined from the depôt.

In July, H.R.H. Prince Maximilian of Bavaria landed at Valetta, and on the following day examined the barracks and every part of the interior economy of the 92nd, with which he was much pleased.

On the 30th November the regiment lined the ramparts at St

---

[1] On the 19th September 1836, the good conduct warrant, dated War Office, 18th August 1836, was promulgated to the regiment. Soldiers enlisted on or after 1st September are to have no claim to additional pay after any length of service ; rewards of pay and badges for good conduct are granted in lieu, as well as to such already enlisted as should relinquish their claim to additional pay for length of service.

1837.—At this period the sergeants were directed to wear double-breasted jackets, without lace. Taken into wear, 1838 (some time after, they had lace round the waist of the jacket, but not on the breast) ; lace to be white, without a coloured worm. From a correspondence between Lieut.-Colonel MacDonald and Major Rose it would appear that the regimental purses were altered, probably to black goatskin instead of grey, and five tassels instead of six ; the officers' had been altered about 1822 to white and gold. The breastplates seem also to have been altered—the original oval giving place, about 1818, to a square silver one, with a crown above XCII, and a thistle below it ; about 1830-2, to a gilt one, having a silver thistle star, which was worn till 1881.

Elmo while H.M.S. *Hastings*, seventy-four guns, entered the harbour, with Her Majesty the Queen Dowager on board. And when Her Majesty landed on the 1st December, and returned on board, the 92nd was formed as a guard of honour in the square in front of the palace. On the 4th, Her Majesty landed amid the rejoicings of the inhabitants, and took up her residence in the palace, the town being splendidly illuminated in the evening.

On the 12th, Her Majesty held a levee, when all the officers were presented. Earl Howe, the Lord Chamberlain, having intimated Her Majesty's desire to see the Gordon Highlanders, when it could be accomplished without attracting a crowd, the officers immediately after the levee repaired to their companies, and the battalion was formed in review order on the Floriana Parade. After marching past in slow and quick time and in column at quarter distance, and having performed several movements, the Queen expressed herself as highly delighted, and declared she had never seen " anything so beautiful and at the same time so warlike " as the appearance of the corps. The Lord Chamberlain having intimated that Her Majesty intended to honour by her presence an evening party and private theatricals (by the n.c. officers and soldiers of the regiment) at Colonel MacDonald's quarters in the Auberge de Castile, the light company, with the Queen's colour, was formed at 8.30 p.m. as a guard of honour, and lined the grand staircase and entrance, which was illuminated by variegated lamps representing the Star of the Order of the Thistle. The Queen expressed herself much gratified and surprised to find so much intelligence in the ranks of any regiment as the performers had evinced. The play was " Rob Roy," and next day, when Colonel MacDonald was at the palace, Her Majesty said she had been particularly struck by the histrionic powers of the soldier who acted the part of " Bailie Nicol Jarvie," and wished to see him in his ordinary dress. " He is there, madam," answered the colonel, pointing to the stalwart sentinel below, for it so chanced that he was on guard, and on that post at the moment.

I saw the play-bill many years ago, when visiting the colonel (then General Sir John MacDonald) at Dunalastair, but I forget the Bailie's name.

The regiment having removed from Valetta to Isola Gate, San Francesco de Paolo and Salvatore Barracks, in January 1839, on the 31st Her Majesty, attended by a numerous suite, again reviewed them on St Clemente, and expressed her admiration and that of all present at their appearance and the steadiness with which they moved and kept their ranks, notwithstanding that it was blowing almost a hurricane at the time.

The Highlands had not yet become the playground of the

South, and the Queen's ladies, unaccustomed to the Highland dress, were somewhat taken aback at the display of manly limbs when the regiment formed square, front rank kneeling, opposite the royal carriage. "The Queen," said the narrator, "was a real lady, and looked straight at us ; but we took it ill when the maids of honour put their hands before their faces. But," added the sergeant, with a malicious smile, "I weel believe they keekit through their fingers ! "

In May they were inspected by the Lieut.-Governor, accompanied by H.R.H. Prince George of Cambridge. His Excellency spoke in the most flattering terms of their movements and appearance, saying it was the most perfect thing he had ever seen. The following extract from the Duke of Cambridge's journal is taken from his Memoirs published in 1906, and shows that H.R.H. was equally gratified :—" I have never seen a Scottish Regiment before, and cannot express how agreeable an impression the beautiful garb made upon me. I have never seen anything so beautiful and they manœuvred admirably. We then visited their barracks and the Colonel—MacDonald—gave us a small luncheon."

Several n.c. officers and soldiers were sent home for change of climate.

In October 1839, the service companies received new arms of the " Land Regular Pattern." [1]

Sergeant-major J. Forbes was promoted quartermaster, and was succeeded by Colour-sergeant Donald MacQueen.

In March 1840, there were in the service companies 100 men with good conduct badges and pay, and 7 with badges only.

In April, Captain Caldwell, 1 lieutenant, 1 ensign, an assistant surgeon, 2 sergeants, 1 drummer, and 63 rank and file joined from the depôt.

In August the regiment was held in readiness to embark for the West Indies. In October a draft under Captain Donald

---

[1] The establishment was augmented, in November 1839, to six service companies of 100 rank and file each, 7 staff sergeants, 4 sergeants per company (including colour-sergeants), and 10 drummers and fifers ; four depôt companies of 50 rank and file each, 16 sergeants (including colour-sergeants), 4 drummers and fifers. Recruits for Highland regiments to be allowed £3, 15s. bounty for their equipment on final approval, independent of 10s. on intermediate approval, and 2s. 6d. on attesting.

Extract from Monthly Return of the Service Companies, 92nd (Highland) Regiment, Malta, 1st January 1840.

	Sergeants.	Drummers.	Corporals.	Privates.	TOTAL.
English,	1	2	0	12	15
Scottish,	25	6	22	374	427
Irish,	1	0	0	12	13
Foreigners,	0	0	0	0	0
	27	8	22	398	455

Stewart, 1 lieutenant, 1 ensign, 2 sergeants, and 129 rank and file joined from the depôt.

In November they were inspected, under Brevet Lieut.-Colonel Winchester, K.H., by His Excellency Sir H. Bouverie, who desired him to make known to all ranks how much he was pleased by their performance, " a pleasure which he invariably experienced since he had been connected with the 92nd Highlanders, and caused him on all former, as it would on the present occasion, to make a most favourable report of them to the Commander-in-Chief."

On the 9th January 1841, the First Division, under Brevet Major Stephen Noel, embarked on the *Somersetshire* transport, and arrived at Barbadoes on the 4th April, after a stormy passage of three months ! The headquarters, on board the *Cornwall*, sailed the 23rd January, anchored at Gibraltar after a boisterous voyage of thirty-six days, and arrived at Barbadoes on the same day as the *Somersetshire*.

Headquarters were stationed at St Vincent, with detachments at St Lucia and Dominica, relieving the 52nd Regiment.

In June 1841, a letter was received by Lieut.-Colonel Winchester, commanding at headquarters, conveying the thanks of the two branches of the Legislature of the island " for the prompt and efficient assistance afforded by the officers, n.c. officers, and privates of the 92nd Regiment in putting down a lawless mob, whereby the town of Kingston was protected and the public peace preserved." A presentment made by the Grand Jury of the island of St Vincent to the same effect was also received.

In August yellow fever appeared at Dominica. Application was made for ground on which to encamp the troops, but the owners refused to lease it. The detachment was withdrawn to Barbadoes in November, having lost, out of two companies, 2 lieutenants, 1 ensign, 1 drummer, and 42 rank and file.[1]

On the 14th November, Sergeant-major Donald MacQueen was promoted ensign in the 92nd. Ensign MacQueen became quartermaster, December 1844, and finally retired on full pay with the rank of captain. He became tacksman of Blinkbonnie, on the Brodie estate, where " the captain " was much respected, and often called upon to settle differences among neighbours. I spent a day with him there, and he told me with pardonable pride that he had been herd on that very farm before he enlisted ; he had also been employed as " look-out " by smugglers in the hills, before illicit distillation was put down ; but as soon as he was eighteen he walked off and enlisted with the nearest party of the 92nd. His account

---

[1] Sanitation was not then understood ; beds in some barracks were in two tiers, as in a ship. Good drainage, pure water, greater space, and better ventilation have now rendered the West Indian stations healthy.

of his promotion was characteristic. One day Colonel MacDonald had been giving them the rough edge of his tongue at drill, and was afterwards standing with the adjutant in the square when Sergeant-major MacQueen passed, and the colonel called him. " I dare say," he said, " you think I was rather hard on you to-day, sergeant-major ? There are some men that are not worth damning, but I 'll make something of *you* yet ! " When on leave some time after, the colonel went to the Horse Guards and asked that one of three death vacancies should be given to a sergeant, when he was told that they were already promised to others. He expostulated roundly, saying that those who had borne the rough should have a share of the smooth, and that if he could not hope to reward deserving n.c. officers he would resign his command ; it ended in the sergeant-major being gazetted senior of the three. Captain MacQueen was a tall, fine-looking Celt, a native of the parish of Ard Clach. He died at Nairn towards the end of the century.[1]

G.O., Dominica.—The Officer Commanding the troops would not presume to pass any eulogium on the conduct of a detachment of so distinguished a regiment as the 92nd Highlanders, had not circumstances arisen owing to the dreadful malady which has deprived Her Majesty of so many gallant soldiers, inducing him thus publicly to offer his unfeigned thanks not only for their own uniform good conduct, but also for the unprecedented, manly, and generous feeling which the officers, n.c. officers, and privates evinced towards His Excellency when himself and his family were suffering under a similar dispensation of Providence.[2]

In December the fever attacked the headquarters at St Vincent. The troops were at once encamped on Lomond's Ridge, which checked the progress of the disease.

In January they were embarked on H.M. frigate *Cleopatra*, having lost 1 sergeant, 1 drummer, and 12 rank and file.

On the 27th January 1842, Lieutenant and Adjutant Kenneth Douglas MacKenzie, Lieutenants William Dalzell, Hope-Johnstone, and Gordon, Ensign Charles Edward Stewart Gleig, 2 sergeants, and 59 rank and file arrived from the depôt in Scotland.

The detachment from St Lucia returned to Barbadoes in July and encamped, having lost four privates. The officer command-ing the troops at St Quein attributes the unusually good health of the detachment " to the cleanliness of their barracks inside and out, and to the watchful and unremitting care which Captain Cald-well had taken of the interests of his men, often under peculiar

---

[1] At Barbadoes three corporals were transferred as sergeants to the First West India Regi-ment. One of them, William Thomson, soon got a commission, retired as major, and died in Edinburgh, 1895.

[2] The kind and manly conduct of the soldiers on this as on former occasions, when their comrades were attacked by this fearful fever, was in marked contrast to the selfish dread of infection often lamentably exhibited by the civil population in the Highlands.

difficulties " ; and he praises the men for their ready and cheerful attention to duty and general good conduct.

In February the fever again appeared, particularly in the officers' quarters. At Colonel MacDonald's recommendation, these were vacated and the troops encamped. Altogether, the regiment lost in the year April 1841 to April 1842, Lieutenants Munro, J. Caulfield Gordon, William Dalzell, and Ensign J. Davies, 7 sergeants, 2 drummers, and 68 rank and file. Among them was Corporal Fraser, from near Beauly, a perfect giant ; said to be the tallest man in the army.

In July a letter was received, dated Horse Guards, 22nd June 1842, addressed to Lieut.-General Maister, commanding at Barbadoes, acknowledging his confidential report after his inspection of the 52nd and 92nd—

the perusal of which has afforded Lord Hill the greatest satisfaction. The efficient state of these two distinguished regiments, notwithstanding the calamitous effects of the epidemic to which they have been recently exposed, I am commanded to assure you His Lordship considers to be extremely creditable to the exertions of their commanding officers, Lieut.-Colonel Blois and Colonel MacDonald, and characteristic of that admirable system of interior discipline which has been long established in both these corps.

(Signed)   JOHN MACDONALD, Adjutant-General.

In March 1843, Ensign Allan M'Donald and sixteen men, all artificers, were sent to Antigua to repair the damage done in that island by a fearful earthquake on the 8th of February.

In 1843 the following extract from a letter, dated Horse Guards, 28th June, relates to a report to the Commander-in-Chief[1] by the Lieut.-General :—

And with regard to the 92nd, the report is altogether so highly recommendatory that His Grace has only to express the satisfaction he has derived from observing that this grand national corps continues to maintain its long established character for efficiency and discipline, notwithstanding its protracted service within the tropics.

(Signed)   JOHN MACDONALD, A.-G.

On the 22nd May the headquarters embarked on H.M. troopship *Crocodile*, and landed at Trinidad on the 26th, where Colonel MacDonald assumed command of the troops. Detachments of the regiment were at Tobago, Grenada, San Fernando, and St. Joseph.

The *Gazette* of the 31st May 1843 announced the appointment of Lieut.-General Sir William Macbean, K.C.B., to be Colonel of the 92nd Regiment, *vice* the Earl of Stair, removed to the 46th.

In June the yellow fever again appeared, and Sergeant-major

1 The Duke of Wellington had again become Commander-in-Chief, *vice* Lord Hill, deceased.

Forgie, 1 sergeant, and 19 rank and file died at St James' Barracks. A monument was erected in the graveyard with the following inscription:—

Sacred to the memory of Sergeant-major Andrew Forgie, 92nd Highlanders, who died 28th June 1843, aged 33 years. Erected by his brother sergeants in testimony of their high esteem.

The following extract from Regimental Orders will show the feeling was not confined to themselves alone :—

Colonel MacDonald invites the officers to accompany him in paying the last tribute of respect due to the remains of one who has served, for upwards of fourteen years, under him as a non-commissioned officer of this regiment. " Mors omnibus communis."

More than forty years after, Colonel Man Stewart, Third Battalion Gordon Highlanders, was commanding in Trinidad, and knowing that the 92nd had been quartered there, he cleared the graveyard to see if there were any memorials of them. The sergeant-major's was the only one, and he had it repaired and set up on its old site.[1]

In November intimation was received that the transport *Java* might be daily expected to convey the regiment to England. Preparations were made accordingly. In December they were relieved by the 71st Highland Light Infantry. The *Java* sailed on Christmas Day with the whole regiment, arrived at Spithead on the 3rd February 1844, and the following day proceeded to Leith, where she anchored on the 15th. Next morning, Nos. 1 and 2 Companies, under Brevet Major Mark Kerr Atherley, transhipped to a steamer, landed at Queensferry, marched to Kinross, and next day occupied Perth Barracks. The steamer *Duke of Richmond* took the headquarters and flank companies to Aberdeen, and the same vessel landed Nos. 3 and 4 Companies, under Captain P. MacLeod Petly, on the 18th at Fort-George. The depôt ceased to be considered as such, but its four companies remained at Dundee as a detachment of the regiment.[2]

I well remember the account of their arrival at Aberdeen, given me by Lance-sergeant Imlach fifty years ago. How numbers of parents had arrived from Strathspey, Moray, and Banffshire, the meetings between mothers and sons—some of them as " yellow as gowans "—and the sad duty of the sergeant of the guard replying to anxious inquiries, " Died at St Lucia," " Died at Dominica." Many of the soldiers belonged to the district through which the

---

[1] Letter from Colonel Man Stewart, 1898.

[2] The strength of the regiment was :—Colonel, 1 ; Lieut.-Colonel, 1 ; majors, 2 ; captains, 10 ; lieutenants, 12 ; ensigns, 8 ; staff, 6 ; sergeants, 47 ; corporals, 40 ; drummers, 12 ; rank and file, 777. 119 men with badges and pay, 40 with badges without pay. Being 22 men above the establishment, recruiting was suspended.

Inverness mail coach passed, and so respected was the regiment that the guard told me they carried free the little presents with which their families greeted their return.   The late Colonel K. D. Mackenzie, who was then adjutant, told me of one old lady, dressed in the well-ironed " mutch " and picturesque scarlet cloak worn by country women in the north at that time, who consulted him on the subject of her son's discharge.   He told her how certain sums, amounting to £20, should be lodged with the War Office. " Twenty pund ! " cried the dame, " that's clean oot o' the question " ; then, giving him a confidential nudge with her elbow, and looking up knowingly in his face as if her argument would certainly settle the matter, she continued, " Ye juist tell the auld Cornal, an' he 'll lat oor Jamie slip quietly awa', *it 'll be as guid as three pund in 's pooch* ! "   The argument had not the effect she expected ; at any rate, I knew " oor Jamie " some years later, a six-foot grenadier, with three good-conduct badges.

We left the depôt companies, under Major Winchester, in August 1833, at Londonderry.   From there they went to Scotland, and were quartered at Greenlaw (now Glencorse).   On April 28th, 1834, they marched for embarkation at Newhaven, but such was the severity of the weather that they were countermanded *en route*, and returned to barracks.   On May 1st they embarked, and landed at Fort-George on the 2nd.   At these stations they were reported on for " soldierlike appearance," " orderly demeanour," and the " cleanliness of barracks."   They remained at Fort-George till June 18th, 1835, when they embarked for Perth in two divisions.   On May 23rd, 1836, Major-General Hon. Patrick Stuart was so pleased with the depôt that he pardoned the only prisoner in the guard-room, Private W. Dewar, who was to have been tried by court-martial.   On July 5th, 1836, the depôt left the Fair City for Ireland, and marched to Glasgow.   Embarking there on the 9th, they arrived at Londonderry on the 10th.   I remember, in 1852, an Atholl man, then a corporal in my company, describing this his first march as a recruit.   " No railways at that time—the train 's a grand marcher ; the civilians were very kind to us sodgers —too kind sometimes in the matter o' drink."

19th May 1837.—The depôt marched to Armagh, one company being detached at Monaghan.

15th September 1837.—Depôt marched to Mullingar, arriving 22nd.   11th May 1838, marched to Nenagh, arriving 23rd, a subaltern's detachment being at Killaloe.   14th September 1838, they marched (two days) to Limerick.[1]

---

[1] There was little luxury in these Irish barracks.   At Birr there was no kitchen ; they cooked in the barrack-rooms.

At these various stations they were favourably reported on, and when they left Nenagh an address, signed by forty-two of the leading inhabitants, was presented to Lieut.-Colonel Winchester, K.H., the officers, n.c. officers, and men, assuring them that they had endeared themselves to the inhabitants of Nenagh " by your general bearing and uniform urbanity," and testifying to the good feeling between the people " and all ranks of the depôt of the gallant 92nd."

January 31*st*, 1839.—The depôt marched from Limerick and arrived on February 4th at Birr, with detachment at Banagher. Here they remained till January 21st, 1840, when they marched to Mullingar, where they were inspected by Major-General Sir W. P. Carroll, K.C.B., who alluded to their efficiency under arms, etc., which he stated he " had never seen exceeded in the oldest established corps," and " that the return of crimes was less than in almost any instance he had known."

In June 1840, the depôt moved to Glasgow, remaining there till July 6th, when it marched to Stirling. May 3rd, 1841, embarked at Alloa, and landed at Fort-George on the 4th.

June 12*th*, 1842.—Embarked at Fort-George and landed next day at Dundee, where, in August, the cordial thanks of the magistrates were conveyed to the officers, n.c. officers, and men for the prompt manner in which they had been assisted by them in preserving the peace of the town. (Signed) WILLIAM BARRIE, Town-Clerk.

August 31*st*, 1842.—On the occasion of H.M. Queen Victoria's visit to Taymouth Castle,[1] a guard of honour under Captain Mark Kerr Atherley, Lieut. Archibald Neil Campbell, and Ensign Edward Peter Mann, 4 sergeants, and 50 rank and file marched to Taymouth, where they encamped and remained during Her Majesty's visit. On their return to their quarters in Dundee, Major-General Sir Neil Douglas, K.C.B., commanding H.M. forces in North Britain, thanked Lieut.-Colonel Winchester for the appearance and conduct of the guard, of which Her Majesty had expressed her approval, as had H.R.H. Prince Albert.

A subaltern of the guard told me how the neighbouring gentry, to show their loyalty, had brought their tenants and retainers armed and in the Highland dress, and wished their clansmen to take the soldiers' place in guarding their Sovereign. This could not, of course, be allowed, but double sentries were posted—a regular and an irregular Highlander. During the day they were equally in evidence, but when he went the rounds *at night* he found only his own men ; the others had left that uninteresting part of the programme entirely to the redcoats.

---

[1] This was Her Majesty's first visit to Scotland.

The Marquis of Breadalbane treated the guard with true Highland hospitality, both officers and men.   The rations of the latter were supplemented by liberal supplies of game and venison, with casks of ale *ad libitum*, while crowds of country people showed their goodwill by unlimited offers of whisky.   Still, though a Gordon Highlander of that time dearly loved a dram, his sense of what was due to his regiment on such an occasion prevented his exceeding. Though the liquor was free, not a single soldier was seen the worse of drink.   And yet, some of these very men got drunk at their own expense on the night they returned to their quarters.

February 7th, 1844.—The depôt was amalgamated with the service companies.

1823.   1828.   1835.
(Field Officer)

OFFICERS' UNDRESS UNIFORM

CHAPTER IV

1844-1846

I HAVE in my possession some interesting notes of the Life of the Regiment written by an officer during his service from ensign to captain—1843-1848. He mentions the long journey in snowy weather by coach from Newcastle, where the railway from London ended, when, as a lad of sixteen fresh from Eton, he joined at Aberdeen. Changing coaches at Edinburgh in the early morning,[1] he arrived at Castle-Hill Barracks as the pibroch, announcing the officers' dinner (at seven), was being played. He describes his kindly welcome by the adjutant, Kenneth M'Kenzie, who took him into the brilliantly lighted mess-room where the officers, in gold epaulettes, sashes, and dirks, were at dinner, and presented him to the colonel, " with iron-gray hair, clean shaved, eyes like a gled, a resolute mouth and chin, and one arm in a sling." Soon the head-waiter told him that the colonel requested to take wine with him ; having bowed to his commanding officer, a like invitation was brought from the major, and by degrees every officer in turn paid him the same compliment.

After being instructed and drilled three times daily for four months, he was examined by the colonel and sent to duty.

Before railways did so much to cement the Union, Scottish gentlemen were educated nearer home than in recent times. Though many of his brother officers were members of well-known Scottish county families, only one besides himself had been at one of the great English public schools. The officers lived, he says, quite a family life together, with the colonel always looked up to and loyally supported. The " Chief," as he was called, left the discipline of companies very much to their captains, who in their turn encouraged and required the subalterns to be acquainted with everything concerning the subdivisions in their charge. The duty was carried on in a manner which gave every one the responsibility of his position. As in " Fassiefern's " time, Colonel MacDonald insisted on the books of the companies being kept in the writing of their commanding officers. " This was unusual in the army, but writing out a subject impresses the memory, so our captains were thoroughly up in all details connected with their companies."

Both the social and the sporting instincts of the officers found plenty of occupation offered to them—many balls and carpet dances

---

[1] The " Defiance," by Queensferry and Perth to Aberdeen, had been established in 1829. The speed, then thought wonderful, was ten miles an hour, doing the journey from Edinburgh in 12 hours 35 minutes, a great improvement on the six miles an hour of its predecessor, whose driver was known as " Ca' awa' Robbie."—*Nimrod's Northern Tour.*

A daily mail replaced the three days a week coach from Edinburgh to Inverness in 1836—starting at 3 p.m., arriving 10.30 a.m. Prior to 1840, a letter of *one sheet only* cost 1s. 0½d. from Inverness to Edinburgh.—*Post Office Recollections,* by A. P. Hay, Inverness Postmaster (private circulation).

—champagne not so common at the suppers as now, but a beverage called "plotty," made of hot spiced red wine. Hosts and partners were kind, and they thoroughly enjoyed their stay in Aberdeen.

Having sketched the life of the officers, we will now describe that of the n.c. officers and men, who also enjoyed the time. Furloughs were freely granted on their arrival, and if all were like one I met on a hill road near the Spey, they did credit to their regiment. In his bonnet and green hackle, waving tartan and buckled shoes, his manly bearing and martial air made as deep an impression on my boyish memory as no doubt it did on the winsome lassie who accompanied him.[1]

At this time the enlistment was unlimited as to place or period, but the soldier was generally discharged to pension after twenty-one years in infantry, and twenty-four in the other branches. The standard height for the regiment was in general 5 feet 6 inches, occasionally raised to 5 feet 8 inches, and at the colonel's discretion a few lads under the standard were taken ; the grenadier company standard varied from 5 feet 10 inches to 5 feet 11 inches, and their average height from 5 feet 11½ inches to 6 feet and upwards. The light company was chosen for intelligence and marching powers, not for height ; their average was from 5 feet 7¾ inches to 5 feet 9 inches, according to the choice of the captain who picked the men.[2]

A recruit received free—greatcoat, red coat, white jacket, and pair of shoes ; the last three articles were renewed annually, the greatcoat at certain periods. All other articles were paid for by the soldier, including his knapsack, and a plaid every third year, his bounty (£4) being mostly thus expended. Four yards were considered sufficient for a kilt, but some men bought an additional yard, or even two. The kilts were not cut out at the back, so after a year's wear the whole stuff could be used for fatigue trousers and vests, or for adding to new kilt, saving any outlay for these. Three months after enlistment the recruit was credited with £1 10s. to supply himself with a bonnet ; this was insufficient for a new one complete, but he generally bought the feathers of non-effectives, or men about to be discharged, often going to considerable expense to have handsome feathers, which, however, lasted for many years. Indeed, a recruit was often in debt and on 1d. a day for pocket-money at first. A board, consisting of a subaltern, the quartermaster, and an old private, examined the tartan, feathers, and all articles of necessaries supplied by the regimental tradesmen

---

[1] A Badenoch song by a girl whose sweetheart was in the 92nd is given in Appendix II. The 92nd were often called "The Duke's Regiment."

[2] Major R. Bethune, Sir George Warrender, Bt., both former captains light company, Major Jas. Gordon, formerly colour-sergeant light company, and others.

before they were issued. Bonnets and all articles of dress down to the wire pins that fastened their kilts, except coats, shoes, and purses, were made up by soldiers, who were paid accordingly. There was also a yearly allowance " in lieu of Highland articles " granted about 1845—to sergeants, 15s. 6d. ; to rank and file, 8s. 6d. The men's walking-out dress was, on week-days, white jacket and kilt without a purse, and buckled shoes ; full dress with bonnet on Sundays. From about 1846 the purse was worn walking out, but never a greatcoat. By an army order of an earlier date, private soldiers no longer carried side arms except on duty, but officers and n.c. officers never appeared in public without them.

The bread and meat were contracted for by the commanding officer every month with local tradesmen, and the cost of the ration was published in regimental orders and charged to the soldiers ; it consisted of $\frac{3}{4}$ lb. beef and 1 lb. bread. In the sergeants' mess the meals were always good and ample, the cost per member seldom exceeding 1s. a day. The men's messing was managed by a committee elected in each company, consisting of a corporal and two privates, who purchased meal and milk, vegetables and groceries ; they kept a mess book, which was examined weekly by the commanding officer. It was always arranged to keep the cost of messing at such a figure as to allow at least a clear 4d. a day pocket-money to each, besides any good conduct pay he might be entitled to. When provisions were cheap the messing was better, when dear it was not so good, but the men were satisfied because they had the management themselves. There was no variety in the bill-of-fare—porridge and a pint of sweet milk for breakfast, barley broth, beef and potatoes for dinner. There was no regular evening meal, but men would club together to buy potatoes and dripping, etc., which they cooked for themselves. About 1846 an evening meal of coffee and bread was established.[1] Altogether, taking pensions into account, the soldier's position compared favourably with that of a farm-servant or workman at the time.[2]

In August 1844, the regiment was held in readiness to move. On the 17th No. 3 Company marched from Fort-George, arriving in Aberdeen on the 24th. No doubt marching troops encouraged

[1] From notes by Major J. Gordon, formerly sergeant-major ; ex-Colour-sergeant A. Anderson, and others who served at this time. Major Gordon said that when he joined (1839) a large Gaelic Bible for the use of the men was kept by the pay-sergeant of each company.

The proposal for a regular evening meal was at first not at all popular. A committee of officers at the Horse Guards asked a number of soldiers their opinion, which was thus voiced by a guardsman. Being asked if he thought it a good plan, he cordially agreed ; but on its being explained that the men were to pay for it, said, " *Pay* for it, sir ? No, sir, he must be a very slovenly looking guardsman who can't get his tea for nothing ! "

[2] About 1840, labourers' wages in Mull were 8d. a day for a lad and 1s. for a man. In 1850, an underkeeper or forester on the mainland had 10s. a week, and a few years later 12s. and lodging.

1840-45

CORPORAL IN MARCHING ORDER, WITH PRICKER AND BRUSH HANGING FROM CROSS BELTS
TO CLEAR VENT AND PAN OF FLINT LOCK—DISUSED 1845.

SERGEANT, LIGHT COMPANY, IN SUNDAY WALKING-OUT UNIFORM.

PRIVATE, GRENADIER COMPANY, IN WEEK-DAY WALKING-OUT UNIFORM.

PRIVATE, BATTALION COMPANY, IN FATIGUE CLOTHING.

The details of bonnets and other items of the Highland dress differed from time to
time, according to the taste of the Commanding Officer and, to a certain extent, of the
individual.

military ardour in the districts through which they passed. It certainly did so in my own case. I well remember leaving my tutor and my books to see the evening parade of this company opposite the " Gordon Arms " at Elgin : the officers in blue frock coats, tartan trousers, and white gaiters ; the cased bonnets and nut-brown knees of the soldiers, and their military bearing as they " recovered arms " and dismissed.

The headquarters marched from Aberdeen on the 24th August for Glasgow, where they arrived on the 5th September. They were well treated on the road. Harvest was in full swing ; bands of men and women came from Skye and the north (before the days of reaping machines), to " shear " the corn with the sickle on the fertile straths between Stonehaven and Stirling. One day as the regiment passed along, a party of buxom lassies, excited by the music, joined the ranks and insisted on carrying the soldiers' muskets for a considerable distance, amid much banter and laughter on both sides. Unfortunately good feeling sometimes found a less harmless vent and severely tried the men's sobriety. A certain grenadier, whose overnight potations and morning dram, though they prevented his being allowed to take his place in the ranks, did not make him forget that *esprit de corps* which, drunk or sober, is ever present in a Gordon Highlander—" I ken fine," he said, " I 'm naething but a drucken grenadier, but I wad rayther be a grenadier o' the 92nd than Gustāvus Adolphus, King o' Sweden." He was a great character, Jamie M'D——, could turn a somersault in marching order—all but the bonnet ; he was well educated ; he made a song about every quarter, which he sang as they left it ; discharged to pension before the Crimean War, he joined the Land Transport Corps, served the campaign and so got additional pension.

There were, however, exceptions to the cordiality of civilians, especially where the Chartist element prevailed. A big rough, with abusive language, shoved a dirty snuff-box in the face of a young officer, but the next instant was sent sprawling in the gutter by a blow straight from the shoulder of one of the light company.

On the 6th September the regiment was united at Glasgow with the exception of detachments at Fort-George, Fort-Augustus, and Fort-William. At these places numbers of 92nd pensioners came to pay their respects to their successors, telling them their adventures in the French wars. Dumbarton Castle was also occupied by a subaltern's detachment, and on the 23rd two companies marched to Paisley. These companies returned to Glasgow on the 8th October by railway, this being the first time the Gordon Highlanders had been so conveyed.

On that day the regiment formed part of the procession for

inaugurating the equestrian statue of the Duke of Wellington then erected in front of the Exchange.

May 1st, 1845.—New arms with percussion locks and a new style of bayonet spring replaced the flint lock which had been hitherto in use. The percussion caps were carried in a leather pouch, at first in a pocket on the right side of the jacket and afterwards on the pouch belt.

At Glasgow they were quartered with the Scots Greys, and the historical association of the two regiments was kept up by many tokens of mutual regard between all ranks. During their stay in the great industrial centre of the west, the officers received much hospitality from the city magnates. On one occasion Major Lockhart was the guest of a wealthy bachelor of the old school. When the dinner was announced, the Major modestly gave place to his elders. " Na, na," cried the host, " step awa', Major— Warriors afore Weavers ! "

During the winter, a sergeant and three rank and file, all MacDonalds, were sent on a recruiting tour to the islands of Mull, Skye, and Uist ; they got several recruits in Uist, but few in Mull or Skye, though the population of these districts was then greater than ever before or since, and though at that time there were so many pensioners in the latter island that their pay-day looked like market-day in Portree.[1] Probably the feeling still existed as mentioned in the old Statistical Account of Scotland, that parents in Skye objected to their sons enlisting even when idle, unless with the sons of the lairds or tacksmen in their neighbourhood.

In July 1845, the headquarters proceeded by rail to Edinburgh, with a subaltern's detachment at Greenlaw. The detachments in the Highlands rejoined during the month, and in August a company occupied Stirling Castle. The same month a subaltern's detachment marched to Dunfermline, where some disturbances had taken place, and were quartered in half billets.

Among the many changes in the social life and manners of the country, none perhaps is more marked than the increase of smoking among the upper classes. For long after 1845, few houses had a smoking-room. If gentlemen wished to smoke they went outside by day, at night to the kitchen. The Duke of Wellington had a great dislike to the weed, and published the following order :—

G.O., 1845.—The Commander-in-Chief has been informed that the practice of smoking, by the use of pipes, cigars, and cheroots, has become prevalent among the officers of the army, which is not only in itself a species

---

[1] " Brave Men of Skye."

At this time a steel pistol, ornamented with silver, was added to the arms of the officers, and carried on the dirk belt. It was proposed also to have a *sgian dhu* ; this Colonel MacDonald would not permit, saying it was the weapon of a *ghillie*, not of a gentleman.

of intoxication occasioned by the fumes of tobacco, but undoubtedly occasions drinking and tippling by those who acquire the habit, and he entreats the officers commanding regiments to prevent smoking in the mess-rooms of their several regiments and in the adjoining apartments, and to discourage the practice among the officers of junior rank.

Colonel MacDonald, though he took snuff freely, disliked smoking, and was about to comply with the Duke's request—for it was not a command—when Major Lockhart remarked that if he did so, the officers, instead of remaining together in the ante-room after dinner, would break up into coteries in their own rooms—a most undesirable result. Smoking, cigars only, was therefore continued in the ante-room (cigarettes were then unknown).[1]

April 6th, 1846.—A letter of thanks was received from the Magistrates and Commissioners of Police in the city, for the promptness and efficiency with which the piquets of the regiment under Captain Sutherland attended and assisted in saving property during a serious fire in the New Town of Edinburgh.

The regiment being under orders for Ireland, three companies under Major Forbes proceeded by rail to Glasgow, and embarked at the Broomielaw[2] on a steamer for Belfast, where the headquarters under Colonel MacDonald arrived on April 11th, two companies under Captain Mackenzie on the 16th, and the remainder under Major Thorold on the 18th. When the regiment left Scotland a general order was issued by Sir Neil Douglas, K.C.B.[3] It was couched in the most flattering terms as to the good conduct of both the depôt and the regiment while under his command.

" The smartness of all ranks—in appearance, in drill, in the general wish to excel—was beyond anything I ever remember in the service," says the officer from whose notes I have quoted.[4]

August 1846.—Headquarters proceeded to Enniskillen, having detachments at Belleek, Ballyshannon, Omagh, Killishandra, Cavan, Rutland, and Drogheda.

1845.—The 34th Regiment having at this time received authority to bear " Arroyo-dos-Molinos " on its colours, Colonel MacDonald, with apparent justice, claimed the same distinction for the 92nd, in a correspondence which is given in Appendix VII, Vol. i.

[1] Many of the sergeants and older soldiers at that time carried a snuff-box. I have seen one made of the end of a horn, that had been carried through the Peninsula.

[2] There used to be a marching song (tune, " Wha wadna fight for Charlie ") :—
Ha'e ye seen the Ninety-Second sailing frae the Broomielaw ?
Mony a lass would fain gae wi' them that was forced to bide awa'
Frae them that wear the feather bonnets, tartan hose, an' plaids an' a'.

[3] Sir Neil was very particular about the men's messes, and at an inspection of those of the light company he exclaimed, " How is this ? I don't see that the men have any mustard ! " Before Major Sutherland could frame a suitable reply to this unexpected criticism, the oldest soldier in the room, with ready wit, saved the situation, and standing at the stiffest attention, said, " Please, sir, the light company never take mustard ! "

[4] The late Sir George Warrender, Bart., of Lochend, formerly in the 92nd and Coldstream Guards.

On the 13th November 1846, the following regimental order by Colonel J. MacDonald, C.B., was published :—

Belfast, 12th Nov. 1846.—Colonel MacDonald, having seen his promotion to the rank of Major-General announced in the public newspapers, takes the earliest opportunity of expressing to Major Forbes, the officers and n.c. officers collectively and individually, his lively sense of their merits, and grateful thanks for the zeal, assiduity, and cordiality with which they invariably supported him in the performance of his duties during the last eighteen years, the result of which has been to render the regiment the most (certainly one of the most) trustworthy, efficient, and well-conducted in the whole British army. He felt truly proud of them, and he thinks they knew it, and also felt proud of themselves ; let the same feeling continue to animate them, and keep them steadfast in the performance of their respective duties, zealously, soberly, submissively, cheerfully and unitedly, and the 92nd Highlanders will ever be honoured and respected wherever they go. Although during the Colonel's time no opportunity offered for testing the regiment before an enemy in the field, yet having repeatedly marked their manly and soldier-like bearing in the midst of pestilence and disease peculiar to foreign climes, and where there was neither honour nor glory to excite, he felt sure that in the hour of trial they would emulate the deeds which he saw performed by the corps during the war, and he would not hesitate to face them against any foe. It is with the deepest regret, even upon promotion, that the Colonel takes leave of a corps in which he has served so long and happily. He will, however, still have the honour of being designated " from the 92nd," etc.

Though Colonel MacDonald's eighteen years of command had prevented promotion in the senior ranks, it had been of lasting benefit to the 92nd. His system of interior economy was acknowledged by the men to have made service in the regiment most comfortable, for though he insisted on a smart and soldier-like appearance, he studied to prevent any unnecessary expense to the soldier. Of a kind and generous though fiery nature, he was not a man to be trifled with, and could be severe on either officer or soldier where severity was required ; but, like the old Highland chiefs, he would never allow one of his people to be wronged.[1] Full of the old Highland spirit, he was as good a landlord as he was an officer, and more than one pensioner of his regiment held a farm on his estate. Private letters from Lord Raglan, the Military Secretary, which I have seen, show the high estimation in which he was held by the Duke of Wellington. Feared by the bad men, he was liked by the good, and I never heard one who had served under him speak of Colonel MacDonald without respect.

Two of his sons were also in the 92nd, and in all nine of the

---

[1] A refrain used to be sung by the men about the colonel which, after describing the very forcible language in which he sometimes rebuked them, was to the following effect :—

| But if a cockit hat ere reckoned | He 'd rue the day and hour he spoke |
| To meddle wi' the Ninety-Second, | And raised the birse o' " Heather-Jock." |

family wore the Gordon tartan.[1]   Colonel Gleig tells the following
anecdotes of MacDonald : Once coming out of church in Glasgow
he was close to the colonel when some of the men put on their
bonnets before leaving the sacred building.   MacDonald rebuked
them : " Have ye no respect to the House of God and be
d——d to ye ? "   On another occasion he had pitched into the
officers very severely on parade, and their silence at the luncheon
table was the measure of their resentment, which the colonel
observing, said, " Gentlemen, I thought that ye knew by this
time that the old man's bark is worse than his bite " ; so all went
well again.   Colonel Gleig sums up his character as follows :—
" He had a personal magnetic command of men and officers which
can only come from a man of original power."

[1] See Appendix V, which shows the very remarkable record of the Dalchosnie family,
where in four generations eight members fought against, and two for, the House of Hanover,
while in the three following generations fifteen members fought for it.   It appears that in these
seven generations every male member of the family was, for a time at least, a soldier.

SERGEANT—Drill Order, with Percussion Lock Fusil.   PIPER—Review Order
PERIOD, 1846

CHAPTER V

1847-1857

THE command was now assumed by Lieut.-Colonel John Alexander Forbes.

The reports by inspecting officers had been invariably favourable during the stay of the regiment at Enniskillen. In May 1847, it moved to Island Bridge Barracks, Dublin. While here a letter came, addressed to " Ensign Falconer, 74th, attached to 92nd Regiment." No one of that name and rank being known, it could not be delivered, till Major Lockhart, who had an inkling of the matter, authorised Colour-sergeant Falconer to open the envelope. It contained his commission in the 74th Highlanders, of which it was his first intimation. Colonel Fordyce, commanding the 74th, had asked General MacDonald to recommend a 92nd sergeant as adjutant. After being senior captain of the 74th, Major Falconer was well known for many years in connection with the Volunteer movement in Dundee.

On the 18th October the regiment was inspected for the first time by Major-General H.R.H. Prince George (afterwards Duke) of Cambridge, who expressed his approbation.

In December 1847,[1] the regiment marched by divisions to Limerick. Detachments were sent to various places, and occasionally they were employed in aid of the civil power. The country was in a very disturbed state. An officer shooting alone had just fired both barrels when two men rushed on him demanding his gun. " Certainly," he said, " and you may as well take my powder flask, shot-belt, and game-bag also." Then, pulling a pistol from his pocket, he marched them both to the nearest police barracks. Except to possess themselves of arms, however, the peasantry never attacked soldiers, but they hoped to intimidate magistrates and land agents by occasionally shooting one. An officer detached for the prevention of such crimes asked a man, " Why don't the boys shoot me, who am here to keep order ? " " What 'ud be the use, yer honour ? Sure there 'd be another man in your place to-morrow ! "

The population of the Highland counties had enormously increased, that of Inverness, which in 1801 amounted to 72,672 souls, in 1841 numbered 97,799, while the means of subsistence had not increased in proportion.

There was a grievous famine during 1846-47 in the West Highlands and in Ireland, principally owing to the decline in the

---

[1] In 1847 the " Peninsula Medal " was issued to the survivors of the various campaigns against the French.

At this period the yellow stripe in the sergeants' sashes was discontinued and a plain crimson sash adopted.

kelp industry, caused by the free importation of Barilla, followed by the potato disease.   Many landlords, notably Macleod of Macleod, spent large sums in importing food for the people, and subscriptions were opened all over the country for that purpose. Officers and men of the regiment had subscribed liberally to the funds for their starving countrymen, and at Limerick they distributed what food they had to spare at the barrack gate, on which it was found one morning that the poor people had written, " God bless the 92nd."   When Captain Miller's Company was on Detachment at this time, he found that his men were in the habit of giving their porridge to the starving poor.   He told them that he was responsible for their health, and that they could not perform their duties without breakfast.   They replied, " We cannot sit down to breakfast and see the people about us starve." The people showed their gratitude in every possible way.[1]

Major-General J. E. Napier, commanding at Limerick, while highly approving, in his report to the Commander-in-Chief, of the regiment in general, called attention to the pipers shown in the state, as not being allowed by regulation.   The Duke of Wellington answered that he was surprised that an officer who must have seen the gallant deeds performed by Highland regiments, in which their pipers played so important a part, should make such a report.

In 1847, Sergeant-Major John Stewart was discharged to pension.   He afterwards received a commission as quartermaster, Haddington Militia.[2]

December 1848.—The regiment marched to Clonmel, and was again under its late colonel, Major-General MacDonald having been appointed to command the Kilkenny district.   Detachments were at Fethard, Cashel, Ballinamult, and Carrick-on-Suir.

The disturbances known as Smith O'Brien's Rebellion caused a great deal of hard work to the military at this time, till the leader was captured by the determination and coolness of Captain K. D. Mackenzie of the 92nd (then on the staff).

In November 1849, Lieut.-Colonel Forbes retired, and Major Mark Kerr Atherley was promoted lieut.-colonel of the regiment.

[1] Related by Captain Miller to General Sir Martin Dillon, G.C.B.

[2] 1847.—Candidates for commissions were now required to pass a qualifying examination, in addition to being recommended by a general officer and certified to be Christians and gentlemen, which had hitherto been the only requirements.

In 1847, life enlistment was done away with, and the soldier now enlisted for ten years, with the option of re-engaging to complete twenty-one years for pension.

July 1848.—Officers' blue frock coat was ordered to be discontinued, and a scarlet shell-jacket to be adopted ; also, in place of the blue cloak, a grey one of the same colour as the men's (as had been used in the Peninsula) " to be worn when the men are permitted to wear their great-coats."   The " cathdath " cloth hose, which had hitherto been worn by the men, were changed for stocking hose of the same red and white colour.   The art of making the cloth hose is now lost, both in the regiment and in the Highlands, as is also that of making the " brogan gaelach."

In April 1850, the regiment marched to Kilkenny, having detachments at Callan, Castlecomer, and Carlow.

This year Sergeant Duncan MacPhail was appointed pipe-major. Up to this time the pipers were in charge of the drum-major, though for musical purposes they were under a lance-sergeant or corporal, who had only the honorary title of pipe-major. He carried on grand occasions the regimental banner on his pipe, each company piper carrying that of his captain ; still, they were not officially acknowledged by the War Office till 1854, when six of their number were ranked as " pipers," and received pay accordingly. On guest nights one piper only, generally the pipe-major, played a pibroch in the officers' mess-room ; no quick-step or reel was allowed unless by permission of the senior officer. No drum was played with the pipe at any time. Band, drums and fifes, and pipes played separately, except in marching past in slow time, when each piper played a " salute " as his company passed the General. Another curious old custom existed in the regiment. When a funeral passed out of barracks the regimental guard, after presenting arms, faced about and stood with their backs to the funeral party, just as in old times in the West Highlands it was customary for a man to doff his bonnet and stand with his back to a funeral as it passed, or, if riding, to dismount, uncover, and stand looking over the horse's shoulder with his back to the procession.[1]

The regiment had never been more thoroughly *Scottish* than at this period, but *Highlanders* were in a decided minority. The few of English and Irish birth in the ranks were mostly soldiers' sons enlisted as boys.

The regiment being about to proceed on foreign service, on February 1st, 1851, in accordance with orders from his Grace the Duke of Wellington, Commander-in-Chief, the depôt companies [2] were formed under Major G. E. Thorold, and on the 4th marched to Carlow, having a detachment at Castlecomer.

February 4th.—A letter was received by Lieut.-Colonel Atherley from Major-General MacDonald, C.B., expressing the satisfaction

---

[1] Alexander Carmichael, author of " Carmina Gadelica." This custom has been seen by the author even in the 20th century.

[2] Field officer, 1 ; captains, 4 ; lieutenants, 4 ; ensigns, 4 ; staff, 1 ; sergeants, 16 ; corporals, 16 ; drummers, 5 ; privates, 161.

Extract from Monthly Return of the 92nd (Highland) Regiment of Infantry, Clonmel, 1st January 1850.

	Sergeants.	Drummers.	Corporals.	Privates.	TOTAL.
English,	0	1	1	11	13
Scottish,	46	11	39	677	773
Irish,	0	4	0	15	19
Foreign,	0	0	0	0	0
	46	16	40	703	805

the regiment had afforded him in every respect since their arrival in the district, and desiring to assure the officers and men that his heartfelt and very best wishes will accompany them. During the days their mess was shut up previous to departure, he kept open house for the officers.

On the 10th, 11th, and 12th of February the regiment marched by successive divisions for Fermoy, preparatory to embarkation at Cork.[1] On the 16th the following address was received from the worshipful the Mayor of Kilkenny :—

> To Lieut.-Colonel Atherley, the Officers, N.C. Officers, and Men
> of the 92nd Highlanders.
>
> We, the undersigned, cannot permit your departure from Kilkenny, where you have now been quartered for nearly twelve months, without testifying our sincere regret upon your removal, at the same time taking occasion to express how much that regret is enhanced, owing to the uniform urbanity of the officers and the steady and peaceable demeanour of the men, which has won upon the regard and gained the esteem of all.
>
> Satisfied that such conduct as your regiment has pursued here will always uphold the honour of the British army and the credit of the Empire, we have only earnestly to hope that the 92nd Highlanders may be protected through all perils and dangers, safely to return home, so that you may again earn, amongst your brother civilians, the same respect and attachment which is now so deservedly borne away from all classes here.
>
> Signed by   MICHAEL HYLAND, Mayor,
>   THE EARL OF DESART, and eighty
>   of the nobility and gentry of the
> 14*th Feb.* 1851.   County and city of Kilkenny.

The Royal Irish Constabulary now performed much of the work formerly done by the troops, and though the state of the

Extract from Inspection Return of the 92nd (Highland) Regiment of Foot, 16th May 1850.

Feet. Ins.		Sergeants.	Corporals.	Drummers.	Privates.
6	0 and upwards	7	2	0	28
5	11	1	1	0	22
5	10	7	9	0	52
5	9	13	7	2	90
5	8	10	10	1	182
5	7	7	7	0	147
5	6	2	3	2	142
5	5	0	1	3	36
Under		0	0	8 (lads)	8
		47	40	16	707

Colonel F. Macbean, who was captain of the grenadier company in 1850, wrote that the smallest man in the company was an officer's servant 5 feet 10½ inches, all others being 5 feet 11 inches and upwards, and the tallest 6 feet 4 inches.

[1] Hitherto for many years the officers were not permitted to wear the Highland dress on the line of march. They did so on this occasion, and ever since.

"Marching money" was allowed to soldiers at the rate of 10d. a day in England ; 5d. in Scotland ; 4d. in Ireland.

country caused a good deal of unpleasant duty to the regiment, their tour in Ireland had not been without its distractions. There had been a cordial exchange of courtesies between the country gentlemen and the officers ; there was plenty of hunting, which was encouraged both by the general and by the lieut.-colonel, as promoting decision of character and an eye for country. Most of the officers kept horses, and though some of them were perhaps " better in their wind than on their pins," others were good enough to win the Conyngham and Kilrue Cups, then the great steeplechase events of Ireland. Rough shooting was to be had for the asking, while woodcocks in the preserved demesnes formed the *raison d'être* for many a cheery party. On the morning after one of these, where claret had flowed and dice rattled till the " wee sma' hours ayont the twal'," the voice of the old gamekeeper was heard adjuring his sleeping master : " Get up, sorr, for the honour of ould Ireland. Sure the wood does be full of cock, and thim divils of Scotchmin are atin' their breakfast as if they hadn't touched the drop or the dice for a month o' Sundays ! " At that same rather lively establishment, a dispute arose as to the merits of the horses there stabled for the next day's meet. It was moonlight—why not put the question to the trial there and then ? and a second edition of the famous moonlit Leicestershire steeplechase was enacted. One of the party, a well known pedestrian,[1] afterwards walked back to his barracks in the morning, and in passing through the park he met his host and hostess, who had been to early mass on an outside car. A low gate barred the way, but instead of waiting for it to be opened, the horse was sent at it, and over or through it they went, car and all !

The n.c. officers and men were equally well received by the people, who, though disaffected to the Government, were at that time very civil to the soldiers, and made them welcome and comfortable in billets. Private Gladow, in his journal of that date, particularly mentions this, as also the convivial meetings with the farmers on market-days. There were then no recreation rooms or gymnastic appliances in barracks, but there were fives courts, and the men played football. They were proficients in the classic game of quoits, and occasionally practised putting the stone and throwing the hammer, and were capital dancers ; cricket was then unknown in the regiment.

.   .   .   .

At Fermoy, where the officers were honorary members at the mess of the 1st Regiment (Royal Scots), they erected a cairn on a neighbouring hill as a memorial of their stay in Ireland. On February 28th, 1851, the regiment marched to Cork, and on March 3rd,

[1] Lieutenant (afterwards General) J. R. S. Sayer, King's Dragoon Guards.

headquarters and four companies under Lieut.-Colonel Atherley embarked on the *Apollo* troopship at Queenstown ; and on March 29th (having been eight days in quarantine on account of smallpox on the ship), three companies landed at Corfu, the band in the leading boat playing the " Garb of Old Gaul."

In 1851, Sergeant-major Daniel Morrison was discharged to pension and appointed barrack sergeant at Greenlaw.

The two companies which had been left at Cork arrived on the freight ship *Edmonston* on the 17th May.

The destination of the 92nd had nearly been changed by the outbreak of the Kaffir war, of which the news arrived soon after the *Apollo* sailed. If she could be stopped at Gibraltar, her course was to be diverted to the Cape. A fair wind, however, had sent the old ship [1] beyond the reach of this order, and the 74th, then at Cork, got this chance of active service.

The regiment occupied the Citadel, having a company at Vido. In 1852 the gold fever, then raging in England, attacked some of the corps in garrison at Corfu, so that men committed offences in the hope of being transported to Australia and then making their escape to the " diggings." To such an extent did this reach that an example had to be made, and a soldier of the garrison was shot by sentence of court-martial for gross insubordination, but so entirely free from the complaint were the Gordon Highlanders, that it was not thought necessary for the regiment to witness the execution. The assistant surgeon of the 92nd, being in medical charge of a detachment of other troops at this time, happened to overhear a conversation among the servants. One of them was speaking disrespectfully of his superiors, and proceeded to mention the officers of the 92nd in the same terms, when the doctor's man intervened with—" An' ye say the like o' that aboot oor officers, I 'll ca' the face aff ye ! "

At Corfu the officers kept a yacht. The advent of the fleet caused lively evenings at mess. There was splendid shooting in Albania, and the many English who then wintered there made agreeable society. The members of the sergeants' mess had many friends, and gave and received entertainments ; a private's journal calls it " a delightful quarter for soldiers, fruit and wine very cheap —beautiful country—splendid bathing—the fleet often in." They

---

[1] Said to be the same *Apollo* which had taken part of the regiment to the Peninsula in 1810.

April 1st, 1851.—The cost to the soldier of his rations was reduced on foreign service to 3½d. a day.

AUTHOR'S NOTE.—In compliance with a Horse Guards order of August 4th, 1851, the glengarry was taken into wear in September 1852 in place of the round forage cap, which was, in fact, the Highland bonnet without feathers. The glengarry was found a handy head-dress, but the men lost much of the appearance of height given by the large dice of the old one. Sergeants had a silver thistle on the glengarry ; other ranks had nothing, except the flank companies, who wore a grenade and bugle.

were very sorry to leave for Gibraltar, which they did in March 1853, the three divisions arriving on April 16th and 18th at Gibraltar, where they occupied Rosea Barracks and afterwards " Town Range " and " Wellington Front." [1]

The several inspections held at Corfu had been particularly satisfactory to all concerned. During their stay various n.c. officers and men had been sent home for change of climate or discharge, their places being filled by drafts from the depôt. By War Office letter of 21st February 1854, the establishment was augmented to 1120 of all ranks. In addition to the drum-major and 15 drummers and fifers, a pipe-major at 1s. 10d. per day and 5 pipers at 1s. 1d. per day (beer-money being in addition to these rates) are included, this being the first official recognition of pipe music. The other pipers remained as they were. In 1854, Sergeant-major James Stewart was discharged to pension, and afterwards became captain and adjutant, Ross-shire Militia. He was succeeded by James George, who was soon appointed ensign and adjutant, then paymaster, 92nd ; afterwards paymaster, 21st Hussars ; retired lieut.-colonel.

A cloud had now appeared on the peaceful horizon of Europe, which soon was dark with the storm of war.

Russia had long coveted Constantinople and the harbours of the Bosphorus, whence her fleets might dominate the Mediterranean. A dispute about the Holy Sepulchre at Jerusalem had long existed between Russia and Turkey. The Czar now asserted his protectorate over all the Christian subjects of the Sultan, about fourteen millions ; to this Turkey refused to agree ; the Czar therefore ordered his troops to cross the frontier river, the Pruth, (which they did on the 2nd of July 1853), and occupy the Dalmatian provinces. The Western Powers intervened in the hope of averting war. The Ottoman Porte demanded the evacuation of the provinces within fifteen days, and their demand being disregarded, a state of war between Russia and Turkey ensued in October 1853 ; and on the 30th November, a Turkish squadron of six small vessels at anchor in the harbour of Sinope was attacked and entirely destroyed, with their crews, to the number of 4000 men, by six Russian ships of the line.

These proceedings had aroused the indignation of the English and French nations, who were equally anxious to prevent the power of Russia being increased by the possession of the Dardanelles. On the 27th February 1854, they sent an ultimatum to Russia

---

[1] Disembarked :—Field officers, 2 ; captains, 5 ; lieutenants, 7 ; ensigns, 0 ; staff, 5 ; sergeants, 32 ; drummers, 11 ; rank and file, 538.

October 1852.—Belts of a new pattern were adopted—a waist belt and buckle replacing the cross belt and plate for the bayonet—the cross belt for the pouch being retained. Officers and staff-sergeants retained the cross belt and claymore, but sergeants received sword bayonets.

demanding the evacuation of the Dalmatian provinces by the 30th April. No reply being vouchsafed, they immediately declared war.

During the long peace the British army had been reduced to the lowest requirements. Most regiments consisted of one weak battalion, which, when it was ordered for active service, had to be filled up from others.

Orders came to Gibraltar that the battalions who had been longest on the Rock were to be made up to war strength by volunteers from those lately arrived ; consequently, the n.c. officers and men of the 92nd were offered the opportunity of seeing active service by volunteering. The offer was accepted by :

SERGEANTS.	CORPORALS.	PRIVATES.	
2	4	95	for the 30th Regiment.
1	1	122	,, 55th ,,
0	0	9	,, 44th ,,
3	5	226	

leaving the service companies with under 300 privates, while the depôt was in an even worse state.

The 93rd, then in England, was the first Highland regiment held in readiness, and was made up by volunteers from the 42nd and 79th. Shortly after, these and many other regiments were added to the expedition, and the 92nd depôt was called upon. It consisted at that time of a particularly fine body of young men, and almost every one that was fit volunteered for service, all choosing the 79th, except ten, who went to the 42nd.[1] Thus a corps avowedly unsurpassed in efficiency was for the time destroyed, while its soldiers went as strangers to the ranks of other regiments. I remember when, in 1851, some young officers were regretting not being sent to the Kaffir war, they were comforted by a senior, who said that, though never sent to the Far East, the 92nd had not, since it was raised, missed a European campaign, and would as certainly be employed in the next. When their regiment was thus broken up, the feeling of grief, amounting almost to despair, may be imagined better than described. By some it was never forgotten. The disappointment was, if possible, increased by the arrival at Gibraltar of a letter (as I was informed) by which the 92nd was excepted from the volunteer offer. It was too late, the men had departed ! This terrible blow would never have fallen had regiments been composed of two or more battalions.

[1] I asked the reason for this preference, and was told it arose partly from tradition, the regiments having been raised very much in the same districts, but chiefly because in the 42nd the men appeared in the kilt at morning, and in *good* trousers at evening, parade, which caused extra expense and troublesome changes of raiment, while the 79th customs were less costly, like those of the 92nd.

In availing themselves of what they supposed to be their only chance of active service, the men behaved like the good soldiers they were ; so good that I have heard an officer of a regiment to which a number went speak of them as men of a very superior class, and that most of the privates were fit to be n.c. officers. Many of them distinguished themselves, and after the war numbers of those who were able to do so rejoined the 92nd, saying they volunteered to see service, not for the purpose of leaving the regiment. One of them (W. Caulfield), who in his journal speaks of his time in the 92nd as " the brightest and happiest of my whole service," says, " Those volunteers could not take the colours of the regiment with them, but they went themselves."

In June the establishment was increased to twelve companies, with 60 sergeants, 25 drummers, and 1200 rank and file.

In December the regiment was divided into six service and six depôt companies, but in January 1855 it was reorganised in eight service and four depôt companies ; and in February, Brevet Lieut.-Colonel Lockhart, one lieutenant, an ensign, and 134 n.c. officers and men joined from the depôt. In April 100 rifled muskets, with fifty rounds of ammunition for each, were received for the use of the regiment. The men were all practised with these weapons, which were, however, divided among the best marksmen of each company.

June 20th, 1855.—Lieut.-General John MacDonald, C.B., from Colonel of 53rd Regiment, was appointed Colonel of the 92nd, *vice* General Sir William Macbean, K.B., deceased.

During the stay of the regiment at Gibraltar several drafts had arrived from the depôt ; still, when they embarked on the steam transport *Orinoco* for the Crimea, on August 19th, 1855, under Lieut.-Colonel G. E. Thorold, they could only muster 489 n.c. officers, drummers, and privates ; but though weak in numbers, their quality was such that Sir Robert Gardiner, the Governor, wrote to Lieut.-Colonel Thorold, " You ought to be proud of the regiment," and he forwarded a most appreciative message from the Commander-in-Chief. Great exertions had been made by the field officers to get to the front, and Sir Colin Campbell had been induced to apply for them. When nearing their destination they could see great clouds of smoke and dust rise from the blowing up of the Russian forts, but unfortunately they only arrived at Balaclava on the 9th September, too late for the fall of Sevastopol on the previous day. On account of a storm their ship ran out to sea, and they did not land till the 15th.

After being supplied with Minié rifles at Balaclava, they marched to Kamara and joined the Highland Brigade, to which in point of numbers they were a poor addition, but their discipline and char-

acter were remarked on by a Guards' adjutant, a very good judge :
" They were a weak battalion, and had many young soldiers, but
one could see it was a regiment with a system." At first they were
in tents ; then in huts, eighty men in a large one ; the weather
became excessively cold, but they had two stoves in the large huts
and one in the small ones.

September 24th.—Lieut.-Colonel Atherley arrived and resumed
the command. In October 1855, a notification was received that
the establishment was increased to sixteen companies of 2150 n.c.
officers and men.

Various drafts joined while the regiment was in the Crimea.

At the time the 92nd arrived it was supposed that though the
first phase of the war had passed, a spring campaign would see the
allies fighting their way to Moscow ; but the Gordons' hopes of
adding fresh honours to their colours were dashed by the Treaty
of Paris, which was signed on the 30th March, peace being
proclaimed in the Crimea on the 2nd April 1856. The loss of
both French and British had been great, that of the Russians
enormous. " For a whole generation the world continued to have
the benefit of the war in the enforced quiescence of Russia." [1]

Though some of them were occasionally under fire, the 92nd
had taken no active part as a regiment in the Crimean War. They
had not, however, been without worthy representatives. Captain
A. M. MacDonald, aide-de-camp to General Pennefather, was
wounded at the Alma ; Captain the Hon. Walter Charteris, aide-
de-camp to Lord Lucan, was killed in the Balaclava charge ; Brevet
Major K. D. MacKenzie was the hard-working and popular Deputy
Quartermaster-General at Balaclava. Between 300 and 400[2] Gordon
Highlanders served through the campaign in the ranks of other
regiments. Private Thomas Beach, a Forfarshire man, gained the
Victoria Cross,[3] and brought it back with him, when, at the expiry
of his first period, he rejoined his old corps. Among others who
distinguished themselves was a sergeant, of whom General A. M.
MacDonald, in a letter to the Commanding Officer, 2nd Battalion
Gordon Highlanders, dated January 19th, 1894, writes :—

There was a splendid, brave, tall fellow (I think Alan [4]) M'Donald, a
sergeant, killed at the Alma, a 92nd man, and volunteered for, I think, the
55th, in our brigade. His conduct excited quite a *furore*, and after the battle
was much spoken of. Some note should be made of such heroes. There was
a great sprinkling of 92nd men in our brigade. One, an hospital orderly,
came to give me some soup, and said, " What will your father say at your

---

[1] Sir E. Hamley, " The War in the Crimea."
[2] I am unable to state the exact number of volunteers from the depôt.
[3] The Victoria Cross was instituted by H.M. Queen Victoria on 29th January 1856.
[4] M'Donald's name seems to have been John, not Alan.

getting so wounded ? " Another, a so-called bad character, MacDivott, in the land transport, I heard make a long speech descriptive of the campaign before an immense audience at Glasgow. He had a great sense of humour.

Colonel M'Pherson of Glentruim, who was a lieutenant in the 30th, writes that Sergeant M'Donald, on volunteering, was made colour-sergeant of the grenadier company of that regiment—not the 55th—that he was conspicuous from his great height and splendid physique, and displayed great gallantry while the flank companies covered the front of the battalion exposed to a heavy fire of musketry and artillery. The captain being severely wounded, the lieutenant found the experience and assistance of the colour-sergeant of the greatest value. M'Donald died of cholera on the very night of the battle, and " it was understood that had he survived, he would have been recommended for a commission."

May 22nd, 1856.—The service companies, under Colonel Atherley, embarked at Balaclava [1] for Gibraltar, where, after picking up a draft at Malta, they landed on 4th June, and found a draft of 3 ensigns, 3 sergeants, 2 drummers, and 208 privates.

In November the establishment was reduced to eight service and four depôt companies, in all 1000 rank and file.

Pioneers were increased to 1 corporal and 12 privates, all tradesmen, and not to carry muskets.

At this time Sergeant-major John Dewar was promoted quartermaster.

During 1857 the regiment remained quietly at Gibraltar. Although the demand for men was so great in Scotland at this time that more than one Highland regiment had been obliged to send a recruiting party to London, the success of the very special exertions made by the 92nd to keep up their nationality as well as their numbers is shown by the Return of January 1st, 1857—Headquarters, Gibraltar :—Sergeants, drummers, and rank and file, and depôt, Fort-George—together, English, 7 ; Scottish, 1043 ; Irish, 40—total, 1090.[2]

---

[1] Strength :—Field officers, 3 ; captains, 7 ; subalterns, 13 ; sergeants, 45 ; corporals, 40 ; drummers, 20 ; privates, 553.

[2] *April 1st*, 1856.—The new pattern Highland doublet, without epaulettes or wings, was taken into wear. At first it was double-breasted, and had lapels which could be buttoned back from the fifth button, showing the regimental facing, or worn buttoned across, showing only red. The buttons were diamond-shaped. It was an improvement to regiments wearing trousers, as it afforded greater warmth than the coatee to the loins and stomach, but as these were protected by the pleats and double cloth of the kilt, there was no need for it in regiments wearing that dress. It is certainly not so becoming to the soldier. All infantry at this time adopted a sash over the shoulder instead of round the waist, officers wearing it on the left and sergeants on the right shoulder. The sergeants of Highland corps were ordered to conform, and they were no longer supplied with sashes of the Highland pattern. At this time the duty of supplying the soldiers' clothing was transferred from the Colonels to the State. In April 1857 the tunics were altered to single-breasted, with round buttons.

CHAPTER VI

1858–1862

THE 92nd was one of a certain number of regiments which, during the Duke of Wellington's life, had always been kept within reach, and had never been sent to the more distant parts of the Empire ; but now a crisis arose which required the presence in India of every British soldier that could be spared.

Early in May 1857, the world was startled by the mutiny of the native army of Bengal ; reinforced by contingents from the more warlike populations, and led by discontented or ambitious native princes, they ruthlessly murdered numbers of Europeans without distinction of age or sex, and it seemed for a moment as if the small British garrison must be overpowered. The gallantry both of the European and loyal native troops saved India. Reinforcements were poured into the country, and for the first time the Gordons were ordered to the East. They embarked, 20th January 1858, on H.M.S. *Urgent*,[1] under Lieut.-Colonel Archibald Inglis Lockhart.[2]

Lieut.-General Sir James Ferguson, K.C.B., Governor of Gibraltar, in General Orders of January 14th, " desires to place on record the good opinion he has formed of the regiment." Major-General Rumly, in Brigade Orders, " is confident, from personal observation of the *esprit de corps* which animates all ranks of the Gordon Highlanders, that opportunity alone is needed to make them emulate their predecessors," etc.

The *Urgent* encountered a storm and put into Malta to repair damages, but arrived at Alexandria, January 30th. Here they remained on board ship, where the officers gave a ball, till the 14th and 15th of February, when they went by train to Cairo in two divisions, arriving at the terminus of the railway next morning, when they rested at a standing camp. Private Gladow in his journal expatiates on the luxurious meals and the excellence of the coffee and grog supplied to them *en route*. After the heat of the day they were mounted, " the officers on horses, the men on donkeys : kilted and in feathered bonnets as they were, it was a comical show." [3] They played at being cavalry, giving the word " At a walk—march ! " resulting in ridiculous scenes and much laughter. Embarking on the P. & O. steamship *Oriental* at Suez on February 17th, they landed at Bombay on March 6th.

The right wing, under Lieut.-Colonel Lockhart, proceeded to Colaba, and the left wing, under Major Robert M'Leod Suther-

---

[1] Embarkation strength :—Lieut.-Colonels, 2 ; major, 1 ; captains, 7 ; lieutenants, 10 ; ensigns, 4 ; staff, 5 ; sergeants, 43 ; corporals, 39 ; drummers, 22 ; privates, 688.

[2] Colonel Atherley had been promoted Major-General, and Brevet Lieut.-Colonel Thorold to the 42nd.

[3] Major R. Bethune.

land, went on field service to Surat (they rejoined headquarters the
8th June).[1]   Neither officers nor men had been in India, and they
were entirely ignorant of the language and customs of the natives.
Colonel Lockhart used to tell how, on first arrival, while smoking
his post-prandial cheroot on the verandah, he heard a soldier ask
a turbaned Oriental where he could get water.   The native did not
understand, and regarded him with a stony stare, when, by way of
making his meaning quite clear, and speaking loudly, he said, " Od,
man, can ye no' gie 's a drap watter to tak' the glaur aff my
spats ? " !

Surgeon-General Landale, then assistant surgeon, 92nd, mentions that on the way up country with a detachment, as the officers
were sitting outside the tent at nightfall, they noticed that a
number of fires were lighted round the camp.   On the sergeant
coming to report that all was well, a young officer asked what
the fires were for.   " To keep off lions," answered the sergeant.
" Nonsense," said the officer, " there are no lions in this
country ; the noise you hear is made by jackals."   " D' ye
no' ken, sir, that the jaickal is the lion's provider, an' whar'
the t'ane is, the t'ither will no' be far awa' ; it 's aye as weel to
mak' sure."

On the 30th March, Lieut.-Colonel K. D. MacKenzie arrived,
bringing a reinforcement of 178 of all ranks, a large proportion of
whom were English and Irish volunteers from various regiments.
The misconduct of some of them on the way out had caused remarks
in the Press to the discredit of the 92nd, which prevented their
being welcomed as cordially as would otherwise have been the
case.

Two drafts from the depôt also joined early in May under
Lieutenants Hunter and J. C. Hay.[2]

June 8th.—Orders were received from headquarters to proceed
on the 12th by bullock train to Mhow on field service, by divisions
of two officers and from forty to fifty men ; two men on each
hackery.   Though in white clothing, they suffered from the heat
and dust.   The first party arrived at Mhow after various small

---

[1] This was the last occasion on which feathered bonnets were worn or packs carried by the
regiment on active service in India.   The 42nd, 79th, and 93rd wore the bonnet throughout
the Mutiny campaign ; they had khaki shades on the left side.   Lieut.-General Sir J. Ewart,
K.C.B., who was then in the 93rd, writes, " Personally I always liked the feathered bonnet as
a head-dress.   It is, I think, a good protection from the sun.   Whilst I was with the 93rd no
man ever suffered from sunstroke."   Captain Cooper of the 93rd said his bonnet saved his
head from a sword-cut.   The bonnets of all regiments had been much reduced in size for
service in the Crimea.   At the Review before the Queen at Aldershot on the return of the
army, the Guards and Highlanders were the only infantry who had retained their head-dress ;
the others were all in forage caps.

[2] Major Haines, with his draft from the depôt, seems to have arrived about the same time
as Lieut.-Colonel MacKenzie.

adventures, very stiff and tired, on the 19th, where Major-General Michel, C.B., was in command.[1]

The back of the rebellion in the north had already been broken ; in Central India, Sir Hugh Rose had captured Jhansi and Banda [2] in May, and taken the fortress of Gwalior in June.   Apparently the campaign was ended, and Sir Hugh proceeded to take up the office of Commander-in-Chief of the Bombay Presidency, leaving the command to General Robert Napier, who soon found the security was but temporary ; and for nine months that remarkable man Tantia Topee kept six columns of troops in constant movement.

The regiment remained at Mhow till the 22nd of August, when, having received sudden orders, four companies, forming part of a column composed of Bengal Artillery, part of the 17th Lancers, with some Bombay cavalry and native infantry, all under Lieut.-Colonel Lockhart, marched by Indore, and reached Oojein [3] on the 25th.   All being quiet there, the column proceeded to Mundesore to protect that city against a rebel army under the Rao Sahib and Tantia Topee.

Rain had laid the dust ; the country was green, and marching agreeable.   On reaching Kholsheira, intelligence was received that the enemy had crossed to the right bank of the Chumbal River, and in consequence the column was directed upon Augur, which it reached on the 28th, having accomplished a march of fifty miles through a most difficult country in thirty-eight hours.   Here they halted ; the men rested, bathed in the lake, and amused themselves, though a storm at night upset the tents, leaving the inmates to flounder out of the wet canvas in the dark as best they might.   On the 31st the column advanced, and encamped to the east of the walled town of Soosnier.   This move was made in consequence of the rebel army having taken the fortified town of Jhalra Patan and deposed the Raj Rana, who escaped to the British camp.   He represented the rebels to number 15,000 men, of whom from 7000 to 8000 were well armed, and they had thirty-two guns.   As there was no support within 100 miles, and as implicit reliance could not be placed on the native portion of the force in an attack on such superior numbers, the column entrenched themselves, and waited at Soosnier for another column of the same strength which had left Mhow under Lieut.-Colonel Hope of the 71st Highland Light Infantry, which was also placed under Lieut.-Colonel Lockhart. On September 9th a squadron of 17th Lancers and two guns Royal Artillery from Hope's column joined at Soosnier by forced marches,

---

[1] Strength of service companies:—Field officers, 4 ; captains, 10 ; lieutenants, 14 ; ensigns, 6 ; staff, 7 ; sergeants, 55 ; drummers, 23 ; rank and file, 998.

[2] Banda was actually taken by General Whitlock.

[3] Now spelt Ujain.   All spellings in text are as given in the Order-Book and are consequently in the old style.

and Lockhart determined to attack the enemy the following day, where he was posted on strong ground at Rampora, fourteen miles distant ; but the rebel leaders, hearing of the reinforcements, abandoned their position and retreated to Machilpore on the right bank of the Golconda. The column marched to Mulkera, ten miles south of Machilpore, and also on the right bank of the Golconda, where it was reinforced by the infantry of Hope's column. The two columns thus united were in a position either to attack the enemy, to guard the rich city of Malwa, or to pursue in any direction.

Major-General Michel, C.B.,[1] commanding the Malwa Division, joined the force that night and assumed the command, fully approving the position taken up by Lieut.-Colonel Lockhart. The rebels having moved towards the south-east, the force left Mulkera on the 12th in pursuit, and on the 14th reached Bailwarrah, where a reconnaissance ascertained that the enemy was encamped seven miles off ; but men and horses were so much exhausted by the long march and intense heat (many of the native troops having suffered from sunstroke), added to the late hour, that the force encamped for the night. The 92nd suffered less than the other troops ; their cap covers were thickly padded, and the screen was so made as to stand out from the head and come down nearly to the shoulders. In the course of this march they forded a river about 300 yards broad ; the water took tall men to the armpits and little men to the chin. They crossed holding hands, while the other hand held the bundle of coat, kilt, rifle, and ammunition on the head ; a strange scene, men tumbling about on the rough bottom, and only their heads above water ; but all got safely over and encamped in the jungle. A spy dressed as a woman selling milk was caught here and afterwards shot. About midnight orders were given to get under arms quickly without noise or lights, and at 2 a.m. on the 15th August the force marched upon Rajghar, a company of the 92nd forming the advanced guard. On reaching the town, which was fortified in the native style, no one was on the walls, but the gate was found to be closed. A gun was brought forward to blow it down, when it was at once opened, and a messenger from the Rajah informed the General that the enemy in great strength was encamped on the opposite side of the river. The cavalry crossed immediately, followed by the rest of the force ; but the camp was abandoned, fires still burning, tent-poles, etc., left on the ground, showing that the rebels' flight had been precipitate.

The European infantry halted for breakfast and grog was served out, while the General followed the rebels with the cavalry,

---

[1] Private Gladow's journal says the men soon found General Michel to be " not only a good general, but a soldier's friend."

artillery, and native infantry. Soon heavy firing was heard ; the infantry at once pushed on, passing several guns taken by those in advance and a few of the enemy's killed, and reached a height where the other troops were halted, by which time the heat was tremendous. The enemy had made a stand in a difficult and jungly country, and kept up a well-sustained fire of round shot, which, however, generally passed over our men.

The 92nd, under Captain R. Bethune, and the 4th Bombay Rifles, deployed into line and advanced, covered by their own skirmishers (picked shots from each company), and supported by the 71st H.L.I. and 19th N.I. in quarter-distance column. The country being covered with jungle, the skirmishers were ordered not to fire unless they could actually see their opponents. When the country became more open, five of the enemy's guns in position were seen, but after a few rounds from our artillery they were abandoned, and the line again advanced. The enemy were now in full retreat, and were pursued by our cavalry, many prisoners and guns being taken. The infantry, after a short halt, proceeded to Beora, where they encamped, very tired, having marched twenty miles under a burning sun by which many were struck down. The sick following in rear were suddenly attacked in the jungle by a party of the enemy, but the invalids, being armed, drove them off with loss. Two men of the regiment, Privates Ferguson and M'Kenzie, had a marvellous escape from death. Though knocked down by a round shot, one was but slightly wounded ; the other had concussion of the brain, and was invalided.

But though the British had been so far victorious, they suffered an ignominious defeat on the march to Beora. A hornets' nest was disturbed ; they attacked horse and foot, and, causing more fear than human foes could do, put them to flight, so that it was some time before the ranks could be re-formed.

Major-General Michel congratulated the troops on the brilliant result of the day's operations on the plains of Rajghar, " the result of the steady gallantry and endurance by which they had captured thirty guns and dispersed the enemy with heavy loss." The action of Rajghar was politically of great importance, for had Tantia Topee, Feroze Shah, and the Rao Sahib succeeded in crossing the Nerbudda at the head of an unbroken army, Southern India would probably have risen against us.

The Bombay Rifles were sent to Mhow with the captured guns, the rest of the force being formed into one brigade under Lieut.-Colonel Lockhart.

September 18*th*.—The brigade marched from Beora by Denora and many other places, till on the 2nd October it reached Seronje, where the enemy had again appeared in great strength under the same leaders.   On this march the men suffered from want of shoes, but they bought native ones, which they found were good for marching and did not blister the feet.   One of the officers who had a spare pair of shoes gave them to one of his men.   The grateful soldier afterwards brought him a jewelled dagger, which he had picked up in a camp from which they had driven the enemy.   Halting at Seronje to obtain intelligence, the force marched again on the 6th.   At Bhadapore the camp was picturesquely pitched among shady trees on the banks of a clear river; here they bathed and baked scones, and saw the comet of 1858.

On the morning of the 9th October they reached Mungrowlie, and were pitching tents, when the cavalry vedettes reported the enemy advancing in force within half a mile of the camp, from which they could not be seen owing to the nature of the ground. The only cavalry then present were the squadron of 17th Lancers, which was at once pushed forward, rapidly followed by the artillery and infantry, the 92nd [1] being commanded by Captain R. Bethune.

The enemy retired to an eminence crowned by a ruined village, about three miles from Mungrowlie, where they made a determined stand, covering their front with six guns placed in a strip of jungle which was filled with cavalry and infantry for the most part dressed in British uniforms.   Our infantry deployed, and, covered by skirmishers, advanced through the jungle upon the enemy's position.   Their guns opened and they kept up a well-sustained musketry fire, but the shot crashed through the trees above the heads of the Highlanders, who, steadily advancing, directed their fire on the guns, whose position they ascertained by their smoke. Meanwhile the enemy endeavoured to turn our left, and, favoured by the jungle, had actually succeeded in getting in rear of it, when a troop of the 17th was ordered to charge along the rear of our line, and the opposing cavalry gave way, leaving their infantry to be severely handled by the Lancers.   The line continued to advance, the six guns were taken by a rush of the skirmishers, many of the gunners being bayoneted, the enemy retired and the ground becoming more open, our guns came into action with effect ; while the rifles at long range also did some execution on the main body of the rebels, who commenced a rapid retreat.   There being so small a number of cavalry with the brigade, and the enemy being strong in that arm, it was impossible to pursue to any distance, and the force returned to Mungrowlie, where the men had a refreshing bathe, and were glad of their dinner and a dram. [2]

[1] The adjutant of the 92nd, Lieutenant Eddington, when placing his revolver in the holster, was shot through the thigh, but insisted on being carried in a doolie along with the regiment.

[2] Early in the action a standard-bearer with a large flag crossed the front of the 92nd, pursued by Assistant-Surgeon Landale on foot.   Captain Bethune, who was mounted,

One of the 92nd, walking unarmed at some distance from the camp, was attacked by several armed *budmashes* ; he rushed at one, knocked him down, took his sword and marched the lot as prisoners to the camp.

Major-General Michel thanked Lieut.-Colonel Lockhart and the troops under his command for the great success " achieved, owing to their steadiness, without any material loss " . . . " and should any extraordinary cases of special bravery have occurred, he requests that the same may be brought to his notice by Lieut.-Colonel Lockhart." That most chivalrous officer is reported to have said that where all had done their duty well, to single out any for distinction would be invidious.

It being ascertained that the enemy had crossed the Betwa and were on the right bank of that river, the Major-General arranged with Brigadier-General Smith, commanding a field force in the Chandaree district, that a combined movement should take place, and that their forces should be divided into three distinct columns, the right column, under Brigadier Smith, to move down the left bank of the river, prepared to cross to the right if necessary. The cavalry and horse artillery of both brigades formed the centre, under the immediate command of Major-General Michel, and were to cross the ford by which the enemy had retreated ; the right, composed of the infantry and field artillery of Lieut.-Colonel Lockhart's brigade, crossed at Khungia Ghaut : the river was broad, deep, and rapid, but by using the same precautions as on the former occasion, nothing was lost but a sergeant's kilt ! They proceeded by Balabet, where they encamped under fine trees in a pretty country, to Narkut, which they reached October 17th, and next day were joined by the General with the cavalry and horse artillery. On the morning of the 19th they marched on the village of Sindwaho, twelve miles distant, where the enemy was reported to be in strength. The infantry, which was in front, halted half a mile from the village ; orders had been given that no bugle should sound, but this was misunderstood by the cavalry, who, on coming up, halted by bugle call. The enemy, thus apprised of the approach of troops, were soon discovered drawn up in order of battle to the right of the village, and the horse artillery and cavalry moved forward to the attack ; while the remainder, under Lockhart, advanced upon the village, which was supposed to be still held. The infantry were in line, with skirmishers in front ; the 71st, covering Le Marchant's battery, passed to the right, the 92nd through the village and the thick enclosures on its left ; the enemy

galloped up just as the standard-bearer had wheeled round with uplifted sword to strike Landale, but he paid for his temerity with his life. Two Sowars afterwards rode up and asked if they might take the standard to General Michel, to which Captain Bethune consented.

abandoned the village, but many were shot by the skirmishers. The nature of the ground now made it necessary to continue the advance in echelon ; the 71st moved to the right, and as the troop of artillery was seriously pressed, the 19th N.I. was sent to their assistance.   The enemy's guns did some damage to our cavalry, against which his fire was principally directed, and his numerous horsemen held their ground obstinately, and tried to turn the right of our cavalry.   The 92nd, now commanded by Captain A. W. Cameron, advanced in the face of a large body of cavalry posted on a wooded rising ground.   They frequently threatened to charge, coming out into the open, but regained their shelter when our fire told on them.   The 92nd was now quite separated from the rest of the force.   Le Marchant's battery was sent to join them, and as the enemy still threatened to charge, the skirmishers were recalled, and volleys were fired by companies, the artillery throwing shot and shell into the *tope* of trees occupied by the enemy, thus causing them to retire.   The artillery and 92nd then joined the rest of the force. The enemy were in full retreat, pursued by our cavalry and infantry, the latter firing as long as their light-footed foes were within range. The 92nd had suffered much from the great heat, and were glad to quench their thirst under the shade of an enormous banyan tree. Afterwards they encamped at Bahra, where, on the 20th, General Michel congratulated the troops on " the signal success of yester-day near Sindwaho, when an army of 10,000 men was defeated with the loss of all their guns."   " Lieut.-Colonel Lockhart's ability in handling his brigade elicits his warmest approbation, nor can he refrain from expressing his admiration of the infantry, whose zeal and gallantry made them forget entirely distance, heat, and fatigue, when an enemy was in front." [1]

On October 21st and 22nd the pursuit was continued.   At 1 a.m. on the 23rd the infantry left Lullutpore, followed an hour later by the cavalry, and reached Maltawa, a distance of thirty miles, in the afternoon ; on the 24th to Dugorial, whence the General, wishing to surprise the rebels, marched at 2 a.m. on the 25th, and at dawn discovered their army, unconscious of the British approach, crossing his front near Koraie ; the cavalry, whose horses had suffered from fatigue more than the infantry, had been given an hour's extra rest, and they had just come up when the infantry under Lockhart, having cut the enemy's line of march, had dispersed them.   The cavalry pursued, while the infantry followed, clearing the villages for five miles.   About 350 rebels were killed, and numbers threw down their arms.   The 92nd was commanded by Captain Cameron.   In his dispatch to the Commander-in-

---

[1] The Victoria Cross was awarded to Lieutenant Wood, 17th Lancers, for his gallantry at Sindwaho (afterwards General Sir Evelyn Wood, K.C.B.).

Chief, Major-General Michel says : " The infantry, by 1 o'clock p.m. on the 25th, had traversed sixty-two miles in sixty hours, the last twelve of which was over broken ground, skirmishing with the enemy. I solicit to bring this fact prominently to his lordship's notice, as a proof of the excellent spirit and devotion of the troops." During these long marches they forded several rivers, but moonlight and good roads made the men tramp along cheerily to the sound of the pipes or marching songs,[1] though when the sun was up they welcomed the mid-day halt, dinner, and grog. Latterly the road was rough and bad, and the soldiers stumbled along, stiff, thirsty, and tired.

The regiment arrived at Bhilsa on the 2nd November, where a much-needed supply of stockings and shoes was received. While here one of the men was so affected by bad news in a letter from his family in Scotland that he shot himself, the sad event casting a gloom over his comrades. From the 9th to the 15th they rested at Goolgong, in a shady camp by a lake where they could bathe at all hours ; then to Bhopal, where the Ranee gave a grand entertainment to the officers, and sent sweetmeats to all the men. At the durbar held by the Ranee was a guard of honour of the 92nd Grenadiers. She remarked to Colonel Lockhart that if she had such handsome men in her country, they would not have been allowed to leave it. Here also, among other strange birds and beasts, they saw a white elephant. This part of the country being quiet, they marched on the 23rd to Sehore, where in the woods were many apes and peacocks, which latter made an agreeable addition to the soldiers' fare.

Tantia Topee had meanwhile crossed the Nerbudda, but had been repulsed at Candeish. Major Sutherland, with a small column, including 100 of the 92nd, crossed the Nerbudda, and was joined at Jeelwana by 50 of the 92nd and 50 of the 71st, mounted on camels. On the 24th, Major Sutherland, having ascertained that Tantia Topee was on the road to Rajpore, pushed forward the Highlanders on camels, but so rapidly were they followed by those on foot (both Europeans and natives), that they overtook the riders in time to advance with them direct on the strong position which the rebels had taken up. Two guns commanded the only approach, but the Highlanders, supported by the native troops, at once rushed up the road under fire of grapeshot. The gunners stuck to their guns till cut down, but the rest, abandoning the position and their artillery, fled across the Nerbudda, having wounded only a few of their assailants, among them Lieutenant and Adjutant Humfrey, who had ridden ahead of the regiment and attacked one of the enemy's leaders ; missing him with his revolver, he threw it at him, then

---

[1] The band had been left at Mhow.

turned to draw his claymore, but it had been jerked out of the scabbard—he was unarmed ! The man slashed him across the arms with his sword, when Humfrey jumped off his horse, ducked under its belly, and catching hold of his adversary's leg, pulled him off his horse ; and when some men ran up to the adjutant's assistance, they found him sitting on his prostrate foe and hammering his head on the ground, so that he was already dead. The pursuit was now taken up by a column under Brigadier Parke, and Major Sutherland, after remaining at Cooksee till December 27th, was ordered to join headquarters at Mhow.

Meanwhile Lockhart's Column had returned to Mhow, December 6th, having detached No. 10[1] and No. 3 Companies, under Captain Bethune, forming part of a column (17th Lancers and a troop R.H.A.) under Brigadier Somerset, to follow up Tantia Topee, who had again got together a following, among them a regiment of cavalry of the Gwalior contingent.

The Highlanders were mounted on riding camels, two on each ; some of them were smooth-paced, and the men soon got used to their action, but others were so rough that some men preferred jogging alongside, saying, " I didna 'list for a horse sodger," or " I wad rather march five-and-twenty miles than ride that muckle brute ten minutes." They underwent great privations and fatigues in the rapid pursuit. On the last night of 1858, they managed to get some arrack to drink a good New Year, and on New Year's Day, 1859, they came up with the rebels at Burrode, but were scarcely dismounted to attack when the enemy beat a rapid retreat, being, however, considerably cut up by the pursuers. These companies did not rejoin headquarters till May 24th.

On March 2nd, headquarters marched from Mhow for Jhansi, but at Bursud they were directed by Sir R. Napier to leave the heavy baggage in charge of a company, and proceed in light order to assist in clearing out the rebels located in the jungles of that neighbourhood ; when they had performed this duty they resumed their march, and arrived at Jhansi on 7th April, leaving two companies at Lullutpore under Major Sutherland, where they were actively employed for some time.

On June 10th, No. 7 Company was detached to Seepree, and on the evening of the 30th, forty men under Ensign Emmet, mounted on elephants, went with a mixed force under Major

---

[1] The grenadier and light company were now officially No. 1 and No. 10, but regimentally the old titles were used, and the badges worn till they left India in 1863.

The captain of the light company could, with the approval of the C.O., select any man from a battalion company, taking only smart men who were also good marchers and shots, so that to wear the green hackle and bugle was considered a sort of promotion. The last time this privilege was exercised was at Bombay, in 1858, by Captain R. Bethune.

Meade, senior officer at the station, to surprise a numerous party of rebels in a village twenty-eight miles distant, situated on a height and surrounded by jungle. They reached it at 5.30 the following morning, and at once attacked the rebels, who kept up a fire of musketry from the loopholed walls of a large stone-built house, and were not finally subdued till the house caught fire. In this affair four men of the 92nd were wounded. Major Meade, in reporting the circumstance to the officer commanding the 92nd, says, " I cannot speak too highly of Ensign Emmet and your men. Their coolness and steadiness were most conspicuous."

October 14th.—Two companies on camels, part of a small force under Lieut.-Colonel Lockhart, left Jhansi to clear the district of Bundelkhand of rebels, acting in conjunction with six other columns. Some difficult and harassing marches were made, and the rebels were scattered, but could not be brought to action.

In the course of these various expeditions in pursuit of a fugitive foe the regiment lost several men from sunstroke, but none by the sword, though a few officers and men were wounded. Their life was one of constant change and adventure, visiting a vast number of towns between the Nerbudda and Jeypore, generally well supplied with sheep, bread, and fruit, sometimes depending on the peafowl they shot, and on flour porridge and buffalo milk. Once they were a long time without tobacco, till an officer earned the thanks of the smokers by bringing a large supply from Nusserabad. Often tired and weary from hard marching they sometimes rested for days, on which occasions pony races, shooting alligators, and bathing amused and refreshed officers and soldiers. Nor did they lack vocal and instrumental music to cheer them in march, combat, or bivouac ; Surgeon-General Landale testifies to the inspiriting effect on the men, and the warlike feeling engendered by the sound of the bagpipes.

Tantia Topee was at length betrayed by a friend while hiding in the jungles of Seronje, was tried for complicity in the Cawnpore massacres and hanged, and the last embers of the fire of revolt were stamped out. Tantia Topee was undoubtedly a marvellous guerilla leader, and as Pipe-major Duncan MacPhail aptly described him, " a maist ubeequitous character." [1]

For their services in these operations Lieut.-Colonel Lockhart and Major Sutherland were made Companions of the Order of the Bath, and Captains Bethune and St John (who had acted as brigade-major) were made brevet majors. All ranks received the medal, but the regiment had not had the good fortune to be present at any

---

[1] During the campaign officers and men wore the Highland dress, even when on camels, with white cotton jackets and forage caps, provided with a screen from the sun. They carried only arms, accoutrements, and water bottles.

engagement of sufficient importance to be emblazoned on its colours.

At Jhansi the regiment was inspected, and afterwards H.R.H. the Commander-in-Chief remarked on the "excellent and most satisfactory report of Brigadier-General Sir R. Napier upon this distinguished corps, which deserves great praise."

Sir Robert afterwards endorsed his opinion of the regiment by placing his two sons (the late Lord Napier of Magdala and his brother), when appointed to the Indian army, with the 92nd as a good school of duty.

Lord Clyde also reported, after inspecting the regiment in December 1859, that "their state of the highest order, after the recent continuous and arduous duties, reflects great credit on every rank of the corps."

Though while on the move the Gordons enjoyed perfect health, when the excitement was over a reaction set in ; they suffered from climatic diseases, and the mournful notes of "Cha till mi tuilleadh"[1] too often floated on the evening breeze, as some good soldier was borne to his last resting-place at Jhansi or Lullutpore. However, New Year's Day, 1860, was kept with the usual festivity ; a large hall was fitted up as a theatre ; some men were good scene-painters, and many were good actors, and they often played to full houses. These distractions, together with the long walks which some took in the beautiful country, bathing by the way, had the best effect on their health.[2]

The Lullutpore detachment having rejoined under Captain M'Grigor, the regiment, under Lieut.-Colonel Lockhart, left Jhansi, March 15th, 1860, and arrived at Dugshai, April 28th, after a forty days' march by easy stages, during which they waded the broad Scinde River, and halted near many towns, among them the fortress of Gwalior. They admired the famous Taj Mahal at Agra, the beautiful city of Delhi, and the magnificent mountain scenery above Kalka, arriving at their new quarters in the best of health and spirits. In this salubrious climate they luxuriated in

---

[1] "I will return no more."

[2] Extract from Monthly Return of the Service Companies, 92nd Regiment of Highlanders, Jhansi, 1st January 1860.

NUMBER OF EACH COUNTRY.

	Sergeants.	Drummers.	Corporals.	Privates.	Total.
English,	3	1	0	91	95
Scottish,	46	12	44	737	839
Irish,	0	8	4	121	133
Foreign	0	0	0	0	0
	49	21	48	949	1067

The English and Irish were mostly volunteers from other regiments.

European fruits and vegetables, while neither drill nor education were neglected.[1]   Officers and men made many excursions in these Highland hills, the former sometimes using a kilt of khaki-coloured cloth.   In their walks the soldiers made collections of butterflies, which, arranged in neat cases, they sold for a lot of money to visitors.   The officers held pony races, the men had ponies to ride, and kept poultry, pigeons, and pet dogs (the latter often taken by leopards).   Cricket, which was beginning to make its way in Scotland, as golf was becoming popular in England, was played by the officers, and they gave some bats, balls, and stumps to the men, by whom, however, the game was at first rather imperfectly understood.   Two soldiers were seen practising, and the bowler managed to hit the wicket more than once.   At last the batsman shook his fist at him, saying, " I 'll tell ye what it is, Sandy—an ye ca' doon thae sticks again after me juist pittin' them up, I 'll bash yer heid for ye."   When the rains prevented outdoor exercise, daily dancing classes were got up, and each company gave a ball in turn, from grenadiers to light company, vieing with each other in the taste of their decorations, and in the quaintness of their fancy dresses, to the admiration of their guests from Subathu and Kussowlie.

November 28.—The regiment marched four days to Umballa, some dandies who had their shoes too small feeling the downhill more than the uphill journey, " but," says one of them, " determined not to fall out, for the credit of the old corps."

In 1860, Sergeant-major James Gordon was promoted adjutant, Haddington Volunteers, and afterwards retired as major.

A draft, ninety-eight of all ranks, under Ensign D. M. M. Crichton, landed at Calcutta on December 30th, and was taken on the strength January 1st, 1861.   On that day they had " plenty of good cheer, and every one was as happy as merriment, songs of their native land, and contentment could make them." [2]

April 2nd, 1861.—The regiment marched for Dugshai, " our Indian Highland home."

In September a letter was received from the Adjutant-General, dated 4th July 1861, acquainting the commanding officer " that Her Majesty has been pleased to authorise the 92nd Regiment being designated, in addition to its numerical title, ' The Gordon Highlanders,' by which name it was popularly known at, and for some time after, the period of its being raised."

On November 11th the regiment was inspected under Lieut.-

---

[1] " The Council of Military Education having called the attention of the General Commander-in-Chief to the School Report of the 92nd Highlanders for the month of July last, I am to inform you that H.R.H. considers the same as highly creditable to the officers and soldiers and to the n.c. officer acting as schoolmaster."—Letter from Adjutant-General of 8th December 1861.

[2] Private Gladow.

Colonel Lockhart, C.B., by His Excellency General Sir Hugh Rose, K.C.B., Commander-in-Chief in India, who expressed in the warmest terms his approbation of all he had seen of "my old regiment."

November 18*th.*—The Gordons bade adieu to Dugshai, and on the 24th, Major-General Sir R. Garrett wrote in Divisional Orders expressing his approval of the "good conduct, discipline, and soldier-like bearing" of the 92nd Gordon Highlanders while in his division. "His admiration of that bearing dates as far back as 1811, when he first saw them, forming, together with the 50th

1857

and 71st Regiments, one of the most renowned brigades, under the command of Sir Kenneth Howard, in the Great Duke's army."

On the march they were joined by a draft under Lieutenant Cockburn M'Barnet. Passing Umballa, Delhi, and camping at many other places, on December 13th they met the 42nd *en route* to Dugshai. The regiments halted for half an hour, so that the many friends and acquaintances should have a chat. The 42nd were in review order, with feathered bonnets, red coats and plaids, the 92nd in forage caps and white cotton jackets. "We did not think English winter dress good for marching in India."

At Agra the regiment availed itself of the newly-made railway, and reached Allahabad at midnight on the 31st December, the band playing " Here's to the year that's awa' " as they went to their tents.   After keeping the New Year in Highland fashion, and seeing the sights of the city, they marched, January 3rd, 1862, and arrived at the interesting city of Benares on the 10th.   Early in March the headquarters, under Lieut.-Colonel Lockhart, C.B., left Benares, embarked at Rajghat on two steamers with flats in tow, and proceeded down the Ganges to Sahibgunge, whence they arrived by train at Calcutta on the 20th.   The division under Captain Wallace and that under Major C. M. Hamilton went by the Sunderbunds, arriving on the 24th March and 10th April at Calcutta, where they joined headquarters in Fort-William.   The journey had been agreeable.   Each evening the boats were tied to the bank for the night ; by day, the sight of towns and villages, shooting at alligators, getting aground, and such little adventures, lent variety to the voyage.   At Calcutta a letter was received from the Adjutant-General conveying the remarks of the Commander-in-Chief on the confidential reports on the various corps for the first period of 1861 : " Those on the 7th Hussars and 92nd Regiment are deemed by H.R.H. highly creditable and satisfactory." [1]

[1] The details of the service of the regiment in India are principally taken from the Records of the Regiment, letters from Major-General D. Crichton Maitland, Major R. Bethune of Nydie, Surgeon-General Landale, Lieut.-Colonel Robert Bruce M'Ewen, the journal of Private Gladow, and oral evidence.

CHAPTER VII

O N December 15, 1862, the regiment was held in readiness to return to England, and the men desirous of extending their service in India were allowed to volunteer, receiving a bounty. To those whom the climate suits there are many attractions in the East, and 500 men sent in their names. They were allowed three days to consider their decision, and 104 of them on second thoughts " elected to return to the good old corps, and many of those who left were sorry for doing so many a time," says a private's journal.

January 24th, 1863.—Headquarters and seven companies embarked on the sailing ship *Middlesex*, and on the 28th the remaining three companies under Major Haines embarked on the *Surrey*,[1] dropped down to Garden Reach, and next day " up anchor and three cheers for home." After encountering a storm, they sighted land at Natal ; at Cape Town they remained four days, bum-boats supplying fresh bread, milk, and fruit, and they caught numbers of fine crabs, which varied the bill of fare ; touching at St Helena and Ascension, where they caught sharks, they called for orders, May 16th, at Falmouth, having made a favourable passage of 112 days. On May 30, 1863, the headquarters landed at Portsmouth and were quartered at Gosport, this being the first time the regiment had been stationed in England since August 1816, after its return from Waterloo, an interval of nearly forty-seven years. The second division disembarked at Gravesend on May 18th, and proceeded by rail to Gosport.

The regiment being below its establishment owing to the number who remained in India, H.R.H. the Commander-in-Chief approved of " natives of North Britain being allowed to volunteer to the 92nd from infantry regiments serving at home which are not Scottish corps. " No man of bad character shall be allowed to volunteer, or any soldier medically unfit for service." The usual bounty of £1, 1s. to be given.

In consequence of the circulation of this letter, 134 Scotsmen from English regiments joined the 92nd.

July 10th, 1863.—The regiment embarked at Portsmouth on H.M. steamship *Orontes*, landed at Granton at 5 p.m. on the 13th, and marched to Edinburgh Castle. They were welcomed by their countrymen, who filled the streets all the way. The crowd became dense at the Mound, was nearly impassable in the High Street, " but the Esplanade beat all, and it was with the greatest difficulty that we, at last, got through the gateway to the Castle." Friends came from far and near to see them, and there was much merry-making, " but not forgetting to be moderate and no' get

---

[1] Total embarked :—Field officers, 2 ; captains, 5 ; subalterns, 16 ; staff, 5 ; sergeants, 44 ; drummers, 19 ; rank and file, 448 ; women, 23 ; children, 58.

fou," says the private whose journal I quote. Many of the men had saved a deal of money, of which some made a good use, while others made it and their badges fly in the dissipations of Gosport. " It was a great pity," says an officer, " they were not sent straight to Scotland, when their savings would have been better spent among their friends when they went on furlough."

On the 31st July the regiment was inspected by its colonel, General Sir John MacDonald, K.C.B., who was delighted to find it in such good order.

In consequence of inadequate accommodation at the Castle, No. 8 Company, under Lieutenant L. M. Lockhart, proceeded to Greenlaw.

April 16th, 1864.—The regiment was formed in Review order to be presented with new colours. Major-General Walker, C.B., and Staff, General Sir John MacDonald, the veteran and revered colonel of the regiment, accompanied by Lady MacDonald and other members of his family, were present. After the marching past and trooping the old colours, the religious ceremony was performed by the Rev. James Miller, chaplain. The colours were then placed by the Major-General in the hands of Lady MacDonald, who addressed the regiment, alluding to their past career, and concluding by referring in a few touching words to " the many happy years I spent among you, and the pleasure it gives me to see you again." Lieut.-Colonel Lockhart, after thanking Lady Mac-Donald, shortly addressed the regiment, and the Major-General having expressed his satisfaction at the way the ceremony had been performed, the regiment returned to quarters. In the evening a ball was given by the officers in honour of the occasion.

On the 24th June, headquarters and four companies occupied barracks in Glasgow, having been preceded there by three companies under Major Haines, who then proceeded to Ayr, while two companies under Captain Wallace went to Paisley.

On the 30th July the headquarters and Paisley detachment took part in a great Volunteer review in Renfrewshire, and were much complimented on their appearance and the precision of their movements by Colonel M'Murdo, Inspector of Volunteers.[1]

Since the Crimean War several changes had taken place in the life and habits of the regiment. Tea, when it was first introduced

---

[1] Volunteer corps were authorised to be raised, by circular letter of 8th July 1859, addressed to the Lords-Lieutenant of counties by General Peel, Secretary of State for War. They succeeded after a long interval the volunteers of the time of the Napoleonic wars, at a time when there was a distrust of Napoleon III. At first their discipline was defective, but they gradually became a very valuable addition to the forces of the country. The movement has not only been extremely beneficial to the population, both physically and morally, but has done much to popularise the profession of arms, and has provided employment as instructors for many deserving n.c. officers.

in Scotland, was denounced by the Lord President of the Court of Session (Forbes) and others as an abominable drug, and drinking it a pernicious custom likely to destroy the nerve of the people ; they also feared, if it was allowed to take the place of ale as the usual beverage, it would prove injurious to the agricultural interest by destroying the market for barley. Notwithstanding these prognostications, " the new China drink " had gradually become popular among all classes, and bread and tea now replaced the more nutritious meal and milk on the men's breakfast-table. Excess in strong drink, which had become comparatively rare among the gentry, was also less common in the ranks. The dram, which was formerly offered at breakfast in the houses of Highland gentlemen, was still the fashion among the older farmers, but the old soldier no longer considered his " morning " as the best refreshment after parade. Some, indeed, were abstainers, but the opinion of the majority was expressed by one to whom an advocate of total abstinence was expatiating on the delights of the tea-table and the pity of spoiling good water by mixing it with whisky. The soldier, wishing to be polite, so far agreed, saying, " No doubt good water is a good thing, and too much whisky—'specially bad whisky—is not a good thing ; but for my part I never saw a very cheerful party round a pump ! "

In matters of dress, shoe buckles had been given up by the rank and file, chin straps were added to the bonnets, and the pipers' uniform was changed. The 79th had for some years adopted for their pipers a doublet the colour of their facings, which were green, and this now became universal in Highland corps. The Highland bonnet and feathers which had been worn by pipers even in regiments where it was not worn by officers or men, was replaced by the modern glengarry forage cap, distinguished from those of ordinary civilian pipers only by a blackcock's tail. The 42nd pipers, however, with truer military instinct, retained the head-dress which could only be worn by a soldier.

August 30th.—Headquarters and the Paisley detachment went by rail to Perth for the inauguration of a statue of the late Prince Consort, at which Her Majesty was present. The regiment furnished a guard of honour for the Sovereign, and the troops afterwards marched past in slow and quick time, and were put through a variety of manœuvres, returning to their quarters the same day.

January 25th, 1865.—The regimental depôt, under Brevet Major Forbes Macbean, joined headquarters on the breaking up of the 22nd Depôt Battalion.

CHAPTER VIII

1852–1865

HAVING followed the fortunes of the service companies during their twelve years of varied service abroad, I will now describe the life of the four companies at the depôt, and the very important work they performed at a critical period in the life of the regiment. They were commanded by a field officer, having an adjutant and a paymaster, who also acted as quartermaster, with a corps of drums and fifes, and pipers. Two of the four colour-sergeants acted as sergeant-major and quartermaster-sergeant, being paid and clothed as such. The depôt was used as a battalion for general military service, but the principal responsibility of the officer commanding lay in the selection of recruits, their professional education and that of young officers joining, on which the future character of the corps so much depended. That education was thorough as far as it went, but was limited, for an officer, to regimental duties, including an intimate knowledge of the men in his sub-division or company, and attention to their conduct and comfort in quarters and on the line of march ; military law ; and, for all ranks, drill, which was old-fashioned, intricate, and complicated as to movements and commands. Light infantry drill[1] was, however, much practised, but above all things *steadiness* in the ranks was enforced. The long peace had resulted, perhaps, in drill being considered as itself the end rather than a means—a very important means—towards efficiency. The soldier had little opportunity to practise musketry, that most necessary part of his business ; very little ammunition was allowed, with which he fired ball once a year at from 80 to 200 yards distance. It is only wonderful how well many did shoot under such adverse circumstances. Some, no doubt, had handled a gun to some purpose before enlisting. " Man, Davie, ye wouldna hae dune yon an' it had been a roe on the hill o' Finavon," was the remark I heard made by his comrade to a man who had missed the target.

The n.c. officers were men of experience and judgment, and their instruction and advice was most useful both to young officers and soldiers.[2]

A recruit was not considered fit for duty for six months, and not a finished soldier for much longer. Recruit officers were

---

[1] At drill in the barrack square the men wore a leather knee-cap on the right knee.

[2] These instructors were often enthusiasts in their profession, who, like Digby Grand's sergeant, thought no object in nature so beautiful as a well-carried musket ! One, who on leaving the regiment added to his means by teaching calisthenics and drill to the children of the gentry round Dingwall, was invited to a tenants' ball, where, observing one of his pupils, a daughter of the house, stooping as she stood, he gently reproved her, adding, " Now what could be nicer, Miss ——, than to see a young lady standing gracefully ' at ease,' and when her partner comes to claim her, springing smartly to ' attention ' ! " (giving as he spoke an example of these soldierly positions).

drilled with the men, and defaulters did their extra drills in the advanced squad of recruits to steady them.   The defaulter's fault generally arose only from his fondness for whisky, and he not only gave an example of perfect drill, but while standing easy would instil into his juniors his own *esprit de corps*.   " Wait till you see the colours of your regiment," he would say to a lad who seemed to repent having enlisted.   " Man ! yon 's a bonny dress ! " exclaimed my youthful neighbour in the ranks, as a party of the 17th Lancers rode into the square.   " Hoots, haud yer tongue ; it 's no' half as bonny as yer ain ! " was the jealous rebuke of an old Gordon.

The old soldiers would impress upon recruits the numerous "honours" of their regiment, and its superiority to others, especially to " horse sodgers," though they were quite ready to drink with them, and it was not uncommon to see Lancer and Highlander exchange head-dresses as they walked home conversing in clipped English and broad Scotch.   I sketched one couple seen after a farewell entertainment—a tall, whiskered dragoon in kilt and hose all too short, while a sturdy little Scot in overalls much too long stumbled over the unaccustomed spurs.

The depôt was first at Carlow, with a detachment at Castlecomer.   General MacDonald had a habit of paying surprise visits of inspection.   On these occasions nothing escaped his eye for praise or blame, the latter administered sometimes with severity, though in a fatherly manner, to the errors of youth, as I myself experienced.   But he hated deceit.   Having so lately commanded the 92nd, he knew personally many of the men, and once, while visiting the hospital, as the door of a ward was thrown open, he observed a man whom he knew to be a very bad character seize a Bible and pretend to be studying it.   The General walked straight up to the patient's bed, and, taking snuff as his manner was, said, " Do you think, sir, you can *sneak* into Heaven ? "

June 2nd, 1852.—The headquarters and two companies went by rail to Naas, and two companies marched from Castlecomer on the 3rd, arriving at Naas on the 4th.

The General had noticed the recruits as a particularly fine body of young men, and the general conduct and willingness of all, both headquarters and detachment, as excellent.[1]   As in all societies, there were, however, a few bad characters.   One of them was guilty of a crime so disgraceful to the uniform that but for the guard he would have been lynched by the soldiers.   He was sentenced to corporal punishment and to be " drummed out."   Never shall I forget the impression made on all who witnessed the ceremony. After the regimental buttons and facings had been cut from his

---

[1] Sixty-six men had good-conduct badges, from one to four each.

jacket, a rope was fastened round his neck ; with the drums and fifes playing the " Rogues' March " behind, he was led by a drumboy between the lines of those who had been his comrades, who hissed as he passed to the gate, when a pioneer held out to him his " ignominious discharge " document in a pair of tongs—and he was no more seen.

In July, Captain Hugh Scott's company was employed for a fortnight at Philipstown in aid of the civil power, and on the afternoon of Sunday, August 19th, a dispatch arrived ordering Lieut.-Colonel Thorold with 5 officers and 130 n.c. officers and men to proceed at once by rail to Limerick. Buglers were sent out into the country to sound the assembly; officers and soldiers rushed back to barracks, and were soon *en route*. During elections in Ireland it was a part of military duty not only to prevent disturbances, but to protect voters from the fury of the opposite party. This disagreeable work had, at the Clare election, devolved on the light company of the 31st, and at Six-Mile Bridge they were attacked by an immense mob, armed with picks, scythes, and shillelaghs, who stoned the voters and the soldiers ; some of the latter were badly hurt, and the former in great danger. The troops at length fired, when two of the rioters were killed and several wounded. There was tremendous excitement in the district, and a strong force of cavalry and infantry was sent to keep the peace. They encamped at Six-Mile Bridge for a week, when, after an amusing picnic, the detachment returned to Naas, where the depôt was soon after inspected by Major-General Cochrane, who was much astonished at seeing the whole of the officers, n.c. officers, and men do the sword exercise. At this time there was no bayonet exercise, and no gymnastics were taught except " setting up drill " ; fencing was therefore practised in the 92nd as the best means of teaching activity.

On the 14th September 1852, died the great Duke of Wellington, Commander-in-Chief. By desire of the Queen the funeral was delayed till the meeting of Parliament, in order that " such honours should not emanate from the Crown alone, and that the two Houses of Parliament should have an opportunity, by their previous sanction, of stamping the proposed ceremony with increased solemnity, and of associating themselves with Her Majesty in paying honour to the memory of one whom no Englishman can name without pride and sorrow." [1]

The Duke was buried on the 18th of November in St Paul's Cathedral, near the grave of Nelson. A party from every regiment in the army attended the funeral, the Gordon Highlanders being represented by Lieut.-Colonel Thorold (commanding the detach-

[1] Sir H. Maxwell's " Life of Wellington."

ments from Ireland), one captain, one subaltern, one sergeant, and seven rank and file.

February 1853.—The depôt moved to the province of Connaught ; Captain Lyon's company left Naas on the 17th, marched to Kilcock, went by rail next day to Galway, and marched on the 19th to Oughterard, followed on the 22nd by headquarters and two companies under Lieut.-Colonel Thorold, who occupied Galway Barracks on the following day. One company under Ensign Greenhill remained at Naas till St Patrick's Day, when they marched to Kilcock, and, after spending a fraternal and lively evening with the people in honour of their Saint, arrived by rail at Galway, March 18th.[1]

Galway was an exceptionally pleasant quarter. There was fox-hunting with the Blazers, shooting and fishing galore (some of the men were first-rate anglers), and a pack of harriers was kept by the officers, who were received throughout the county with true Irish hospitality. The country people, who adhered to their picturesque costume—the men in " caubeen," tail-coat, knee-breeches, and shoes, the women in blue cloaks and red petticoats—were most friendly to the Highlanders ; all spoke Irish Gaelic, many had no English, and on market-days a painter would have revelled in the picturesque groups of pretty girls flirting with those of the Highlanders who could speak Gaelic. The old-fashioned barracks had no modern conveniences ; the soldiers might be seen on a frosty morning in shirts, kilts, and bare feet, washing their necks and legs at the pump.

In June, Captain Hamilton's company marched to Ennis, in aid of the civil power at the Clare election, and Lieut.-Colonel Thorold followed with another company, returning July 8th. There was also a party of twenty men and some dragoons at Gort, under Ensign Greenhill.[2] Besides these excursions, subalterns were often detailed with small parties for a week or ten days to escort ammunition. These marches were instructive preparation for active service both to officers and soldiers ; they were always in heavy marching order, for it sometimes happened that before their return headquarters had moved, but it was a point of honour with the soldier never to fall out or put his pack on a cart. I remember a sad event arising out of an exaggeration of this soldier-like feeling. A most respectable old soldier named M'Kay had lately come out of hospital when his company marched. In the morning he was

---

1 In April there were 264 privates at the depôt.

A squad book of No. 6 or Captain W. C. Lyon's Company depôt, 92nd Highlanders, 1852, gives 62 n.c. officers and men, of whom 61 were Scottish, 1 Irish, no English—average height, 5 feet 8 inches ; average age, 27 years.

2 The old landlady of the Inn at Gort said the last Highlanders they had there was in 1798, when the Glengarry Fencibles marched in with their priest at their head.

cheerful and said he felt quite fit, but was after a while affected by the sun, and obliged to ride in the cart. He was greatly distressed, and told his comrades that if he was not fit to carry his pack he was not fit to soldier in the 92nd. They thought nothing of it, but it so preyed on his morbid state of mind that he shot himself that evening in his billet. He was within a year of his pension, and all were shocked that a good man should, in a melancholy moment of weakness, have committed such a dreadful act.

These expeditions were enlivened by the hospitality and sometimes by the wit of the natives. A young officer on reaching his billet found himself the centre of a little crowd, and thinking, no doubt, that in his full Highland dress he was worthy of their admiration, he paused on the doorstep to gratify it, when an old fellow approached him, hat in hand, and with the pleading accents of a beggar said, " Av ye plase, sor—I 'm a poor man—would your honour, sor, give me " (the officer's hand sought his sporran) " your breeches, sor, *when ye 've done wid them* ! " On another occasion, an officer driving to dine in the neighbourhood of his billet found fault with the pace, telling the carman his horse was a bad one. " He has the good drop in him anyhow," pleaded the owner ; " sure, sor, I thought about entering him for the Hunter's race." " Hunter, be d—d ! might have some chance in a *donkey* race perhaps " ; but the officer owned himself defeated, when, with a polite touch of his hat, Paddy quickly retorted, " Not if yer honour was in it, sor, I think."

In the spring of 1854 the depôt was reduced to a few men, by volunteering for active service to the 42nd and 79th, as mentioned in the account of the service companies. In July the depôt moved by rail to Belfast, where Brevet Lieut.-Colonel Lockhart replaced Lieut.-Colonel Thorold in the command.[1]

To bring the regiment to a strength which would enable it to take a part in the war was now the problem. Recruiting parties were as usual employed in Scotland, but there are in the north of Ireland districts where the population is largely descended from the Scots who were planted there in the time of James I (VI of Scotland).[2] The militia, which had never been called out since

[1] Moustaches, first introduced in the British army as part of the foreign uniform of Hussars, had been worn for some years by all the cavalry, who, when they left the service, generally shaved them, for it was not thought respectable for a civilian to wear them. In the autumn of 1854, *permission* was given to the infantry to grow moustaches ; most of the officers took advantage of the permission, but the men of the 92nd disliked the idea, and few of them sported " whiskers under the nose," though they liked to show them on their cheeks. They were afterwards *ordered* to wear them, and the hirsute appendage soon became general in all classes.

[2] A lawyer, himself of Scottish descent, gave me an instance of how entirely these immigrants kept the character and dialect of their origin. An old lady who had never left her native place in Tyrone was a witness in an incendiary case. She said, " I saw the licht o' the

1816, were now embodied, and the Antrim Rifles offered volunteers. Should the depleted ranks be filled with this excellent material? Lockhart consulted Sir John MacDonald, colonel of the regiment, and, after consideration, it was decided that the general rule of taking only natives of Scotland should be adhered to, and the result proved the decision to be right. Application was made to the Commander-in-Chief to be moved to Scotland, and on the 18th January 1855, the depôt embarked clad in greatcoats, with trousers under their kilts, for they slept on the deck. The scene as the ship went up the Clyde was a droll one, the preparations for landing being made not so much by dressing as by undressing.

On the 19th they occupied Edinburgh Castle, when there were only 164 privates.

Colonel Lockhart's speech on parade before going on shipboard was an example of brevity and point. " My lads," he said, " we are going to our own country. There are many temptations in Edinburgh, and I would have you to remember that it is neither Donald nor Jock that is seen drunk in the High Street, but a *Ninety-Second man.*"

Great exertions were at once made to recruit. Besides the regular parties,[1] all the n.c. officers and men were allowed to enlist (the recruiter's fee for each recruit was a guinea). It became known that the regiment was particular as to the class of men taken, which had the best effect. Officers were sent to the Scottish militia regiments, getting many volunteers. The Inverness Militia, then as now, had few townsmen, but was filled with country-bred Highlanders (though they did not then wear the Highland uniform), and the officer commanding the depôt wished to get some of these men from the districts where the regiment had been principally raised, and with which it had always kept up its connection. An officer who spoke Gaelic offered to undertake the journey (by coach from Perth), but the recruiting sergeant at Inverness wrote that it was not necessary, as over seventy men had given him their names for the 92nd ; on the volunteering parade, however, the son of their

---

lum alow." Asked if she considered a certain man trustworthy, " Wha ? Jamie ? " said she ; " na, na, I dinna lippen till him ava." My friend was called on to interpret. He told me that they called themselves Scottish in the sense of descent, but Irish in the ordinary meaning. They and the original Irish race went down the stream of life like oil and water, side by side without intermixing.

[1] Parties were at Stornoway, Tain, Inverness, Campbeltown (Argyll), Huntly, Perth, Edinburgh, Glasgow, and Hawick.

More *Highlanders* were enlisted at Glasgow than anywhere ; a Gaelic-speaking sergeant used to meet the *Clansman* on her weekly arrival from the West Highlands, when she constantly brought young men in search of employment.

New Year's Day, 1855, at Belfast passed without a single man being confined drunk. The usual Hogmanay festivities and New Year entertainments were held, but during the day Highland games took up the men's time and thoughts, showing that occupation is the handmaid of temperance.

adjutant, who had the promise of a commission in another regiment on condition of bringing men, induced them to go with him, and the Gordons only got about seventeen.   It was always found that an officer was more successful than a n.c. officer.   The bounty had been raised to £11 ; short leave was often given to a smart young fellow who, with money in his pocket and bonnet on his head, gave a favourable impression of the regiment to his friends at home.

As usually happens in war-time, young men of mettle wanted to see the fighting.   One young fellow was found, on being measured, not to touch the standard.   " Go home, my lad," said the colonel, " take more milk to your brose, and come back when you 've grown."   " Oh, sirs," entreated the lad, " an' ye 'd juist tak' me !   I 'm *wee*, but I 'm *wicked* ! "   Lockhart could not resist this appeal, and I hope the lad's enterprise met with the success it deserved.[1]

So many joined that the tailors could not clothe them fast enough, and on the 30th January 1855, a draft of 4 officers and 135 n.c. officers and men, under Lieut.-Colonel Lockhart, left for Gibraltar, where their equipment and drill were completed.   Many parents came to see these young lads off.   Among others I spoke to was an old man with white hair and a blue bonnet, giving his son his blessing and telling him in Gaelic " never to turn his back on friend or foe."   He was a farmer from Rannoch, who had served at Waterloo as sergeant in the 92nd.

Captain A. W. Cameron took command of the depôt.[2]

An incident which occurred to the writer at this time shows how different were the ideas of society as to after-dinner conviviality to those of the present day.   He dined at the Royal Company of Archers' Hall in the Old Town as the guest of one of the members, a gentleman well known for his legal acumen and his literary talent. The dinner hour was about six, and on leaving in the light of a summer evening no cab was at hand.   The host was not very steady on his legs, and had to take the arm of his guest, who was conspicuous

---

[1] During the two years I was adjutant at the depôt in Ireland and Edinburgh, only two Englishmen were enlisted as ordinary recruits, one at Tain and one in Edinburgh.   The enlisters were reprimanded and the recruits asked to go to other regiments, but they declined. An English regiment being opened to volunteer for the 92nd, by order of Colonel Lockhart I wrote privately to the adjutant that, without meaning any disrespect to his men, they would not be welcome unless natives of Scotland, of whom a few n.c. officers and privates came. More recruits came from the Highlands than for some years, and the drill instructors might often be heard explaining their orders in Gaelic.

[2] Captain Cameron, by desire of Lieut.-Colonel Atherley, selected a pattern of grey-ribbed stocking hose for ordinary wear, the red and white being continued for Sunday, etc. These were replaced a year or two later by the red and black still (1928) in use.   The men's purses were altered to a smaller size—same pattern.   The height of the bonnets was also greatly reduced in view of active service.

in gold epaulettes and dirk. Many and various were the remarks of the passers-by, such as, " Eh, losh keep 's a', woman, here 's the Shirra' fou—wi' a sodger ! " on which that official, striking an attitude, exclaimed, " Is it not hard that the Sheriff of Edinburgh is the only man in the city that can't get drunk with impunity ! " But though they looked leniently upon occasional excess in drinking, the citizens had a rooted objection to Sunday music and the band was not allowed to play outside the Castle, even marching to church.

In August, 5 officers, 3 sergeants, and 185 rank and file, under Captain Cameron, embarked at Liverpool for the Crimea, the depôt being commanded by Captain C. M. Hamilton.

In February 1856, 3 officers, 1 sergeant, and 232 rank and file, under Captain J. A. MacDonald, embarked at Liverpool to join the service companies ; and in April, 3 officers, 3 sergeants, 2 drummers, and 208 rank and file embarked for Gibraltar.

So successful had been the recruiting that on January 1, 1856, the sergeants, drummers, and rank and file of the service and depôt companies numbered 991 Scots, 4 English, and 41 Irish.[1]

In August the depôt under Major Robert M'Leod Sutherland embarked at Granton and landed next day at Fort-George, 246 of all ranks. In November, Major Sutherland embarked at Fort-George with a draft for Gibraltar. The depôt remained in the Highlands, recruiting and sending out drafts, till the 10th September 1857, when it embarked, and arrived at Stirling Castle on the 13th, where it was under Major Haines till February 1858,[2] when, the service companies having been increased to ten companies and the depôt reduced to two (Nos. 11 and 12), Major Haines, with 4 other officers, 5 sergeants and 233 rank and file, proceeded via Alexandria and the overland route to Bombay.

October 1859.—A guard of honour under Captain Gibson Stott, Lieutenant C. MacBarnet, and Ensign D. Makgill Crichton, was present at Loch Katrine when Her Majesty Queen Victoria opened the Glasgow Waterworks there.

In 1860 the depôt under Captain Forbes Macbean moved to Perth, and though several drafts had been sent to the service companies, it numbered 265 of all ranks.[3]

On their return to Stirling in May 1861, the Provost and magistrates of the city of Perth addressed a letter to Captain Macbean, commanding the depôt 92nd Highlanders, in which they

---

[1] W.O. Records, Public Record Office.

[2] In 1858, recruits received as bounty £3, a free kit, and a bonnet.

[3] At this time the depôt (two companies), with the 42nd and 71st depôts, formed the 22nd Depôt Battalion, of which the headquarters were at Stirling, one of the depôts being detached at Perth.

express " our sense of the peculiarly excellent and orderly character of the soldiers belonging to that gallant regiment during the
time they have been quartered here.   The best evidence of this is
to be found in the fact that the city authorities have not been
troubled with a complaint against any one of them, which is more
than can be said for the soldiers of any depôt quartered in Perth
for very many years. . . ." They attribute the good understanding between the inhabitants and the soldiers to the high state of

1852
OFFICER—MARCHING ORDER

discipline of the latter, " and tender our best thanks to yourself
and the officers, n.c. officers, and privates under your command
for so pleasing a state of matters."   The letter concludes by an
expression of gratitude to Captain Macbean for his " many acts of
kindness in connection with public objects in this city, and for
those deeds of philanthropy which so well mark the character of
the Christian gentleman and the Christian soldier " ; and with
good wishes to all—" we feel assured these sentiments are shared
by the entire community over which we preside, and who will part
with the 92nd with much regret."   (Signed) WILLIAM IMRIE,
Lord Provost.

In a letter to the depôt dated Dunalastair, 1861, Lieut.-General Sir John MacDonald, colonel of the regiment, expresses the great satisfaction it has afforded him " that the Magistrates of my own county town should so highly prize those who have never stood beneath their own standards, but who will ultimately uphold them with honour and glory as of old, of which their conduct in Perth is a sure guarantee."

On the breaking up of the 22nd Depôt Battalion, the depôt under Brevet Major Macbean proceeded from Stirling to Glasgow on the 25th January 1865, and joined the headquarters stationed there.

CHAPTER IX

O N March 6th the regiment embarked at Glasgow, transhipped to H.M. steam troopship *Himalaya*, arrived at Portsmouth on the 10th, where each rank was entertained by the corresponding rank of the 31st Regiment, and the same day proceeded by rail to Aldershot.

March 14th, 1865.—Colonel Lockhart, C.B., retired on half-pay, and was shortly after promoted Major-General. Having joined while there were still officers and soldiers who had served in the Peninsula, he formed a link between the Waterloo period and the more modern life of the regiment. A man of first-rate abilities, he adapted himself to changing circumstances ; tall, manly, and full of chivalry, tempered by a rich vein of Scotch humour, his fine features could look stern enough on occasions, which were, however, rendered rare by the tact, temper, and justice which governed his actions. He was an ideal commander of a national corps.

The command of the regiment devolved on Lieut.-Colonel Haines, who retired in the following September, and was succeeded by Lieut.-Colonel C. Monteith Hamilton.

At Aldershot, Sergeant-major (afterwards Captain) Dods took leave, after twenty-two years' service, amid every demonstration of respect, on being promoted quartermaster in the Monaghan Militia. He was succeeded as sergeant-major by Alexander Yeatts.

Here all ranks of the Gordons and Greys renewed their traditional friendship. At a dinner which was given by the officers of the 92nd to those of the Greys, in proposing the health of all ranks of that regiment, Lieut.-Colonel Hamilton presented the officers with a handsome gold quaich. Colonel Darby Griffith, in returning thanks, said the Greys well knew how to appreciate the friendship which it symbolised, and drank to the officers, n.c. officers, and soldiers of the Gordon Highlanders. When the health of the Greys had been proposed, numbers of 92nd men, who had congregated outside the officers' mess, lustily took up the cheering, thus contributing their share in the compliment to their gallant compatriots. The Greys presented the officers of the 92nd with a snuff-box made from a hoof of their last Balaclava charger.[1]

March 1st, 1866.—The regiment embarked at Portsmouth on H.M. troopship *Simoom* for service in Ireland, and landed at Kingston on the 5th. They proceeded by rail to the Curragh, but after three days returned to the Royal Barracks, Dublin, where the Greys were also quartered. On the regiment's departure from Aldershot, Major-General Lord Henry Percy, V.C., reported,

---

[1] Still an honoured possession of the 2nd Battalion officers' mess.

" that during the time the 92nd have been in the brigade under my command, I can report most favourably of them ; they are well drilled, their conduct sober, orderly, and soldier-like, discipline good, and all that one can desire in a well regulated corps."

General the Hon. J. Yorke Scarlett, commanding the division, reported, for the information of H.R.H. the Commander-in-Chief, to the same effect, adding—" They left camp without an absentee or a drunken man, and were placed in the train within seven minutes from the regiment entering the station." [1]

On the 25th June 1866, the Right Hon. Hugh, Lord Strathnairn, G.C.B., G.C.S.I., was appointed Colonel of the Gordon Highlanders, *vice* General Sir J. MacDonald, K.C.B., deceased.[2]

In December 1866, at Ship Street Barracks, the regiment was armed with the Snider Enfield breech-loading rifle in place of the Minié muzzle-loading rifle.

The duty in Dublin was rendered unusually severe by the Fenian disturbances, and the men were glad when, on July 15th, 1867, the regiment moved to the Curragh Camp, where, in the intervals of field-days, games of all sorts were encouraged by Lord Strathnairn, the Commander-in-Chief in Ireland, and where the regiment was very healthy.

The first annual regimental races were held, along with those of the Greys and 9th Lancers, at Baldoyle racecourse in 1866. A Regimental Challenge Cup was subscribed for, and among other events was a welter race, for which a challenge cup was given by Lieutenant H. V. Brooke, to be run for by horses carrying not less than thirteen stone, owned and ridden by officers of the regiment. Lieutenants Macgregor and Papillon distinguished themselves at Punchestown, where the latter officer owned and rode the winner of the light-weight Military Steeplechase. The regiment also furnished a large contingent at the meets of the Kildare Hounds, and during their tour of home service they kept a Regimental Coach.

August 20*th*, 1867.—A Horse Guards letter informed the commanding officer that 156 volunteers from the 42nd had been transferred to join the 92nd on its arrival in India, to which it was

---

[1] *April* 1*st*, 1866.—The regiment was reduced from twelve to ten companies, officers, n.c. officers and men to be borne as supernumeraries till absorbed ; the new establishment to be— Field officers, 4 ; captains, 10 ; subalterns, 20 ; staff, 5 ; sergeants, 49 ; corporals, 40 ; drummers, 21 ; pipers, 6 ; privates, 640—total, 756. In May 1867, the establishment was again increased to twelve companies, with a total of 1045 of all ranks.

[2] This famous old Highland warrior died in his native land, and the old colours of his regiment hung for some years over his tomb in the Episcopal Church at Kinloch Rannoch. It is much to be regretted that no portrait of him suitable for reproduction appears to exist.

now ordered. By a Horse Guards letter of September 7th, inspecting officers of recruiting districts were informed that recruits for general service were to be posted to the 77th and 92nd Regiments. The consequence of this order was an influx of general service men, of whom very few were Scots. Major Forbes Macbean, in Lieut.-Colonel Hamilton's absence, at once wrote to remonstrate, and the result was that a memo., dated Horse Guards, 31st October, was received, stating that H.R.H. the Commander-in-Chief had directed that recruiting for the 92nd should be stopped, except in Scotland. The want of a second battalion was again felt, and whenever the recruiting was taken out of the hands of the officer commanding the regiment, its nationality suffered.

It has often been said, both in Parliament and in the Press, that recruits are not the best workmen, and seek service only when in difficulties. This may be true, to a certain extent, for lads of eighteen have not had time to make their mark in life, and the high-spirited are apt to be restless at home ; but it is a great mistake to suppose that the same spirit which induces so many young officers to serve their country in preference to more lucrative professions is not also the motive of the rank and file. I remember, in 1852, a sergeant-major telling me that Grant's " Romance of War," lately published, had brought several recruits to the regiment, and Mr Ross Martin, formerly sergeant, who joined at the Curragh, 1867, tells how, when he was a boy, the minister at Inverness gave him Grant's book, and how he and his young friends got a man to read it aloud to them in the evenings. He determined to be a soldier when old enough, and that there might be no mistake about the regiment, had " 92 " tattooed on his arm ! When the time came, he and twelve other lads agreed to go together. Not wishing to enlist at Inverness, where most of them were apprenticed, they walked to Fort-William, took steamer to Glasgow, where they knew the recruiting sergeant (M'Intyre), who had been stationed at Inverness, and enlisted with him.

November 24th.—The regiment was divided into ten service and two depôt companies.

On the 31st December great preparations had been made by the Gordons to celebrate their last New Year's Day before going abroad. The materials for the dinner had arrived, the men were putting the last touches to the decoration of the rooms for next day's festivities, but—there 's many a slip between the cup and the lip—to their dismay, at 5 p.m. a telegram was received ordering five companies to proceed immediately by special train to Cork in aid of the civil power, and they started, bag and baggage, that evening under Major A. W. Cameron, while at the same time E and F

Companies,[1] under Captain A. Forbes Mackay, proceeded on similar service to Tipperary, where they were quartered in the Court House. No wonder that a soldier's journal says—" The Fenians would have suffered if we had got the chance."

The depôt companies proceeded, on January 27th, 1868, to join the 15th Depôt Battalion at Aberdeen, with a total of all ranks of 158.

On the 25th January 1868, headquarters entrained at 11 p.m., and being joined at Cork by the detachments, the service companies under Lieut.-Colonel C. M. Hamilton, embarked on the 26th on H.M. troopship *Crocodile*, in which they were much more comfortable than on the voyage home from India ; after touching at Malta, they landed at Alexandria on the 9th February, proceeded by rail to Suez, and embarked on H.M.S. *Malabar*. In the Red Sea they passed the 42nd, homeward bound. At Bombay, where they arrived on the 26th,[2] they were transhipped in two divisions, and, after a hot and uncomfortable voyage, the headquarters reached Karachi on the 8th March, thence went by rail to Kotree, whence they embarked on flat-boats, which were towed by steamers up the river Indus. A pleasant trip ; the officers got shots at the alligators basking on the banks ; there was plenty of mutton, fish, and fruit for all. Sometimes they had time to land and stretch their legs by a country walk, and on the 27th they reached Multan ; whence by train, spending the night in rest camps, being well cared for on the journey to Amritsar ; from there they marched, getting a view of the Himalayas by the way, to Jullundur, where they arrived 30th March. A number of men who had volunteered from the 42nd came out to meet their new regiment, and three of them who were pipers played them in. " These volunteers were splendid men." The other part of the regiment from Meean Mir joined on the 7th April. Detachments were sent to Fort Phillour, Fort Gavindghur, and Amritsar.[3]

Private Gladow's journal says the men were very happy in their new quarters, the rooms were comfortable and airy, with broad verandahs, the regiment had a good library and a reading-room,

---

[1] At this time the companies were distinguished by letters instead of numbers, as heretofore.

About this time (1866-8) " beer money " was discontinued on a slight addition to the pay being given. A blue patrol jacket was adopted for officers in place of double-breasted frock coat, and steel scabbards in place of leather for infantry officers' swords.

[2] At Bombay they received white linen coats and white helmets, which had now become the universal headgear of British troops in India.

[3] In 1868 the size of regimental colours was reduced to 3 feet 9 inches flying, and 3 feet on the pole. The fringed colours with *Crown and Lion* on the staff, 4 feet 6 inches flying and 4 feet on the pole, were introduced in 1858. From 1751 till 1855, colours were 6 feet 6 inches flying and 6 feet on the pole Those made in 1855 were a trifle smaller.—" Colours and Standards of the Army," by S. M. Milne.

where all sorts of papers and periodicals were taken, a game room with billiard and bagatelle tables ; also a regimental theatre.   They kept the New Year (1869) as usual, the officers visiting the rooms, " the old songs of Scotland sounding sweeter when far from home, and everything done to make men happy."   Duty and drill were not neglected, and General Beatson, after inspecting on the 2nd February, said, " He had for long heard of the high character of the regiment, and that now on making its acquaintance, it quite came up to his expectations."

The severe penalties in civil life had been much modified since the early years of the century, but it was only in the reign of George IV that Sir James M'Intosh brought into the House of Commons a measure for abolishing the punishment of death in cases of the stealing of property to the value of five shillings.[1]   In the army corporal punishment had, in 1847, been reduced to a maximum of fifty lashes, and confined to a few disgraceful offences, and was done away with in 1868, except on active service.   It was entirely abolished in 1881—a form of punishment no longer suited to the times, but it was not generally disapproved by the old soldiers, for the offender's duty did not fall on his comrades as it did when he was imprisoned.   When punished a man was not called in question for anything he chose to say.   " Odd, sir, ye micht hae peety—on a puir drucken cratur like yersell ! " was, on one occasion, the remark of a culprit to the senior officer on parade, who had the reputation of being a two-bottle man.

At Jullundur they were visited by Shere Ali Khan, Amir of Afghanistan, who was on his way to meet the Viceroy in Durbar. He saw the regiment reviewed, and forty men fired 200 rounds volley firing, with only seven misses.   The Amir was in the butts and was astonished, and afterwards spoke to the men, saying, " Very good, brave boys, very good ; well done."   He was also delighted by an exhibition of Highland dancing.[2]

Sickness set in at this time, and several n.c. officers and men died.   On the 18th April a detachment of young and sickly men, 182 of all ranks, under Captain Forbes Mackay, marched to Dalhousie in the Chumba Hills, for change of air.   It is many days' march, but they enjoyed the walk in the early mornings, and the " good breakfast and dram of rum " on arrival in camp.   They remained five months, and were employed in the healthy occupation of road-making, for which they got working pay.

In October 1869, Lieut.-Colonel Hamilton took leave of the

---

[1] " History of the Four Georges," by Justin McCarthy.

[2] It is said that when the officials went out to meet the Amir on his arrival, they were accompanied by the senior ladies of the station ; on which His Highness remarked, " I see your custom is the same as ours at Kabul, where on such occasions we leave our young beauties at home."

regiment, " officers and men being very sorry to part with him," and he, in an eloquent and touching order, expressed his regret at parting with them.   The command devolved on Lieut.-Colonel Forbes Macbean.

March 3rd, 1869.—Lieut.-General John Campbell was appointed colonel of the regiment, *vice* Field-Marshal the Right Honourable Hugh, Lord Strathnairn, transferred to the Royal Horse Guards. Although Lord Strathnairn now became colonel of the " Blues," he remained an enthusiastic " Gordon " to his dying day.

February 1st, 1870.—The regiment, under Lieut.-Colonel Forbes Macbean, went by special train to Meean Mir, and was encamped along with other troops for the reception of H.R.H. the Duke of Edinburgh.   The 92nd furnished the guard of honour at Government House, Lahore, and also formed the guard of honour at the Durbar next day when the native princes were received. H.R.H. dined with the officers, when 200 men, having provided themselves with ropes, took the horses out of the carriage and drew it up the approach to the mess-tent, which was lined with piles of arms and illuminated with coloured lamps, the pipers playing " Oh, but ye 've been lang o' coming ; welcome, royal Charlie ! "   One of the Gordons made a poem of welcome, of which H.R.H. desired a copy to be sent to the Queen.[1]

A Soldiers' Industrial Exhibition took place, where drawings, models, furniture of all sorts, upholstery, saddlery, shoemakers' and tinsmiths' work, needlework, stuffed birds, patchwork, etc. etc., all made by soldiers and their wives, were shown.   There was a review of the troops, European and native ; also garrison games, in which the Gordons gained several principal prizes, and theatricals at night.   The regiment returned to Jullundur on the 19th.

In February a draft of 5 officers, 2 sergeants, 2 corporals, 1 drummer, and 100 privates arrived from Scotland.   In June the establishment was raised to 10 companies, 1058 of all ranks.

At this time a General Order was issued allowing natives of North Britain in regiments under orders for England to volunteer to the 92nd, and a considerable number of n.c. officers and soldiers from time to time took advantage of the opportunity to join a national corps.[2]   About this time too the hard spun regimental

---

[1] Private Gladow.

[2] In 1870 we imitated the Prussian system by allowing a large portion of the standing army to pass to furlough after serving six years with the colours.   They were called Reservists, and were still on their army engagement.   The new rule was impressed on the sergeant-major by one of a draft whose stupidity had aggravated him.   " If you don't do better I 'll keep you at drill all your twelve years," said the angry instructor.   " Ye canna do that," replied the lad, " I 'm just listed for sax ! "

The standard for recruits was reduced at this time from 5 ft. 8 in. to 5 ft. 5½ in. (G.O. 8 and 74 of 1870) ; in 1871 to 5 ft. 5 in. (G.O. 47 of 1871).   The standard was often changed, and growing lads were always allowed to be taken under it.

tartan was replaced by the much more comfortable, though less durable and showy, soft tartan.   The hue of the soldiers' coats was also changed from red to scarlet.

In January 1871, a draft of 86 n.c. officers and men, under Lieutenant D. F. Gordon, was taken on the strength, to replace invalids and time-expired men going home.   Among the latter was Private Gladow, whose journal now ceases.

The regiment erected a memorial in St Luke's Church, at Jullundur, to the memory of the officer, n.c. officers, men, women, and children who had died since leaving Ireland, January 1868.   To aid in defraying the cost a play, "The Beggar's Petition," was performed, a prologue being written for the occasion by Private J. Sawyers.

Detachments were constantly sent to Dalhousie for change of air and road-making.

December 1871.—Headquarters, under Major G. H. Parker, went by rail to Delhi for the camp of exercise, and were posted to the First Brigade (Colonel Walker, V.C., 3rd Buffs) of the Second Division, commanded by Major-General M'Murdo, C.B.   A detachment, under Captain Maxwell, composed principally of sickly men, with the married women and children, had moved meanwhile to Chakrata, there to await the headquarters.   At the

Extract from Monthly Return of the Service Companies of the 92nd Regiment of Gordon Highlanders, Jullundur, 1st January 1870.

	Sergeants.	Drummers.	Corporals.	Privates.	TOTAL.
English,	3	4	3	95	105
Scottish,	40	14	35	563	652
Irish,	3	5	0	47	55
Foreign,	0	0	0	0	0
	46	23	38	705	812

NUMBER OF EACH SIZE.

Ft.	In.		Sergeants.	Drummers.	Corporals.	Privates.	TOTAL.
6	0 and upwards		8	0	0	18	26
5	11		2	0	3	20	25
5	10		3	0	5	60	68
5	9		4	2	5	40	51
5	8		8	2	3	107	120
5	7		11	3	7	162	183
5	6		6	4	9	184	203
5	5		3	3	5	90	101
Under			1	9	1	24	35
			46	23	38	705	812

1871.—Purchase of commissions was abolished.   Hitherto officers (unless promoted from the ranks and certain other exceptions) had, besides passing an examination, to pay a considerable sum on appointment, and a further sum (with certain exceptions, such as death vacancies) on promotion to each rank, so that their pay was really interest on their capital, of which they were liable to be deprived by being cashiered for misconduct.   Extra sums were constantly paid by junior to senior officers to induce them to retire, and when purchase was stopped, the flow of promotion had to be kept up by granting retiring allowances.   The change was a boon to the officers, but a great cost to the country.

termination of the camp of exercise, the Brigadier issued an order, of which the following is an extract :—" The last six weeks have added to the interest I have for many years taken in the career of my old friends the 92nd Highlanders "; and he thanks Captain Chalmers for his valuable services as aide-de-camp.

December 29*th*, 1871.—Lieut.-General George Staunton, C.B., was appointed colonel of the regiment, *vice* Lieut.-General John Campbell, who was the last officer in the 92nd who served at Waterloo, where he was in the 44th Regiment.

February 2*nd*, 1872.—The regiment left Delhi by march route to Chakrata, which they reached on the 4th March. In November a draft under Lieutenant A. D. MacGregor was taken on the strength. About 1872 a stag's head with the word " Bydand " replaced the Sphinx with the word " Egypt " as cap badge. It is remarkable that a most honourable cognisance won by the regiment on the battlefield, given by the King and adopted as cap badge while Lord Huntly was colonel, should have been exchanged for the crest of his family after all connection with it had ceased except the name, to which the regiment had added so much honour, and not least by the deeds which won the Sphinx. From notes kindly sent by the Earl of March, it appears that various heralds give the meaning of " Bydand " as " biding," or " abiding," in the sense of " enduring," " lasting," or " biding the time." [1] In this year the white coats of the band were exchanged for scarlet.

On 17th April 1873, Major-General Travers, V.C., inspected the regiment under Major Cameron, and noted " the splendid appearance of the regiment and the very good behaviour of the men." Indeed, Inspecting Generals, since their arrival in India, seem to have been unanimous in their good opinion.

At the regimental games held at Chakrata, Colonel MacDonald, of the Indian Army, gave a prize for a race to be run by natives of Inverness-shire and men of the name of MacDonald. There were a great many entries. The winner was Private Colin Macrae.

On the 1st April 1873, an important change was made in the life of the regiment by the introduction of the system of linking together two regiments of one battalion. They were to retain their individuality as regiments, in number, name, and uniform, but the officers and men now joining were liable to serve in either, and the latter were no longer to have regimental, but brigade numbers. The 92nd was fortunate in being linked with so good a Highland corps as the 93rd, and recruits were enlisted for the 56th Depôt Brigade. It had long been evident that a regiment of

---

[1] 1872.—Pantaloons and boots, also a sabre-tasche, were ordered to be worn by mounted officers of infantry.

one battalion is unworkable in war time, but it was not generally considered that this system of linking was a satisfactory solution of the difficulty. Colonel Kenneth MacKenzie, then Assistant Adjutant-General at the Horse Guards, who had been long adjutant of the 92nd, and who added to an unusual amount of common-sense great experience of the discipline and recruiting of a Highland corps, expressed his opinion in the strongest terms. " It will never do," he said ; " far better unite all the kilted battalions into one regiment, with one title and uniform ; in time they will agree as well as the battalions of the Rifle Brigade, but two separate regiments linked will never answer."

On November 22nd, 1873,[1] they marched under Major Cameron for Multan (495 miles), and arrived January 13th, 1874, a detachment being sent to Dera Ismail Khan.

A Horse Guards letter, with remarks by the Commander-in-Chief on the confidential report on the 92nd at Chakrata, says, " The highly creditable and satisfactory report on the corps reflects much credit on Major Cameron, who commanded the regiment since last inspection."

In December 1873, Lieut.-Colonel Forbes Macbean retired after thirty years' service, and was succeeded in the command of the regiment by Lieut.-Colonel A. W. Cameron.

The Gordons remained at Multan during 1874 and 1875, during which time the Commander-in-Chief expressed his satisfaction with them.

In 1875, the time-honoured rank of ensign was exchanged for that of sub-lieutenant.

In the course of this year Captain H. V. Brooke and Lieutenant Dick-Cunyngham were among the first Englishmen to visit Gilgit and the Tibetan frontiers in pursuit of markhor, ibex, and ovis ammon, of which they obtained many magnificent specimens ; and at various places officers had good sport, killing, besides smaller game, tigers, leopards, bears, and deer of the various Indian varieties.

On the 13th January 1876, headquarters and a wing, under Major Parker, proceeded by rail to Lahore to be present on the occasion of H.R.H. the Prince of Wales's visit to that place. On arrival, a guard of honour of 100 n.c. officers and men, with the band and pipers, under Captain H. V. Brooke and Lieutenant

---

[1] By G.O. 79 of 1873 the standard height for infantry was reduced to 5 ft. 4½ in.

Till 1873 the surgeon and assistants belonged to their regiment, wearing its uniform, with slight differences ; in the 92nd they wore tartan trousers, black belts, and a black hackle in their bonnets. They were generally most popular among their brother officers, and the unofficial knowledge they had of the constitutions and characters of the soldiers was of great use to the commanding officer. After this period, medical officers were attached to stations or regiments, but were no longer regimental officers.

F. G. Kinloch, was encamped in the grounds of Government House, the other companies being on the racecourse. The wing returned to Multan on the 26th. Previous to his departure, H.R.H. expressed himself greatly pleased with the clean and smart appearance of the men, and desired Major Parker to make the same known to the regiment.

October 31*st*, 1876.—The following farewell order by Lieut.-Colonel A. W. Cameron, dated 5th September 1876, was published :—

> I cannot leave the Gordon Highlanders without expressing how high an honour I shall always esteem it to have been privileged for nearly thirty-two years to serve in its ranks, and, above all, that I was entrusted with the command of it. Circumstances compel me now to resign the charge which it was the ambition of my life to obtain, but wherever the regiment goes, there will my best hopes and wishes accompany it. It will always afford me the greatest pleasure to learn that mutual goodwill, ready and willing obedience to authority, and zealous and fearless discharge by all of the duties of their several stations, continue, as heretofore, to mark the character of the regiment. Comrades, there are now a great many young soldiers in your ranks, and not so many " old hands " with whom in former times it rested in a measure to hand down the traditions of the regiment. I would therefore recommend you, as a last parting word of advice, to make yourselves intimately acquainted with the history of your regiment, to take well to heart the great name (second to none in the British Army) which our forefathers earned for it, and always to remember that you have that name in your safe keeping. I need hardly say that to add to that name should be the ambition of every individual in the corps, no matter what his standing is, etc.

Colonel Cameron was a son of Sir Alexander Cameron of Inverailort, who was wounded at the battle of Alexandria in the 92nd, and Colonel Cameron, like his Peninsular namesake of Fassiefern, was a true Highlander, understanding the feelings and speaking the language of his countrymen. Like him, too, he had a foster-brother named M'Lean, a soldier in the regiment. Unfortunately he died at Kilkenny, and Cameron never could speak of him without showing the distress he felt at his untimely end, and he supported the mother till her death. Colonel Cameron died in Inverness-shire, July 1888,[1] and was buried among many of his name and of his regiment at Kilmallie. He was succeeded in the

---

[1] A characteristic story of Colonel Cameron was told me by Lieutenant (afterwards Major-General Sir Hector) MacDonald. When a corporal he was sent for by the colonel, who said, " Corporal MacDonald, there is a vacancy for a sergeant, and though you are a young soldier I intend to make you, but I would have you remember that a sergeant in the Gordon Highlanders is at least equal to a member of Parliament, and I expect you to behave accordingly ! " Corporal MacDonald mentioned the circumstance to the sergeant-major, and asked what the colonel meant by his being equal to an M.P. " Oh, my lad," said the sergeant-major, " he only means that he respects us, and he wants us to respect ourselves."

command by Lieut.-Colonel George Hubert Parker. During the absence of Cameron and Parker, the regiment had been commanded for some time by Major G. Stewart White.

November 2nd, 1876.—Headquarters and six companies, under Major J. C. Hay, marched to Delhi to take part in the Imperial Assembly, followed by D Company from Multan and B Company from Dera Ismail Khan. On November 2nd the following order was published :—

Brigadier-General MacPherson, in taking leave of the Gordon Highlanders, begs to express his high appreciation of their soldier-like conduct since he has had the honour to command them. The admirable spirit which pervades all ranks, so clearly manifest to all who have had the good fortune to be associated with the 92nd, is due to the traditions of the corps, so ably maintained by the judgment and energy of Major White, assisted by the loyal support of all whom he so happily commands.

December 6th.—A draft of 2 lieutenants, 1 sergeant, and 65 privates from the 56th Depôt Brigade was taken on the strength—chiefly from the northern counties of Scotland, but three were Englishmen.[1]

December 19th.—The regiment encamped $3\frac{1}{2}$ miles from Delhi, within half a mile of the Imperial dais, and took part in the " Imperial Assemblage " on the occasion of H.M. Queen Victoria being proclaimed Empress of India, in addition to her other titles.

" It is difficult to overrate," says Lord Roberts, " the political importance of this great gathering." Princes and Chiefs of every race, from all parts of India, met to do homage to the Queen-Empress, and united in their expression of loyalty to her as their sovereign. They vied with each other in the magnificence and numbers of their retinues ; their elephant housings were of cloth of gold ; some brought war-elephants, whose tusks were tipped with steel, with shields on their foreheads and breastplates flashing in the sun, mounted by warriors clad in chain-armour. The guests were received by the Viceroy, Lord Lytton, and the scene was brilliant beyond description ; British uniforms mingled with gorgeous Eastern costumes set off by a blaze of diamonds and other precious stones. Never in all its eventful history had Delhi witnessed an assemblage at once so immense, so varied, and so unanimous.

The 92nd took a prominent part in the various ceremonials and reviews which took place on this historic occasion. A commemoration medal was presented to a sergeant of each regiment present, the Gordon Highlander selected for this honour being Colour-sergeant James Drummond. Before the camp broke up the British troops took part in a two days' competition in athletic games.

---

[1] Regimental Record.

Sergeant MacFadyen took the first prize for throwing the hammer, Private John MacGregor for the stone; Private Malcolm MacAulay won the mile, and Private Colin MacRae the quarter-mile race, while many seconds and thirds were gained by Gordons ; the great event, however, was the Viceroy's prize—a watch and 100 rupees, for sword *v.* bayonet, and sword *v.* lance. In this contest Regimental-Sergeant-major May, of the 11th Hussars, who had been champion man-at-arms in India, was defeated by Private Matthew Thompson of the Gordons, who therefore received the prize.[1]

February 22*nd*, 1877.—Headquarters, under Lieut.-Colonel Parker, arrived at Sitapur, while half the battalion was quartered at Benares.

In May, Martini Henry rifles were issued in place of Sniders.

During these years n.c. officers and men had been constantly discharged at the expiry of their service, and latterly to the reserve, being replaced by drafts from the Depôt Brigade, or from the 93rd, and by Scotsmen from regiments going home. Among those who left at this time was Gregor Fraser, a pipe-major of the old school, whose quaint remarks and pithy sayings were long remembered in the regimental family. He seems to have agreed with another Highlandman who, when offered water with his dram, preferred to " tak' her as she was porn." He retired to pension as private, and lived at Culloden Moor.

---

[1] Strength at Delhi :—Field officers, 2 ; captains, 6 ; subalterns, 12 ; staff, 4 ; sergeants, 36 ; corporals, 30 ; drummers, 20 ; privates, 586.

PIPER, 1865

CHAPTER X

1878-1879

AT this time a misunderstanding had arisen between the British Government and Shere Ali, Amir of Afghanistan. Russia had for many years been advancing towards India ; in 1873 she had annexed Khiva, and her southern frontier was now nearly coterminus with the northern frontier of Afghanistan. The Amir had been pleased with the magnificent reception given him by the Viceroy, Lord Mayo, on the occasion of his visit to India in 1869 ; but the political result of the conference was unsatisfactory to both parties, and he had since become dissatisfied with the British, who had refused to acknowledge his favourite, but younger, son as his heir, or to give him a direct promise of protection in case of an invasion of his territory. He therefore determined to throw in his lot with Russia, whom he now believed to be dreaded by England as much as by himself, and he received a Russian mission at Kabul with every demonstration of honour.[1] The Government of India, on hearing of this proceeding, wrote to the Amir announcing that a mission of British officers, headed by Sir Neville Chamberlain, G.C.B., G.C.S.I., would be sent to Kabul. Major Cavagnari, Commissioner of Peshawar, was desired to inform the Amir that the object of the mission was friendly, but that a refusal to grant to it the same free passage that had been accorded to the Russian Envoy would be considered as an act of hostility. The Amir decided not to allow the British mission to enter his dominions, but did not communicate his decision to the Viceroy, so that the mission started from Peshawar on the 21st of September 1878, and encamped near the Khyber Pass. Major Cavagnari rode on to Ali Masjid, ten miles beyond, and demanded leave to proceed from the Commander of the Afghan troops ; but permission was refused, and it required all Cavagnari's tact and decision to prevent bloodshed.[2] The mission was dissolved, and it was decided that as political efforts had failed, military measures must be resorted to. Sir Donald Stewart was recalled from England to command a column which was to advance on Kandahar, and Major-General Roberts took command of another column at Kohat to operate in the Kurram Valley. He had but a small force, and the country offered many almost impregnable positions of defence ; but notwithstanding these natural difficulties, Roberts, by his indomitable energy and skilful generalship, surprised his enemy after a night march, and by a bold turning movement (which, though for a time it exposed his communications, was amply justified by the results

---

[1] Field-Marshal Lord Roberts' " Forty-one Years in India," and Malleson's " History of Afghanistan."
[2] Lord Roberts.

attained) defeated him at the Spingawi Kotal. He was again victorious at the Peiwar Kotal in November, and took possession of the Shutargardan Pass on the 8th December 1878. The conduct of this campaign was not the least brilliant of the General's many exploits, and resulted in the flight of the Amir from Kabul, accompanied by the Russian mission.

It was under these circumstances that the Gordon Highlanders were ordered to Afghanistan.

December 18*th*, 1878.—Headquarters and four companies, under Lieut.-Colonel Parker, left Sitapur *en route* for Afghanistan, leaving a depôt under Captain Robertson. Headquarters arrived at Lucknow on the 23rd December and halted the 28th and 29th at Jhelum, where they were joined by the half battalion from Benares under Major J. C. Hay. On January 8th, 1879, the regiment reached Lawrencepore, and on the 15th a draft, 108 in all, under Captain D. F. Gordon, having arrived in India, was taken on the strength.

On the 21st they were at Kohat,[1] where they were inspected under Lieut.-Colonel Parker by the Commander-in-Chief, General Sir F. Haines, K.C.B. ; and, after complimenting them on their smart and soldier-like bearing under arms—" His Excellency was pleased farther to express his very great satisfaction at the reports which have everywhere been brought to his notice of the good behaviour of the men on the line of march." Lord Roberts, in his " Forty-one Years in India," says, " Towards the end of February 1879, I paid a visit to Kohat, and had the pleasure of welcoming to the frontier that grand regiment the 92nd Highlanders, which had been sent up in readiness to join my column in the event of an advance on Kabul becoming necessary."

March 25*th*.—The regiment marched from Kohat, under Lieut.-Colonel Parker, by Kurram and the Peiwar Kotal, and on April 18th they arrived at Alikhel. On this march Peter M'Pherson, a drummer boy, was so footsore that Colonel Parker told him to fall out, be carried in a doolie, and get his feet bathed. The lad's soldierly pride was hurt, and, sobbing, he said, " Na, na, sir, I can carry a side o' the big drum as weel as ony man ; I 'll never fa' oot till I wash my feet in the Caspian Sea ! "[2]

In February 1879, the Amir, Shere Ali, died, and his eldest son, Yakub Khan, who had assumed the reins of government on his father's flight, wrote that he wished for the friendship of the British Government. The rectification of our frontier and the rendering

---

[1] Strength, March 12th, 1879, at Kohat :—Field officers, 3 ; captains, 7 ; subalterns, 14 ; staff, 6 ; sergeants, 38 ; corporals, 35 ; drummers, 21 ; privates, 703—total, 827.

AUTHOR'S NOTE.—By G.O. 110 of 1878 the standard was again raised to 5 ft. 6 in.

[2] Told by Sir G. White, V.C., G.C.B., and by Jas. Roddick, D.C.M., late drummer 92nd. Drummers take it in turn along with the big drummer to carry his instrument.

India secure against foreign aggression was the policy of the Viceroy (Lord Lytton) ;[1] and accordingly he was told that the Viceroy was prepared to enter into negotiations for peace, provided that he renounced all claim to the Khyber and certain other places, to authority over the independent tribes of the territory on the main routes to India, and agreed that the Kurram district should remain under British control.

It was agreed that instead of the British mission going to Kabul, the new Amir should visit our camp at Gandamak, thirty miles on the Kabul side of Jalalabad, which he did on the 8th of May ; the Treaty of Gandamak was signed on the 26th, and so ended the first phase of the second Afghan War.

By the terms of the treaty Yakub Khan agreed to the cession of territory considered necessary by us, and bound himself to conduct his foreign policy in accordance with the advice of the British Government, while on our side we promised to support him against external aggression.   It was further arranged that a British representative with suitable escort should reside in Kabul, and that the Amir, if he desired it, should in like manner depute an agent to the Viceregal Court.[2]

The British Government, however, always anxious for peace, sometimes forgets in dealing with an Oriental foe that he must be made to fear as well as respect our power, or, as in this case, the peace will not be permanent.

General Roberts had endeavoured to impress the neighbouring clans by inviting them to witness the Queen's Birthday parade of his troops, to the number of 6450, on the 24th of May ; and in the afternoon an impromptu rifle meeting was got up, at which the Afghan marksmen found they could not hold their own against our good shots armed with Martini Henry rifles.   Athletic sports were frequently held, also a horse show, at which General Roberts' Arab charger carried off the first prize.   In the evenings open-air concerts round a huge bonfire were enjoyed by all ranks.   Detachments were occasionally employed on reconnaissance duty, and in June two companies were detached at Kudi Kheyl.

On the 15th July, Major Cavagnari, who had been selected as the " Envoy and Plenipotentiary to His Highness the Amir of Kabul," arrived in Kurram with his Staff.   In order to do honour to the Envoy, an escort, consisting of two companies each of the 67th, 72nd, and 92nd, the 5th Gurkhas, a mountain battery, and a squadron 12th Bengal Cavalry, under Brigadier-General Dunham Massy, accompanied him to the limit of our territory ; when General Roberts, who had also accompanied them, bade adieu to the mission, with forebodings of their fate, which were not, however, shared by

[1] Lord Roberts.   [2] *Ibid.*

Cavagnari, who appears to have had confidence in the intention and power of the Amir to protect him.   His last telegram to the Viceroy, dated September 2nd, concluded with the words " All well," but on the 5th the awful news reached Simla of the massacre at Kabul of Cavagnari (now a K.C.B.) and his gallant companions, which struck the whole civilised world with grief and indignation.

Sir Donald Stewart's troops, except a small number, had left Kandahar for India.   The Kurram force was the only one in a position to reach Kabul quickly, and General Roberts, then at Simla, was ordered to proceed at once and resume his command there.   Brigadier Massy, who was in temporary command, was ordered to move troops to the Shutargardan, and Stewart to stop all regiments on their way to India, and himself to hold fast at Kandahar.[1]

The Kabul Field Force, assembled at Alikhel under Major-General Sir Frederick Roberts, K.C.B.,[2] C.S.I., was composed of two batteries Royal Horse Artillery, a battery Field Artillery, and two Gatling-guns, Lieut.-Colonel B. L. Gordon commanding.

The Royal Engineers were commanded by Lieut.-Colonel A. E. Perkins, C.B.

Brigadier-General W. Dunham Massy commanded the cavalry, consisting of the 9th Lancers, 5th Punjab Cavalry, 12th Bengal Cavalry, and 14th Bengal Lancers.

The First Brigade of Infantry comprised the 67th Foot, 92nd Highlanders, and 28th Punjab Infantry, under Brigadier-General Herbert Macpherson, V.C., K.C.B.

The Second Infantry Brigade, Brigadier T. D. Baker, C.B., commanding :   72nd Highlanders, 5th Gurkhas, 5th Punjab Infantry, 3rd Sikhs, and 23rd Pioneers.

Meanwhile the Amir Yakub Khan had written to Sir Frederick Roberts to the effect that the massacre by his troops had taken place without his knowledge or consent ;   that he was deeply grieved and feared the country would be ruined, and that he looked to the Government (of India) for assistance and advice.   At the same time, Sir Frederick was aware that he had really been inciting the Ghilzais and other tribes to oppose us, and that, though he may not have actually planned the massacre of the Embassy, he had taken no steps to oppose it, and was, in fact, playing us false. Roberts therefore issued a proclamation to the Chiefs and people, explaining that by treaty, and by the special request of the Amir, a British Envoy and suite were located at the Kabul Court, and the Amir had guaranteed that they should be honourably treated and protected ;   that, as the Amir had not been able to protect them

[1] Lord Roberts.
[2] General Roberts had been made K.C.B. after the first phase of the war.

even in his own citadel, thereby showing the weakness of his authority, therefore the British were entering Afghanistan for the double purpose of punishing the murderers and of strengthening the authority of the Amir, on condition that His Highness loyally used those powers for the maintenance of friendship with the British Government. The tribesmen were assured that no one would be injured except persons who had joined in the massacre, unless they offered opposition, and that full price would be paid for supplies.

Meanwhile Sir Frederick had ordered the Second Brigade to entrench themselves at Shutargardan ; roads were being improved and supplies collected.

On September 20th, Sir Frederick received a letter from the Amir by two confidential agents, who affirmed their master's friendly feeling to the British Government and his wish to be guided by their advice ; but it became clear that his real object was to stop the advance, and gain time for the tribesmen, who were hurrying up on all sides, to defend the approaches to their capital.

On the 24th, the regiment, under Major White, in Colonel Parker's temporary absence, marched from Alikhel, and next day encamped at Shutargardan, C Company, made up to 100 rifles, under Captain McCallum and Lieutenant Grant, being sent to occupy Karatiga Fort. There was no proper camel food in this district, and numbers had died and were lying among the rocks, their heads twisted painfully back and downwards in the throes of death, presenting a singular appearance, which being remarked upon by a soldier, his comrade was heard to say, " D'ye no' ken that a cawmel aye stands on his heid when he 's gaen to dee ? " The stench was so powerful that many of the troops were actually sick from it. On the 27th, D Company, under Captain Oxley and Lieutenant Ramsay, was dispatched to the Sukar Kotal to hold the Pass during the passage through it of Sir F. Roberts, and returned to Shutargardan on the completion of that duty.

After a correspondence with the Amir, in which he still gave His Highness credit for good faith, and expressed the determination of the British Government to protect him against his own troops, over whom he had lost control, Sir Frederick, having completed his arrangements and impressed on his troops the necessity for prompt payment for supplies, set out on the 27th of September for Kushi, where Baker was now encamped. He was escorted by a squadron of the 9th Lancers, the 5th Punjab Cavalry, and detachments of the 5th and 28th Punjab Infantry, but, anxious to reach camp on the Shutargardan Pass before dark, the General pushed on with the cavalry. He was, however, met by twenty-five men of the 92nd, under Lieutenant Grant, who brought a note from

Colonel Perkins, R.E., in command on the Shutargardan, warning him that he was sure to be attacked ; and he had not proceeded far through the wooded mountains, where a few resolute men might check an army, when in the Hazar Darakht defile (Pass of the Thousand Trees) the passage was found to be blocked by some 2000 tribesmen, and as the British General approached, a volley was fired at him by a party concealed in the rocks ; Sir Frederick escaped, but Dr Townsend, to whom he was talking, was severely wounded. The Highlanders, in skirmishing order, supported by dismounted cavalry, cleared away the enemy to the north, but as they clung to the precipitous hills on the south, it became necessary to wait till the main body of the escort came up, when they were quickly dispersed.

Meanwhile some tribesmen had cut the telegraph wire near the Karatiga Fort, and had ambushed a party of Sikhs sent to repair it ; four of the Sikhs were killed, and as the hills were swarming with men, a party of the 92nd (about eighteen men) under Colour-sergeant Hector MacDonald, and a detachment (forty-five) of the 3rd Sikhs under a native officer (himself an Afghan), were at once sent out from Karatiga. MacDonald, taking command of both parties, worked them into position. The enemy were greatly superior in numbers, and commenced a charge downhill on the Highlanders and Sikhs, who, waiting till they were at close range, received them with a steady rifle fire ; some thirty of the enemy were killed and many wounded, and they were driven over the hill in full retreat. "The manner in which the colour-sergeant and the native officer handled their men gave me a high opinion of them both."[1]

On the 28th September the regiment, under Lieut.-Colonel Parker, arrived at Kushi,[2] ten miles from the top of the Shutar-gardan. On the Shutargardan, Roberts heard that the Amir, desiring a personal interview, had arrived in General Baker's camp at Kushi, attended by his son of seven years old, his father-in-law, and Daoud Shah the Commander-in-Chief of the Afghan army, with an escort and suite of 245 men. As he came ostensibly as our ally seeking refuge from his mutinous soldiery, whatever suspicions the British General might entertain as to his good faith, it was neces-

[1] Roberts' "Forty-one Years in India." Colour-sergeant MacDonald was specially mentioned in dispatches, dated 16th October 1879 (*London Gazette* of 16th January 1880), and was afterwards promoted second lieutenant in the 92nd. At an enthusiastic meeting of the Gordon Highlanders' Society of Glasgow, in 1898, at which MacDonald, then Colonel and Brigadier-General, was present to meet his old comrades, one of the members told me that on the return of this party to camp inside Fort Karatiga a man called out, "We'll mak' ye an officer for this day's work, sergeant!" "Aye," cried another, "and a General too!" prophetic words which showed that the soldiers were, like their General, good judges of character. MacDonald was a native of Mulbuie, Ross-shire.

[2] *Kushi* signifies "delight."

sary to treat him as an honoured guest, and he was lodged at first in the centre of the camp, but afterwards in a separate camp outside.

On the 28th, Sir Frederick, leaving a mountain battery and two regiments of native infantry under Colonel Money to hold the Shutargardan, rode to Kushi, where, on the 29th, he had his first interview with Yakub Khan, who returned the visit in the afternoon, when every attention was shown to him. A guard of honour of the Gordon Highlanders, with the Queen's colour, was drawn up to receive him. "The Amir was lost in admiration of his guard, and he may well be pardoned for his earnest study of the men ; the Gordon Highlanders are in physique and bearing perfect specimens of British soldiers."[1] "In the evening the band of this regiment, turned out in their usual faultless manner, played before the Amir's tent."[2]

Sir Frederick's interview had not been very satisfactory ; the Amir urged him to delay his advance, his object, as proved by subsequent events, being to gain time for the development of plans for opposing it. Sir Frederick declined to accede to his wishes, and on 30th September marched with the Cavalry Brigade to Zerganshah, the first halting-place on the way to Kabul, returning in the evening to Kushi. He issued a proclamation to the people of Kabul, telling them that if his army was allowed to take peaceable possession of the city, well and good ; if not, the city would be seized by force, and that as the British Government does not make war on women and children, they should be removed beyond the reach of harm ; that while full retribution would be exacted from those who took part in the murder of the British Envoy and his followers, all classes would be treated with justice, and their religious feelings and customs respected ; but after the receipt of this proclamation, all persons found armed in or about Kabul would be treated as enemies.

Sir Frederick, also in orders to his army, desired general officers and officers commanding corps to impress upon all officers under their command the necessity of preventing "irregularities likely to arouse the personal jealousy of the people of Kabul, who are, of all races, most susceptible as regards their women." . . . "The deep-seated animosity of the Afghans to the English has been mainly ascribed to indiscretions committed during the first occupation of Kabul, and the Major-General trusts that the same excellent discipline so long exhibited by the troops under his command will remove the prejudices of past years," etc.[3]

---

[1] Hensman's "Afghan War, 1879-80."

[2] Duke, "Recollections of the Kabul Campaign."

[3] "It was a matter of intense gratification to me that the whole time we remained in Afghanistan, nearly two years, not a single complaint was made by an Afghan of any soldier in my army having interfered with the women of the country."—Lord Roberts.

On the 1st October the whole of the Kabul Field Force was assembled in the Logar Valley. It consisted of 192 British officers, 2558 British n.c. officers and men, and 3867 native troops.[1] The 92nd numbered 17 officers and 717 n.c. officers and men.

On the 2nd a general advance took place, and after a short march of eight miles through a desolate country, they encamped at the village of Zerghanshah, where there is a stream of good water. The Amir and his Sirdars were with them, and no doubt were impressed by the fitness and discipline of the soldiers. Meanwhile Colonel Money had a successful affair at the Shutargardan, where he repulsed the enemy with considerable loss.

On the 3rd they marched fifteen miles to Zahidabad, where they could see the fortified hill above Kabul. On this march a determined attack on the rear guard was made by the clans inhabiting the neighbouring villages, but they were driven off by the 72nd Highlanders. The advance was delayed by the insufficiency of baggage animals, rendering it extremely difficult to keep up the supplies ; a halt was therefore made on the 4th. The Amir, though pretending to be seeking our friendship and protection, was constantly receiving messengers from Kabul, and through them inciting the people against us.

On October 5th the regiment, 712 of all ranks, under Lieut.-Colonel Parker, after a short march during which the rear guard had a slight skirmish, arrived at Charasia, a pretty village nestling in orchards and gardens, with a rugged range of hills towering above it a short distance beyond. This range descended abruptly on the right to where the Logar River ran between it and the precipitous cliffs on the other side, forming a gorge named *Sang-i-nawishta* (the "written stone"), distant five or six miles from Kabul. Intelligence was brought that large bodies of troops were moving from that city to oppose the British advance, and though the Amir, who was still with Roberts, pretended to disbelieve this, Sir Frederick was not taken in by his assurances. Owing to the transport difficulty, Macpherson's Brigade was still a march behind, except the 92nd, which had come up.

The road through the gorge having been reported impassable, before dawn on the morning of the 6th a party consisting of twenty men of the 9th Lancers, a squadron of 5th Punjab Cavalry, a wing of the 92nd under Major White (200 rifles), with two guns of No. 2 Mountain Battery, was sent as escort to the 23rd Pioneers, who were to make the way practicable for guns, all under Colonel Currie of the Pioneers. Soon daylight discovered large numbers of Afghan troops in regular formation crowning the hills which Roberts had not been in a position to occupy the previous evening, and which

---

[1] Lord Roberts.

commanded the road ; so that as the Pioneers were unable to fulfil their task of repairing it, Colonel Currie returned with them to camp, and they afterwards joined in Baker's attack.   Major White, who now commanded the party, got permission to take on his four companies of the 92nd in support of the cavalry, who were in contact with and watching the enemy.   The cavalry patrols were fired upon and obliged to retire, and immediate action became necessary, for if the enemy were allowed to remain in undisturbed possession of their position for a night, their numbers would certainly be largely increased.   Sir Frederick therefore deemed it wise to attack at once, while Macpherson was ordered to follow with the least possible delay.   After the men had breakfasted, General Baker, with the guns of No. 2 Mountain Battery, two Gatling-guns, a detachment of the 12th Bengal Cavalry, the 72nd Highlanders, 5th Gurkhas, 5th Punjab Infantry, and a company of sappers and miners, went to make an outflanking movement to the Afghan right, and to dislodge the enemy in that direction, while Roberts distracted their attention by making a feint to their left.   With this object, Major White, who commanded the party near the *Sang-i-nawishta* gorge, was ordered to threaten the pass, and to prevent the enemy occupying any part of the Charasia Village ; to advance within artillery range of the enemy's main position above the gorge ; and when the outflanking movement had been fully developed and the enemy was in full retreat, he was to push the cavalry through the gorge and pursue.   General Roberts, with six guns (R.H.A.), 450 cavalry, and between 600 and 700 infantry, including the headquarters of 92nd, remained to keep open communication with Macpherson, and for the protection of the camp, which was in rear of Charasia and was threatened by masses of tribesmen.   He was still handicapped by the presence of the Amir and his untrustworthy following.

About 11.30 a.m. Baker's troops emerged from the enclosures about Charasia, and were immediately engaged with a crowd of Afghans, both regulars and irregulars.   A company of the 72nd was sent to turn the Afghans off a succession of peaks, situated at right angles to the ridge they were occupying on their right ; these almost inaccessible peaks formed the key of the position, and their defenders had to be dislodged at all hazards before anything else could be attempted.   The 72nd with much difficulty fought their way up and gained a footing on the first peak, where they were obliged to pause until reinforced by two companies of the 5th Gurkhas, when, advancing together, they cleared the enemy from each successive point, while the remainder of the 72nd breasted the hill, and under cover of the Mountain guns attacked the position in front.   The enemy were obstinate, and the difficult nature of the ground, which was very steep and rocky and without trees, somewhat checked the gallant Highlanders, when General Baker sent two companies of the 5th Gurkhas and 200 of the 5th Punjab Infantry to their assistance, while the 23rd Pioneers were brought up on the right as a support. At 2 p.m. the Highlanders and Gurkhas could no longer be resisted, and gained possession of the ridge which was the real point of attack. "The brunt of this affair," says Lord Roberts, "was borne by the 72nd, admirably led by their company officers, under the skilful direction of Lieut.-Colonel Clarke and his adjutant, Lieutenant Murray." Private Mac-Mahon, 72nd, by his coolness and daring gained the Victoria Cross. The general advance was now sounded ; the enemy fought desperately, charging down on the Gurkhas, by whom they were repulsed with heavy loss. The Afghans then took up a position 600 yards in rear of that from which they had been driven, where they made an obstinate stand for half an hour ; but they were again forced back, on the attacking party being strengthened by two companies of the 92nd sent by White under Captain Oxley, who came in with great effect on the enemy's left.

Meanwhile Major White had seen and seized his opportunity ; his feint on the right had been turned into a successful attack. Skirting the east of Charasia, White found the enemy taking cover among the trees, and holding the hills to the right and left of the gorge. His three guns were soon in action, and, with the fire of the skirmishers thrown out among the gardens and trees, drove the enemy to the shelter of the sangars they had built in the hills. Our artillery made beautiful practice, one shell dismounting an Afghan gun and killing two horses standing near it, while others dispersed some bodies of the enemy and prepared the way for the infantry attack. This was led by Major White, who, having examined the ground, at the head of only fifty Highlanders charged the first hill, on which several hundred Afghans were strongly posted, outnumbering his force by about eight to one. It was a perilous undertaking, and looked, perhaps, impossible ; but that word is not recognised in the Gordons' vocabulary. The Highlanders went up in skirmishing order, climbing from rocky terrace to rocky terrace under a severe fire of musketry, and the enemy waited in the protection of his sangars, as if to receive them at the point of the bayonet ; but when they were within six yards the Afghans turned and fled, and were shot in the back as they made for the next hill. The success of this bold attack was mainly due to White's personal gallantry, of which the following is an instance. Not caring to expose his men, who were rather blown, in a particularly steep bit of ground which was enfiladed by a few Afghans securely placed in rear of some rocks, he took a rifle from one of the soldiers and " stalked " the enemy, followed by his leading files. Cautiously climbing, he reached the rocks forming a natural sangar behind which they were concealed, and as he showed himself they jumped up and ran, doubtless in the belief that he was the leader of many. " Look out, sir," cried a soldier just behind White as one man, the Afghan officer, stayed to fire ; but he missed his aim, and as he turned the Major shot him through the back, and some of the 92nd took his sword and gave it to their leader. This hill was named " White's Hill " in memory of his daring.

The guns were now able to advance nearer the pass, and the Major having given his men breathing time, and being reinforced by 100 men [1] under Major Hay and Captain D. F. Gordon, he again went forward and captured the other hills in gallant style. It was at this juncture, when Baker's troops, having carried the main position, were proceeding to attack that to which the enemy had retreated, that White was enabled to send on two companies of the Gordons, under Captain Oxley, by whose timely aid the determined foe were at length driven from this point of vantage also. The troops followed up their success and advanced at the double, while our guns shelled the shaken masses. The Afghan right and centre gave way completely, and by 3.45 we were in possession of the whole ridge. The first objective having been thus gained, the troops, pivoting on their right, brought round their left, and advanced against the now exposed flanks of the enemy's left wing ; at the same time White advanced from his position in front of the gorge, and a little after 4 p.m. had gained possession of the pass and twelve Afghan guns.[2] Completely outflanked and enfiladed, the left wing of the enemy made but little resistance, but abandoned the height and retired across the river, pursued by the small body of cavalry attached to White's force, and by a party of the 92nd under Major Hay.

The headquarters of the 92nd, under Lieut.-Colonel Parker, had been with Sir F. Roberts for the defence of the camp, and while the fighting was going on upon the heights in front of Charasia, the hills on both flanks were crowded with the enemy watching the result. One party of them caused so much annoyance by firing into the piquets that it became necessary to dislodge it—" a service which was performed in a very daring manner by a few of the 92nd under Lieutenant Grant and Colour-sergeant Hector MacDonald, the same n.c. officer who had a few days before so distinguished himself in the Hazar-darakht defile." [3] They had to climb a bare

---

[1] White had sent back a message to General Roberts that, if reinforced, he could act with considerable effect against the enemy's left.

[2] For the honour of being the first to lay hands on these guns there was a race between the Gordons and the Pioneers. It was won by a Sikh Pioneer.—Duke.

[3] Lord Roberts.

hill, so steep that they were sometimes on all fours, the enemy firing down on them the while, but when the Highlanders, breathless as they were, reached the top they soon cleared it of the enemy.   They were reinforced by a company of the 67th, who brought them meat and drink, and held the hill, being occasionally fired at, till the morning, when they rejoined the column as it marched.

Major White's force bivouacked on the ground it had won. Our casualties were wonderfully few, only eighteen killed and seventy wounded.   The Afghans were armed with Enfield and Snider rifles, and some with matchlocks.   The Gordons had three men killed, viz. Privates Henry Burness, Malcolm Gellately, and James Meek, and six wounded, of whom Private J. Cockburn died of his wounds : the regiment having about 300 men engaged.[1] During the fight the infantry expended 41,000 rounds, of which 20,000 were fired by the 72nd.

Major White was mentioned in Sir F. Roberts' dispatch of November 20th, 1879, for the able manner in which he conducted the right, consisting of half of G3 Royal Artillery, a wing of the 92nd Highlanders under Major Hay, and 100 men of the 23rd Pioneers.   Captain Oxley was also mentioned, as were Lieutenant Grant and Colour-sergeant MacDonald, for the skilful manner in which they handled their piquets.   Major White was recommended for the Victoria Cross.

To the promptness of General Roberts' action, the able manner in which his plan was carried out by the officers, and the spirit and gallantry of the troops, must be ascribed the comparatively slight loss sustained in this victory over a force advantageously posted and greatly superior in numbers.   Many of the tribesmen, on seeing the Afghan army defeated, returned to their homes, but the greater number waited about Kabul to assist any further stand by the regular troops.   At dawn on the 7th October, the regiment under Lieut.-Colonel Parker marched, along with other troops who accompanied Sir F. Roberts, through the *Sang-i-nawishta* defile, where Major White met Sir Frederick and explained his part in the action of the previous day.   Roberts was accompanied by the Amir, to whom White had the satisfaction of showing his own guns ; he did not look diverted !   " From my inspection of the ground, I had no difficulty in coming to the conclusion that much of the success which attended the operations on this side was due to White's military instincts, and, at one supreme moment, his extreme personal gallantry." [2]

The troops encamped at Beni Hissar, a considerable village, surrounded by orchards, gardens, and cornfields, two miles south

[1] The 72nd had about 800 men engaged.—Duke.
[2] Lord Roberts.

SERGEANTS OF THE 92ND GORDON HIGHLANDERS
AFGHANISTAN, 1879

[For list of names see other side

1. Sergeant ALLAN MARTIN.
2.   ,,   WILLIAM STEPHENSON.
3.   ,,   JOHN M'LAREN.
4. Provost-Sergeant JAMES TAYLOR
5. Sergeant JOHN MACFADYEN.
6.   ,,   RICHARD FRASER.
7. Drum-Major CHARLES FLINT.
8. Colour-Sergeant THOMAS SMITH.
9. Sergeant JOHN BELL.
10. Colour-Sergeant JAMES DRUMMOND.
11.   ,,   HECTOR ARCHIBALD MACDONALD
12. Sergeant JOHN CAMERON.
13.   ,,   JAMES COUTTS.
14. Pioneer-Sergeant PRINGLE TAYLOR.
15. Colour-Sergeant THOMAS NICOL
16. Sergeant JAMES FORBES
17.   ,,   WILLIAM COCHRANE.
18. Hospital-Sergeant WILLIAM ANDERSON.
19. Colour-Sergeant JAMES STEWART.
20.   ,,   ROBERT HART.
21. Sergeant ALEXANDER MORRISON.
22. Colour-Sergeant JOHN M'INALLY.
23. Sergeant JAMES LAWSON.
24.   ,,   WILLIAM GILLANDERS.
25.   ,,   WILLIAM M'GILL.
26.   ,,   JOHN GASKARTH.
27.   ,,   MURDOCH MACLEAN.
28.   ,,   WILLIAM MILNE.
29.   ,,   JOHN MACGREGOR.
30.   ,,   JAMES WILSON.
31.   ,,   JAMES MACLACHLAN.
32.   ,,   CHARLES ROSS MARTIN.
33   ,,   THOMAS MACDONALD.
34.   ,,   ARTHUR GORDON FORBES.
35. Musketry-Sergeant WILLIAM CRAWFORD.
36 Sergeant CHARLES BAKER.
37. Colour-Sergeant WILLIAM FRASER.
38. Armourer-Sergeant JAMES TAYLOR.
39. Paymaster-Sergeant EDWARD MACDONALD.
40. Sergeant-Major JAMES ROSS.
41. Orderly-Room Sergeant WILLIAM NOBBS.
42. Sergeant HARRY DE ARCY ADAMS.
43.   ,,   JAMES WILLIAMS

Note.—The Photograph was given by the Gordon Highlanders' Society in Glasgow, and the names examined and corrected by several of the members.

of the far-famed citadel of the Bala Hissar, and enjoyed the first
regular square meal since they left Alikhel. A Company, under
Captain Cotton, and 40 men of D Company, under Captain D. F.
Gordon, with the 5th Gurkhas and four Mountain guns, were left
to guard the heights of Charasia till Macpherson's Brigade had
passed.[1]

On entering Beni Hissar the General sent out cavalry patrols,
who brought the pleasing news that his rapid advance had had the
desired effect, the Bala Hissar had been evacuated, and the part
of the citadel of Kabul visible appeared to be deserted. Having
received intelligence that the enemy, if again defeated, intended
to retire towards Turkestan, Sir Frederick directed Brigadier-
General Massy to move at 11 a.m. on the 8th and place himself
across their line of retreat. Massy, avoiding the city and heights,
made a detour through the richly cultivated plain by Siah Sang to
the Afghan cantonment at Sherpur,[2] which he found deserted, the
magazine blown up, and seventy-five abandoned guns inside the
enclosure. Continuing his march, he skirted the Asmai heights
on the western side, and sighted the Afghan camp pitched on the
slope of the hills, a mile from Deh-i-Mazang. He reported by
heliograph, and was informed that Brigadier-General Baker would
be dispatched to drive the Afghans from their position, while he
was to be ready to intercept them.

The headquarters of the 92nd (six companies), 370 rank and
file, under Lieut.-Colonel Parker, formed part of the small force [3]
which Roberts could spare to Baker, who moved from Beni Hissar
at noon ; but so difficult was the ascent that it was nearly 4 p.m.
before the Mountain guns got into action, and it was still later before
the Gordons reached the village to the west of Deh-i-Mazang. On
the way up the regiment was marching in fours with the colours
cased ; a shell fell just to the left of the colours, but did no harm ;
the colonel then formed open column of companies. The enemy
were in greater force than was expected, and the 92nd were ordered
to await reinforcements. Although the enemy opened fire from
two breech-loading guns, the shot flew so high as to cause only
amusement to the Highlanders as they took up a position on a spur
of the Shahr-i-Darwaza heights, where marksmen were posted at
sheltered points, whose aim was so good that the Afghan gunners

[1] Macpherson had arrived at the village of Charasia at dusk on the evening of the fight.
[2] The fortified camp of Sherpur is built at the base of the strong Bimaru Hills. Three
sides are fortified, the hill in rear forming a sufficient defence in that quarter. The thick mud
wall, about a mile and a half long, is twenty-five feet high, with bastions for guns and a parapet
to shield the defenders. The four strongly guarded entrance gates are lofty structures, and
wide enough for five horsemen to ride abreast, and each is defended by a curtain built like the
outer wall. On the inside space more than 20,000 men could be paraded. There are large
barracks, where the roofs are arranged for musketry.—H. Hensman.
[3] Part of the 72nd, the 23rd Pioneers, two Gatling and two Mountain guns.

left their guns. The reinforcements did not reach General Baker till 5.30 ; between him and the Afghan camp was the precipitous gorge, 1600 feet deep, through which flowed the Kabul River ; it was getting dark, and he was reluctantly obliged to postpone his attack. The Gordons occupied the gorge above Baber's Tomb, where they bivouacked, and each man supped on what he happened to have in his haversack.

At 4.30 a.m. on the 9th October, Captain Oxley, with a patrol of fifty men, forded the Kabul River and proceeded up the Asmai heights, which he found had been deserted during the night—the enemy had given them the slip and evaded the British cavalry, leaving their camp standing with twelve guns, some elephants, camels, mules, and ponies, a prey to the pursuer. The regiment followed and encamped at Siah Sang, on the opposite side of the city, where the detachment left at Charasia rejoined, making the total strength 729. The name of Lieutenant I. S. M. Hamilton, 92nd, orderly officer to Brigadier-General Massy, commanding the cavalry, was brought forward by that officer as having rendered valuable aid, and Lieut.-Colonel Parker received the thanks of Sir F. Roberts in his dispatch dated 20th October 1879. In the same dispatch Sir Frederick spoke in the highest terms of the conduct and discipline of the troops, their " good spirit and proper soldierly feeling caused all difficulties to disappear, and made the work of the Commander easy."

Kabul, with the picturesquely situated Bala Hissar, the fortified walls of the citadel, and the city with its 50,000 inhabitants, lay below the camp at the mercy of the British troops, who, however, knew little of the political difficulties which, far more than his military task, were a source of anxiety to their General. His instructions were that the punishment of those who had taken part in the murder of the Embassy was to be " swift, stern, and impressive, without being indiscriminate or immoderate." He was charged not only with the protection of his own camp, but with the security of the well-affected population, the general maintenance of order, and, as events had proved that the Amir had lost his authority or failed to make use of it, Sir Frederick was desired to assume and exercise supreme authority in Kabul.

Some of the villagers who, after pretending friendship, had treacherously fired at our soldiers, were made an example of as a warning to others, but the country people being made aware that only those who misbehaved would be punished, confidence was restored. The camp was soon made lively by merchants hawking their wares, especially poultry, fruit, and vegetables, and, for a very small sum, the soldiers could purchase many luxuries, large luscious-looking bunches of grapes costing a mere song.

Here the army remained for some time. The situation was healthy and picturesque ; from the camp could be seen the fertile Chardeh Valley, backed by the lofty mountain towards Turkestan ; its canvas streets were daily thronged by gaily-attired Orientals on horseback and on foot, on business or on pleasure bent, while order was enforced by the smart European sentries, and routine work went on as usual. In the evening one of the bands played, till the day closed with the strains of " God Save the Queen."

ON the 12th October the regiment, under Lieut.-Colonel
Parker, took part in the triumphal march through Kabul,
when Sir Frederick Roberts read the proclamation announcing the
intentions of the British Government to the Sirdars and people
from the steps of the Hall of Audience at the Bala Hissar. He
desired to make the ceremony as impressive as possible by the presence of all the troops, who, though their late duties had been severe
and continuous, turned out as clean and smart as their General
could wish, to line the road to the Peshawar Gate. The F./A.
Battery Royal Horse Artillery was drawn up opposite the entrance,
and next the gate came the senior regiment, the soldier-like 67th ;
then two living walls of bronzed and bearded Highlanders, the
72nd in their tartan trews, the Gordons in their Highland dress, all
three in red. There stood the nine-pounders of G3 Royal Artillery
which had been so effective at Charasia, the Gatling and Mountain
guns on their mules, sappers and miners with their tools, stalwart
Sikhs in their high turbans, active little Gurkhas, whose green
contrasted with the red coats of the 28th N.I. and the khaki of the
23rd Pioneers. The cavalry prolonged the line towards the camp ;
first the 9th Lancers in their handsome uniform ; then the 14th
Bengal Lancers, 12th Bengal Cavalry, and the 5th Punjab Cavalry ;
all in their semi-oriental costumes, the glint of their weapons showing through the branches of the trees, making altogether an impos-
ing array as the General rode along, justly proud of his followers.
The Union Jack was hoisted over the gate, the artillery fired a
salute of thirty-one guns, the bands played the National Anthem,
the bagpipes a " salute," and the troops presented arms. A company of the 67th, with the band, led the way for the procession,
followed by Sir Frederick and staff, accompanied by the Amir's
little son,[1] Daoud Shah, the late Afghan Commander-in-Chief, and
a number of the Sirdars in silken attire of many colours. The
narrow streets would not admit the artillery, but the other troops
passed along through a crowd whose " silent, somewhat sullen, but
orderly acceptance of the situation struck me," says an officer of the
Gordons. In the Hindu Bazaar, however, the merchants well
knew the advantage of the British *raj*, and expressed their satisfaction by sundry salaams.

---

[1] The Amir was to have attended, but early in the morning he had asked for an interview
with the General, when he announced that, finding himself incapable of ruling his turbulent
countrymen, he had determined to resign the Amirship, and begged to remain in the British
camp, and that his son might take his place in the procession that day. Sir Frederick gave
him time to reconsider his decision, but finding he had finally made up his mind, Roberts
telegraphed to the Government, with the result that the Amir was afterwards sent to India,
where he lived surrounded by every comfort at Mussoorie.

On October 13th a telegram was published from the Viceroy to Sir Frederick Roberts, congratulating him on the brilliant and important action of the 6th, and requesting him to convey to the officers and men engaged at Charasia His Excellency's appreciation of their conduct, to which Sir Frederick added an expression of his own " satisfaction and pride " in knowing " that he has troops under his command capable of such achievements."

On the 14th a telegram was published from the Commander-in-Chief, communicating to Sir Frederick and the officers and soldiers a gracious message from the Queen-Empress, expressing Her Majesty's " warm satisfaction " with her troops, her sorrow for those of their comrades who fell at Charasia and in the recent brilliant exploit at Shutargardan, and her anxiety for further information as to the condition of the wounded.

On the morning of the 16th the camp was startled by a most terrific explosion in the upper part of the Bala Hissar, which was occupied by the 5th Gurkhas, while the 67th Foot were encamped in the garden below.   The General at once sent orders to these troops to clear out without even waiting to bring away their kits, for 250 tons of powder was dangerously near the scene of the explosion, which had resulted in the death of Captain Shafto of the artillery (who was examining the war material stored there), a private of the 67th, a native officer of Gurkhas, and nineteen natives.   A second and still more violent explosion took place two hours and a half later, by which several Afghans were killed at a considerable distance by the falling stones.   The cause of the disaster was never discovered, but it was the occasion of an example of the good feeling which prevailed between the European and native troops.   The men of the 72nd not only provided their Gurkha comrades, who had lost everything, with a sheep for each company, but, the night being bitterly cold, they generously lent them their greatcoats.[1]

After the Amir Yakub Khan's resignation, Sir F. Roberts was charged with the government of the country, and it became necessary that he should take possession of the treasury.   An immense sum in rupees, Russian five-rouble and other gold pieces, besides jewellery, was found.   In 1884, Sir Hector (then Lieutenant) Mac-Donald told me that he was employed with a fatigue party to fill boxes and sacks with gold coin and bar gold together with other valuables; that the soldiers could have filled their pockets with gold, but, so far as he was aware, they resisted the temptation, believing

[1] Roberts.
At this time Sir Frederick was given the local rank of Lieut.-General, and was placed in command of all the troops in Eastern Afghanistan.

it to be prize-money which would be given to the army. It was, however, afterwards refunded to the Afghan Government of Abdur Rahman. Had the men been aware of this, they would perhaps hardly have been so particular !

On the 1st of November the headquarters, with the artillery and infantry, moved into Sherpur Cantonment, about a mile and a half from Kabul, where they encamped until the barracks were cleaned for the Europeans, while the native corps, assisted by Hazara coolies, built huts for themselves. The cavalry were quartered outside for a time.

On the same day Brigadier-General Macpherson marched with 1800 men to join hands with the troops who were advancing from the Khyber Pass, but though the Gordons belonged properly to this brigade, they were retained at headquarters.

A little snow fell on the 11th, and the weather having become very cold, the elephants belonging to the army were sent back to India, as were the invalids and time-expired soldiers, while every possible preparation was made to enable the troops to face the rigours of an Afghan winter.

On the 21st the regiment (500 rifles), under Major White, formed part of an expedition which marched to Maidan under Brigadier-General Baker, C.B., to protect over 2000 baggage animals employed in carrying forage collected in this fertile district. Here retributive justice was meted out to the inhabitants of a village who had nearly succeeded in treacherously entrapping Baker and his staff while on a reconnaissance. These people offered milk and fruit and were talking to him in pretended friendship, while a force was approaching to surround him. It was, however, observed in time by Mahomed Hussein Khan,[1] the British Agent, who accompanied the party, which only escaped after a sharp skirmish. A vedette of the escort was afterwards asked how it was that he had not kept a better lookout and seen the enemy. " I seen 'em right enough, sir," said the Lancer, " but I thought they was only a ram-sammy sort of a wedding ! "

There were rumours of armed gatherings in the south ; several of the village headmen had been insolent, and on the afternoon of the 23rd a party of cavalry were fired on in the direction of Bamian. The chieftain responsible for this action was Bahadur Khan, who had already given much trouble, trusting to the inaccessible situation of the valley, where he had a considerable body of well-armed men in his fort eight miles from Maidan. His villages were fortified by towers and enclosures from which our foraging parties might have been attacked, and General Roberts, who had come out to visit the force, decided that it was necessary to break up the

---

[1] Hussein Khan was murdered shortly after.

gathering of the clans before it grew to serious proportions, and that an example must be made of Bahadur Khan.

Accordingly at daybreak on the 24th, tents were struck and baggage left (as was the Horse Artillery, the roads being impassable for wheels) under a guard of 300 men from the 92nd and Native Infantry, and the little column of 400 Gordons, 600 Native Infantry, a troop 9th Lancers, with some native cavalry and four mountain guns, marched, carrying one day's provisions, but unencumbered by transport.

The morning was bitterly cold as the Sepoys stripped their legs and the Highlanders lifted their kilts to wade through the floating ice of the Kabul River and the Darra Narkh stream which falls into it ;[1] the road was commanded by high hills, which were now found to be deserted by the men who had occupied them the previous evening, and a *malik* volunteered the news that Bahadur Khan and his followers had fled over the hills, taking their movable property with them.   When the Lancers, however, pushed on into the valley, they saw a body of men coming down to within range, emboldened, no doubt, by supposing that they had only to do with horsemen who could not follow them to the mountains ; but when the leading company of Highlanders appeared round a corner, they hurriedly took to the higher hills.   The company advanced in skirmishing order and occupied a rocky eminence overlooking the fort ; troops were sent round the other side, but the place was found to be deserted.   It was destroyed, along with some ten of Bahadur Khan's villages, in which no inhabitants had remained.   A high wind fanned the flames, and the valley was soon filled with smoke, while the Sikhs and Sowars were ransacking every place, though with scant success, for hidden treasure.   Exciting duck-hunts and chicken-chases furnished an addition to the dinners of the infantry, while the cavalry brought in some cattle and sheep from the more distant places.   After about three hours the order to march was given.   A few shots were fired at the rear guard, but the troops reached camp in the evening, having tramped seventeen miles over difficult ground, and through half-frozen streams, without loss.

Force is the only argument appreciated by these wild tribes, and the punishment of Bahadur Khan, showing that the remotest glens were not safe from our troops, had a great effect on the other chiefs and their people.[2]

[1] On the previous night the rum froze in the barrels, and the hard-boiled eggs in the haversacks that day had to be thawed in the hand before they could be eaten.

[2] Sensational articles on this foray were published in the class of newspapers which delight in traducing their countrymen, describing how old men, women, and children were turned out to die in the snow.   There was no snow, and no old men, women, or children.   There were forty or fifty other villages in which they had taken refuge.   These falsehoods aroused great indignation among men who felt they deserved the good opinion of their countrymen.—Hensman.

The camp at Maidan was about 8000 feet above the sea, and the cold in the tents was intense. The force remained there till the 1st December, when they returned to Sherpur. The men, cold and weary, had towards the end of the march arrived at that stage of fatigue when singing and joking had ceased, and as the Gordons broke the ice to wade across a river, Major White overheard the soliloquy of a soldier near him—an expression of his own feelings rather than a communication to others—" My God, I wish I had the sergeant that 'listed me by the lug the noo ! "

Meanwhile the feeling of unrest increased throughout the country, and the General was aware that only the mutual jealousy of the chiefs prevented their combining against him. The priests, particularly the aged Mullah named Mushk-i-Alam (Fragrance of the Universe), preached a *jehad* or religious war, and denounced the English in every mosque ; the Afghan successes of 1841-2 under somewhat similar circumstances were recounted, and the people were assured that if they would only act together, they would be rewarded by the plunder of the British.

Though his intelligence was defective, Roberts was aware that large bodies of Afghans were advancing from different directions with the intention of possessing themselves of the city and of surrounding Sherpur. Among them Mahomed Jan was near Arghandeh with 5000 men, whose numbers were afterwards increased to 10,000.

Sir Frederick recognised the difficulties of the situation, but there was no feeling of despondency. On the 6th December, the weather being bright and bracing, he gave a picnic to the officers, and afterwards joined in a paper-chase, in which many were unhorsed, including the gallant General himself.

In order to prevent the different sections of the enemy from concentrating at Kabul, a column under Macpherson started on the 8th to attack those coming from the north before they could join those advancing from the west ; and on the following morning, Baker, with a small force, of which the 92nd (450 rifles), under Lieut.-Colonel Parker, formed a part, marched to Charasia, his instructions being to make a feint towards the Logar Valley, but afterwards to turn westwards and place himself on the Ghazni road between Arghandeh and Maidan, ready to intercept the retreat of the enemy if beaten by Macpherson, or to co-operate with that officer. The Gordons, with Baker's force, encamped on the 9th at Charasia, and next day at 8 a.m. the force marched for their appointed position. The bitter cold of the night was followed by the heat of the sun rays reflected powerfully by the barren and waterless hills, and the troops showed signs of fatigue, till on the summit they found water, which trickled down towards the Kabul

River at Beni-Badam (better known as Beni-be-d—d), a short way west of Maidan, where the main body camped in the dark ; but the unfortunate rear guard (a company each of the 92nd and the 5th Punjab Infantry) was delayed by the exceeding roughness of the track, so narrow and rocky in places that the baggage animals could only move slowly in single file, causing constant confusion.   Sunset was succeeded by hard frost, darkness overtook them, and they had to spend the night near the top of the pass as best they could. Piquets were carefully placed in case of an attack, and they reached camp next morning.

Early on the 11th December [1] Baker's Brigade moved towards Arghandeh, only about eight miles distant.   The advanced guard, commanded by Major White, consisted of a half troop 5th Punjab Cavalry and three companies of the 92nd, followed by the rest of the regiment under Lieut.-Colonel Parker, two mountain guns, and the native cavalry and infantry.   The rear guard, commanded by Captain McCallum, 92nd, consisted of two mountain guns, half troop 5th Punjab Cavalry, a half company 5th Punjab Infantry, and 64 rifles of the 92nd under Lieutenant Fraser ; the whole force amounting to about 1300 men.

Rumours of hostilities reached the Brigadier, and a white standard was observed on a hill a mile off.   The force forded the river and took the road for the Arghandeh Kotal, on the far side of which it was intended to encamp.   After the main body had crossed and the baggage was starting, small bodies of the enemy showed themselves on the hills, from which they could see the movements of the column below.   The advanced guard proceeded about four miles without any resistance being offered.   The concealed enemy, however, were tempted by the sight of the main body to fire a few distant shots, which struck the ground unpleasantly near but did no injury ; and the column proceeded and halted under the Kotal, when the Afghans, encouraged at no notice being taken of their fire, became bolder, crept nearer among the rocks, and shot a Sepoy dead.   The country was now more open and the hills out of rifle range, but after proceeding about two miles word was brought forward that the rear guard, which had been threatened all along, was being vigorously attacked where the road ran between the hills. The enemy attempted to seize the eminence on the right of the road, which had to be secured with the bayonet ; the left, towards the

[1] On the 11th December the troops amounted to :—

At and around Sherpur	6352 men	20 guns
At Butkhak and Latabund	1343 „	2 „
On the night of the 11th the Guides Corps reached Sherpur	679 „	0 „
	8374 „	22 „

river, was also attacked, while another body of the foe pressed upon
the rear, yelling their war cries and brandishing their swords and
long knives, and had nearly charged home, but were kept at bay
by the undaunted front shown by the Gordons and Punjab Infantry.
The guns were sent back in time to check the enemy rushing down
from the higher hills, and the baggage was got forward ; the men
holding the eminence they had taken with the bayonet were then
ordered to withdraw.   Hardly had they done so when the Afghans
swarmed up the other side, planted their standards, and fired down
on our men, who were ordered to double for 400 yards, their skirmishers in rear facing about at intervals to check pursuit ; and in
spite of the number of bullets fired by the Afghans only one of our
men, a Bengal Cavalry trooper, was killed, and one man was
wounded.   Dr Duke, from whose " Recollections of the Kabul
Campaign " much of the above is taken, mentions a soldier of the
92nd named MacKenzie, who was brought to him shot through
the thigh, just before they left the eminence.   As he was lifted
from the dooly he said, " I fear the bone 's broken, I felt it click " ;
and next day, when the doctor told him that he would never more
march with the regiment, two tears silently trickled down his
cheek ; but he lighted his pipe and manfully pulled himself
together for the amputation.

The continued attacks caused confusion among the baggage
animals, the difficulties and delays increased as darkness set in,
and the rear guard, bringing the baggage safely, only arrived
in camp at 7.30 p.m.

While this was going on, the advanced guard had arrived near
the intended camping ground at 3 p.m.   A gorge intervened which
was held on both sides by the Afghans.   The two guns opened fire,
and the Gordons, led by Major White, Captain D. F. Gordon, and
Lieutenant the Hon. J. S. Napier, " advancing in their usual
straight manner," rapidly cleared the heights.   Major White
observed the enemy gathering on a hill where, if allowed to hold it,
they would have an exceptional opportunity of commanding the
ground selected for the camp, and of opposing next day's march.
He accordingly ordered Lieutenant Napier to seize this hill and
hold it with his company as a piquet till further orders.   This
service was gallantly performed, and E Company remained there
all night.

On this adventurous day the Gordons had two men wounded,
but the enemy sustained far more loss than he had inflicted.   Major
George Stewart White, Captain George Kellie McCallum, and
Lieutenant the Hon. John Scott Napier were favourably mentioned
in Sir F. Roberts' dispatch of 25th January 1880, for their conduct
on this occasion.

Baker had now gained the position at Arghandeh which he had been directed to occupy, but instead of meeting a routed enemy, his rear guard had been attacked all day. Meanwhile Macpherson had carried out his instructions, and on the morning of the 10th December, with his column of about 1500 men and four guns, had defeated and dispersed the Kohanistani levies near the Surkh Kotal, and encamped on the ground he had won. On hearing of Macpherson's success, Roberts sent him orders to march next morning —the 11th—in Baker's direction towards Arghandeh, and informed him that Massy (whose force was 350 men, all Cavalry and Horse Artillery, with four guns) was directed to leave Aushar at 9 a.m. to co-operate with him *via* the Arghandeh and Ghazni road against the army of Mahomed Jan.

A misapprehension of these orders brought on a premature cavalry combat, resulting in a loss of four British officers, 16 British and 9 native rank and file killed, and 4 British officers, 1 native officer, 20 British and 10 native rank and file wounded. The guns were taken by the enemy, but afterwards rescued.

On December 12th, soon after daybreak, Baker marched from his position, which was twelve miles from Kabul. He was unaware of the events of the previous day, but he felt that the proposed combinations must have failed, for the enemy, instead of retreating, were persistently following him ; and he informed Roberts by heliogram from Kila Kazi that he was on his way back to Kabul.

The rear guard of native cavalry and infantry, under Major Pratt, was soon exchanging shots with the enemy ; as the latter became bolder, Pratt ordered his infantry skirmishers in rear of the baggage to give them a volley at 600 yards ; several Afghans fell, and the rest did not venture nearer, though they fired long shots, by which a Sepoy was wounded. As the column proceeded, the hills on each side were cleared, those on the right being held by parties of the 92nd, who accounted for several of the enemy. The last hill occupied was high, and an artillery officer mistook them for one of the bodies of armed men to be seen hovering on all sides ; he sent a shell at the Highlanders, which fortunately passed over them, and the gunner found out his mistake before he had corrected his aim.

When they neared Kabul they could see the flash of guns at the Bala Hissar and fighting on the Shahr-i-Darwaza heights, where Macpherson with 560 men, made up of the 67th, 72nd, and native regiments, with two mountain guns, was gallantly attempting to dislodge the enemy from the Takht-i-Shah. " They 'll need the kilties yet for that job, I expect," remarked one of the officers, as he observed the formidable nature of the Afghan position ; and, in fact, Roberts, seeing that it could not be carried without great loss,[1] ordered the assault to be deferred, and Macpherson to hold the ground he had gained till Baker could co-operate the next morning. The Gordons, with Baker's Column, entered Sherpur in the evening, after a march conducted with scarcely any loss, which was wonderful considering that Mahomed Jan's forces were all round them.

It was only now that Baker's men heard the particulars of yesterday's disaster—how the small force of the 9th and 14th Bengal Lancers had charged the formidable array of the Afghan army—how the guns had stuck in the ditches of Bhagwana and were spiked and abandoned—how Roberts appeared on the scene at the critical moment of the action, and was himself only saved from an Afghan knife by the ready pluck of a Mahometan soldier. The Lancers could tell the Highlanders how Parson Adams,[2] strong in arm as in argument, had dragged their wounded comrades from under their fallen chargers and saved their lives at the risk of his own ; how Hills[3] galloped to Sherpur to tell the state of affairs to Sir Hugh Gough, commanding there ; with what speed Colonel Brownlow of the 72nd had left Sherpur with 200 of his regiment and arrived in the nick of time to stem the tide which threatened to submerge them at Deh-i-Mazang ; of the skilful and gallant defence of the gorge there till the arrival of Macpherson's Brigade, when the abandoned guns (which had been rescued by Macgregor, Chief of the Staff, with a party of the 67th and some artillerymen and Lancers) were brought safe into Sherpur. Sir Hugh Gough's cool and confident bearing had prevented any panic among the garrison, and when Roberts rode in after dark on the evening of the 11th, he found every possible arrangement had been made for the defence of the cantonment.[4] No attack was made upon it, but the picket at the Bala Hissar was assailed on all sides, and suffered considerable loss in holding that post, so that the arrival of Baker's Brigade on the 12th relieved the General of some anxiety. A sharp lookout was kept, and the night passed in comparative quietness.

During the night Mahomed Jan, who had received large reinforcements, occupied the villages between the Bala Hissar and Beni Hissar and along the road to Charasia. His troops still held the Takht-i-Shah (*King's Throne*), a natural fortress about 7500 feet above sea-level, and 2400 feet above the plain ; it was strengthened

---

[1] Three officers and ten rank and file were killed and wounded in the attempt.

[2] Chaplain the Rev. J. W. Adams afterwards received the Victoria Cross.

[3] General Hills, Governor of Kabul, had ridden out with Roberts.

[4] It is said that when things looked bad, the Rev. Father Brown, R.C. Chaplain, went round the hospital telling all who could carry a rifle to turn out. " It 's Jesus Christ against Mahomet, and we 're sure to win."

by well-built *sangars* (walls) of great thickness, which with the rocks extending down the steep face of the mountain afforded secure cover to its defenders. It is the highest point of the Shahr-i-Darwaza heights, which extend from the river opposite Deh-i-Mazang on the north to Beni Hissar on the south. Macpherson still occupied ground on the north side, and Roberts now determined to attack the stronghold from the south, General Baker being entrusted with the task. His force[1] was formed up at 8 a.m., when the Brigadier explained his plan to the senior officers, and informed Major White that he was to take four companies and lead the advance. A loud cheer rose from the ranks when they heard that once more " The Gordons hae the guidin' o't." The men divested themselves of the rolled greatcoats they carried, and the column took the road to Beni Hissar.

Immediately above that place the ridge rose to where there was a dip caused by a ravine 200 feet above the plain, and above this dip the ridge became much steeper towards the Takht-i-Shah. Below the village were thick orchards, and the country was intersected by ditches lined with willows. Major White was ordered to advance against the village, which was strongly held by the enemy, with two companies extended and two in support. A marsh caused a slight delay to the Highlanders, and some shots were fired at them by the Afghans, who apparently expected the attack to be directed against their friends on the hills, for as soon as they saw the intention of the British, they evacuated the village and made for the dip in the heights above, from which they could dominate the British advance. White, with the instinct of a true soldier, took upon himself the responsibility of changing the order of attack to suit the altered circumstances, and at once changed front to the right ; the right company of skirmishers and the right company of supports covering the new front as skirmishers, facing the position to which his opponents were fast advancing, and recognising its importance, he ordered his officers to try to intercept the enemy at the dip on the ridge. It was now a race between Highlanders and Afghans, which was watched with breathless interest by their comrades under Lieut.-Colonel Parker who were with the guns, and the other troops in the plain. The artillery covered the advance with their fire, but the Afghans threw themselves behind shelter, and when a shell had burst, jumped up and fired at the advancing 92nd ; but when the latter gained the base of the hill they also had some cover, and rapidly climbed the steep

---

[1] Four guns G3 Field Artillery, 4 mountain guns ; 1 squadron 9th Lancers, 5th Punjab Cavalry ; 6 companies 92nd (350 rifles), 300 3rd Sikhs, and subsequently 150 of the 5th Punjab Infantry.

ascent.[1]   Lieutenants Forbes, Grant, and Dick-Cunyngham were leading, when from below Surgeon-Major Duke, who was watching with his field-glass, could see an officer on the extreme right, with a few men, gain the summit and without taking breath run eagerly along the hill.   Young, active, and armed only with sword and pistol, he outstripped his more heavily-accoutred followers, and made straight for a red standard surrounded by a number of Afghans.

I can recall now how I saw him on the sky-line, his drawn sword waving from side to side keeping time with the swing of his kilt ; two Gordons are on his right and two on his left, each grasping his rifle ready for the foe. . . . An old Afghan boldly urges on his followers and only fifty yards intervene, when the men with the standard open out and take cover—the Highland officer runs steadily towards them just a little ahead of his men ; he is evidently determined to capture the standard.   Only thirty yards intervene, when from behind a rock I can see an Afghan slowly rise on his knee and take deliberate aim.   The officer appears to look only at the standard—I feel inclined to shout to him.   A puff of smoke issues from the rock, and he falls backwards, his sword still grasped in his hand—he makes an effort to rise—my glasses drop, for the Afghans are rushing upon him ! but another officer who continued looking told me that a Highlander stood over his fallen body and bravely defended him, shooting one and endeavouring to bayonet another, who seized the Highlander's rifle, and a deadly struggle took place, during which he was cut down from behind and killed, and then the officer he had tried to save.   Such is the manner in which Lieutenant St John Forbes and Colour-sergeant James Drummond met their death.[2]

At the same time that this scene was being enacted, Lieutenants Grant and Dick-Cunyngham, with their men, were in rear of Forbes' section, below the rocks held by the enemy, whose numbers were rapidly increasing, but they were separated from Major White and the rest of his command by a spur of the hill, Lieutenant E. C. Bethune's company being on the left ; on getting close to these rocks they found themselves enfiladed from another

---

[1] Early in the day Private J. Shairp was shot in the ankle, and, leaning on his rifle, hopped back to the shelter of a rock shouting for a dooly. The Rev. Mr Manson, Presbyterian Chaplain, ran up holding out his hands to help him. Thinking the minister was holding out his hands in the position of prayer, Jock said—" Ye needna pray the noo, sir, I 'm no' gaen to dee yet ; rin an' get me a dooly—rin an' get me a dooly ! "

[2] Lieutenant Forbes was son of Colonel Forbes, late Coldstream Guards, brother of Forbes of Callendar.

Colour-sergeant Drummond had twenty-one years' service ; he was a native of Stanley in Perthshire, and an athlete who excelled in putting the stone and throwing the hammer.

NOTE.—Having sent the above account of Lieutenant Forbes' death to his family for their approval, I received a letter from Mr Drummond Forbes of Millearn stating that he had always understood that his brother was killed in trying to save the wounded sergeant, and in support of this enclosed cuttings from Indian newspapers of the time and a letter from Lieutenant Dick-Cunyngham. Knowing how those who have taken part in exciting scenes necessarily differ in their description of details, I took the evidence of several persons who were present, which is given in Appendix IV and confirms the account in the text.

sangar on their left by a heavy fire in addition to that from their front. With the naked eye those below could see the Afghans crowding upon them in the bravest manner ; a bullet at fifteen or twenty yards struck the metal top of Grant's sporran with such force that it knocked him over, apparently killed (though he was soon able to pick up the rifle of a wounded man and return the compliment). Two of the three officers were down, the breathless men were falling under the furious fire ; there was naturally a momentary hesitation, but it was only for a moment, for Dick-Cunyngham rushed forward, waving his sword, and called out, " Don't retire, come on, lads, follow me ! " With a wild shout on they went and rushed the sangar, jumping into it, Cunyngham first.[1] Some of the Ghazis [2] fought desperately, but their red standard went down, its defenders being shot or bayoneted, and the rest were driven over the further side of the hill.

The above incident occupied less time than it takes to describe it. Major White had gained the ridge, but the honour of scattering its defenders was shared by the Guides under Colonel Jenkins, who supported his advance.

By this movement the enemy's line was cut in two, while the cavalry and 3rd Sikhs prevented the fugitives from rallying in the direction of Beni Hissar. Dr Langridge dressed the hurts of the wounded Gordons, and they were sent down from the ridge, on which the Mountain Battery soon arrived. After a very short breathing time the 92nd and the Guides proceeded on their perilous undertaking against the Takht-i-Shah ; for some distance the ground was open along the ridge which rose to commanding knolls, each fortified by a sangar, and as the 92nd advanced, those in rear momentarily expected to see them receive the fire of the concealed foe, but on nearing the breastwork an officer was seen to seize the flag, which had been left to deceive the British. There were still 400 yards of precipitous mountain to ascend before they could carry the peaks, which bristled with the enemy ; but the very steepness of the hillside, with its boulders and crevices, gave cover to the assailants, who had very few casualties as they steadily advanced covered by the fire of the mountain guns in rear and of the field artillery below, though the shells mostly fell short of the standards of the defenders. The enemy's attention was now turned to his left, where some of the 72nd Highlanders, 3rd Sikhs, and 5th Gurkhas, under Lieut.-Colonel Money, had fought their way from the Upper Bala Hissar. The men of the two Highland corps

---

[1] Lieutenant Dick-Cunyngham afterwards received the Victoria Cross for his conduct on this occasion.

[2] Fanatical Mahometans who think that they merit Paradise by killing a Christian, and fear not death if they can attain that object.

vied with each other who should be first on the top, an honour which fell to Colour-sergeant Yule of the 72nd. The enemy made a determined stand, and it was only after a severe struggle that they were driven off.

Although defeated, they were not thoroughly routed, and at some distance began to get together again, beating their drums. Roberts, from his position at Sherpur, had witnessed the success of his troops, but could now see large bodies of armed men moving towards Siah Sang, whence the road between the Bala Hissar and Sherpur would be commanded ; he ordered Macpherson to move from Deh-i-Mazang and protect the Bala Hissar with six companies of the 67th Foot, while the remainder of his force went to Sherpur. To Baker he signalled orders to leave a small party on the Takht-i-Shah under Lieut.-Colonel Money, and to move with the rest of his troops towards the cantonment, driving the enemy off the Siah Sang on the way. As White and his men made their way down the steep descent, the boom of cannon and the rattle of musketry was heard from the plain ; the guns were threatened by Afghans who had been concealed in the villages and ditches, but the villages were shelled, two companies of the 3rd Sikhs under Major Griffiths kept the enemy back, while the 92nd cut off their retreat, killing some of them. As White's advanced company approached a village which looked deserted, and had almost reached the gateway, they were suddenly fired upon from the loopholes of the wall. The Highlanders ran to cover in the ditches and lay ready, but two of them who were on the left, John M'Leod from Kintail and an Aberdonian named James Henderson, rushed up to the wall, got under the loopholes, and kept firing at any head that appeared on the wall till they afterwards rejoined their company unhurt ; meanwhile the artillery fired at the gate, but the shot only made holes in it. The difficulty was solved by an officer of a native regiment, who, taking a lighted torch made by the gunners, gave it to a villager who had been taken —then, pistol in hand, he drove the man before him so that the enemy could not fire at him without hitting their countryman until the gate was reached, and some straw which lay there was set on fire. While the doors were burning, the 92nd (the two wings being now united) was ordered into Sherpur, leaving the 5th Punjab Infantry to capture the village, which they afterwards did with great slaughter. Meanwhile the cavalry achieved a signal success, driving the enemy from the neighbourhood of Siah Sang, though not without loss, especially to the 9th Lancers.

Major-General Baker thanked Major White for the service rendered by the Gordons under his command, and the name of Lieutenant and Adjutant C. W. H. Douglas was mentioned in the

Brigadier-General's dispatch, dated 19th December 1879, as having done good service.

The Gordons lost Lieutenant St John W. Forbes, Colour-sergeant James Drummond, Private William Diack killed, and nineteen n.c. officers and men were wounded.[1] One of them, Private J. M'Nab, had been lying down to fire when he was hit from above, on the end of his back. Dreading the jokes of his comrades and that it might be said in his native Islay that he had

5th Punjab Infantry   3rd Sikh Infantry
SEPOYS—1880

turned his back to the foe, he refused to go to hospital, till he had to be carried there. Among many narrow escapes was that of Lance-corporal Duncan M'Lennan, who was struck on a button of his jacket, which deflected the bullet. It made a mark like a whip round his body and came out at the back of his kilt. The body of the 92nd private was afterwards found in one of the villages they had passed in the morning ; the man, who was sick and fell out, was supposed to have been enticed to enter by the offer of milk, and then brutally murdered and mutilated in a manner which excited feelings of horror and revenge among his comrades.

---

[1] Total loss on 13th December :—Two British officers and 12 men killed ; 2 British officers and 43 British and native soldiers wounded.

On the evening of the 13th Lieut.-Colonel Parker, in Regimental Orders, expressed the deep regret of the regiment for the death of Lieutenant Forbes " whilst leading on his company foremost in the advance which the Brigadier-General has described as the most brilliant he has ever witnessed." With the name of that most promising young officer, the Lieut.-Colonel coupled that of Colour-sergeant Drummond, who " fell beside his officer," and who " has always been held in the highest esteem in the regiment." [1]

[1] In the summer of 1880 I happened to be at a party in London where the ladies were making much of a wounded officer of Lancers, and begging him to relate his warlike experiences. With military modesty he avoided speaking of his personal achievements, but I heard him describe in graphic language the conduct of the Gordon Highlanders, which he had witnessed on this occasion—" as if one was looking from the stage of a theatre at the gallery." " That," he said, " was the grandest performance I ever saw." On being introduced to him, I mentioned that I had once been in the 92nd, when he remarked, " It is a most extraordinary regiment. They are always ready for work—they always turn out as neat as new pins—their discipline is strict, while the good feeling between officers and men is remarkable." He was Captain Scott Chisholme, who is mentioned by Lord Roberts as having remained in the saddle and brought his regiment (the 9th) out of action though severely wounded in the charge at Siah Sang on this occasion. He was killed as colonel commanding the Imperial Light Horse at Elandslaagte, 1899.

FINDING that the heavy losses sustained by the enemy had not broken up the combinations against him, Sir Frederick Roberts telegraphed for Charles Gough's Brigade, and directed the detachment at Butkhak to return to Kabul, while Colonel Hudson was directed to hold Lataband, an important post on the road from Jalalabad by which Gough would arrive. The night of the 13th December passed quietly, but at dawn on the 14th it became apparent that the numbers of the enemy were increasing enormously—the sky-line was alive with men who were concentrating on the Asmai heights, evidently preparing to deliver an attack in great strength from that quarter.

To cut the enemy's communication with Kohistan and drive him off the Asmai heights, Roberts dispatched Brigadier-General Baker at 9 a.m. with a force [1] of which two companies of the 92nd formed a part. They were commanded by Captain D. F. Gordon, who was under the orders of the officer commanding the 72nd. The heights extend from Deh-i-Afghan close to Kabul, for a considerable distance westwards between Sherpur and the Chardeh Valley ; they are divided by a dip or pass, on the north side of which is a conical hill. Covered by the fire of his artillery, to which the Afghan mountain guns replied, Baker seized this hill with a party composed of the 72nd, one company of the 92nd (the other remaining with the artillery), and the Guides Infantry, all under Colonel Jenkins, who was thus placed on the enemy's line of communication.

Leaving two mountain guns, 64 men of the 72nd and 60 of the Guides, under Lieut.-Colonel Clarke, to hold the hill, Jenkins proceeded to attack the enemy, who, protected by formidable rocks and by sangars, held the opposite height. Setting a " stout heart to a stey brae," the British toiled steadily up the steep hillside, utilising the cover afforded by boulders and shelving rocks to return the fire which met them from above. Roberts, who was watching the attack from the walls of Sherpur, brought four guns into action near the north-west corner of the cantonment, and ordered Macpherson, who was on the north end of the Shahr-i-Darwaza, to assist Baker's people by sending the 67th across the Kabul River to threaten the enemy's left rear. The guns made good practice, and when the enemy saw the glittering bayonets of the stormers near the top, many sought safety in flight, but not all ; a number of Ghazis still held the sangars, but though well posted, strong and

---

[1] Four guns Field Artillery ; 4 guns Mountain Artillery ; 14th Bengal Lancers, 72nd Highlanders (192 rifles), 92nd Highlanders (100 rifles), Guides Infantry (460 rifles), 5th Punjab Infantry (470 rifles).

brave, the defenders of the first could not withstand the rush of British infantry, and to a man they met the death they sought. In another sangar, which was on the peak of the hill and unusually strong, were forty or fifty men, who by their fire checked for a time the advance along the ridge, and their stronghold had to be taken. Major Stockwell (72nd) and Captain Gordon (92nd) got together some men of their regiments and of the Guides. Between them and the sangar a bit of open ground intervened which was swept by such a fire that the bravest might have hesitated ; they did not hesitate, but contending who should be first, rushed at the wall, where a stubborn hand-to-hand fight ensued. Corporal Sellar of the 72nd seized a standard ; its bearer on the wall wounded him with his long knife and then jumped down on him—they closed, and rolled over together, when another Highlander bayoneted the Afghan. It was a tough tussle, but the bayonet made short work, and the sangar was filled with dead men. " I saw M'Laren slay at least three," says Major Gordon, of a stalwart sergeant from the Braes of Balquhidder, who (in allusion to his being but a second-class shot) called out, as his bayonet broke through an Afghan's guard, " If I canna shoot, lads, I can stick ! "[1] The whole summit was now held by Baker's troops, and only those who have seen the ground can realise the difficulties they had overcome.

It was now a little past noon, and Roberts became anxious about the party left on the conical hill, as Macpherson had helio-graphed that large bodies of Afghans were moving in that direction ; he signalled this information to Baker, who detached part of the 5th Punjab Infantry to reinforce Clarke, and Roberts sent 200 of the 3rd Sikhs for the same purpose, but before the re-inforcements could arrive, Clarke's men had been outnumbered and almost surrounded, so that notwithstanding the extreme gallantry of its defenders the conical hill was lost. Captain Spens of the 72nd was killed in an encounter with Afghan swordsmen ; the mountain guns had to be abandoned, the mules carrying them being shot, and the overmatched party retired slowly and steadily, closely followed by the enemy, who were, however, checked by the troops from Baker's Brigade. While this was going on the enemy began to collect on Siah Sang and to make their way round the eastern flank of the cantonment ; they were charged by some of the 5th Punjab Cavalry, who were led in such a brilliant manner by Captain Vousden that he received the Victoria Cross. Two Horse

---

[1] Captain Gordon, when laid up at Sherpur from the effects of his wounds, asked Colonel Parker and the adjutant to come to his quarters and interview M'Laren, with a view to his being recommended for the silver medal. The question was whether he or Corporal Sellar of the 72nd was first man over the wall of the sangar, to which the sergeant replied—" Weel, sir, I couldna just richtly say, I was that thrang slaughtering ! "

Artillery guns and a party of the 92nd were also sent in pursuit. Roberts now heliographed to Macpherson to inquire in which direction the enemy were moving, and their numbers. He replied that large masses were advancing from north, south, and west, and the officer in charge of the signalling station added, " The crowds of Afghans in the Chardeh Valley remind me of Epsom on Derby Day." Sir Frederick, realising that the retention of the Asmai heights would entail great loss of life, decided that he must for the present act on the defensive, and concentrate his forces at Sherpur. At 2 p.m. his two Generals were ordered to retire. Macpherson was to hasten back with all his force by the Deh-i-Afghan suburb, while Baker was to hold on to a village he had occupied since the morning, till all the other troops were within the cantonments.

On seeing the retirement commence, the enemy, full of confidence in their numbers, swarmed down on the handful of men retreating before them, shouting cries of victory and brandishing their weapons, so that had there been the smallest unsteadiness or confusion among any of the British detachments, a disaster would certainly have occurred. Major Stockwell with a small party of Highlanders was sent to a position from which he kept up a hot fire on the advancing masses, and when ordered to withdraw there was no appearance of undue haste ; the men of the 72nd, 92nd, and Guides alternately forming up with perfect regularity, and covering the others with their volleys as they scrambled down. The deafening sound of volley and independent firing lasted for fifteen minutes. Many splendid acts of courage were performed. Captain Hammond of the Guides held a knoll with a few men, killing several Afghans with his own hand, thus saving the wounded from their murderous knives, and earning the Victoria Cross. Captain Gordon (92nd) was severely wounded, and Lieutenant Gaisford (72nd) was killed. All the wounded and the dead were safely brought in, and the hazardous operation was successfully accomplished. Macpherson's Brigade had behaved equally well, and Jenkins' force being now in safety, they and Baker's rear guard completed the retirement, being covered as they crossed the plain by a wing of the 92nd from Sherpur. The British loss during the day was 19 officers and men killed and 88 wounded ;[1] of the 92nd Company engaged, Captain Gordon and 3 rank and file were wounded. Sergeant John M'Laren and Corporal Edward M'Kay[2] were afterwards awarded the " Distinguished Conduct Medal " for their great personal gallantry.[3]

---

[1] Lord Roberts.
[2] Corporal M'Kay volunteered to carry an important message under very heavy fire.
[3] Regimental Record.

Once inside the walls there was no cause for anxiety for the safety of the troops, and by their General's care supplies of ammunition, food, and firewood, sufficient for nearly four months, had been collected. The perimeter of Sherpur, four and a half miles, was rather large for the garrison of 7000 effective men, but the defences, both natural and artificial, were considerable, their weak spot being on the eastern face near the village of Bimaru and its adjacent heights. The village was loopholed, shelter trenches were made on the heights, the unfinished part of the wall was secured by abattis and wire entanglements, and the troops were employed in generally strengthening the place and safeguarding the hospitals. The defences were divided into five sections, under Brigadier-General Macpherson, Colonel Jenkins, Brigadier-General Hugh Gough, Major-General Hills, and Colonel Brownlow. Brigadier-General Massy was given the centre of the cantonment, and Brigadier-General Baker commanded the reserve (composed of a wing of the 67th, a wing of the 72nd, the whole of the 92nd, and six squadrons of cavalry), which was formed at a depression or gorge in the Bimaru heights, that he might be able to move rapidly to either end of the ridge, the weakest points in the defences. Meanwhile the enemy were resting on their laurels and looting the bazaars of Kabul ; additional forces were constantly joining them, and they apparently considered the total destruction of the British as merely a matter of time.

The 15th December did not pass, however, without active employment to a company of the Gordons who, under Captain McCallum, were sent to bring in a quantity of grain which was stored in a fort on the Kabul road, about 700 yards from the cantonments. While Captain McCallum superintended the loading of the camels, the enemy, who tried to prevent him, were kept off by the fire of the rest of the company who, under Lieutenant Grant lined the road. In performing this service, Private W. Davis was killed.

Each day and night brought its alarms and adventures to the beleaguered garrison. On the 17th, the enemy showed in force at Siah Sang, but were dispersed by artillery fire from the Sherpur side of the river, which, as a soldier remarked, made them " rin like skelpit bairns " ;[1] there was also a skirmish in the afternoon, in which some native infantry drove the enemy, who had been annoying the garrison, from the King's Garden. This was the scene of another spirited skirmish on the 18th, when the Afghans also threatened the eastern bastion ; and on the 19th they opened fire from two forts, from which they were driven by General Baker, who then blew up the forts. In this sortie there were several casualties, among them Lieutenant Montanaro, who continued to give orders

[1] Hensman.

to his gunners as he lay mortally wounded. On the 21st, news arrived of the approach of Gough's Brigade, and as their road lay through an open country, the 5th Bengal Cavalry were sent out at 3 a.m. on the 22nd to assist their advance : a perilous march in the dark over roads slippery with snow and ice through a district possessed by the enemy, which they executed with the loss of three men killed and three wounded.

On this day the enemy showed great signs of activity, and the spies brought information that numbers of scaling ladders were being made, that in all the mosques the mullahs were appealing to the people to make a final effort to exterminate the infidel, and that the aged Muskh-i-Alam had promised to light, at dawn on the 23rd (the last day of the *Moharram*, when religious exultation amongst Mohammedans is at its height), the beacon fire which was to be the signal for the assault.

During the night the troops remained accoutred, and lay rolled in their waterproof sheets and blankets near their arms, ready for any emergency ; those on duty had thick sheepskin jackets provided, and by the General's order tinned soup or cocoa was issued so that they could have a hot morning or evening drink instead of rum. On the night of the 22nd the sentries could hear the cries of the Afghans and the noise of the wooden scaling ladders being dragged over the frozen snow ready for the assault. Before daybreak on the 23rd the troops were under arms at their posts. The distribution of the 92nd was as follows :—" Two companies, under Major White, lined the entrenchments from the valley of Bimaru to the fort on the top of the Bimaru ridge ; two companies, under Captain McCallum, held the gorge between the Bimaru heights ; two companies, under Lieut.-Colonel Parker, remained in reserve in the centre of the cantonments." [1] The companies under White were along with the 67th Regiment, and the Guides and 28th Punjab Infantry were also there. The cold was biting as the troops waited for the dawn, talking in whispers and looking for the expected assault. It was with a feeling of relief that, just as the first faint glimmer of day appeared, they saw the flames of the signal fire shoot up from the Asmai heights, while single warning shots rang out from Deh-i-Afghan and the various villages. The enemy now opened fire from the King's Garden and against the southern face, and large bodies of men with ladders made for the wall, but were repulsed by the fire of Gorham's howitzers and of the infantry and dismounted cavalry stationed on that side. This, however, was only a feint, and soon a mighty shout, as if from 50,000 throats, the flashes of musketry and the boom of cannon, announced that the real attack was being made on the east flank, where Sir Hugh

---

[1] Regimental Record.

Gough and Colonel Jenkins commanded and where the Gordons were stationed.   From beyond Bimaru the roar of many voices and incessant rifle fire told the position of the assailants, but it was yet too dark to see clearly, till Gough's guns fired star shells, which revealed the numbers of the advancing masses at 1000 yards.   On they came, filling the air with the cry of " Deen, deen ! "   " Allah il allah ! "   The native infantry opened fire at 600 yards, but the 67th and 92nd waited till the dense array of Afghans, firing and waving their swords with howls of defiance, appeared through the morning mist ;   then at last the order was given to fire, and the effect at close range was awful.[1]   Still the Ghazis tried to rush the defences ;   the din of the artillery, the crash of the volleys, the yells of the Ghazis, and the rolling roar of the masses behind them made a terrific accompaniment to the fighting.   " Repeated attempts were made to scale the south-eastern wall, and many times the enemy got up as far as the *abattis*, but were repulsed," . . . " heaps of dead marking the spots where these attempts had been most persistent." [2]   The Afghans had recoiled before the fire of the breech-loaders, and about 10 a.m. there was a lull in the fighting.   An hour later, however, they resumed the assault.   Roberts resolved to attack them in flank.   He sent out four guns and the 5th Punjab Cavalry over the hollow in the Bimaru hill to open fire on the enemy's troops near the village of Kurja Kila ;   these wavered and broke, the attack became weaker, and by 1 p.m. it had ceased, and the enemy were in full flight.

Massy was now ordered to pursue with his cavalry, and before night the neighbourhood had been cleared of the enemy.   At the same time a party was sent to destroy the forts and villages, which had caused much trouble, and whence it was necessary to drive the enemy before the entrance of Brigadier-General C. Gough next day.   They were occupied by Ghazis, who refused to surrender, and the buildings were blown up.   Captain Dundas, R.E., V.C., and Lieutenant C. Nugent, R.E., were killed in performing this duty.

" It was calculated by those best able to judge that the combined forces exceeded 100,000, and I myself do not think that an excessive computation." [3]   The enemy lost about 3000 men in killed, wounded, and prisoners.   Owing to their being sheltered from the Afghan fire, which the accuracy of their own rendered less effective, the British had few casualties ; between the 15th and 23rd December their loss was 2 officers, 9 rank and file and 7 followers killed, and 5 officers, 41 rank and file and 22 followers wounded.[4]

---

[1] Major White saw about seventy dead Afghans after the repulse.
[2] Lord Roberts.   [3] *Ibid.*
[4] Sir H. Gough was knocked over by a bullet, but was able to do his duty without being returned as wounded ; his thick sheepskin coat saved him.

On the 23rd the Gordons lost Private Thomas White killed, and 5 rank and file wounded.

In General Orders Sir Frederick expressed his high sense of the services of his troops. " All and every night in most severe weather officers and men were at their posts or sleeping with their arms in the vicinity of the trenches." . . . " Hardships and exposure were cheerfully borne . . . The skill exhibited by the rapid march upon Kabul and in the advance upon the other lines of action reflects the highest credit upon officers and men of my British and native forces."

In his dispatch dated January 23rd, 1880, the Lieut.-General mentioned the good service performed by Lieut.-Colonel Parker and Captain Duncan F. Gordon ; and Brigadier-General Macpherson brought to Sir Frederick's notice the name of Captain A. D. M'Gregor (92nd), his orderly officer.

Christmas was passed amidst seasonable surroundings, with six inches of snow on the ground, but the festivity of the day was toned by the thought of comrades lost, and of the sufferers in the hospital. On New Year's Eve (Hogmanay), however, the Gordons, according to ancient usage, went round the cantonments with band and pipers ; at the General's quarters they cheered, calling him out, and Sir Frederick obeyed, saying, " You have always answered when I called on you, and now I answer your call as readily."

Next day's dinner did credit to the cooks, and there was grog and Kabul wine in which to drink a Happy New Year. Food, indeed, was always plentiful, but during the siege tobacco became so scarce that men smoked tea leaves and such substitutes. The Afghans had plundered the shops in the capital, but as soon as the road was open, merchants from India arrived bringing luxuries, for which they found a profitable market, the troops having plenty of money.

All enclosures within 1000 yards of Sherpur were razed to the ground, the Bala Hissar was reoccupied, and precautions were taken for the protection of the city and cantonments by building forts on the Bimaru, Siah Sang, and Asmai heights.

In the frosty weather there was skating and sliding, the native soldiers soon learning to join their European comrades on the ice. Fresh snow provided ammunition for a mimic war in which the forts were attacked and defended by the various regiments, beating cooking-pots for drums and carrying captured Ghazi flags for colours. A large tent was pitched, its sides built up with walls of mud and brick, having doors, windows, and chimneys complete, which was used as a Club, where all the officers of the army could meet. A theatre also was improvised ; minstrel bands gave concerts, and, though like true Britons they sometimes grumbled, the troops made the best of things ; when spring brought milder weather, there were steeplechases, polo, and cricket.   Some of the handy soldiers made canoes, and disported themselves on the neighbouring lake ; in the streams and irrigation culverts fishing was enjoyed by both officers and men, but the votaries of the gentle craft went armed, and one of the party always was posted to look out for a prowling enemy.   In these ways the monotony of cantonment life was relieved.

An incident described to me by an eye-witness as having taken place at Sherpur is worthy of being recorded as both picturesque in itself and creditable to all concerned.   When the *Gazette*, announcing Colour-sergeant H. A. MacDonald's promotion to sub-lieutenant, was published, the men of his company carried him shoulder high to the officers' quarters, their piper at their head and the other soldiers turning out to cheer ; then each man in turn marched up, stood at attention and saluted him.

The officers afterwards presented him with a sword, and the sergeants with a dirk.

Time-expired men and invalids were sent home as occasion offered, and in April a draft of 1 sergeant, 2 corporals, and 79 privates arrived in India *en route* to join the regiment, while, by the *Gazette* of 16th April 1880, General Mark Kerr Atherley, from the 93rd, succeeded General G. Staunton, deceased, as colonel of the 92nd, in which he had served many years, and of which he had been lieutenant-colonel.

CHAPTER XIII

1880

ALL this while, however, the General's thoughts and time were more seriously occupied in the pacification of the country, and correspondence with Government on the political situation. For the protection of India from invasion from the north-west, it is necessary that the ruler of Afghanistan should be friendly to the British Government, and to a certain extent under its control. As soon as such a ruler could be placed on the throne of Kabul, the British were ready to withdraw ; he was found in the person of Abdur Rahman, a grandson of Dost Mahomed, the Amir before Shere Ali. This arrangement was acceptable to some of the tribes, but others wished for the return of Yakub Khan.

To make such a show of strength as would overawe the country, Sir Donald Stewart was desired to march with his division from Kandahar to Kabul, there to take part in the general pacification of Northern Afghanistan. He started on the 30th March, and on the 16th, Roberts dispatched a small column under Major-General Ross, C.B., to meet him at Ghazni with supplies. There being considerable excitement on the question of the Amirship, and the clans of the Logar Valley being against Abdur Rahman, Sir Frederick, with a view to prevent them from joining in any attack on General Ross, sent a force 1200 strong, under Colonel Jenkins, on the 20th April, in the direction of Charasia. With Colonel Jenkins marched a wing of the 92nd (9 officers and 266 men), under Major White ; they encamped on the left of the road from Kabul, opposite to Childukteran, one of the villages on the plain of Charasia, and about fourteen miles from Sherpur.

On the 22nd, the welcome news was received that Sir Donald Stewart had fought a successful engagement at Ahmedkhel on the 19th, and had arrived at Ghazni. Roberts hoped that this intelligence would have a quieting effect on the people around Kabul, but in this he was disappointed. Jenkins' force had been watching the tribesmen about Charasia, and on the night of the 24th he heard that he was to be attacked by the Logaris under Mahomed Hasan Khan. Soon dropping shots were fired into the camp from the hills; tents were struck, and the baggage and followers placed under cover of a small hill in rear of the camp, guarded by a half company of the 92nd under Lieutenant the Hon. J. S. Napier, who at once built a sangar on the hill. Jenkins sent a party of cavalry to reconnoitre, strengthened his pickets, and sent a message to inform General Roberts of the situation. Soon the enemy were reported to be advancing, from 4000 to 5000 strong. The men had breakfast, which was fortunate, as they got nothing more till night, and then Major White took possession of a dry watercourse in front of the camping-ground, and extended two companies in skirmishing order under Captain Robertson, to cover his front. The remaining company and a half formed a support under Lieutenant Macbean. The Guides Infantry were extended to the left flank ; on the right a fortified house was held by a few Sepoys with some cavalry close by ; the two guns were 400 yards in rear with a guard of cavalry.

At daybreak the action began. The enemy advanced under cover, bringing their standards to within 200 yards of the line, beating drums, waving standards, and constantly attempting to break the defence; but they were kept at bay by the steady fire of the defenders. " Ye micht hae waited till I was through," expostulated Sergeant Lawson, as a bullet spilled his drink of tea by smashing the canteen as he put it to his lips, and wounded him in the neck.

This state of matters lasted till 1.30 p.m.

Meanwhile Roberts dispatched Brigadier-General Macpherson to their aid with four mountain guns, followed later by two more guns and a troop of Punjab Cavalry ; he had 962 infantry, of which the other wing of the 92nd, under Lieut.-Colonel Parker (8 officers and 278 men) formed the European portion, while Gough's Cavalry and Horse Artillery were ordered to take up a position on the way to Charasia as a support. The Gordons were waiting for church parade when they heard that their friends were in danger of being overpowered by numbers ; they were ordered to fall in under arms, and in twenty minutes they were on the road and marching as fast as they could to their comrades' assistance. They reached the high ground beyond the Sang-i-Nawishta gorge at one o'clock, whence they could see that the enemy formed a complete semi-circle round Jenkins' small force and had got very close to it. Macpherson, with quick perception of the position of affairs, tackled the enemy on his weakest point. He extended part of his troops — the Gurkhas — to the left to try to get in touch with Jenkins' men and also to conceal his real attack, which was made from his right on the left of the enemy in the village of Childuk-teran, which was carried. White's men and the Guides rose from their shelter, and joining Macpherson's people, together with them drove the enemy to his right, thus crumpling up the horn of his half-moon, and though the Afghans stood for a little, they were soon hopelessly broken and in retreat; they were pursued by the infantry for a considerable distance and by the cavalry and horse artillery for four miles. By four o'clock not a living Afghan was in sight, and over 200 had been killed ; while our casualties, owing to the way the skirmishers took cover, were only four killed and thirty-four wounded, of whom some died. Of that loss the Gordons' share was two killed, viz. Colour-sergeant Thomas Smith and Private John Keane, and six wounded. Two horses of mounted officers of the 92nd were hit, Colonel Jenkins' horse was killed, and the cavalry had eight horses killed and twenty-four wounded. The shooting of our skirmishers was particularly good ; the enemy who were opposite E Company of the 92nd could hardly look up from their cover without being shot in the head, and, in fact, the majority were so killed. When the enemy were running away, however, the excitement was too great for good shooting. The red coat of one of the Afghans was a mark which many missed, and when its wearer got to shelter he waved his head-dress in defiance.

Altogether it was a most creditable and well-managed affair.

General Roberts arrived just as the fight was finished, and, confident from its decisive character that a retirement could not be misunderstood, he ordered the troops to return to Sherpur, fourteen miles distant ; so that when Macpherson's men arrived there they had done twenty-eight miles, besides the active afternoon's fighting, and were quite ready for their dinner, for they had had nothing to eat since early morning. Near Sherpur they halted in the dark, and the tired men lay resting on the ground, when the pipers of the 72nd came out to meet them and struck up " Gillean an fheile " ; the music put new life into the exhausted soldiers, and they sprang up and stepped out to the invigorating sound.

The following officers were mentioned in dispatches :—Lieut.-Colonel Parker, who " led the attack in the most determined manner," Major White, Captain M'Gregor (orderly officer to Brigadier-General Macpherson), and Captain Singleton. Lieut.-Colonel Parker favourably mentioned Lieutenant and Adjutant Douglas, and Lieutenant Ramsay, the latter " for his conduct in bursting open a house in which a number of the enemy had taken refuge and were preparing to make a stand."[1] Sir F. Roberts remarked on the excellent spirit displayed by the troops during the long and exhausting day.

On the 5th May, Sir Donald Stewart reached Kabul, and, being senior to Sir Frederick Roberts, he took over the command of the Kabul Field Force[2] in addition to the troops he brought with him. Sir Frederick retained the command of two divisions, with Major-General Ross as second in command, while the brigades

[1] It was really a walled garden, not a house, and Ramsay, leading his men, burst in the gate and dashed into the garden—a plucky act, as he did not know the number of the enemy it might contain ; one of his men was killed.

[2] On April 30th the Kabul Field Force amounted to nearly 14,000 men and 38 guns, besides 15,000 men and 30 guns on the Khyber line under the immediate command of Major-General Bright.

from Kandahar formed a third division under Major-General Hills. In order to relieve the pressure on the commissariat caused by the increased number of troops at Kabul, and to open up the roads, a strong brigade, of which the 92nd with a total strength of 597 formed part, marched from Sherpur on the 9th July for Mullah Gaffoor in the Maidan district, and returned on July 31st.   Some of the troops when on similar excursions had lost rifles, stolen from the tents by the clever Afghan thieves ; to avoid this happening to them, each man of the Gordons had a lanyard attaching his rifle to his left wrist while he slept.

Meanwhile it appeared that the adherents of Yakub Khan, finding that there was no hope of his being reinstated, had espoused the cause of his younger brother, Ayub Khan, who was in the neighbourhood of Herat, where a number of chiefs had placed themselves under his leadership and induced him to proclaim a *jahad* or religious war.   On the 29th July the astounding and lamentable intelligence reached Kabul that Brigadier-General Burrows, who had gone out from Kandahar to prevent Ayub from getting to Ghazni, had been defeated at Maiwand on the 27th with a loss of 934 killed and 175 wounded and missing out of the 2476 men engaged, besides followers, two guns, and an immense number of baggage animals, and quantities of arms and ammunition.

This disaster to our arms naturally caused great excitement in Afghanistan and throughout the Indian border.   It was of supreme importance that Kandahar, which was invested by Ayub Khan, should be relieved, and that the reverse to the British arms should be retrieved ; but the Government of India hesitated to weaken the British strength at Kabul till matters were finally arranged with Abdur Rahman, and inclined to Quetta as the place from which Kandahar could be most conveniently succoured.   Both Sir Donald Stewart and Sir Frederick Roberts felt that Ayub Khan's superior numbers, elated by their victory, should be opposed by the best and most experienced troops ; and, being aware that these were not at the time to be found in Baluchistan, communicated with the Viceroy through the Commander-in-Chief by telegraph, stating that Stewart had organised a force sufficient to overcome all opposition *en route* to Kandahar ; that its march through the country would show our strength, and that the simultaneous movement of the rest of the Kabul Field Force towards India might take place without giving rise to misunderstanding in Afghanistan or elsewhere, as the withdrawal of the whole force from Kabul to India would certainly do.

A meeting between Sir Lepel Griffin, Chief of the Political Staff, and Abdur Rahman took place sixteen miles from Kabul, and the delicate and difficult negotiations were brought to a successful conclusion.

On the 3rd August a telegram from the Viceroy (Lord Ripon) authorised the dispatch of a force to Kandahar, to be commanded by Major-General Sir F. Roberts, who at once set about his preparations. General Stewart had allowed him to choose his regiments, and from these every man not likely to stand the strain of prolonged marching was weeded out.

The force numbered 9986 men of all ranks and eighteen guns. The Infantry were in three Brigades :—

1ST BRIGADE.
Brig.-Gen. Macpherson, V.C., C.B.
92nd Highlanders.
23rd Pioneers.
24th Punjab Infantry.
2nd Gurkhas.

3RD BRIGADE.
Brig.-Gen. MacGregor, C.B.
2nd Battalion 60th Rifles.
15th Sikhs.
25th Punjab Infantry.
4th Gurkhas.

2ND BRIGADE.
Major-General Baker, C.B.
72nd Highlanders.
2nd Sikhs.
3rd Sikhs.
5th Gurkhas.

CAVALRY BRIGADE.
Major-Gen. Sir H. Gough, V.C.
9th Lancers.
3rd Bengal Cavalry.
3rd Punjab Cavalry.
Central India Horse.

Colonel C. A. Johnson commanded the artillery ; the roads being impassable for wheels, only screw guns carried on mules were taken. Colonel Perkins, R.E., commanded the sappers, and Colonel Chapman was Chief of the Staff. There were also about 8000 followers, and for the transport 8000 animals, mostly ponies and mules, were required. Large supplies of bread-stuff, preserved vegetables, tinned meat and soup, tea, sugar, salt, rum, lime-juice, etc., were taken, numbers of sheep were driven with the force, and nearly 5000 were purchased on the march. The men's kits [1] were carried for them, so that the soldier had only his arms and seventy rounds of ammunition to carry. For each man thirty rounds were in reserve with his regiment and a hundred in the field park.

On Sunday the 8th August the regiment, under Lieut.-Colonel Parker, moved out of Sherpur to Beni Hissar, where the First and Third Brigades encamped preparatory to the march, General Roberts' headquarters being with them. On the morning of the 9th they began the march of 320 miles, by the Logar Valley route to Kandahar. The strength of the regiment on leaving Kabul was :—Field officers, 2 ; captains, 4 ; subalterns, 11 ; staff, 3 ;

---

[1] The greatcoats were carried by the men "en banderole," but were carried for them occasionally ; the belts were kept washed on the march.

sergeants, 39 ; corporals, 20 ; drummers, 20 ; privates, 560 ; total, 659.[1]

This day they revived the memory of their October and April adventures in the neighbourhood of Charasia, and camped at Zahidabad. The 92nd was on rear guard, and, though the actual distance was moderate, the constant halts while the baggage was being got forward caused them to be under arms for fourteen hours, which was the more unpleasant that a dust storm raged all the afternoon.[2] Major White (who in June had gone as Military Secretary to the Viceroy of India, and when he heard of the expedition to Kandahar, had returned rapidly) here rejoined the regiment, and was received with cheers as he rode into camp.

The Logar district is fertile, food and forage could be bought in plenty, and the climate was bracing, so that part of the journey was not unenjoyable ; the stages at first were short, in order that man and beast might be gradually hardened before entering the difficult country where forced marches were inevitable ; and when it is remembered that 18,000 men and 11,000 animals had to be fed daily after arrival in camp, that fuel for cooking had often to be brought from long distances, and that a limited time was available for meals and rest, it will be seen that some practice was required before every one learned to know exactly what to do and how to do it. Each day the " rouse " sounded at 2.45 a.m., and by four o'clock tents had been struck, baggage packed, and all had breakfasted and were ready to start.[3] The cavalry generally covered the movement, two of the regiments being about five miles in front and the other two on either flank. Two infantry brigades came next, each accompanied by a mountain battery ; then the field hospitals, ordnance, and engineer parks, treasure, and the baggage according to the order in which the brigades were moving. The remaining infantry brigade, with its battery and a detachment of cavalry, formed the rear guard. An interval of ten paces, when in column of fours, was always kept between each company to allow of air, while, if the ground permitted, they marched in open column of companies. A halt was called for ten minutes at the end of each hour, prolonged to twenty minutes at eight o'clock for a snack, the men carrying food in their haversacks, with coffee or tea in their water-bottles, and each had occasionally a tot of

---

[1] Regimental Record.

[2] As soon as Sir Donald Stewart heard that Roberts had safely entered the Upper Logar Valley, he evacuated Sherpur, and the Second Division, consisting of two batteries R.A., one brigade of cavalry, and three of infantry, marched by the Khyber Pass for India. Abdur Rahman having been finally proclaimed as Amir of Kabul, he had the support of the Mullah Mushk-i-Alam, whose son accompanied Roberts' force.

[3] The Adjutant always inspected the " Staff Parade," *i.e.* n.c. officers and musicians, by the light of a lantern before marching off.

rum at night.   Men who fell out on the march were mounted on ponies, but the few who did so were unmercifully " chaffed " by their comrades and they got no rum.   On arrival at the camping ground for the night, the front face was occupied by the brigade which had been rear guard during the day, and which became the leading brigade on the morrow ; thus each had its turn of the arduous and troublesome rear-guard duty.   Want of bridges caused great delay in getting the baggage across streams ; towards the end of the longer marches the footsore followers would give in and lie down, and the officers and soldiers had to encourage them or put them on baggage animals to prevent their lagging behind, and being murdered by Afghans who hovered about on the look-out for plunder, so that the rear guard had a hard time of it, and sometimes did not reach the camping ground till late.   Then there are no idlers—every man has his place, and within half an hour the mules are unloaded, fires lighted, and dinner prepared ; then arms are cleaned, pipes lighted—stories, songs, and laughter— till all turn in, and no sound is to be heard but the challenge of the wakeful sentries from the piquets posted on the neighbouring heights.   The variations of temperature (sometimes as much as eighty degrees), the scarcity of water (which was generally brack-ish), the constant sandstorms and suffocating dust raised by the columns, added greatly to the fatigue.

On the 12th August the force crossed the Zamburak Kotal, 8100 feet high, and so steep that it was most difficult to get the baggage animals over ; in order to lighten their loads, the men carried their blankets themselves.   On the 15th they crossed the Sher-i-Dahan Pass.   Owing to the darkness and the nature of the road, the Gordons went first in place of the cavalry, who followed till the southern end of the pass was reached.   Some of them then trotted on to reconnoitre the country towards Ghazni, where the Governor handed the keys of the fortress to General Roberts, and the troops encamped in the neighbourhood.   This part of the country was very different to the wild mountains they had lately passed through, being rich in corn and fruit, the people bringing quantities of delicious grapes for sale.

While the Gordons were passing through the streets of Ghazni with the pipes playing, a white man in Afghan dress was observed dancing.   He could speak no English beyond that his name was Dawson.   It appeared that he had been stolen when a child from Peshawar and brought up as an Afghan.   He was employed at the officers' mess till, on the regiment returning to India, he went off and was never heard of more.   Here a large and handsome dog attached himself to the regiment.   He was named "Ghazi," became a great favourite, was wounded at Majuba, and died in Guernsey.

The next march was over a barren but open country, where the brigades marched in parallel columns of route. A terrific dust storm was blowing, the First Brigade lost its way and the rear guard did not get into camp till long after dark, men and beasts much exhausted ; indeed, many soldiers were so done up that they did not attempt to cook, but slept supperless. It being now moonlight, they turned out at 1 a.m. and marched at 2.30 in order to get in early and avoid the heat of the day, though the rear guard did not arrive till the afternoon. Still the troops had ample time to collect fuel, for which sometimes houses had to be bought and pulled down, and to cook the liberal rations supplied (each company had three native cooks). All not on duty turned in at 7.30, but the piquet duty was heavy, and the men seldom had more than three consecutive nights in bed.

From Mukar to Panjak on the 20th was one of the worst marches, not so much on account of the distance (twenty-one miles) as from want of water and the excessive heat of the sun, from which there was no shade on the arid plain ; and many, especially of the native troops and followers, suffered terribly from thirst. On the 21st, camp was on the bank of the river Turnak, where they heard of an unsuccessful sortie made from Kandahar on the 16th, in which General Brooke and eight other officers had been killed. On the 23rd the column reached Kelat-i-Ghilzai, and the British garrison[1] was withdrawn by Sir F. Roberts, who saw no advantage in holding the place longer ; and, finding that there was no imminent danger at Kandahar, the General gave his army a day of welcome rest.

On the 25th the march was resumed, the heat becoming greater daily as they descended to a lower level. At Tirandaz next day the General was informed that Ayub Khan had raised the siege of Kandahar, and was entrenching himself at Mazra in the immediate neighbourhood of the city. Some fear was felt that he might retreat towards Herat without fighting, but the spies afterwards reported that he had determined to wait and give battle.

It may be here mentioned that the General's guard throughout the march was furnished by twenty-four Gordons under Lieutenant Forbes Macbean and Sergeant J. MacFadyen.

On the 27th the General was obliged by an attack of fever to be carried in a doolie, and was unable again to sit a horse till he got to Kandahar. On this day the 3rd Bengal and 3rd Punjab Cavalry marched thirty-four miles to Robat, where heliographic communication was established with the garrison of Kandahar. They were

---

1 Two guns R.A., 145 rifles, 66th Regiment, 100 of the Scinde Horse and 2nd Baluch Regiment—639 ; commanded by Colonel Tanner.

joined next day by the main body.   The column halted at Robat on the 29th, which being Sunday the troops attended divine service. A short march brought them to Momund on the 30th, and on the 31st of August they marched thirteen miles to Kandahar, cheered when they saw the city, and by 9 a.m. the First Brigade had piled arms outside the Shikarpur gate, where the whole garrison turned out to welcome their deliverers.   The defeats they had suffered had depressed and demoralised them, and they expressed their gratitude to the General and his troops for having come so quickly to their assistance ; while, though they were not very cheerful themselves, they provided good cheer in the shape of the best square meal the Highlanders had enjoyed since they left Kabul.

This famous march, in which 10,000 soldiers had been lost to view in an enemy's country, and of whom no intelligence had been received for nearly three weeks, occupied twenty-one marching days and two halts—twenty-three days in all.   The longest march was twenty-two and a half miles to Robat on the 28th, and the average fifteen and a quarter.[1]   It was not the distance so much as the nature of the country and its inhabitants—the choking dust storms and latterly the tremendous heat—the constant piquet and fatigue duties—the length of time under arms and the exertions required of the rear guards in getting the followers and baggage forward—added to the want of sleep, that made it so great a trial of endurance in the troops, and of judgment and determination in their General.   There was little sickness among the Europeans, except such as was caused by the bad water, but more among the native troops and followers, of whom a few died and five were missing, supposed to have been murdered by the country people.

Roberts halted the troops for rest and breakfast outside the south wall of Kandahar, where they were sheltered from the long-range fire of the enemy.   The position of the latter was two and a half miles north of the city.   His line extended for a mile and a half along a high range of hills from the Baba Wali Kotal on his left, to Pir Paimal hill and village on his right ; his camp being pitched at Mazra on the far side of the Baba Wali Pass, while some of his troops occupied hills four miles to the eastward ; a mile west of Pir Paimal was the road to Herat ; in the intervening country was the village of Gundigan, surrounded by walled enclosures and orchards.   There were batteries in position on Pir Paimal and at the Baba Wali Pass ; and on a low hill between the latter and Kandahar was the village of Gundi Mulla Sahibdad, also strongly held by the enemy.   Between Gundi Mulla and the city was a

[1] Duke.

ridge on which were two detached eminences known as Picket Hill on our right and Karez Hill on our left ; the ground was partly enclosed, and through it ran the Herat road, which led by Gundigan to the Argandab Valley.

Roberts determined to take up a position to the west of the city so as to cover it, where was a good water supply and where he would be within striking distance of Ayub Khan's camp ; accordingly the First and Third Brigades occupied Picket Hill, Karez Hill, and the north-east spur of the hill above Old Kandahar. A few shots were fired at the advance guard, and the ground proved to be within range of the enemy's artillery on the Baba Wali Kotal, but it was the only place where water was to be had in sufficient quantity. Large numbers of men were seen crowning the Baba Wali Kotal, and constructing shelter trenches along the crest of a ridge which jutted out into the plain. Piquets were sent to occupy high ground which commanded the road to Gundigan, and also the deserted villages across the valley in front of the British camp.

Having examined the enemy's position, Roberts saw that the Baba Wali Kotal could not be carried by direct attack without great loss : he therefore determined to turn it : and in order to decide how this could best be done, he sent Brigadier-General H. Gough with two guns, the 3rd Bengal Cavalry and the 15th Sikhs, to make a reconnaissance. He started at 1 p.m., accompanied by Lieut.-Colonel Chapman, who, having been at Kandahar with Sir Donald Stewart, knew the country well. Leaving his infantry at Gundigan, Gough advanced with his cavalry towards Pir Paimal, which was found to be strongly entrenched ; he then fell back on his infantry, and brought his guns into action to check the enemy, who were passing into the gardens near Gundigan. The little force then retired within the pickets, the Afghans following in such strength that Roberts ordered the Third and part of the First Brigade under arms, including a contingent from the 92nd. The enemy were driven back after a good deal of skirmishing by the infantry, the 15th Sikhs greatly distinguishing themselves. " Foremost among the many, there could be distinguished the gallant Colonel of the 92nd (Parker), who led on his men ten yards in front, steadily breasting the mountain . . . carrying each successive defence at the point of the bayonet," [1] while in the plain Gough's squadrons charged with great effect, and before dark the troops were back in camp with a total loss of only five killed and fifteen wounded.

From the information obtained by the reconnaissance, Roberts found that it was practicable to turn the enemy's right, and he decided to attack their position the following morning. The

[1] " The Kandahar Campaign," by Major Ashe, 1st Dragoon Guards.

retrograde movement of Gough's party was construed into a defeat by the Afghans, which increased their confidence ; and occasional bursts of musketry during the night, along the line of piquets, showed that the enemy had reoccupied the villages they held before.

PRIVATE, GORDON HIGHLANDERS, AFGHAN WAR, 1879-80

CHAPTER XIV

1880

ON the morning of the 1st September the whole of the troops
were under arms an hour before daybreak, and at 6 a.m.
Roberts explained to Generals Ross and Primrose (the latter commanding the garrison of Kandahar) and the officers commanding
brigades, his plan of operations, which was to threaten the enemy's
left (the Baba Wali Kotal), while the real attack in force was to be
made first by clearing the gardens in front of Gundi Mulla Sahibdad,
then by storming that village,[1] then by turning the Pir Paimal, and
finally taking the Baba Wali in reverse, and Ayub's camp at Mazra
in flank.

At 7 a.m. the troops breakfasted, and officers were desired to
see that each infantry soldier had one day's cooked provisions in his
haversack, and that his water-bottle was filled (the cavalry, who
might probably pursue to a greater distance, had two days' food).
Major Ashe, who was on Roberts' Staff, mentions that he visited
the officers of the Gordons at breakfast, and partook of their oat-
meal porridge. " It was impossible not to be struck with the
splendid appearance and peculiarly fine physique of the Highland
regiments ; their chest measurement, muscular development, and
the bronzed hues of sun and wind giving them a martial appearance
beyond all the other corps."

At eight o'clock the regiment paraded (402 rifles [2]) under
Lieut.-Colonel Parker, and, with the other troops, took up their
ground (tents having been previously struck and baggage stored
in a walled enclosure). The infantry of the Kabul Column, who
were to carry the enemy's position, were formed up in rear of the
low hills which covered the front of the camp, their right being at
Picket Hill and their left resting on Chitral Zina. The cavalry
of the Kabul Column were drawn up in rear of the left, ready to act
by Gundigan and the Arghandab, so as to threaten the rear of
Ayub Khan's camp and his line of retreat. Four guns of E
Battery R.H.A. and six companies of native infantry were also
under Sir Hugh Gough's orders. Lieut.-General Primrose,
leaving guards in the city, was, with Brigadier Daubeny's Brigade,
to take the place of the infantry of the Kabul Column as soon as
they advanced to the attack. He was to place the remains of
Burrows' Brigade and No. 5 Battery 11th Brigade R.A., under
Captain Hornsby, and his cavalry under Brigadier Nuttall, in a
position north of the cantonment, from which the forty-pounders
could be brought to bear on the Baba Wali, while the cavalry could

---

[1] The villages were all fortified.
[2] Regimental Record. Hensman gives 501 of all ranks.

PEN AND INK SKETCH OF BATTLE-FIELD OF KANDAHAR
1st September 1880
FROM
HILLS overlooking GUNDIGAN

KANDAHAR
CITY

GUNDIGAN

watch the pass called Kotal-i-Murcha. About 9.30, Hornsby's guns opened fire on the mass of Ghazis on the Kotal. This feint having the desired effect of attracting the enemy's attention, Roberts gave the order for Major-General Ross to make the real attack with the First Brigade (in which was the 92nd) under Macpherson, and the Second under Baker. The Third, under Brigadier Macgregor, was held in reserve. General Ross entrusted Macpherson with the duty of capturing Gundi Mulla Sahibdad, and of driving the enemy from the enclosures between it and the Pir Paimal hill; while Baker advanced to the west, keeping in touch with Macpherson's Brigade, and clearing the gardens and orchards in his own immediate front. Under cover of the fire of C2 Battery R.A. and the screw guns, Macpherson moved the 2nd Gurkhas and the 92nd towards Gundi Mulla Sahibdad. The 23rd Pioneers remained with the guns, and the 24th Punjabis were in support of the leading battalions ; the Gordons advanced on the right along the foot of the hills, exposed to the fire of the enemy collected above, whose leaders could be seen urging them on, and a portion of them did come down, when some desultory but warm fighting took place. The regiment at the same time met the fire from the walls and roofs of the village in front, which, however, they hardly paused to return. Here Colour-sergeant Richard Fraser was killed ; Private Strachan, severely wounded, was afterwards found dead from sword cuts, still grasping the Afghan who had inflicted them, and who was also dead. Colour-sergeant Coutts was knocked over by a bullet, but his cross-belt saved his life ; while on the ground an Afghan attacked him, but was shot by the sergeant, who, when his wound was dressed, rejoined the ranks. Two companies of the 92nd under Major White, and two of the Gurkhas under Lieut.-Colonel A. Battye, carried the village, the Highlanders and the hillmen of Nepaul rivalling each other in their efforts ; the Gurkhas on the left, having the shorter distance to go, were the first within the walls. The enemy retired slowly, fighting, but a number of Ghazis stood to receive a bayonet charge of the Highlanders, while many shut themselves up in the houses and fired on our men as they passed, and some splendid hand-to-hand fighting occurred. In the *mêlée* Lieutenant Menzies found himself in a courtyard, at the end of which was an open door, and beyond it another door which was locked, but, voices being heard within, the lock was burst by a shot from the officer's pistol, and the door swung open ; instantly a shot from the inside hit Menzies in the groin, and he fell. The only man near at the moment was Drummer Roddick, whom he asked not to leave him. " You're all right, sir, as long as this blade lasts," replied Roddick, as with his drawn claymore [1] he stood over his wounded officer.   A number of Afghans rushed out, and the leader fired, the bullet knocking off Roddick's helmet ; the man then made for him with the muzzle of his rifle, but the stalwart drummer parried the blow, and ran him through with his sword.   At this moment Private Dennis came up ; not liking to put the wounded man in the house, where a lot of bags of grain might conceal a foe, they laid him in the slight shade given by the wall of the court.   Just as they had done so, an Afghan rushed from behind the bags, making a slash at the officer as he passed and cutting his shoulder ; but, fortunately, his blade hit the wall, which broke the force of the blow, and the man was shot by Dennis.   More men joined them, Roddick and Dennis carried the lieutenant to a doolie, and immediately rejoined their company.[2]

The active little Gurkhas delayed here some time, determined to leave nothing in the village alive, and Colonel Parker, taking advantage of this delay, brought his regiment rapidly to the front, extending beyond the village and taking the lead.   While passing close to the village two men, John Fraser and Donald MacLean, clambered up the wall to the flat roof of a low house, on which Ghazis were popping up from below to fire, and the two were seen doing bayonet exercise to good purpose, but their captain called them back, saying, " Leave that work to the Gurkhas."

The regiment, having the 23rd Pioneers to their left, advanced skirmishing, first over a bit of open ground, then through orchards and enclosures intersected by water cuts, some dry, but some containing water which, though muddy, was welcome in the great heat to the thirsty soldiers.   One of them, Lance-corporal Martin M'Lachlan, setting his rifle against a hut, knelt down to drink, and rose to find himself confronted by a tall, fierce-looking Afghan between him and his arms, who at once attacked him sword in hand ; M'Lachlan received the stroke on his left arm, then dashed at the Afghan's throat, knocked him down, and before he could rise had seized his rifle and bayoneted his opponent, when he coolly rejoined his company, but soon had to fall out from loss of blood. While Private Dyer, an Englishman, was passing a broken bridge, an Afghan concealed below fired up at him, but missed ; Dyer aimed at his enemy, but saying—" You 're not worth a bullet, I 'll give you the steel "—he bayoneted him.   Many such dramatic incidents illustrated the nature of the fight, and on such a stage tragedy goes hand in hand with comedy.   " What are you doing

---

[1] The drummers and pipers had claymores ; the band were partly employed with the ambulance, or were in the ranks and carried rifles.

[2] The account of this incident was told me by the late Major (then Lieutenant) Menzies and by Drummer Roddick.   A fine picture has been made of the incident by Skeogh Cumming, which has been reproduced.

there, MacKenzie ? " cried Sergeant-major Ross. "Takin' a deid man oot o' the watter before he 'll be drooned !" replied the Highlandman. The tip of a man's nose was shot off, and as he returned from the ambulance with a bit of burnt cotton stuck on his proboscis to stop the bleeding, his appearance caused great laughter, which in the case of one poor fellow was his last, for a bullet struck him in the mouth at the moment, and killed him.

The enemy were so many on a ridge towards the village of Pir Paimal, and their musketry became so hot, that the regiment was held for a few minutes. General Macpherson remarked on the severity of the fire, and marksmen were told off, who by their steady shooting to some extent checked it ; the General then asked the commanding officer to bring up the pipers. Piper Middleton, who happened to be near, sprang forward and struck up, being quickly joined by others, and the regiment, inspirited by the strains of "The Haughs of Cromdale," rose from cover, dashed on with a cheer and pushed the enemy back. "Fat 's wrang wi' the auld wife the day ?" wondered Middleton as, after a few paces, his pipe refused to speak—a bullet had pierced the bag !

Colonel Parker led his regiment swiftly forward, and the First and Second Brigades joined in the attack on Pir Paimal, for Baker's troops on the left had been threading their way through the narrow lanes and loopholed enclosures which lay in the line of their advance ; they had encountered a continued and stubborn resistance, and overcame it with persevering gallantry, the 72nd Highlanders and the 2nd Sikhs frequently carrying positions, and stopping with the bayonet the desperate rushes of the Afghans. Colonel Brownlow of the 72nd and several other officers and men were killed before both brigades emerged at the point of Pir Paimal hill.

Bringing their left shoulders forward, they pressed on, the Gordons hugging the slope of the Pir Paimal ; while they were advancing, a body of the enemy were stealing down under cover of the trees to attack them in flank, when Private Grieve, who was on the right of the line, noticed the top of their standard and gave the alarm. He was the first of the men who jumped an intervening ditch and repulsed them ; Grieve killed the standard-bearer, but, being too busy to stop, the men did not pick up the standard. The brigades, supported by artillery, swept the enemy through the thickly-wooded gardens which covered the western slopes, and by noon the village had been captured, and the whole of the Pir Paimal was in their possession.

Being now assured of General Ross's success, and there being no further need to detain the Third Brigade, Roberts pushed on with it to join Ross, but that officer, knowing how thoroughly he could depend on his troops, followed up the retreating foe without waiting to be reinforced.   It was difficult ground, and the fighting was continuous, the troops being sometimes stopped by water-courses or walls, from which they fired.   On one of these occasions Private Chapman cautiously raised his head for a shot, when, to the astonishment of his comrades, " the Loon," as he was called, jumped up, dancing about like a madman, with smoke coming out from a hole in his helmet, crying, " My heid 's aff, chaps ! "   It appeared that he carried his pipe and lights in his helmet, and a bullet had ignited the matches and set his hair ablaze, he being more frightened than hurt by this close shave.   During this part of the action, Lieutenant and Adjutant Douglas's horse was shot under him.

At the other side of the Baba Wali Kotal the Afghans made another determined stand.   Ghazis in large numbers flocked from the rear to an entrenched position on the plain ; the enemy's guns on the Baba Wali were brought to bear on our men, who were also exposed to the fire of artillery from their front.   The advanced companies of the 92nd, led by Major White, were lying under fire behind a line of willows, having a small bank and in some parts a ditch, which, however, gave little protection.   White, who was on horseback, could see the muzzles of the latter guns right in front of him in a natural position of great strength ; he could see the enemy were in solid columns a good distance behind their artillery, and he felt that if these masses had time to deploy, and lined the watercourse and bank where their two guns were in position, they could not have been defeated by a frontal attack without great loss and delay.   Now was the time to take it by storm.   He rode along the line, a conspicuous mark to the enemy, saying, " Now, men, we 've got to chalk a ' Ninety-two ' on these guns ! "   The signal was given, and they advanced with a rush in extended order over the level but fire-swept intervening space, supported by a portion of the 2nd Gurkhas and 23rd Pioneers, and covered by the fire of the screw-gun battery.   Once they halted and lay down for a minute to take breath, then the Major called for " Just one more charge to finish the business," when, with a yell rather than a cheer, they up and at it, the pipers swelling the sound as their comrades raced for the guns.   Many fell, but the gallant Major seemed to bear a charmed life as he rode on in front, put his horse at the ditch, and with difficulty scrambled up the opposite bank as his men jumped into the water.   An Afghan, who fired at him as he did so, was killed with others where they stood ; but their gunners left the guns, and Bandsman Gray sat waving his helmet on one, while a Gurkha, who had joined White's men in the charge, put his cap on the muzzle of the other, and catching the Major's stirrup, said to him in Hindustani, "Write down my name, Sahib, for the Order of Merit," which he afterwards got.

Meanwhile Lieut.-Colonel Money with his Sikhs (belonging to the Second Brigade) captured three other guns ; but the nature of the ground made it impossible for General Ross to realise how completely the enemy were routed, and he ordered the First and Second Brigades to halt and replenish their ammunition, and then advance towards Ayub Khan's enormous camp. On nearing it the Gordons, again together, recognised with a cheer the two guns lost at Maiwand on the 27th July, which, with thirty other pieces of artillery, were taken. The whole camp was left standing. When the 92nd came to the splendid tent of Ayub Khan they were horrified to find the body of Lieutenant Maclaine of the Horse Artillery, who had been taken prisoner at Maiwand, lying with the throat cut near Ayub's tent ; he had only socks on his feet, and had evidently been dragged out of his tent and murdered.

Further pursuit by the infantry being valueless, they halted on the far side of Mazra, where the Gordons, with the First Brigade, remained for the night to protect the captured guns and stores, while the other brigades returned to Kandahar, and the cavalry, under Brigadier Hugh Gough, pursued across the Arghandab.

Three British officers and 21 n.c. officers and men were killed in action, and 11 British officers and over 90 men were wounded ; 22 native officers and soldiers were killed and 99 were wounded. Of the total British loss, the Gordon Highlanders had 11 n.c. officers and men killed in action, and Lieutenants S. A. Menzies and Donald W. Stewart and 69 n.c. officers and men were wounded,[1] of whom 9 died of their wounds.[2]

KILLED IN ACTION

Rank and Name.	County.
Colour-sergeant Richard Fraser	Argyll.
Corporal Lewis W. Friendship	England.
Private Alex. Easton	Aberdeen.
Private Thomas W. Kerr	Perth.
Private John M'Kenzie	Born in the regiment at Gibraltar.
Private Robert M'Kenzie	Ross.
Private Wm. Reid	Dumbarton.
Private Neil Ross	Perth.
Private James Scott	Aberdeen.
Private John Strachan	Edinburgh.
Private William Wilson	Lanark.

[1] Regimental Record.
[2] Public Records Office. Birthplaces from Lieutenant Macfadyen (Govan Police) and Mr C. Ross Martin, both at Kandahar in 92nd.

DIED OF WOUNDS

Rank and Name.	County.
Sergeant H. E. D. A. Adams (had been lieutenant in Militia)	England.
Corporal Donald MacPhail	Argyll.
Private Duncan Brimber	Fife.
Private Wm. Davelin	Ireland.
Private Wm. Dixon	England.
Private Wm. Henderson	England.
Private Peter Hoey	Forfar.
Private Allan MacDonald	Argyll.
Private James Wilson	Renfrew.

" It was difficult to estimate the loss of the enemy, but it must have been heavy, as between Kandahar and the village of Pir Paimal alone 600 bodies were buried by us." [1]

It has been seen that the regiment had no small share in the success of the operations by which General Roberts had restored the prestige of the British nation in the East, prevented the interference of Russia, and relieved the defeated and depressed garrison of Kandahar. To commemorate their conduct throughout the campaign, the Royal authority was afterwards received for the words "Charasia," "Kabul, 1879," "Kandahar," and "Afghanistan, 1878-80," to be inscribed on the regimental colour.

Her Majesty the Queen-Empress was graciously pleased to confer a special war medal, with clasps for the various actions, on the officers, n.c. officers and soldiers, European and Indian, and also a bronze star for the march to Kandahar.

Brigadier-General Macpherson reported favourably of the following officers of the 92nd, viz. :—Lieut.-Colonel G. H. Parker, Major G. S. White, Surgeon-Major S. B. Roe, Captain A. D. M'Gregor, D.A.Q.M.G., and Lieutenant and Adjutant C. W. H. Douglas.

In recognition of their services during the campaign, Lieut.-Colonel George Hubert Parker and Major George Stewart White were afterwards made Companions of the Most Honourable Order of the Bath. Major White was promoted Brevet Lieut.-Colonel, and the decoration of the Victoria Cross, inscribed with the dates October 6th, 1879, and September 1st, 1880, was conferred upon him " for conspicuous bravery " on those two occasions, as has been described above.

Lieut.-General Sir F. Roberts recorded his opinion of the excellent services performed by Major White, Captains Singleton, Darvall, and Hon. J. S. Napier, Lieutenant and Adjutant Douglas, and Lieutenant Dick-Cunyngham.

[1] Lord Roberts.

Captains Loftus Corbet Singleton, Alexander Donald M'Gregor, Duncan Forbes Gordon, the Hon. John Scott Napier, and Charles Whittingham Horsley Douglas were afterwards promoted Brevet Majors.

The medal " for Distinguished Conduct in the Field " at Kandahar was conferred on Corporal William M'Gilivray, who, during the whole day, showed an example of bravery which was the admiration both of his superiors and his comrades—a native of Pettie, Inverness-shire ; Drummer James Roddick, from Ecclefechan, Dumfriesshire ; Privates John Dennis and David Gray, from Glasgow and Campsie ; and Peter Grieve, from Aberdeenshire (the deeds of these four are described above) ; also James Mackintosh, from Strathdearn, Inverness-shire, who, being wounded in the leg during the early part of the action, was ordered to fall out.   He complied so far as to bandage the wound, when he returned to the ranks ; but as it still bled profusely, he was again told to go to the rear, and appeared to assent, but saying to his comrades, " He 'll no fa' oot when this work 's going on ! " continued to do his duty till, when his company was re-formed at the halt after the charge for the guns, he was found to be unable to stand from loss of blood.   His captain gave him a pull at his flask, and clapping him on the shoulder, complimented him, sent him to hospital in a doolie, and reported his gallant conduct.

Nothing could better illustrate the changing system of military rewards than the number of officers and soldiers mentioned in dispatches at this period, as compared with the time of the great French War, when only those in very responsible positions were noticed, and, with rare exceptions, no names of regimental officers under field rank, or of soldiers, were officially published.[1]

A remarkable instance of the fulfilment of a presentiment is related by Lieutenant MacFadyen of the Govan Constabulary, late sergeant in the Gordons.   On the 23rd August 1880, while on the march to Kandahar, Private Allan MacDonald, G Company, a native of the Island of Coll, Argyllshire, told him in confidence of a dream which had deeply impressed him.   He said he had dreamed the previous night that he was in battle, when a bullet struck him in the forehead, and that he died as it was being extracted.   The sergeant made light of it and tried to cheer him up, but in vain. He had forgotten the circumstance, when on the 28th the man told him that the dream had been repeated.   Shortly before capturing the enemy's guns at the battle of Kandahar, the sergeant, seeing him alive, called out, " Hullo, Allan, you are still safe," and

---

[1] After the battle of St Pierre, the names of a number of officers of junior rank were brought to the notice of Wellington, but he declined to mention them on the ground that he could not do so without being unjust to others.

he answered with a smile, " Oh yes, I 'm all right yet." Never-theless, the dream was fulfilled. One of the last shots from the hill struck poor Allan in the forehead, and a day or two later, as the bullet was being extracted, he died under the doctor's hands. Among the wounded was a young man from Strathspey named Grant, an enthusiastic musician, whose ambition it was to become a regimental piper. Two of his fingers had been shot off ; the surgeon, while dressing the wound, observed a tear in the lad's eye, and remarked that the pain would soon be over. " I don't mind the pain, sir," replied Grant, " but that I will never more play the pipe."

The day after the battle, the regiment encamped outside the city of Kandahar, where they attended the funeral of the officers and soldiers who had fallen. While here they received clothing, of which they were much in need, rested, and had time to write to anxious friends more or less correct accounts of their adventures. " There 'll be a gey heap o' lees sent hame the day," was the cynical remark of a soldier on the correspondents ! The attitude of the people, however, among whom there were many dangerous fanatics, was such that the troops were obliged to do their shopping armed and in parties ; while one made his bargain the others guarded him till each in turn had bought what he wanted.

The following incident of the march shows that the Gordons always kept up their character for smartness as well as for bravery. When they got into heliographic communication with Kandahar, the garrison asked if they could do anything for them, when, to the astonishment of the besieged, who were not in a frame of mind to think much about appearances, Lieutenant and Adjutant Douglas replied, " Buy up all the pipeclay in Kandahar for me." This was done, and the day after the battle the 92nd shone distinguished from the other regiments by belts as white as those of the Queen's guard at St James's.

On the 8th September, Sir Frederick Roberts, who was in bad health, left for Quetta with the Third Brigade. Speaking of his army, he says :—" Never had a commander been better served. From first to last a grand spirit of *camaraderie* pervaded all ranks. . . . Notwithstanding the provocation caused by the cruel murder of any stragglers who fell into the hands of the Afghans, not one act infringing the rules of civilised warfare was committed by the troops. . . . The conduct of the troops will ever be to me as pleasing a memory as are the results which they achieved." [1]

[1] The conduct of the British army in war was thus noticed by Napoleon : " Had I had an English army I should have conquered the universe, for I could have gone all over the world without demoralising my troops."

Again, speaking of Waterloo—" The English won by the excellence of their discipline."
—" Napoleon, the Last Phase," by Lord Rosebery.

In a letter to Lieut.-Colonel Parker, General Roberts said, " You must be proud of commanding such a regiment, which I am sure is second to none, and which I sincerely hope I may have with me if ever I am fortunate enough to hold another command on active service " ; and when made a G.C.B. he, like Sir John Moore, chose a Gordon Highlander as a supporter for his coat of arms, the other being a soldier of the 5th Gurkhas.

On the 14th February 1881, on being presented with the Freedom of the City of London and a sword of honour by the Corporation, Sir Frederick emphasised the advantage to a Commander of having seasoned troops, and instanced the 92nd, whose sergeants, he said, averaged fifteen, corporals eleven, and privates nine years' service. He mentioned that between the first and second phases of the Afghan War some 150 men of the regiment, whose first period of service had expired, expressed their readiness to re-engage on the express condition that they were not to be liable to be transferred to another regiment, according to the then " Brigade " system. The authorities in England, on being referred to, allowed a special relaxation of the rule, with the result that these men, " when every tried soldier was worth his weight in gold," remained in the service.

Like Sir Rowland Hill in the Peninsula, Sir Frederick Roberts not only possessed the implicit confidence of officers and soldiers as their leader, but was regarded by them as their friend. The chorus of a marching song, which was a great favourite among the men, expresses this feeling sincerely, if not very poetically, and alludes to the ungenerous and carping criticisms of part of the English Press in whose eyes those in command are always wrong :—

> There is a jovial Irishman, whose name I need not tell,
> He 's just the man for a brilliant dash, and that we know right well.
> A better we could not have here—no matter how they blame,
> Old England trust him—so do we—and Roberts is his name !

While on the subject of singing, it may be mentioned that a Gaelic song in praise of the Gordons in Afghanistan was sung before an immense gathering of Highlanders in Glasgow, and received with tremendous applause. It is given in Appendix III.

On the 28th September the regiment marched from Kandahar for India,[1] arriving, October 21st, at Meean Mir, where Brigadier-General Macpherson's farewell order was published. In it " he

NOTE.—Throughout the campaign the Highland dress was worn by officers and men, generally with khaki jackets. Officers had "Sam Browne" belts, not so convenient, in the opinion of some people, as the Highland fashion, which carries the sword in a belt across the back. The basket hilt of the officers' claymores was removed to suit the "Sam Browne," thereby losing the most efficient guard for the wrist.

[1] Field officer, 1 ; captains, 4 ; subs., 11 ; staff, 3 ; sergeants, 37 ; corporals, 28 ; drummers, 20 ; privates, 539—total, 643.

offers his best thanks to all ranks of the 92nd for having contributed to make his command of the First Brigade a real pleasure. The conduct of the regiment in quarters has been admirable, and its bearing in action invariably elicited the admiration of our countrymen.   A useful lesson should be gained from the battle of Mazra,[1] for the Brigadier considers that by the determined and rapid advance of the 92nd on that day, an immense loss of life was saved, and Sirdar Eyoob Khan was unable to get away his guns."

RIFLEMAN, 5TH GURKHAS.

He congratulates Colonel Parker on the efficient state in which the regiment was maintained : " a condition for which the only word is—perfection."

[1] Kandahar.

NOTE.—The officers present in the action at Kandahar were :—

Lieut.-Colonel H. Parker.	Lieutenant R. A. Grant.
Major G. Stewart White.	„ A. D. Fraser.
Captain L. C. Singleton.	„ Forbes Macbean.
„ Hon. J. Scott Napier.	„ H. Wright.
„ R. F. Darvall.	„ D. W. Stewart.
Lieutenant S. A. Menzies.	„ H. A. MacDonald.
„ H. Bayly.	„ G. Staunton
„ W. H. Dick-Cunyngham.	„ and Adjutant C. W. H.
„ F. F. Ramsay.	Douglas.

NOTE.—The above account of the Afghan campaign is taken chiefly from Lord Roberts' " Forty-One Years in India," Mr Hensman's and Surgeon-Colonel Duke's narratives.   The details are from the Regimental Record and from notes by Lieut.-General Sir G. S. White, V.C., G.C.B. ; Major-General C. W. H. Douglas, Colonel Oxley, Majors D. F. Gordon and A. D. M'Gregor, Captain the Hon. R. A. Grant ; Lieutenant of Police J. MacFadyen, late sergeant ; Mr Hugh Tulloch, late colour-sergeant ; Mr C. Ross Martin, late sergeant ; ex-Drummer Roddick, and Mr J. Fraser, late private, 92nd.

At Meean Mir a dinner was given to the men of the 72nd and 92nd by the Scottish ladies and gentlemen resident in the Punjab. An address expressing the appreciation of their conduct by their compatriots was read to them ; afterwards the committee called for Scotch and Gaelic songs.   In the latter, Private Angus M'Leod from South Uist and many others were greatly applauded. Games followed, when the Gordons won the tug-of-war after a severe struggle ; also the hammer, the stone, and dancing, besides several second prizes.[1]

5th December.—The regiment arrived at Cawnpore, where they kept New Year's Day, 1881, and as they were under orders for home, those who wished to remain in India were allowed to volunteer.   Two sergeants, one lance-sergeant, and thirty-eight privates were accordingly transferred to other regiments.

[1] Mr Ross Martin, at that time sergeant.

CHAPTER XV

1881

THE adventures of the regiment were, however, by no means over, for on the 6th January the following telegram was received :—" The 92nd Highlanders are to embark for Natal immediately instead of going to England, to be completed in arms and equipment, to take 200 rounds of ammunition per rifle, and the Kabul scale of entrenching tools."

On the 9th of January 1881, the regiment, under Lieut.-Colonel Parker, arrived at Deolali, where, in a farewell order to the 15th Hussars, 2nd 60th Rifles, and 92nd Gordon Highlanders, the regiments leaving India for Natal, His Excellency the Commander-in-Chief said, " To recount the services of the 92nd would be to write the history of the second phase of the Afghan war. From Charasia to Kandahar the 92nd has always been conspicuous for its gallantry and discipline."

At Bombay, ninety-eight invalids and time-expired men were left for conveyance to England ; and it is sad to find that in a body of men so remarkable for their conduct, two should have so disgraced themselves as to be discharged with ignominy. The women and children were also left behind with a view to their being sent to England, and on January 14th the regiment embarked on board H.M.S. *Crocodile* for South Africa, a country destined to be the scene of many most important events in the life of the Regiment, both in the immediate and more distant future.

It may not be out of place to give a slight sketch of the political circumstances which led to such far-reaching results.

The Cape of Good Hope had been discovered by the Portuguese in 1486, and used as a harbour of rest on the road to their Indian possessions. On the decline of the power of Portugal, the Dutch established a colony at the Cape in 1652, which thirty years later received the addition of a number of French Protestants, who may still be traced by such names as Joubert, Du Plessis, Delarey.

Throughout the 18th century the country was governed by the Dutch East India Company, whose rule was tyrannical and harassing to the settlers. The Boers, or wandering farmers, were especially discontented, and in 1795 they broke into open rebellion. The French Revolution found many sympathisers among the Dutch, and, fearing that the Cape might fall into the hands of the French, the British Government took possession in 1795. By the Treaty of Amiens[1] the Cape was given back to the Dutch in February 1803, but shortly afterwards war again broke out between Great Britain, France and Holland, and on January 4th, 1806, a British fleet once

---

[1] See art. Cape Colony, " Ency. Brit."

more anchored in Table Bay.   In the battle of Blueberg, Sir David
Baird defeated the Dutch, and the Governor capitulated.   The
country was ruled as a conquered territory till the peace of 1814,
when, by the general settlement at the Congress of Vienna, the
Kingdom of the Netherlands was restored and enlarged, and a
convention was signed whereby the Dutch possessions in South
Africa were formally handed over to England by the Netherlands,
in consideration of a sum of £6,000,000.   So that England has
possessed them ever since, by right both of conquest and of
purchase.

The British rule, though not altogether satisfactory to the
colonists, was a great improvement on that of the Dutch East
India Company, and there would probably have been no serious
discontent but for the native question.   Slavery was abolished in
1834, the slaves to be entirely free by December 1st, 1838.   The
manner in which the abolition was carried out caused great dissatisfaction, and a large number of Boers determined to seek new
homes, far from modern civilisation.   The Government permitted
them to do so, but did not allow that they thereby ceased to be
British subjects.   They went to Natal, where they set up a
Republic ; but in 1843 Natal, with the consent of the emigrants,
became a British colony, and in 1848 the sovereignty of Queen
Victoria was proclaimed over the whole country between the Orange
River and the Vaal.   The Republican party on both sides of the
Vaal tried to prevent this arrangement, but were defeated, and
retired over the Vaal, where the British Government guaranteed
them the right, but only under certain restrictions, to manage their
own affairs.   In 1854 the British withdrew from the Orange River
sovereignty, and made it into a Republic, entirely against the
strongly expressed wish of the inhabitants, both British and Dutch,
to remain British subjects.

The Transvaal had been split into four Republics, till in 1864
they united as the " South African Republic," with Pretorius as
President and Paul Kruger as Commandant General.   In 1876
the Republic was bankrupt, and was threatened with native invasion,
so that a large proportion of the burghers expressed their desire for
British protection.   On the 12th of April 1877, the proclamation
of annexation was read in the Market Square of Pretoria, and was
received with satisfaction both by the people and the Press.   The
result was an immediate revival of prosperity ; the public debt
was paid, British troops protected the country from native risings,
and the Zulu power was broken.[1]   But now that their country was
solvent and flourishing the Boers began to regret their independence,
and this feeling was stimulated by the reactionary party led by

---

[1] The battle of Ulundi, 1879.

Kruger and Joubert ; the British Government had failed as yet to establish the promised representative Government, and there was neither a sufficient police force nor a proper garrison to keep order, or to protect the farmers from being terrorised into joining the irreconcilables.

At the Midlothian election Mr Gladstone had denounced the annexation, which encouraged the Boer leaders ; but when the Liberal party succeeded to power he announced that it would be adhered to. The Transvaal revolted, and the Republic was proclaimed on December 15th, 1880. On the 16th an ultimatum was sent to the Governor (Sir Owen Lanyon) ; on the same day the garrison of Potchefstroom was attacked. On the 20th the Boers laid an ambush at Bronkerspruit for the headquarters (two companies) of the 94th Regiment, who were marching to Pretoria with the band playing, thinking no evil. Colonel Anstruther was told he must turn back, and immediately on his refusal a murderous volley from all sides killed 56 officers and men, including the colonel ; 101 were wounded, and the rest taken prisoners.

A large number of the Boers were against the rebellion, but they were at the mercy of the revolutionists, whose success enabled them to coerce the loyalists. Natal was invaded and Laing's Nek seized. On the 28th January, Sir George Colley, Governor of Natal, attacked 2000 Boers on the Nek with 570 men, and was repulsed with loss.

Such was the state of affairs when, on January 30th, 1881, the Gordon Highlanders, under Colonel Parker, landed at Durban, where they were presented with an address signed by 105 Scottish residents.[1] Next day they reached Pietermaritzburg, where they were cheered to the echo, and handsomely treated by the inhabitants.

On the 8th February, Sir George Colley had moved with a small force of thirty-eight cavalry, four guns and about 280 infantry [2] from his camp at Mount Prospect to reopen his communications, which were threatened, but was obliged to retire from Ingogo with loss.

The 92nd moved to camp at Newcastle, where they arrived on the 16th, on which day Colley was instructed by the Home Government to inform Kruger that " if the Boers will desist from armed opposition, we shall be ready (with reference to certain proposals for the ultimate government of the Transvaal) to appoint commissioners with extensive powers. . . . If this proposal

---

[1] Strength on disembarking—Field officers, 2 ; captains, 6 ; subs., 7 ; staff, 6 ; sergeants, 41 ; corporals, 33 ; drummers, 19 ; privates, 587—total, 701.
[2] Sir W. Butler's " Life of Sir George Colley."

is accepted, you are authorised to agree to the suspension of hostilities." [1]

On the 19th two companies of the 92nd under Major J. C. Hay made a reconnaissance to a drift on the Utrecht road, which they held while Major-General Sir E. Wood, V.C., K.C.B., crossed the Buffalo River and pushed his reconnaissance with the cavalry towards Utrecht and Wakkerstroom.   On the 23rd the regiment arrived at Mount Prospect, where Sir George Colley, who had been to Newcastle, returned and found the Boers were actively fortifying Laing's Nek.   On the same evening he wrote to Mr Childers, Secretary of State for War, that the Boers were occupying more advanced positions, and that he might have to seize some ground between Laing's Nek and Mount Prospect which had been hitherto practically unoccupied by either party, without waiting for Kruger's reply.   " But I will not, without strong reasons, undertake any operation likely to bring on another engagement until Kruger's reply is received."   Colley waited three days for the reply, which never came.[2]

On the 26th, Captain Douglas, with D and E Companies, made a reconnaissance towards Buffalo River, and on the evening of that day Sir George Colley, accompanied by a detachment of his troops, started on the secret [3] expedition which ended so tragically for them and for himself, and which the fateful action of Mr Gladstone's Government turned into a political disaster to the British name and power in South Africa.

Although only a detachment of the Gordon Higlanders was present at the defeat on Majuba Mountain, the incident is specially noticed in the Regimental Record, which states that " the greatest misrepresentation has prevailed about the details of the action and the cause which led to its disastrous result."

The death of Sir George Colley, who fell facing his foes, to a great extent disarmed criticism : some accounts written afterwards were perhaps to a certain extent a plea for the gallant and unfortunate General : descriptions of the various phases of the fight vary according to the point of view of the narrator, and some of the statements published reflecting on the conduct of the troops are characterised by Major (afterwards General) Hay as " utter rubbish " and " pure invention." [4]   He and the other officers of the 92nd who were present are unanimous in not blaming the men, and in this they are borne out by the official report.   " The conduct of the 92nd was excellent throughout."

[1] " Life of the Rt. Hon. H. Childers," by Lieut.-Colonel Spencer Childers.
[2] *Ibid.*
[3] Major M'Gregor, A.D.C. to Colley, writes that when told by the General to warn the troops at 8 p.m., " I had no idea where they were going to."
[4] " Story of Majuba," by J. Cromb.

The following is Sir Evelyn Wood's letter forwarding the report of the action in general :—

From the GENERAL OFFICER COMMANDING, Natal, to the
SECRETARY OF STATE FOR WAR

CAMP, NEWCASTLE, *March* 9, 1881.

SIR,—In submitting the accompanying report from Major Fraser, Royal Engineers, the senior effective officer remaining from those engaged on the 27th February, I desire to bring to your notice the good service rendered by this officer. After being the foremost to scale the mountain, he descended again for the purpose of hurrying up the men, and was one of the last staff officers to quit the ridge. While in the act of withdrawing he fell over a rock and injured his hand, but with great endurance and determination he walked from 1 p.m. on Sunday until 2 a.m. on Tuesday without tasting food, ultimately regaining our lines through the Boer position.

Had Major-General Sir George Pomeroy-Colley survived, he would, I have no doubt, have endorsed all that Major Fraser has written with regard to the conduct of both officers and men in the fight on the Majuba Mountain, and, therefore, although the result of the action was disastrous, I feel confidence in submitting for favourable consideration the names of those mentioned in the report.

To what has been adduced in that report with regard to the conduct of Captain M'Gregor, 92nd Highlanders, I would in addition bear testimony to the activity he displayed during the march up country, conduct which induced me to recommend him for staff employment to Sir G. Colley, who subsequently informed me that he had decided to appoint Captain M'Gregor to his staff as an aide-de-camp.

From independent sources I have heard much of the conspicuous gallantry displayed by Lieutenant Lucy, 58th Regiment, by Lieutenant Hamilton and Second-Lieutenant MacDonald, 92nd Highlanders,[1] by Corporal Farmer, Army Hospital Corps, and by No. 1865, Private John Murray, 92nd Highlanders. I recommend Corporal Farmer to favourable consideration for the Victoria Cross, and Private Murray for the Distinguished Service Medal.

Corporal Farmer showed a spirit of self-abnegation and an example of cool bravery which cannot be too highly commended. While the Boers closed with our troops near the wells, Corporal Farmer held a white flag over the wounded, and when the arm holding the flag was shot through, he called out that he had " another." He then raised the flag with the other arm and continued to do so until that also was pierced with a bullet.

Private John Murray was close to the brow over our line of advance during the final forward movement of the Boers. A Scotsman in the Boer ranks called upon Private Murray to surrender. The latter replied, " I 'll see you d——d first," and jumped down, receiving a bullet wound in the arm. Half-way down the hill his knee fell out of joint, but obtaining the assistance of a comrade to restore it to place, he returned at six o'clock with his rifle and side-arms to camp, where he was seen by Second-Lieutenant Sinclair Wemyss, 92nd Highlanders.[2]—I have, etc.

(Signed) EVELYN WOOD, Major-General,
Commanding Forces in Natal and Transvaal.

[1] Afterwards General Sir Ian Hamilton, Colonel of the Gordon Highlanders, and Major-General Sir Hector MacDonald.

[2] Some fugitives arrived at Mount Prospect without their arms.

PLAN OF COUNTRY
ROUND ABOUT MAJUBA AND LANG'S NEK
SHOWING LINE OF ADVANCE,
26TH FEBRUARY 1881.
REDUCED FROM A SKETCH BY LT. BROTHERTON, R.E.,
AND MAJOR FRASER, R.E.

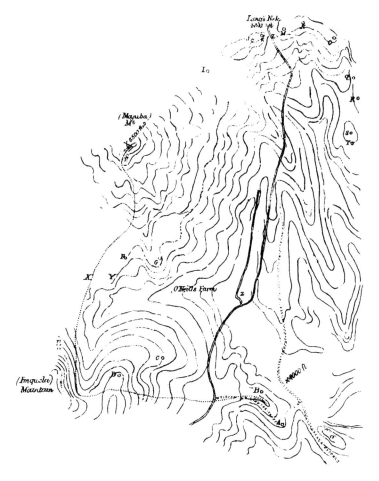

No. I.

About: ⊢———————|———————0———————|———————⊣ 2 miles

From Major FRASER, R.E., D.A.Q.M.G. to the
GENERAL OFFICER COMMANDING, Natal

NEWCASTLE, *March* 5, 1881.

SIR,—I have the honour to report that, at 3.30 p.m., on the 26th instant [ulto.], I was ordered by General Colley to accompany him with a force he proposed to take to the top of the Majuba Height at 9.30 p.m.

This point commands the position of Laing's Nek (*see* map [No. 2]).

Orders were issued at 8 p.m. for the following to parade at 9.30 p.m. (at B, *see* sketch [No. 1]), viz. :—

3 companies, 92nd Highlanders (Major Hay and 180 rifles).
2 companies, 3/60th (Captain Smith and 140 rifles).
2 companies, 58th (Captain Morris and 170 rifles).
Naval Brigade (Commander Romilly and 64 rifles).[1]

The whole were ordered to have greatcoats, waterproof sheets, 3 days' rations, and 6 picks and 4 shovels per company.

I was ordered to lead column, and was furnished with two local guides. The night was bright, but there was no moon.   Our line of advance is marked in yellow on the sketch.   [No. 1.]

We started at 10 p.m. in the following order, viz., 58th, 60th, 92nd, Naval Brigade.

The column halted near " D " at 11 p.m.   Two companies 60th were detached, and left with orders to send some men to occupy the top of Imguela, and to cover the general movement.   The column then moved northward through a defile as far as " E," where it gained the neck between Imguela and Majuba.   The head halted at " X," and I was ordered to fetch a company of the 92nd to " Y," where the General posted it, with instructions to entrench.[2] I reported, from Major Hay, that the rear company 92nd and Naval Brigade were missing, and was told to find them.   I did so at " E," and brought them up to " X."   At 1.30 a.m., column proceeded to the foot of the mountain, whence we ascended some way without difficulty.   The guides were doubtful of the way, but we went straight up along a stone-covered ridge from " H " to (1). (*See* sketch of hill top [No. 3].)   I reached (1) at 3.40 a.m., found hill unoccupied, and took steps to extend the 58th towards (2), to make way for the column.   On the General's arrival immediately afterwards, Colonel Stewart and myself were sent down to hurry up the column.   The men, heavily weighted as they were, had made extraordinary efforts to reach the top, and were extremely exhausted.   On our return they were extended all round the brow, showing on the sky line.   The Boers were entirely ignorant of our movements.   General Colley forbade firing on some of them below

---

[1] Total, 554 rifles.   Of these, the two companies 60th and one company 92nd, detached, numbered together 200 (according to Regimental Record), so that the number who continued the ascent was 354, of whom the 92nd numbered 120 ; but before reaching the top two men had to be sent back with sprained ankles, as mentioned by the late General Hay, and vouched by Sir Ian Hamilton.   So that the 92nd actually on the top amounted to 118 rifles, and the total force to 352 rifles.

[2] Captain Robertson's company.

us, but some shots were fired without orders at about 5.45 a.m.[1] 16 men were posted at " H," and a few at (5). The General now organised the defence as follows :—

To the 92nd was assigned the whole brow from (6) by (5), round to between (4) and (3). One company extended, the other in reserve in rear of the ridge (7), (9). One company of the 58th was ordered to hold the brow from (3) by (2) to (1), the other company in reserve with the 92nd. The sailors extended from (1) to (10), keeping a small reserve with the others. The General thought the troops were too exhausted for any systematic entrenchment, but the extended men made cover of stones and turf, etc.,[2] and two wells were dug where shown.

We looked down upon the whole position of Laing's Nek, and saw three large Boer waggon laagers in rear of it, at 2000 to 3000 yards to north-west ; and a fourth about 1500 yards to west of us. Shortly after 6 a.m. the Boers began a desultory fire. They inspanned their oxen in the laagers, and stood ready to go. At the same time, reinforcements, mounted and on foot, kept coming up. We counted 160 men in one party alone. These all worked up skilfully under cover till within 600 yards from the brow, and then kept up a rapid fire on us. Our men fired very slowly and steadily, to save ammunition. About 10.15 a.m., Colonel Stewart and I went with the General to (11), where Commander Romilly stood, to arrange to start the sailors on an entrenchment at (1). Commander Romilly was shot between us by men from below, firing from the south-west. Finding the ground so exposed, the General did not give the order to entrench. The fire somewhat slackened till 11.30 a.m. By this time the Boers had advanced up the steep slopes, which were unseen from our shooting line. They were massed under cover, and then moved up rapidly. Some 15 or 20 of our men were now sent up the rocky peak (6) on our extreme left, and a few sailors were sent to (1) to guard our rear there. Colonel Stewart, myself, and others took the rest of the reserves and reinforced the shooting line about 12 noon, but not finding room for these supports whence they could shoot down the brow, we withdrew, and posted them on a second ridge (7, 4) about 12.15 to 12.30 p.m. The sailors at (1) now came running down, saying they were attacked from the east. We sent them back to do the best they could. As the Boers closed, General Colley was at (9), Colonel Stewart next him, and I was on the left, towards (7) ; all in the shooting line. We had succeeded in getting the men to fix bayonets. The attack advanced, firing so rapidly we could only see their rifles through the smoke as they crept up. Ours fired repeatedly, and fell fast. They began to retreat and make for the last ridge (12) about 12.45 p.m. Colonel Stewart ran back to rally them, and failing to do

---

[1] Captain H. Wright, in a statement quoted in " The Story of Majuba," by J. Cromb, says the shot was fired from between points 3 and 1 in the Plan " against orders." In reference to this, General Hay wrote : " When the shot in question was fired I thought it contrary to orders, and at once started for the spot where the shot in question had been fired. On my way I met Sir George Colley, and he told me he had given orders or permission for the firing. Captain Wright having received orders that there was to be no firing, would naturally imagine that the shot was fired against orders."

[2] These little entrenchments were afterwards seen by Major Douglas and other officers, and were described as " white with bullet marks."—Regimental Record.

LEFT.

VIEW FROM CAMP EXTENDING FROM MAQUELA TO BUFFALO RIVER.

so was returning to General Colley, when the latter fell.   As the Boers came up to the rocky ridge the remainder of our men fell back after the others.

I now went after our retreating men, walking from the hollow towards the point (11), feeling too exhausted to catch up the men ; as I was near the hollow I saw General Colley, with a few men, moving back near the wells. He turned round to face the enemy, and fell shot through the head by fire from the rocky ridge which we had just left.   When I got between (11 and 1) our men were passing over the ridge (1 and 2).

Fresh firing parties now opened on me from below (6), and in seeking shelter I went down the precipitous hill side, 200 or 300 feet.

About midnight of the 26th-27th, a third company of the 60th, with a small ammunition column, destined by General Colley to come up to us on the afternoon of the 27th, joined the company [92nd] at " Y " ; they were entrenched.[1]   An order was sent from camp about 2 p.m. on the 27th, for these companies to retire.   After leaving their entrenchments, about 3 p.m., they were attacked by Boers advancing from Majuba, but were in part covered by the two companies of the 60th, under Imguela, and by a troop of dismounted Hussars (15th) sent up from camp.   All these troops retreated without much loss.

About 1.30 to 2 p.m., when our retreat was ascertained, two guns and two companies of the 92nd were sent out about a mile north of the camp, so as to check pursuit.

By these means the retreat was partly covered.

I am informed the "assembly" sounded in camp at 3 p.m., and the garrison went into entrenchments.

Throughout the movement, and during the whole of the action, Colonel Stewart seconded the General with great activity and coolness.   Commander Romilly, R.N., Major Hay, 92nd Regiment, and Captain Morris, 58th Regiment, all gave him unremitting support.

The following were conspicuous for gallant conduct, viz. :—

Lieutenant Hamilton, 92nd Regiment, and Lieutenant Lucy, 58th Regiment ; both were exposed to severe fire during seven hours.   Lieutenants Wright and MacDonald, 92nd Regiment, behaved with the greatest coolness and courage, and to the last made every effort to turn the course of events. Captain M'Gregor, 92nd Regiment, exposed himself constantly with the men of his regiment, in addition to performing his duties as aide-de-camp. Corporal Farmer, of the Army Hospital Corps, held a white flag over the wounded as the Boers closed near the wells ; when he was shot through that arm, he called out he had " another," and held up the flag with his other arm till shot through that also.

Nothing could exceed the devotion of Drs Landon and Cornish, both of whom lost their lives in the discharge of their duties.

The conduct of the 92nd was excellent throughout ; many whose names I cannot recall, or did not know, behaved with coolness, and their shooting was uniformly steady.

After submitting causes of failure, the Report adds :—

It is only right I should mention that owing, I presume, to its being

---

[1] See plan No. 2.

constantly patrolled by Boer scouts, the Majuba had not been reconnoitred beforehand. I must also add that, although I saw a few men very short of ammunition, my belief is that many had 20 to 40 rounds remaining before the final attack.—I have, etc.

(Signed)   T. FRASER, Major, R.E., D.A.Q.M.G.

The top of Majuba is thus described by Lieut.-General Sir W. F. Butler in " The Life of Sir George Pomeroy Colley, K.C.S.I., C.B., C.M.G." :—

The shallow depression dipping from the encircling rim occupied almost the entire mountain top. The floor of this depression was from 10 to 40 feet lower than the edge, viz., some 40 feet lower than the south edge of the mountain (that nearest to the British camp), and from 10 to 20 feet lower than the northern, or Boer, side. The rim of this hollow, which measured 900 yards round, was composed largely of rocky outcrop. It was nearly coterminous with the edge of the summit on its south and west sides, but at its northern side (that nearest to the Boers) the space at top sloped for some distance before the steep outer brow of the volcanic hill was reached. Thus the edge of the hollow nearest to the Boer camps was not the edge of the Majuba Hill itself, but on that side there was a grassy roll or slope, descending some 40 feet in a distance of from 50 to 100 yards, between the rim of the basin and the true brow of the mountain. As the inner edge of rocks did not command the steep outer drop of the mountain side, it was necessary to make the line of defence taken by the soldiers follow the outer circuit, which measured about 1200 yards in perimeter. From this outer circuit two or three steep isolated spurs of rock projected. One abrupt rocky eminence, or koppie, stood at the north-western angle of the summit, and another on the western face. On the inner rim also small eminences arose, forming the highest points of the summit—from 6500 to 7000 feet above sea-level. Below the brow the hill plunged down so abruptly that a considerable part of the lower mountain was invisible to men at top.

Sir George and the chief of his staff appear to have considered the position sufficiently good. " This sense of security," says Sir W. Butler, " was the real explanation of the non-entrenchment " ; and their opinion was probably shared by many of the officers and men, but by no means by all, as is evident from the requests made by Major Hay and others to be allowed to entrench.[1] Meanwhile :

The practised eye of Commandant Smidt had discovered that the force holding the mountain was not a large one, and the word had been given to storm the summit. For this duty two small separate bodies of Boers, all tried men and deadly shots, were told off under different leaders. These bands were to climb the mountain at different places and await, at spots not far below

---

[1] In a letter, dated July 30, 1901, Colonel A. D. M'Gregor writes : " The position, you will see from the rough section I give, was a bad one, unless it had been entrenched." He adds, that in his capacity of A.D.C. he was asked by Major Hay and others to get them permission to make some entrenchment ; but the General always said, " Not yet, that it did not require anything very substantial, as it was only against rifle fire."

the summit, the signal for assault. Meanwhile the same steady rifle fire was to be maintained from round the northern and western slopes of the mountain. On the edge of the top, at every puff of smoke and at every figure showing against the sky-line, this unremitting fire was to be kept up.[1] It was not the waste of ammunition the Staff officer's message described.[2] It prevented a full examination being made of the ground below the precipitous drop of the mountain. It covered, almost as well as artillery could have covered, the advance of the small assaulting parties. It kept the strain upon the defenders of the position still tightly drawn. If in this war the fighting General of the Boers had done nothing except the attack he was now directing against Majuba, the manner in which he carried out the movement would suffice to stamp him as one of the ablest leaders of mounted infantry that have appeared in modern war.[3]

About noon the officer commanding the party of the 92nd overlooking the north face noticed various parties of the enemy below moving in closer to the mountain, and he reported this movement. " The accuracy of the fire with which the Boers covered their advance may be judged by the fact that, while crossing the short open space between his advanced line and the reserve, the officer's clothes were cut twice by bullets." [4]

A deer-stalker knows well how difficult it often is to see objects from above on a rough and rocky hillside, even if they are known to be immediately below, and, on the other hand, how clearly they can be seen on the sky-line above. It was impossible to estimate exactly the numbers who had crossed the open beneath, and disappeared in the unseen terraces below the crest of the mountain. " There appeared to be altogether on the mountain a force which, in the opinion of the officer already mentioned, might amount to between three and four hundred men." [5] A body of Boers (about sixty in number) reached, unseen, a position about eighty yards below the koppie [6] commanding the northern face ; concealed by brushwood and rocks, they could see the soldiers above as they

[1] NOTE FROM REGIMENTAL RECORD.—This fire was especially searching from a ridge marked A in Lieutenant Ian Hamilton's sketch, not included in the position, but which was within easy rifle range of its north-west angle. (This ridge A is added to the copy of Fraser's plan given. It was about 500 yards down the hill.)

[2] Sent by Colonel Stewart about 9.30, " All very comfortable ; Boers wasting ammunition."

[3] Butler.

[4] Ibid. The officer alluded to was Ian Hamilton. He could sometimes hear, without seeing, the Boers below.

[5] Ibid.

[6] No. 5, occupied by a few of the 58th and three men of the 92nd.

NOTE.—The Regimental Record states that General Smidt, who commanded, afterwards told two officers that he had 2000 men that day. Of these, no doubt, a large proportion were not near the firing line. Major-General C. W. H. Douglas, however, writes that Smidt told him that 600 were on ridge A. " I believe the storming party consisted of about 200. Of these, however, I cannot say how many reached the top ; of the remaining 1200, parties were, no doubt, detached to fire at parts of the hill not to be carried by assault."

occasionally fired at the Boer riflemen 500 yards beyond.   Having quietly and skilfully completed their arrangements, they fired a well-directed volley point-blank on the few men (less than twenty) who held the koppie, " putting half of them *hors de combat*, and the remainder ran back." [1]   Having taken koppie (5 on plan) the Boers cleared ridge (12) [2] with rifle fire, repulsed by rifle fire an attempt made by the reserve to reoccupy it, and, outflanking Lieutenant Ian Hamilton's company, forced it to retire with terrible loss towards (8).   Hamilton afterwards made a determined effort to retake the ridge (12), but the fire was too hot to enable him and his small following to do so without support. [3]   " By this time the reserve had been greatly decreased by the call for reinforcements from different points to keep down the fire and approach of the Boers, whose parties now nearly surrounded the hill.   The few men left in reserve, chiefly sailors and 58th, were now brought up towards the western face," [4] but before reaching the position from which our men had been driven, they received a volley which stretched out some sixteen or twenty of them. [5]   Confusion ensued, increased probably by the soldiers who had retreated from the crest ; but they were all formed behind the ridge (7, 9, 4 in plan).

The Boers then pushed in force [6] into the gap thus left in the western face, and there established, took the north face in flank and reverse, and rendered it untenable.   Almost immediately after the Boers showed in force on the N.E. angle on a koppie (marked 2 in plan), which is the highest point on Majuba top.   Our men, now formed behind the ridge (7, 9, 4), fixed bayonets, and as the unequal fire-contest could not be long doubtful, Lieutenant Ian Hamilton suggested to Sir George Colley that the men should be ordered to charge.   Sir George answered, " Not yet, wait till they cross the open, and then we will give them a volley and charge."   But the Boers were not likely to give up the advantage of their better position and the superiority of their many rifles to cross the open. . . . All those present state that before the last position was yielded, the numbers must have been reduced to sixty or seventy fighting men, [7] and there was a line of killed and wounded, chiefly 92nd, to mark the ground.   Lieutenant MacDonald, who held an important hillock (6 in plan) on the left of the position, had eight men killed out of twenty, and nearly all the rest wounded. [8]

[1] Regimental Record.

[2] The eastern half of (12) was held by about six men of the 92nd, and they there linked on to the right of the 58th.

[3] Colour-sergeant Tulloch's account, approved by Sir Ian Hamilton.

[4] Regimental Record.

[5] Sir Ian Hamilton.

[6] Sir Ian Hamilton, who saw them plainly, says between seventy and eighty.

[7] Captain M'Gregor shows that, at the very last, the numbers had been still further reduced.

[8] Regimental Record.

Lieutenant MacDonald told the writer that he could not have believed, had he not witnessed it, that human nature could have borne what was borne without complaint, beyond the wish expressed to charge down on the invisible enemy, by the twenty men of his detachment, of

The slope of the ground from the last position to the brow of the mountain concealed the advance of the Boers until they were about forty yards distant from our men, and so well did they take advantage of the ground, and so admirable was their shooting, that nothing was to be seen but the muzzles of their rifles as they fired with unfailing accuracy, while the bullets from our men passed just over their heads.[1]

Captain A. D. M'Gregor, aide-de-camp to Sir George Colley, was, on his return to England, asked by the Military Secretary to make a report to him of what he knew of the action. It coincides generally with the above. He says that in the morning, working parties were every moment expected to be told off to commence entrenchments. He mentions that the western face was all the time exposed to a well-directed fire, the men lay flat behind a stone or two, and the casualties for some time were few, but later the men kept being knocked over from the ridge about 400 yards off, as they were at once hit if they stood up to fire, and they could not see the Boers without doing so. Thus the numbers there were greatly diminished. He made careful inquiry, when taken prisoner before Mr Joubert at the top of the hill, as to the number of killed and wounded between the western brow held by the 92nd and the first position, and was told there must have been about forty to fifty, which accounts for the small numbers at the second position. " When the line broke, the numbers at the new position had dwindled to not more than sixty or eighty, I should say." With reference to this, he writes, November 10th, 1901 :—

I gave that as an outside number. Out of that number I took, as I mentioned, eight or ten men of the 58th to the extreme left, at the head of the ravine, so with the casualties you see there could not have been many left when they retreated. . . . I had on several occasions, by order of General Colley, to move men to either flank ; I never had the least difficulty, I may say even hesitation, on their part when I called on them to move, and they could see as well as myself what their comrades were suffering there, and what they might expect when they got there. The last men I moved were those of the reserve company of the 58th, to the ravine on the left, with whom Lieutenant Lucy went. They were, I hear, all killed, but they and all I ever asked went quite willingly. Men of my own regiment I sometimes called by name, and they always obeyed my call, and wherever I was told to send them I told them, and could not have expected them to go to what appeared certain death more cheerfully if it had been a peaceful field-day.

---

whom every individual, he believed, was killed or wounded except himself and a lance-corporal, and that without the opportunity of fighting. He was constantly listening for the sound of guns in an attack on the Nek, to which he supposed the occupation of Majuba was preparatory. (The above was submitted to and approved by Sir Hector MacDonald, August 1902.)

[1] Sir W. Butler and Major Hay (verbally, soon after the event). Hay also said that at the time of the retreat, Lieutenant Wright and a few men were firing from behind some rocks, and that he had to call them twice before they would come away.

Captain M'Gregor states that up to the end there was plenty of ammunition, but it was being taken from the pouches of the dead and dying, " which, in such a position, I may say, is not encouraging"; and he finishes his report to the Military Secretary, " I hope that these few lines will help to clear the wrong impression held by some of the behaviour of the men on that day."

Ex-Colour-sergeant Tulloch, who was with Lieutenant Ian Hamilton, says they retired from their first position only when their left flank was turned by the occupation by the Boers of the gap left in the western face of the hill, as already described (*i.e.* ridge 12), and that Hamilton afterwards tried to retake the position as mentioned above. The nature of the ground allowed the Boers beyond to fire, without moving from their cover, over the heads of those near the British. He was close to the General when he was shot, just as he appeared to be taking his handkerchief out of his pocket. Then, with Captain M'Gregor, he and the remaining men crossed the zone of fire as best they could. He says there was nothing to call panic [1] among Ian Hamilton's or any other detachment of the 92nd so far as he saw or knew. " At the last, of course, it was every man for himself."

Tulloch and Lance-corporal Hull were standing at bay with their backs to the edge of a precipice. Having broken his rifle to prevent the Boers getting it, Tulloch was defending himself with the sword-bayonet which sergeants then carried, when Hull, shot through the heart, leaped up, and falling on the sergeant knocked him over the precipice. A bush broke his fall, but he was much torn and hurt ; his face was bleeding profusely from the splash of a bullet in the earlier part of the action, and his knee from a slight wound, so that he presented a ghastly appearance as he still tried to defend himself, when an old Boer interfered in his favour, and, thinking his hurts worse than they were, his assailants left him.[2] At night he got down part of the way, and was picked up by a patrol of the 15th Hussars. He and several other men were hit besides those returned as wounded. The regimental dog " Ghazi " was wounded by buckshot used by the Boers at close quarters.

In January 1882, Sergeant Tulloch received a letter from Mr Townsend M. Kirkwood, in Eastern Bengal, in which he said that,

---

[1] With regard to a statement that the first attack was a surprise resulting in a panic, Sir Ian Hamilton writes that " in one sense it was a complete surprise, but some of us knew what was happening, and were not surprised, but overpowered. Had it been merely a surprise and a panic flight, we should not have lost twenty men, as the Boers would only have had a few seconds during which they could have fired with effect whilst we cleared the plateau."

[2] Major Hay said that, being severely wounded, the Boers left him on the hill, saying they could not be troubled with wounded prisoners. Those they took, however, they treated very well, and when it was explained to Joubert that Lieutenant MacDonald's sword had been presented to him by the officers on his promotion, it was generously returned.

" wishing to show my concern for those of our British soldiers who distinguished themselves by their bravery on the disastrous day of Majuba, I have made inquiries from General Sir Evelyn Wood. You are one of six men specially selected as having displayed conduct deserving the highest praise." He enclosed £10 " as a slight recognition on my part of your high merit," asked for his photograph, his birthplace and parentage, and afterwards kept up a correspondence with the sergeant.

Many of the Boers took the regimental purses to hang up as trophies. In 1900, Captain Greenhill-Gardyne, having been wounded with the 1st Gordons, was in hospital at Pretoria, when he was given one of these, which was identified by the number as that of Private James Heggie.

Lieutenant (afterwards Major-General) Forbes Macbean, who was with the burial party next day, said, " I went to the edge of the hill where so many of the 92nd had been killed. . . . The dead were all shot above the chest ; in some men's heads I counted five or six bullet wounds." [1]

Captain M'Gregor mentions that when General Colley desired him, on the evening of the 26th, to warn the companies to take three days' provisions, he asked if he should order some for the General and staff, but Sir George replied that it was not necessary ; " I will take a few biscuits, etc., for us all." He also left the horses for himself and staff at the foot of the hill in charge of orderlies. It seems evident, therefore, that he intended either merely to occupy Majuba in accordance with his letter of the 23rd to Mr Childers, or else that, having occupied it, he intended himself to return to Mount Prospect, where were artillery, cavalry, and infantry, and make a demonstration against Laing's Nek. Had such a demonstration been ordered by heliograph from Majuba, even in the forenoon, it would, humanly speaking, have changed what became a disaster into a success. It appears that however narrators differ in other points, they agree in believing that had three points on the hill been entrenched, the disaster could have been averted.

The victory of Majuba was most creditable to the tactics of the Boer commander, to the resolution of his followers, and to the superiority of their fire ; but the overthrow of the small British detachment engaged has been magnified both at home and abroad into a great battle, and the relative proportions of the combatants have been frequently misrepresented.[2] Its importance to the

---

[1] " Story of Majuba."

[2] Even in the *Times*' " History of the War in South Africa, 1899-1900," 554 British are supposed to have been on the top, defeated by less than 200 Boers, no mention being made of the strong force of riflemen who covered the storming party.

British name and nation was derived not from the defeat of 350 British soldiers and sailors, but from the disastrous and abject political surrender which immediately followed.

The total loss on this melancholy occasion was General Sir George P. Colley and 91 officers and men killed and 134 wounded. Of the five officers of the 92nd on the top,[1] Major J. C. Hay, Captain Singleton (mortally), and Lieutenant Ian Hamilton were wounded, and out of the 118 n.c. officers and men, 33 were killed in action and 63 were wounded, of whom 11 died of their wounds.[2]

KILLED IN ACTION.		COUNTY.
Colour-sergeant Wm. Fraser		Inverness.
Sergeant John W. Baker		London.
,,	George Williams	Aberdeen.
Lance-corporal Geo. F. Hull		From Duke of York's Military School.
Drummer Peter M'Pherson		Inverness.
,,	Fredk. Nobbs	From Duke of York's Military School.
Private	Alexander Bain	Ross.
,,	David Falconer	Elgin.
,,	Wm. Fife	Aberdeen.
,,	John Grigor	Elgin.
,,	Charles Hailey	York.
,,	Henry Hancey	Do.
,,	James Heggie	Fife.
,,	Francis Innes	Aberdeen.
,,	Adam Johnstone	Kincardine.
,,	Wm. Kynoch	Forfar.
,,	Thomas Lodge	
,,	Wm. Low	Forfar.
,,	Jas. M'Arthur	Lanark.
,,	W. M'Lellan	Argyll.
,,	John M'Donald	Inverness.
,,	Patrick M'Donald	Edinburgh.
,,	Alexr. M'Intosh	Nairn.
,,	John M'Leod	Ross.
,,	Colin MacRae	Inverness.
,,	Mitchell Marshall	Fife.
,,	Thos. Mathieson	Caithness.
,,	Peter O'Boyle	Cork.

[1] Not including Captain M'Gregor, aide-de-camp.

[2] It was stated by the Boers, and generally believed, that only one of their number was killed and seven wounded. Colonel M'Gregor writes that when a prisoner he heard that seven dead Boers had been found on one spot, and he felt confident, from other reasons, that there were more casualties than were reported.

AUTHOR'S NOTE.—It will be observed that the above account of the action is largely taken from the statements of those who were present, and who were themselves all individually mentioned by their superiors for their conduct on that occasion.

Killed in Action.	County.
Private Jas Robertson	Perth.
„ John Sawyers	Lanark.
„ Chas. G. Smith	Aberdeen.
„ Peter Walker	Forfar.
„ Chas. Wallace	Perth.

Died of Wounds.	County.
Colour-sergeant Thos. Nicol	Perth.
Private John Abbot	York.
„ Adam Adamson	London.
„ Wm. Campbell	Inverness.
„ Joseph Graham	Stirling.
„ Alexr. Hendry	Aberdeen.
Piper David Hutcheon	Kincardine.
Private John Hutcheon	Do.
„ Kenneth M'Kenzie	Ross.
„ John F. Stewart	Perth.
„ Alexr. Watson	Lanark.[1]

[1] There is no *official* evidence obtainable of the nationality of the men killed, but Mr Ross Martin, who was sergeant in Captain Singleton's company till within three days of the action, states the above to be correct, and the Gordon Highlanders' Society in Glasgow agree. A monument was afterwards erected in St Giles' Cathedral, Edinburgh, to the officers, n.c. officers, and men who were killed in the Afghan and South African campaigns.

CHAPTER XVI

1881–1882

ON March 3rd, 1881, a meeting of those desirous of recognising the brilliant services of the Gordon Highlanders in Afghanistan, and of expressing sympathy with them in the great losses they had sustained during the recent campaign, was held at Aberdeen. A subscription was also opened, on the initiative of Lord Saltoun and other gentlemen in the north, for the benefit of the women who had been so unexpectedly separated from their husbands in India, and had arrived with their children in England at the most inclement season of the year.

On the 28th March the regiment arrived at Newcastle, moved to Bennet's Drift on the 6th May, and on the 29th reached Drakensberg.

At this time the promotion and honours to officers and men, and the additional titles to be borne on the colours for the Afghan Campaign (as previously described) were published.

On Waterloo Day, 18th June 1881, the officers of the Royal Scots Greys celebrated their bi-centenary by a dinner in London, and took this opportunity of commemorating the partnership of the two regiments in that stirring episode of their military history—the " Scotland for ever ! " charge. Many old officers of the 92nd, together with those at the depôt, were invited. General Darby Griffith, C.B. (in the absence of General Sir John Gough, Colonel of the Greys), was in the chair, and after the loyal toasts and that of " Scotland for ever ! ", " Our sister regiment the 92nd Gordon Highlanders " was given by the chairman, and replied to, on behalf of the Gordons, by Field-Marshal Lord Strathnairn, G.C.B. Colonel Forbes Macbean, late of the 92nd, proposed the toast of the evening, " The Royal Scots Greys," and bore testimony to the cordial and kindly feeling which had always existed between the two regiments : and though, he said, there would be great changes in the army on the 1st of July, he felt confident there would be no change in the friendship between the Scots Greys and the Gordon Highlanders. Many old sergeants of the 92nd were also invited to dine with the sergeants of the Greys in Dublin ; return tickets from Scotland being generously offered by the officers of the Greys.

On the 30th June 1881, a very important extract from General Orders, dated 1st May 1881, was published in Regimental Orders, viz. :—

The following changes in the organisation, title, and uniform of the regiments of the line having been approved, are promulgated for general information. The words " Regimental District " will in future be used in place of " Sub-District " hitherto employed. The following alterations in the localisation of line regiments will take place : "The 75th and 92nd will be localised together at Aberdeen.   Soldiers serving in any of the battalions mentioned, previous to the 1st of July 1881, will not be held liable to serve in the other line battalion of their new territorial regiment without their own consent.

"The precedence, composition, and title of the regiment will be—

No. of Precedence.	Title.	Composition.
60	The Gordon High-landers.	1st Battalion 75th Foot.
		2nd „ 92nd „
		3rd „ Royal Aberdeenshire Militia.
		4th Battalion not yet formed."

Regimental Orders.—From to-morrow inclusive all documents, returns, rolls, etc., of this battalion will be made out with the following heading : "2nd Battalion The Gordon Highlanders." The number 92 will no longer appear.

Though the 92nd was to retain its own designation of "The Gordon Highlanders," all ranks determined that the obsequies of the dying number should be celebrated with due pomp and respect ; accordingly, representatives of other corps were invited by the officers to the funeral feast, and at midnight of June 30th, when the number ceased to exist, the funeral oration was pronounced by Lieut.-Colonel Luck, 15th Hussars ; a torchlight procession was formed, the coffin containing a flag inscribed "92" was borne shoulder high, with the officers in full Highland dress as chief mourners, and proceeded, the band playing the "Dead March," to the grave.   Three volleys were fired over it, and the pipers played a Lament.

Next morning it was found that the "body" had been exhumed, and on the flag, in addition to "92" were the words "No' deid yet," while many tents had flags flying with similar mottoes.   Some of the English newspapers were foolish enough to find fault with this innocent and harmless ebullition of *esprit de corps*.

The "linked battalion" system had been found unsatisfactory by all concerned, but experienced soldiers agreed that a regiment of one battalion cannot be made ready for active service without recourse to that worst of systems—completing one regiment by depleting the ranks of another—of which the 92nd had such unhappy experience in Crimean days.   Mr Childers, who was at this time Secretary of State for War, came to the conclusion that the best way out of the difficulty was to adopt the recommendation of a Committee presided over by Mr Stanley in 1877, that instead of *linking* two still separate regiments, they should be *welded*, as it were, into one, each of the newly organised regiments having a district appointed for its recruiting.   Some difficulties arose from regiments objecting to lose their individuality, and this was particularly the case with Highland corps, each of which, like the clans of old, thought itself entitled to the place of honour. They were all on foreign service except the 42nd, whose commanding officer was the only one personally consulted. Colonel Duncan MacPherson of Cluny was both a Highland soldier and heir to a Highland chief. He explained that it was with difficulty that the five kilted battalions could be recruited in Scotland, let alone in the Highlands ; that therefore it would be a mistake to increase the number of battalions wearing the Highland dress ; and that in his opinion, rather than destroy the nationality of all, it would be better to join them in one regiment with the same uniform, having the Northern Counties of Scotland for its territory, and call it " The Highland Brigade." [1]

Meanwhile, I believe, the commanding officers of the 79th and 93rd had been asked by telegram if they would be willing to join another regiment and adopt its tartan, to which they, not having the alternative before them, naturally answered in the nega-tive. A number of enthusiastic Scots resident in London, some of them belonging to distinguished Highland families, but ignorant of the recruiting question in the Highlands, left their places of business to don the Highland dress, and held a meeting of rather a theatrical character at St James's, where, to the music of the bag-pipes, they were reported to have sworn on their dirks to keep the Highland regiments intact. Telegrams were sent to the provosts of towns and other influential people in the north, of whom few had any practical knowledge of the subject, and protests were got up against interfering with the tartan. Mr Childers, in a humorous letter to Lord Reay, writes :—" The tartan question is one of the gravest character, far more important, as your friend suggests, than the maintenance of the union with Ireland. All the thoughts of the War Office are concentrated on it, and patterns of tartans— past, present, and future—fill our rooms. We are neglecting the Transvaal and Ashanti for the sake of well weighing the merits of a few more threads of red, green, or white."

Mr Childers preferred the irresponsible sentiment of the per-fervid Scots to the wise counsel of the Highland Colonel and Chieftain who knew his business ; and four battalions,[2] which in 1809, when they could no longer obtain men in the Highlands, had like sensible people given up the kilt, were now ordered to adopt it when recruiting in the Highlands was still more difficult. I have no doubt the late General J. C. Hay (when lieut.-colonel) ex-

---

[1] Letter from Colonel Ewen MacPherson of Cluny, late 93rd Highlanders, and others. From letters of officers at the time it would appear the 92nd was not consulted as to its fate.

[2] 72nd, 73rd, 75th, 91st.

pressed the feeling of most of the older Highland officers when he said to the writer, " I have worn the Gordon tartan for thirty years, and I should be very sorry to change it ; but I would rather have the right men in the wrong tartan than the wrong men in the right tartan."

The territorial idea is in itself no doubt good, and in populous counties the scheme was a success ; but in the Highlands, the county did not appeal to the *esprit de province* of its inhabitants to the same extent as in the south.   The district of Atholl or Rannoch in Perthshire differed in customs and language from Stormont or the Carse of Gowrie.   The traditions of Appin or Lochiel in Argyllshire were as far apart from those of Inveraray or Cowal as are the geographical positions of Argyll and Sutherland.   Still, had Cluny's suggestion been adopted, the whole Highland district would have been united by *esprit de race* in one really representative regiment.   The practical effect of the change, as applied to the Highland regiments, was to make them all less national and, with two exceptions, to alter their territorial traditions.   The oldest of them, the Royal Highlanders, was given a territory chiefly in the Lowlands ;   the 93rd or Sutherland Highlanders was no longer to recruit in its native district ;   the Gordon Highlanders, who, as we have seen, were principally raised in Inverness-shire, with which and the neighbouring counties it had always kept up its connection, was confined to counties remarkable certainly for the admirable class of men they had given to the army and to the regiment, but of which only a small and thinly populated portion is in the Highlands.[1]

Six regiments only (five kilted and the 71st) had, when left to their own devices, more or less successfully kept up their Highland character, and with rare exceptions (when volunteers from other regiments, or general service recruits, had been given them) had always kept up their Scottish nationality ; but regiments which in 1809 ceased to be called " Highland " were gradually returned to their original designation—the 72nd in 1823, the 74th in 1846, and in 1871 the 91st—this made recruiting more difficult for all. Many people in England do not seem to understand the wide difference between the Highlands and Lowlands, and that the former contains but an insignificant proportion of the population of Scotland.   The territorial scheme for Scotland naturally included the Lowland corps, more ancient and no less distinguished than their Highland brethren-in-arms ; but they had for many years been very partially recruited in Scotland, and the traditions

---

[1] The people of Aberdeen, Banff, and Kincardineshire would strongly object to be called " Highlanders," except those of Upper Dee and Don in Aberdeen, and Kirkmichael, Inveravon, and perhaps part of Mortlach in Banff.

of at least one of them were positively anti-Highland. Yet they were all now for the first time in their history rigged out in Highland tartan trews, and recruited to a great extent in the centres of industry where Highlanders seek employment. These regiments have become more Scottish, but the Highland regiments have become less national than they were. It is no question of the comparative merits as soldiers, of Englishmen, Irishmen, Lowland Scots, or Highlanders, but it does seem inconsistent to put a regiment in Highland dress and call it "Highland" unless it is allowed to recruit in the Highlands and at least a considerable proportion of the men are "Highlanders." Allowing for those who enlist in other branches of the army, no one who knows the present state of the country would say that the Highlands could keep up the necessary supply of recruits for even four battalions of infantry of the line.[1]

I have tried to find the nationality of the 92nd in 1880, but the returns between 1870 and 1890 have not been preserved either at the War Office or Record Office. Those given for previous years show the number of *Scots*, but it is impossible to give with accuracy the number of *Highlanders*. To a certain extent, however, it may be estimated from the following evidence.

In a letter from Brevet Major Cameron, himself a Gaelic-speaking man, then (1860) in India, he said there were more Highland men in his company than there had been for many years, but also more English and Irish, mostly volunteers from other regiments. Ex-Private Morrison, an Argyllshire man, says that when he joined the service companies in 1871, there were 25 Gaelic-speaking men out of between 60 and 70 in his company (E). Mr Ross Martin, General Post Office, Glasgow, formerly sergeant, a native of Inverness, stated that about 1870-1 the sergeants counted the number of Highlanders and found it 400, including all belonging to the Highland counties without reference to language ; and that in 1873-4 there were among the n.c. officers, natives of Inverness-shire alone, 11 sergeants, the pipe-major, 16 corporals and lance-corporals, besides 4 pipers and a number of privates, and he enclosed a nominal roll with particulars of each.[2] Lieutenant J. MacFadyen, Govan Police, an Argyllshire man, sergeant during the Afghan War, stated verbally that there were at that period 350 or 400 High-

---

[1] Mr Stanley's Committee took as the basis of calculation for the territorial scheme a population of 200,000 males for the support of one regiment of two regular and two militia battalions. The male population of the six Highland counties (Caithness, Sutherland, Ross and Cromarty, Inverness, Nairn, Argyll) amounted in 1891 to 149,294. The Highlanders in the partially Highland counties may make the number up to 200,000. There are now twelve regular battalions called "Highland."

[2] There were shooting and other matches between men of different counties. Martin was secretary to the Inverness Association, and thus had intimate knowledge of the men.

landers.   Some time after, being asked if he adhered to the statement, he wrote that he considered 400 nearer the mark than 350.
Mr Tulloch, doorkeeper, Parliament House, Edinburgh, late
colour-sergeant 92nd and sergeant-major 2nd Volunteer Battalion
Gordon Highlanders, an Inverness-shire man, considered that
there were not nearly so many as 350 men who could speak Gaelic
at the Afghan period, though the great majority belonged to the
north of Scotland.

The Rev. G. W. Manson, who was for many years attached to
the 92nd in India as chaplain, writes :—

If you were referring to 1872, when Colonel Cameron was in command,
I should have no hesitation in accepting 400 as a moderate and reasonable
estimate of our n.c. officers and men from the Highland counties.   Later on
we were getting more general service recruits, and I fancy the tendency was
to raise the average proportion of Lowland as compared to Highland men.
In 1879, I should be inclined to put the Highland county men at 300 to 350
perhaps.   That is the nearest guess I could venture in the absence of anything
like statistics.

Major Duncan F. Gordon, Garthdee, late Chief Constable of
Aberdeenshire, did not think there were nearly 400 Gaelic-speaking men, that 200 would be nearer the mark, but that many came
from districts of the Highlands where Gaelic is not so commonly
spoken as it was.   Taking this into consideration, " I should be
inclined to put men from more or less Highland counties at roughly
400."   Major Gordon stated that when he joined in 1867, there
were over 50 Macdonalds, but some were not born in the
Highlands.

Although the number of Highlanders in the 92nd was certainly as great as in any regiment, there is indirect evidence of the
preponderance of Lowlanders, in the essentially lowland sobriquet
" Jock "[1] in place of " Donald " or " Her nainsel," formerly the
familiar appellations of Highland soldiers.   For the diminutive
" Tommy " is a later invention of the evil one, taken from the name
" Thomas Atkins " in a War Office circular showing how soldiers'
accounts should be made up.

Mr Childers had wisely set himself to improve the position of
n.c. officers ;   with short service and no pension, many men well
qualified for promotion did not think it worth while to undertake
the trouble and responsibility of that important position.   They
were now excepted from the ordinary conditions of short service,
and were allowed to serve for a liberal pension.   The rank of
warrant officer, between the n.c. and commissioned officer,
already known in the navy, was established in the army, and on 1st

[1] " Jock " is a word entirely unknown among the Gaelic people.

July 1881, Sergeant-major James Ross and Bandmaster Joseph King of the battalion were appointed warrant officers.

On the 31st October 1881, Lieut.-Colonel Parker, C.B., relinquished the command after twenty-nine years' service in the regiment, and was succeeded by Lieut.-Colonel G. Stewart White, V.C., C.B.

In November the battalion was in camp at Richmond Road, and arrived at Durban on the 22nd December, where they embarked on the 24th on board the s.s. *Calabria*, and landed at Portsmouth on the morning of 30th January 1882, with a total strength of 538 officers and men. They had hoped to be sent to Scotland, where they would be able to visit their homes without the expense of the long journey from Portsmouth, but they remained there quartered in Anglesea Barracks. Here 146 rank and file joined from Aberdeen, where, and at Fort-George,[1] the depôt companies had formed part of the 15th Depôt Battalion when the service companies went to India.

In June 1871, the depôt was attached to the 93rd Sutherland Highlanders at Edinburgh, and in November 1872 it moved to Aberdeen to be attached to the 91st Highlanders, whose headquarters were at Fort-George.

In April 1873, the depôt formed part of the 56th Depôt Brigade, consisting of the depôts of the 92nd and 93rd under Colonel E. S. F. G. Dawson, late 93rd, recruits being enlisted to serve in either corps.

August 26th, 1873.—One sergeant and 8 rank and file proceeded to Plymouth to attend the funeral of Colonel Kenneth Douglas MacKenzie, C.B., Assistant Quartermaster-General, and late of the 92nd, who was drowned during the autumn manœuvres.

August 1874.—Captain McCallum, 4 sergeants, 46 rank and file, twenty rounds ball cartridge to each rifle, proceeded to Fraserburgh in aid of the civil power.

May 6th, 1876.—The depôt, with militia staff and Aberdeen City Artillery Volunteers, paraded in review order to witness the presentation of medals to two of the 93rd and three of the 92nd ; the latter were Sergeant-major James Mather, Sergeant John M'Intyre, and Private William Bulloch.

Drafts were constantly sent to join the home battalion (93rd), from which the foreign battalion (92nd) was reinforced till the territorial regiment was formed in 1881.

---

[1] While the depôt was at Fort-George in 1869, a tradesman in good business, and much respected in Inverness, went to Fort-George and gave himself up to the sergeant of the guard as having deserted from the 92nd in 1826. This was found to be true. He was tried by court-martial and convicted, but under the circumstances he was forgiven, and returned to his home with a conscience relieved of the burden which had so long oppressed it.

CHAPTER XVII

1787–1792

ALTHOUGH this work professes to be a history only of the Gordon Highlanders, it seems very desirable and right that a memoir should be added of the regiment which had now become their First Battalion, and which brought to the united standards the honours it had won by the distinguished part it had borne in the history of the British Empire in the East.[1] I advertised in the Press, and inserted in the first volume of this book, an appeal for journals or other documents which would throw light on its early achievements, and I am indebted to A. A. Gordon, Captain 9th Volunteer Battalion (Highlanders) Royal Scots, for useful matter collected by him ; to Campbell of Dunstaffnage, Captain MacRae-Gilstrap of Ballimore, John MacLachlan, Esq., Tobermory, and H. R. Craufurd, Esq., for information and relative letters ; but otherwise I received no response. What follows is taken chiefly from the abridged Regimental Record.

The state of affairs in the East had made it necessary to send strong reinforcements to the army of India, when, in the autumn of 1787, Colonel Robert Abercromby, son of the laird of Tullibody, was appointed colonel of a regiment to be raised by him in the north of Scotland. The army was unpopular at this period in the south, but English ideas had as yet little effect in Scotland, still less in the north, where the Highlanders were neither jealous of the power of the Crown, nor cared much for the liberties of the people ; they disliked manual labour, and though a man who claimed gentle blood despised mercantile pursuits, he did not consider it derogatory to be an innkeeper, a drover, or a soldier ; thus men of a superior class often enlisted in the Highland regiments. The Highlands were in a state of transition—the new order of relations between landlords and tenants had begun, but the shadow of the clan system survived in the great power and influence over the people still possessed by the gentry, several of whom, among them MacKenzie of Seaforth,[2] assisted Colonel Abercromby in his levy. Not many Highland officers appear to have been appointed to the new regiment, but some received commissions for raising

---

[1] The Royal Tiger superscribed " India," " Mysore " (granted March 1889), " Seringapatam," " South Africa (1835) " (granted September 1882), " Delhi," " Lucknow."
[2] Major Davidson's " History of the 78th."

men,[1] while though Abercromby had no territorial influence in the Highlands, his character as a leader brought to his standard a considerable body of experienced soldiers who had served under him in a light brigade which he commanded in the American War. These men had belonged to the 76th (MacDonald's Highlanders) and other Highland regiments which had been disbanded after the peace in 1783-4.[2]

The regiment was embodied at Stirling,[3] that place being no doubt chosen as convenient to the colonel's home at Tullibody ; there is, however, no evidence that it was recruited particularly in that district ; had it been so, it would not in those days have been designated, as it was, the 75th *Highland* Regiment, sometimes called Abercromby's Highlanders. The regiment moved immediately to England and embarked for Bombay, where it landed, 700 strong, in August 1788.[4]

The uniform was red with yellow facings, with the Highland dress, probably much the same as that of other Highland regiments of the period, but whether in the ancient form of the *breacan an fheilidh* or of the *feile-beg* does not appear.[5] The officers [6] were armed with sword and dirk, .the latter holding a knife, fork, and spoon, the sergeants with sword and halbert—a light kind of battle-axe with a long shaft (replaced in 1792 by the pike). The officers and sergeants of flank companies of infantry at this time carried fusils. The officers wore silver epaulettes, but, as in several other regiments, they had no lace on their jackets ; the belts at that period were generally black, with a buckle ; the hair was curled at the side and tied back with a ribbon at the neck, till queues were

---

[1] It would appear that some of these recruits were not always very willing or not very sober volunteers. A letter, in the possession of Campbell of Dunstaffnage, written by a Mull laird to his cousin who was raising men for a commission, is to the following effect :—" I send a recruit who will, I think, make up your number. As he is a very obstreperous man, he is tied in a cart, and you will please give the carter 5s. and 2s. 6d. for the rope if you do not return it, as it is new." Judging from a letter written in 1771, there was an aversion to soldiering in the Lorn district of Argyll. " There are great numbers of idle fellows that transgress the law by wearing the Highland dress and arms. I dread it will only be by comprehending [apprehending] them for either of these that I can be of any assistance (in recruiting) ; however, I 'll exert myself to the utmost of my power, and try every fair means first."

[2] Stewart's " Highlanders of Scotland," and Regimental Record.

[3] The Regimental Record gives no date. Stewart says in June 1788, which hardly gives time to arrive at Bombay in August. Several regiments, which had no special connection with Stirling, were embodied there, as the older 71st or Fraser's Highlanders, and the 79th or Cameron Highlanders.

NOTE.—The experience gained by the wars in Canada caused the formation of a corps of Light Infantry, picked for their marksmanship from various regiments, and trained in tactics which were regarded as a strange innovation—advancing in loose order and taking cover. They are said to have been first used in 1758 at the siege of Louisburg, then held by the French.

[4] Regimental Record.

[5] See Appendix VII.

[6] Officers of some Highland corps carried a pistol.

HIGHLAND OFFICER, *circa* 1780-90
From a portrait by Copley

introduced.[1] Sergeant's rank was shown by the sash and laced shoulder-knot, or aiguilette, as still used in the Household Cavalry, till chevrons were introduced in 1797-8. It is not known what tartan was worn. Captain John MacRae-Gilstrap of Ballimore writes that he has a portrait of his grandfather, Major Colin Mac-Rae of Conchra, in the uniform of the 75th (Abercromby's Highlanders) ; the colour is faded, but the tartan looks like the Gordon, though the stripe may be either white or yellow. If white, it was probably the " Graeme " ; if yellow, it may have been " Breadalbane," these being used in neighbouring districts to Tullibody. This major had a brother-in-law, Alexander Macra of Huishnish, and a nephew, James Campbell MacRae, also a nephew named Matheson, in the regiment at various times, but there is no list of the original officers.

In the Army Lists of 1788 and 1789 only a few names are entered ; the first complete list is that of 1790.

OFFICERS OF 75TH (HIGHLAND) REGIMENT OF FOOT,
JANUARY 1ST, 1790

Colonel Robert Abercromby.
Lieut.-Colonel James Hartley.
Major George Hart.
Captain Robert Craufurd.
,, John Wood.
,, Daniel Seddon.
,, Alexander Cumine.
,, Robert Kennan.
,, Charles de Castro.
,, John Ramsay.
,, Samuel Auchmuty.
Captain-Lieut. } Zachariah Hall.
and Captain }
Lieutenant Colville Learmonth
,, George M'Kenzie.
,, Benjamin Forbes.
,, Charles Anderson.
,, David Maxwell.
,, J. Charles Halkett.
,, Gabriel Trotter.
,, John Abercromby.
,, Adam Davie.
,, James Dunsmore.
,, John Ross.
,, Thos. Milborne West.

Lieutenant Colin MacRae.
,, John Doherty.
,, Charles Branton.
,, George Douglas.
,, Edmund Filmer.
,, Christopher Hayes.
,, Hon. Quin Brownrigg.
,, Oliver St John.
,, Thomas Drummond.
,, Alexander Stewart.
,, George Laye.
Ensign Donald Cameron.
,, Alexander Wallace.
,, Benjamin Hill.
,, Jonathan Brown.
,, Charles Stewart.
,, Robert Mudie.
,, — Lloyd.
,, John Keirnan.
,, James Towers.
Chaplain John Pritchett.
Adjutant Geo. MacKenzie.
Quartermaster Charles Stewart.
Surgeon Charles Kerr.

---

[1] The fashion of long hair was no doubt inconvenient, but it at least gave the protection to the neck for which it was intended by Nature.

There is no evidence of the nationality till January 4th, 1790, when it was :—

	Officers.	N.c. officers and men.
English	8	73
Scottish	24	437
Irish	8	33
Foreigners	1	5
	41	548

Soon after arriving in India, Colonel Abercromby was appointed Governor of Bombay, and the other field officers to the general staff ; thus the immediate command of the corps was in the hands of Captain Robert Craufurd, son of Sir Alexander Craufurd, Bart. of Newark, Ayrshire, from whom he seems to have inherited a somewhat violent temper. He had served in the 26th, the 92nd (an English regiment which had preceded the Gordons in that number), and the 101st Regiments. While on half-pay he had for four years studied his profession at Potsdam, attending the manœuvres of the Prussian army under Frederick the Great, and visiting the principal theatres of war on the Continent. Craufurd entered on his duties in command with great zeal and energy, but the system he introduced had been formed on the Prussian model, in which fear was the great principle of action, and feeling or sentiment was little regarded.[1]   Though a Highlander of former days would stand with his bonnet off while talking to the laird, it was not from fear but from courtesy to his superior that he assumed the attitude of respect, and he claimed the friendly greeting and handshake as a member of the clan family.   This manner of respectful familiarity and kindly feeling, which to a certain extent has generally been carried into the system of the Highland regiments, has often been remarked and admired.   But Craufurd showed a want of discrimination between the feelings and position of the men of a Highland regiment of the 18th century and those of the class found in the ordinary marching regiments of the time.   The result on the conduct of the regiment was most unsatisfactory, but a military observer of the time remarks—" Whatever means he may have pursued in the system he adopted, he was equally rigid in the impartial justice he rendered to those under his orders.   He was indefatigable in his own exertions, shared in the toils to which officers and soldiers were exposed, and was ever at their head in cases of danger."   There is no doubt that the 75th became one of the best trained battalions in the army, and when the lieut.-

---

[1] " Scotsmen would not easily be brought to bear German punishments."— Papers illustrating the History of the Scots Brigade, issued by the Scottish History Society.

colonel returned, a more suitable system was introduced, and the regiment went honourably through an eventful course of Indian service, as remarkable for good conduct in quarters as for gallantry in the field and smartness on parade.[1]

Early in 1790, the 75th, commanded by Colonel Hartley, who had also two battalions of Bombay Sepoys under his orders, proceeded to assist our ally, the Raja of Travancore, whose country was at that time invaded by Tippoo, the Sultan of Mysore. The quarrel was about two towns on the Malabar coast, which Travancore had purchased from the Dutch, but which Tippoo affirmed belonged to his tributary the Raja of Cochin. The 75th was at Travancore from April to September, when, along with the Bombay troops, they were ordered, under Colonel Hartley, to the relief of some Madras battalions at Pallyghautcherry ; on the march Hartley found the enemy in possession of the Fort of Chowghaset, which he instantly attacked and carried. He afterwards, with his brigade, marched to the Malabar coast, from which Tippoo intended to cut off the British communications. As he approached Calicut, Hartley received information on the 10th December that 14,000 of the enemy under Mahab Khan and Hussein Ali Khan were strongly posted in a jungle at Tervangherry, ten miles distant.

He at once advanced, with the 75th and two native battalions, towards the enemy, who, trusting to superior numbers, did not decline the battle. After a warm engagement, they were driven to the village of Teronkibeel, where they made an obstinate defence, but were compelled to fly to Trincalore Fort, which the Bombay Grenadiers entered with the fugitives. Hussein Ali Khan was taken, but Mahab Khan escaped with his cavalry. The victory was gained without much loss ; I find no complete list of casualties, but among the wounded were Captains Lawson and Blackford, and Lieutenants Powell and Stewart of the 75th.

The result of this success was the capture of Calicut and the Fort of Ferokabad, of which the 75th took possession. While here, the thanks of Earl Cornwallis, Governor-General of India, were conveyed to the regiment for their gallant conduct in this their first action. The Government of Bombay also expressed sentiments equally flattering and honourable to the corps.

On the 22nd February 1791, the Bombay army, consisting of the 73rd, 75th, and 77th Regiments, a regiment of Bombay Europeans, and seven battalions of Sepoys, under Major-General Abercromby (colonel of the 75th), proceeded from the Malabar

---

[1] From a Memoir of Craufurd, lent by H. R. Craufurd, Esq. [a member of the same family, which has now (1902) two representatives in the Gordons], Stewart's " Highlanders," and Regimental Record. Craufurd became the celebrated leader of the Light Division of Wellington's army, and was killed at its head at Ciudad Rodrigo, 1812.

coast towards Seringapatam to take part in the campaign against Tippoo.[1] In the passes of the Poodicheram Ghauts, difficulties which appeared insurmountable were overcome : the battering guns were hauled up by tackles fixed to trees on the hillsides, and a road was cut for them through the forest for sixty miles. The army descended into the plains of Mysore at Ludasier, and on May 16th encamped near Perapatam, a strong fort which the 75th had been ordered to storm, but on their approach the enemy blew up the works and fled.

A native battalion was left to secure the general hospital and stores, while the rest of the army took up a strong position and awaited instructions from Lord Cornwallis, the Commander-in-Chief, who, with the Bengal army, had defeated the enemy on May 15th near Seringapatam. The Mahratta contingent, however, delayed their advance to join him, and other unfortunate circumstances obliged Cornwallis to leave the siege of Tippoo's capital for another campaign.

Abercromby's army, after surmounting so many difficulties, had the mortification of finding their success of no avail ; part of the artillery had to be left, and they retraced their steps, worn by fatigue and exposed to the excessive rains of that season. In this movement the enemy followed with large bodies of horse, who pressed upon the main body and repeatedly charged the rear guard, consisting of the 75th, who suffered some loss in performing their arduous duty.

During the autumn new battering trains were completed and every preparation made for a second advance of the combined armies. The 75th, having received new clothing and necessaries, and being recovered in health, quitted their cantonments on the Malabar coast, and at Canonore, on the 23rd November, they joined the Bombay army, consisting of three brigades and a reserve commanded by Colonel Hartley of the 75th, while the regiment, which was in the First Brigade, was commanded by Captain Craufurd.[2] The rains had destroyed the road in many places, and at one stage of the Ghauts, where they were on the 17th December, it took two days to drag the artillery two miles. Three weeks of constant labour were spent in getting the impedimenta to the top. Here they dug up the heavy guns which were buried when the first expedition was abandoned.

In January 1792, by order of Cornwallis, the heavy guns were placed in battery for the defence of the pass, guarded by a detach-

[1] Abercromby's troops amounted to about 3000 Europeans, 5900 Sepoys, with twenty six-pounder brass guns, two brass howitzers, and a train of fourteen twelve- and eighteen-pounders. 12,000 bullocks were required for the artillery and victualling department.

[2] He left the 75th in 1794 to join a military mission to Austria, and was killed at the assault of Ciudad Rodrigo in 1812 as Major-General commanding the famous Light Division.

MAJOR-GENERAL ROBERT CRAUFURD
Younger son of Sir Alexander Craufurd, Bt. of Newark, Ayrshire
From a bust now at Wellington College

ment of infantry ; and Abercromby proceeded to Ludasier Ghaut, where he encamped till required to co-operate with the army of Bengal, the Mahratta and Mysore contingents.　On February 8th, Abercromby's troops advanced ; on the 11th they forded the river Cauvery at Esatore, about thirty miles above Seringapatam.　On the 13th, they were harassed by the enemy's cavalry, but on the 14th, 4000 horse and a Sepoy battalion joined Abercromby, who united his troops with those of Cornwallis on the 16th.

The fortress of Seringapatam was constructed at the west end of the island of that name, which is formed by the embranchment of the river Cauvery.　The east side was covered by strong outworks and defended by two broad and massive ramparts, both having good flank defences and deep ditches.　It was decided to make the principal attack on the north side, where the defences were weaker, and where the river, though rapid, was not deep. The trenches were opened on February 18th, and at the same time a diversion was made against the enemy's horse encamped on the south side.　On the 19th, the 75th with the Bombay troops (except the 77th and a Sepoy battalion) crossed the river to invest the south-west side of the fort, and prepare to enfilade the south and west faces.　On the 21st the enfilade attack was commenced, and Captain M'Kenzie, with Lieutenants Doherty and Filmer, and 100 men of the 75th, were sent to take post in a redoubt at some distance from the river, with orders to take possession next morning of a tope [1] of trees in front of the redoubt.

At daybreak on the 22nd, M'Kenzie sent Lieutenant Doherty with twenty men to the tope, which was, however, found to be occupied by the enemy, and Captain M'Kenzie followed immediately with the rest of his party.　Finding Doherty warmly engaged, he at once charged, drove the enemy out of the tope, and took post in front of it opposite the batteries of the fort.　About 8 a.m. the guns opened on him, and considerable numbers of the enemy, both horse and foot, advanced so as to take the Highlanders in flank, while the guns of the fort still played upon them.　Two companies of the Bombay Europeans and a Sepoy battalion were sent to their aid ; the possession of the tope was long and hotly contested, till our troops, having expended their ammunition, were obliged to fall back, though in perfect order ; when the enemy, gaining confidence, advanced with loud shouts, and over 2000 of the Sultan's chosen troops (surnamed the *Tiger* battalions) rushed in on all sides.　Captain M'Kenzie would not brook being pressed in this manner, and facing his men about, charged with the bayonet, drove his assailants through the trees and pursued them until

---

[1] Grove.

checked by the fire of the fort.   The enemy, reinforced by still
greater numbers, again advanced and commenced a heavy fire on
the small British force, who, being without ammunition, were again
obliged slowly to retire ; when a battalion of Sepoys arrived with
a supply of ammunition and held the tope till M'Kenzie's men
had replenished their pouches, and the combat was renewed with
determined perseverance on both sides.   Abercromby now sent
the remainder of the Bombay Europeans and another battalion of
Sepoys, who formed on the right and left of the tope, while the

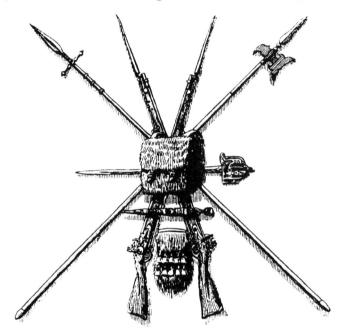

Bombay Artillery also took part in the fray.   After nearly an hour
the enemy's fire slackened, and at sunset they withdrew to the
fort.

The loss on our side this day was 51 Europeans and 53 Sepoys
killed and wounded.   That of the 75th was 1 sergeant, 2 drummers,
and 13 rank and file.

Preparations were now made for breaching the northern face
preparatory to an assault, when, on February 24th, Tippoo, who
had in the course of these operations lost about 4000 men, made
overtures of peace, and hostilities were suspended till a definite
treaty of peace was signed on the 19th March.   Tippoo ceded a
large portion of his territories, delivered up his prisoners, and had
to pay three crores and thirty lakhs of rupees towards the cost of
the war.[1]

----

[1] A " crore " is ten millions, a " lakh " is a hundred thousand.

On the army being broken up, the 75th reoccupied its former station on the Malabar coast, where it shared with the army in the honourable testimony borne to its merits by Lord Cornwallis, in the approbation of the King and the thanks of both Houses of Parliament.

NOTE.—The account of these campaigns is taken from the Regimental Record, and a " Narrative of the Campaign in India, War with Tippoo Sultan, 1792," by Major Dirom, D.A.G., published by W. Faden, 1793.

In 1792 greatcoats were added to the soldier's clothing. Previously watch-coats were kept, to be used only by those on guard.

CHAPTER XVIII

1794–1807

WHEN intelligence was received in India that the Revolutionary Government of France had declared war against England, preparations were made for the conquest of Pondicherry, the most important French possession on the eastern coast ; and in 1794 a part of the Madras army was detailed for the expedition. Meanwhile in the west, the 75th Highlanders were directed to take possession of the Fort of Mahé, after which they occupied Cochin, and protected that place against a French force which threatened it ; but little appears to have happened worthy of record during 1795-6.

In 1797, according to the custom in those days when a regiment was going home, 388 men were drafted into the 75th from the 72nd Highlanders, which was then recruited almost entirely from Ross-shire and the neighbouring counties. This brought the effective strength of the regiment to 880 rank and file.

In April 1798, the Marquis Wellesley became Governor-General of India, and it was soon afterwards discovered that Tippoo, who had constantly shown dislike to the British and friendship for the French, was now in correspondence with the latter Power, with the purpose of expelling the former from India. To possess Seringapatam was of importance to the security of the Carnatic ; to have delayed hostilities would have given time to the Sultan to improve his alliance with the French, whose invasion of Egypt, of which Lord Wellesley was aware, might have been construed into an advantage over us, thus magnifying our difficulties in bringing a war with Tippoo to the desired conclusion. The Nizam, ruler of the Deccan, who had been our ally in the last war, was now under French influence, while Scindia, a powerful chieftain unfriendly to the English, seemed to have complete sway over the mind of the Peishwa, another important native prince.

Hostilities having been resolved on, a force from the Bombay army, of which the 75th formed part, was collected at Canonore under Major-General Stuart, to co-operate with armies from the other Presidencies assembled at Mysore.

Tippoo, with 10,000 men, crossed his frontier, and on the 5th March 1799 arrived at Peripatam, where he found three native battalions, under Colonel Montressor, separated from the rest of the army at Ludasier. The Sultan thought them an easy prey, but they kept him at bay till General Stuart came up with the 77th Regiment and the flank companies of the 75th under Captains Forbes and Dunsmore : Tippoo tried to prevent this reinforcement from advancing to the relief of Montressor, but Stuart, after a severe action, defeated him, and he retreated to Peripatam with the loss of 1500 killed and wounded ; six days after, he fell back on Seringapatam. The loss of the British was twenty-nine killed and ninety wounded.

In a dispatch from the Governor-General to the Right Honourable H. Dundas, the following reference is made to this combat :—
" The victory obtained by the troops at Ludasier must ever be remembered as one of the most brilliant events in the history of British India."

On the 14th April the 75th with the Bombay troops joined the Madras army before Seringapatam ; the united forces, amounting to about 41,500 men, of whom 8000 were Europeans, were commanded by Lieut.-General Harris.

On the 17th it was ascertained that the enemy were busy strengthening a post at the village of Agrar on the north side of the river, which the British General proposed to seize. Accordingly, the 75th with two Sepoy battalions, supported by the 74th Highlanders and a Madras battalion, all under Colonel Hart of the 75th, were ordered to attack : they advanced under a severe cannonade, drove the enemy from the position with the greatest gallantry, and took possession of a redoubt about 900 yards from the north-east angle of the fortress. During the night a battery for six eighteen-pounders was completed at this place to enfilade the enemy's entrenchments on the south side of the river. In this affair the regiment lost eleven men, and on the night of the 22nd the 75th was again in action, and mainly assisted in repelling a formidable sortie of the enemy.

The bombardment began on the 23rd April, and on the 3rd of May, the breach having been reported practicable, Harris issued instructions for the assault on the following day under Major-General David Baird. Two columns of attack were formed ; the left, led by Colonel Dunlop of the 77th, consisted of the flank companies of the 12th, 33rd, 75th, and 77th Regiments and of the Bombay European Regiment, together with ten companies Bengal Native Infantry—in all, 1649 Europeans and 900 natives. The strength of the 75th flankers was 1 lieut.-colonel, 2 captains, 6 lieutenants, 1 assistant surgeon, 6 sergeants, 6 drummers, 200 rank and file. The right column under Colonel Sherbrooke numbered 1200 Europeans and 1100 natives. Before dawn on the 4th the columns were quietly lodged in the trenches, each man having twenty-four rounds of ammunition in his pouch and twelve spare rounds in the boxes ; " the leading companies of each attack to use the bayonet principally, and not to fire but in case of absolute necessity." [1] Scaling ladders were carried by European pioneers, assisted by forty men from the battalion

---

[1] Orders for the assault.

companies of each leading regiment. European and native pioneers with hatchets accompanied each attack, as well as native pioneers with fascines. A forlorn hope, consisting of a sergeant and twelve men (who volunteered for this dangerous duty), preceded each column, followed by a subaltern and twenty-five men. The 75th furnished that of the left column.

The General passed along among the troops, speaking to the men in his usual encouraging and kindly manner, and, the arrangements being complete, the Commander-in-Chief's order for the assault was received, and shortly after one o'clock in the afternoon, Baird led the columns forward and entered the bed of the river, where they were immediately assailed by a tremendous fire of musketry and rockets ; the General encouraging his followers by his coolness and example, and directing their efforts during the difficult passage, the opposite bank was gained. Both parties ascended the glacis and the breaches in the *fausse-braie* together, Baird being close to the forlorn hope. Such was the rapidity of the attack, and the uncompromising bravery of the stormers, that notwithstanding the determined opposition of the defenders, the forlorn hope, closely followed by the leading companies, had in six minutes reached the summit of the breach, and the British colours were soon proudly displayed on the famous fortress of Seringapatam.

In all these affairs the 75th suffered the loss of 16 n.c. officers and men killed in action ; Captain John Gordon, Lieutenants Turner, Broughton, Mather, and Skelton, 64 n.c. officers and men wounded, and 3 missing. Of these, the four subalterns and 50 n.c. officers and men were placed *hors de combat* in the last assault.[1]

Many instances of individual heroism displayed by officers and soldiers of the regiment occurred. The forlorn hope of the left column was led by Sergeant Graham and Corporal Roderick M'Kenzie (the latter survived to attempt the same gallant service at Bhurtpore, where he was killed). Graham being first up the breach thought himself sure of a commission and cried exultingly, " Success to Ensign Graham ! " then exclaiming, " Hang them, I 'll show them the British Flag," he planted it among the broken stones, but next moment was shot through the head.[2] The names of Sergeant Donald Ross and Corporal David Adams have also been recorded for their conspicuous gallantry on this occasion.

Lieut.-Colonel Arthur Wellesley commanded the 33rd Regiment, and was present when Tippoo's body was found, as was also

---

[1] From general return of killed, wounded, and missing of the corps composing the army before Seringapatam from the 4th April to the 4th May 1799.

[2] " Asiatic Register."

Baird, who had, as colonel, been taken prisoner in 1784 by Tippoo's father, Hyder Ali, and kept four years in irons at Seringapatam.

The taking of Seringapatam is among the most important achievements of the British army. Tippoo Sultan was killed, the power of the house of Hyder, which for many years had been used against the English, was broken, and large and valuable territories were added to the British possessions. The treasure taken (besides private plunder) was valued at £1,143,216, also nearly 1000 guns and a great store of ammunition.[1]

The 75th now returned to its cantonments in the west. In September it was employed in reducing the lately conquered districts to their new allegiance. The strong hill-fort of Jemanlabad occupied their attention for a month, when, after a vigorous resistance, it surrendered, and the regiment moved into cantonments at Mangalore.

In 1800 the regiment was again actively employed, under Lieut.-Colonel Alexander Cumine, in the arduous duty of quelling the rebellion of the refractory chiefs of Malabar and Canara. The rebels had seized the above-mentioned fort of Jemanlabad from the Sepoy garrison, and the 75th was for the second time employed in its reduction, which was effected by blockading the upper fortifications and storming the lower defences. In this gallant assault the regiment lost an officer and 50 rank and file in killed and wounded.[2] They remained actively employed, together or in detachments, in Malabar during the year 1801. Lieutenant MacNeil mentions that in this campaign of six months they marched 2500 miles in jungle country, exposed to damps and without tents, having an active enemy to watch. They had relieved Montana with a loss of 69 killed and wounded. On November 21st they took the fort of Pychee by storm with a loss of 2 rank and file killed and 5 wounded. They were then concentrated at Goa, where the thanks of Parliament were conveyed to them for their conduct during the war.

---

[1] " Life of Wellington," by Sir H. Maxwell.
The account of the siege is taken from Lushington's " Life of General Lord Harris," Theodore Hook's " Life of Sir David Baird," and the records of the 73rd, 74th, and 75th Regiments.

[2] " The assault on Jemanlabad took place on the 4th June and was beaten back with a loss of 2 rank and file killed and 25 wounded. Captain Gordon, much bruised, and Lieutenant McKay, shot in the thigh, were with 8 men on a scaling ladder which broke. There was no access to the upper fort except by a narrow staircase admitting only 2 men abreast. The enemy commanded by a dependant on the family of Tippoo Sahib had a six-pounder gun loaded with combustibles pointing down the staircase and a large pile of stones ready to throw down. Our two flank companies made up to 100 rank and file under Colonel Cumine are before it. It was intended to storm it yesterday morning, but the morning was too clear. Our men are determined to take it and say they will not be beaten back again " (letter from Lieutenant Archibald MacNeil of Carksay, Argyllshire, to Colin Macneal of Ugadale, dated 5th June 1800).

In March 1802 the regiment was dispatched to Cambay in consequence of the turbulent proceedings of the chiefs in Guzerat. It became necessary to besiege Fort Kerria, when the entrenched camp and out-works of the place were stormed and carried in a very gallant manner by the 75th under Lieut.-Colonel Grey. The fort afterwards surrendered at discretion, and was occupied by part of the regiment, which lost in this service Lieutenants Mather and Weston and 13 rank and file killed, while 40 men were wounded. In August the regiment served at the recapture of the fortress of Brodera, which had been seized by the partisans of the " Guicowar,"[1] and continued during the year in difficult and harassing services against the Guicowar and his Arab allies. From the laborious nature of the operations, and being in constant contact with the enemy, the regiment suffered severely. Lieutenant Hervey was killed in investing the small fortress of Pankera in July, and in September, Lieutenant McColl[2] died of extreme fatigue, as did Colonel Grey from the same cause the following month. The end of the year found the regiment resting at Brodera, but in the beginning of 1803 they took the field against Conojie, a refractory chieftain, whose fortified camp they attacked on the 6th of February and dispersed his forces, inflicting such chastisement upon them that they never reappeared on the scene of conflict. The regiment returned to Brodera, having lost in the foregoing services 2 officers and 35 men killed, and 75 rank and file wounded.

The following general orders were published, dated Bombay, March 23rd, 1803 :—

On the occasion of the return of the Seventy-Fifth Regiment from the active duties it has for the last twelve months been employed on in Guzerat, the Governor in Council requests that the Commander of the Forces will make offer of the thanks of Government to Captain Brownrigg (its immediate Commanding Officer), and to the officers, for the distinguished gallantry they and the n.c. officers and privates of that regiment have displayed, and for the high and meritorious services they have rendered during the last campaign in Guzerat ; in testimony of the Governor in Council's sense of which, and of the great and continued fatigue and hard duty they have undergone, the officers and men of the regiment are to continue on field allowances for as many days (not exceeding one month) after their return to Surat, as the Commander of the Forces shall think fit to limit.

Major-General Nicholls has great satisfaction in having the opportunity of publishing the Governor in Council's approbation of the conduct of His Majesty's Seventy-Fifth Regiment, and the Governor in Council having been pleased to leave to Major-General Nicholls the naming of the time, within the term of one month, for granting to the high and distinguished corps, field

---

[1] One of the principal Mahratta chiefs.
[2] Lieutenant McColl was the son of the minister of the Island of Tiree, Argyllshire.

allowances after their return to quarters, the Major-General names the last day he has in his power, viz., thirty days after that on which the corps arrived in Surat.

After resting at Surat from May till August, and after sundry movements connected with disturbances in the Guicowar's territory, they joined a force formed for the purpose of watching the motions of Scindia, who was now in arms. He had enlisted a large number of Frenchmen to aid his ambitious views ; there was a combination of the Mahratta chiefs against the British, while the Raja of Berar also declared himself the ally of Scindia, and a junction of their armies was effected. After some delay caused by the insincere and evasive negotiations of the enemy, General Arthur Wellesley began a brilliant series of military operations by the storming of Ahmadnagar on the 8th August ; the battle of Assaye and other victories followed, and in the short period of five months the enemy threw themselves on the generosity of the Governor-General.

The 75th, from their position near Surat, although by no means leading a life of repose, had little opportunity of sharing in these splendid operations of their more fortunate brother soldiers. From Surat a company was detached to take possession of Pamera, and during the monsoon the regiment proceeded, under Major (Brevet Lieut.-Colonel) Watson, to secure the strong fort of Soangurh, and after performing this service, it joined the force under Colonel Sir John Murray.[1]

In February 1804 the regiment embarked at Surat for the Bengal Presidency, arrived at Calcutta in May, and, after a short stay at Fort-William, proceeded in boats up the Ganges to Cawnpore.

The British Government having in vain remonstrated with Holkar, a cunning and powerful prince, as to the advance of his forces to Jeypore, whose rajah was under British protection, the Marquis Wellesley (Governor-General) directed Lord Lake to force him to retire. Holkar proposed terms so extravagant that they could not be granted. He was discovered in efforts to incite several chiefs, dependants of the British, to throw off their allegiance, and hostilities were resolved on.

On the 31st December the 75th, commanded by Lieut.-Colonel the Hon. J. Maitland, joined Lord Lake's army, which was between Deeg and Bhurtpore, where nearly the whole of Holkar's forces were collected.

[1] In a letter dated, Surat, 27th September 1803, Lieut. A. MacNeil writes :—" I have been 3 years and 7 months in the 75th, of which near 3 years on constant active service—11 actions, one storm and one siege. In that time Major Gray, 2 Captains, and 11 Lieutenants have been numbered with the dead." There is no mention in his letter of cholera or any serious sickness.

On January 2nd, 1805, the army encamped to the west of the latter city, which measured about eight miles in circumference and was surrounded by a wall partly composed of earth and partly of trunks of trees knit together with an incredible degree of firmness. The ramparts bristled with cannon and the ditch could be deepened by flooding at pleasure. The garrison was as numerous as the besieging army and well provided. Lord Lake had not sufficient force to invest the place, and it was determined to try to take it by assault. On the side where it was proposed to attack was a garden held by the enemy, which was taken by a party of the 75th under Colonel Maitland on the evening of the 4th of January ; a breaching battery was erected at this spot, which opened fire on the 7th. The breach was reported practicable on the 9th, and about 7 p.m. the storming party, in three columns, moved into the trenches. The 75th formed part of the right and of the centre columns. At eight o'clock they marched to the attack. The left, under Lieut.-Colonel Ryan, was to attempt a gateway on the left of our battery ; the right, under Major Hawkes, was to carry the enemy's advanced guns ; and should these two columns be unable to make their way into the city, they were to turn and support Lieut.-Colonel Maitland, who, with the centre, was to endeavour to surprise the enemy and enter by the breach. Ryan succeeded in driving the enemy from his guns outside the gate, but finding the access to that entrance cut off by a deep drain, he went to Maitland's assistance. Hawkes had also been so far successful, and having spiked the guns, he also turned to support the centre. The ground over which the centre column had to pass was rough and broken by trees and swampy pools, which occasioned delay and also caused the men to open out, so that many lost their way in the darkness. Some confusion arose from the centre and left clashing, and they failed to surprise the enemy, who received them on their arrival at the ditch with a tremendous fire of grape and musketry, which did not cease till near midnight. Some men, indeed, got into the ditch, but the water was breast high, and notwithstanding the inflexible ardour and repeated efforts of the gallant Maitland, who fell near the summit of the breach, the greater part of the troops, exposed to an incessant enfilading fire of grape, could not face the deep water ; and those that did so were powerless to storm the walls. The loss of the British in this attempt was 43 Europeans and 42 natives killed, 206 Europeans and 165 natives wounded. Of the 75th, Lieut.-Colonel the Hon. J. Maitland and Ensign Hatfield were killed ; Major Archibald Campbell, Captains Hessman and Branton, Lieutenants Byne, Tully, M'Lachlan, and Mathieson were wounded, and 91 n.c. officers and men were killed and wounded.[1]

[1] Regimental Record does not give names, merely " 100 killed and wounded."

Notwithstanding this repulse, active operations were at once renewed against another part of the wall. New batteries were erected, which opened fire on the 16th January and broke through the curtain wall, but next morning the breach was found to be effectively stockaded. The batteries again broke down the obstacles, but on the morning of the 18th, new stockades had been erected by the indefatigable defenders, and the fire of the guns was again directed on the breach. On the morning of the 20th a havildar and two intelligent privates of the 3rd Native Cavalry volunteered to inspect the state of the wall, and did so disguised in the dress of the country. Riding out of the trenches pursued by our soldiers firing blank ammunition, they called to the enemy that they were escaping from the " *banchut Feringhees*," and asked to be shown the way into the city ; they were thus enabled to examine the breach, when they galloped back under the fire and the execrations of their dupes. Each man was promoted and received 500 rupees. They reported the breach to be practicable, and noon on the 21st was appointed for the assault ; but the enemy, with wonderful perseverance again stockaded the breach, and it was 3 p.m. before it could be cleared. Parties of men were selected from the 22nd (50), the 75th (120), the 76th (150), and First Europeans (100), supported by the remainder of these regiments and by three native infantry battalions. When, covered by the fire of our batteries, the troops moved out of the trenches to the attack, it was found that a sheet of water of great depth and breadth had been formed by artificial flooding immediately opposite the new breach. Portable bridges, which had been prepared and which were carried by men trained to their use, were now found too short, and all attempts to lengthen them failed. Notwithstanding, several of our men, with indomitable courage, swam across and even mounted the breach. Colonel MacRae of the 76th, who commanded, however, saw the impossibility of conveying such a number across as would be adequate to the service, and he prudently recalled the foremost and retired to the trenches. Throughout the whole time of the advance and delay, a destructive fire of grape, round shot, and musketry was kept up by the enemy, causing a loss to the British of 18 officers and 573 men ; Captain W. Hessman and Lieutenants T. Grant and J. Craig Thomas of the 75th were among the officers wounded, 13 n.c. officers and soldiers of the regiment were killed and 101 were wounded.[1]

General Orders, 22nd January 1805.—The Commander-in-Chief returns his best thanks to the officers, soldiers, and natives, for the gallantry and steadiness they displayed in the attack yesterday, which, though ultimately

---

[1] Regimental Record gives four as the number of officers wounded, but no names.

unsuccessful, reflects the highest credit on the courage and intrepidity of the troops employed, and demands, in His Excellency's opinion, this public testimony of his approbation.   The Commander-in-Chief cannot sufficiently lament the number of brave men who have suffered on this service, when the utmost exertions of their intrepid valour were unequal to surmount the unexpected obstacles which were opposed to them.

By Lord Lake's order extra batta was given to the Europeans next day, and a sum of money to each native corps engaged.

On the 6th of February the army shifted camp to the south-east and prepared to continue the siege ; on the 10th, General Toms arrived from Bombay with reinforcements 5000 strong.   Lake now tried the effect of more regular approaches, and a fresh assault was delivered on February 20th.   The 75th formed part of the principal column of attack, consisting of most of the European force and three Sepoy battalions (under Colonel Don), which was to storm the works ; another column, under Captain Grant of the 86th, with 200 of his regiment and a Sepoy battalion, was to seize the enemy's trenches and traverses outside the town ; while a third (300 of the 65th and two Sepoy battalions) was to escalade the Been Narain Gate.   *Coracles*, or light boats of wicker-work covered with hides, to serve as pontoons, and a portable raft buoyed up by oil-skin floats, were prepared, and approaches were carried on to the brink of the ditch.   Stockades placed by the enemy in the night were knocked off and all moved out about 4 a.m.   Grant's Column carried the entrenchments and captured eleven guns, but the Third Column lost its way from the mistake of a guide, and was so early exposed to a destructive fire that it was obliged to retire.   The First Column (in which was the 75th) was preceded by fifty men carrying fascines to throw into the ditch, then they were to wheel outwards and keep up a musketry fire to the right and left while the stormers were crossing to the breach.   Unfortunately, however, our men were prevented from advancing as intended, owing to the imperfect construction of the approach, while they were exposed to an enfilade fire of artillery from right and left. Moreover, the enemy had sallied out during the night while the approaches were unoccupied, and the report spread that they had mined the ground, so that a feeling of gloom took possession of the minds of the troops who had to pass these approaches, which was increased by the groans and convulsions of dying comrades left exposed to the enemy's fire.   Don did all he could to counteract this impression, but could not at first prevail on the troops to leave the trenches.   At length, headed by some flankers of the 22nd,[1] they advanced to the assault.   The difficulties proved to be almost

---

[1] Captain Lindsay led the 22nd men with his arm in a sling, and he threw away the crutch which supported his leg, lame from a former wound.

insurmountable, but it was found that a bastion on the right was so roughly built as to present a chance of climbing up ; the ladders, however, were too short, and the ascent so difficult that only one man was able to mount at a time, and sufficient numbers could not get up to support each other. Fourteen officers succeeded in clambering up near to the top of the bastion, and the colours of the 12th Native Infantry were planted on it ; but Colonel Don, who saw the uselessness of attempting to carry it without support, recalled the whole party. While this was going on at the bastion, the enemy, thinking our men were nearer, sprung a mine, which made the breach larger, and had the troops left in the approach availed themselves of this by dashing out instantly, the place would probably have been taken. Our loss in this disastrous business was very severe, amounting to 894 killed and wounded. Lieutenant Stewart of the 75th was among the slain, but I have not found a list of the other regimental casualties.

Notwithstanding the loss already sustained, it was determined to renew the attack on the bastion which had been so nearly surmounted, and which they reported might be made easy by battering. Next morning Lord Lake addressed the troops who had taken part in the unsuccessful operations in such appropriate and feeling terms—with " affectionate regret rather than stern severity "[1] as to the opportunity they had lost—that on his calling for volunteers for another attempt, every man answered his call. The storming party consisted of the whole of the European troops of the Bengal army and the 2nd Batt. Bengal N.I., also the 65th, 75th, and 86th Regiments, and some native troops of the Bombay army. They advanced at 3 p.m. on the 21st February under Brigadier-General the Hon. Charles Monson, and as they passed Lord Lake the soldiers cheered him, and expressed their determination to avenge their comrades and carry the place, or die in the attempt. Nor did their conduct discredit this resolution ; but the difficulties were found to be so great that, though the men took advantage of the holes made by our shot and drove their bayonets into the wall to form steps by which to ascend, they were prevented by a terribly destructive fire—they were knocked backwards by logs of wood, round shot, and pots full of combustible materials which, with flaming packs of cotton dipped in oil, were thrown down upon them. Still the fearful contest was continued, efforts were made on the curtain and wherever the soldiers could see an opening promising a chance of success ; in this tremendous struggle and awful scene of death, officers and soldiers evinced an astonishing, even desperate, degree of valour for two hours, when Monson, finding success hopeless, ordered a return to the trenches. The loss of the British was

[1] Thorn's " War in India, 1803-6."

987 killed and wounded; among the latter were Captain E. Engel and Lieutenant and Adjutant Mathieson, 75th. The Regimental Record does not give the casualties in this attempt, but it mentions that the regiment lost nearly half its effective men, killed or wounded, during these operations. After this last failure the siege was converted into a blockade.

Among the many who individually performed acts of extraordinary gallantry, the conduct of Sergeant M'Kenzie and Privates John Grant and Martin struck their officers as conspicuous even among so many brave men, as well as that of Private Walter M'Farlane, whose hand was cut off at the wrist by the blow of a sabre. Sergeant Duncan, having led the assaulting party to the height of an embrasure, had his head blown off by the discharge of a gun as he was trying to enter, and his comrade, Sergeant Wm. Gordon, also received a grape-shot wound at the same moment, and retained the ball in his body for seventeen years.

On the 10th March the Raja made overtures of peace, and the preliminaries were signed on April 18th; on the 21st the 75th marched to Fatehpur, where they were stationed.[1]

The fine spirit of zeal and cheerfulness which animated the Highlanders is shown by a regimental order issued by Major Archibald Campbell, dated "Camp before Bhurtpore, 13th February 1805":—

R.O.—The Commanding Officer listened with much satisfaction to the very handsome declaration of the men of the 75th Regiment who declined receiving any payment for working when on duty in the trenches, but as that duty has been required of them oftener than he expected, and as the other European corps are in the habit of being paid for it, he has also directed that it should be drawn for the men of this regiment, whose willing and regular behaviour at all times entitles them to every indulgence, and is exceedingly creditable to themselves.

The ranks of the Highlanders, so reduced by their losses at Bhurtpore, were recruited by 300 men of the 76th Regiment, which was ordered home; this was not the *Highland* regiment of that number, which had been disbanded, and the number had become that of an English corps. No doubt this circumstance caused the first great change in the nationality of the 75th. Thus reinforced, the regiment, under Major Campbell, marched to Nouringabad, near Muttra,[2] where they were quartered till March 1806. Being now under orders for England, a number of soldiers were drafted

---

[1] The above account is taken from "War in India, 1803-6" and from the Regimental Record.

[2] Captain MacLachlan, in a letter dated Camp, Muttra, 31st January 1806, to his family at Loudle, Loch Sunart, mentions that he had remitted money from a soldier from that district to his father, but that "from the great scarcity of specie, the troops are six months in arrears of pay."

to regiments of cavalry and infantry remaining in India, and the remainder proceeded to Cawnpore and down the Ganges to Calcutta.

On the 13th April 1807, the headquarters reached the Downs and were sent to Leith. Their invalids had been discharged by the end of May, when only forty-four men remained in the regiment. Such was the result of the system of compulsory drafting, so heart-breaking both to the soldiers and their officers.

SUBALTERN OFFICER, 75TH
1809-10

From portrait of Lieutenant H. Malone, lent by S. M. Milne, Esq. (a feathered bonnet belonging to this officer is preserved, probably worn till uniform changed at this period).

CHAPTER XIX

1807–1849

ON July 10th, 1807, the royal authority was received by Sir Robert Abercromby, K.B., Colonel of the 75th, for his regiment to assume, " in addition to any other devices or badges to which it may be entitled, and bear on its colours and appointments the ' Royal Tiger ' and the word ' India ' superscribed, as an honourable and lasting testimony of the distinguished services of that corps in India."

The regiment was stationed at Dunblane, where several recruits and volunteers from the Militia joined, and by November the effective strength exceeded 300, but among them " were but few Highlanders." [1]

A memo., dated Horse Guards, 7th April 1809, states that

As the population of the Highlands of Scotland is found to be insufficient to supply recruits for the whole of the Highland corps on the establishment of His Majesty's army, and as some of these corps laying aside their distinguishing dress, which is objectionable to the natives of South Britain, would in a great measure tend to facilitate the completing of their establishments, as it would be an inducement to the men of the English Militia to extend their service in greater numbers to those regiments, etc.

Consequently it was decided that the 75th " should discontinue in future to wear the dress by which His Majesty's Regiments of Highlanders are distinguished," and that it " should no longer be considered on that establishment." [2]

Accordingly the 75th, then quartered at Haddington, assumed the usual uniform of Regiments of the Line, and was no longer designated as a Highland regiment (by inadvertence the word " Highland " remained for some years in the Army List).

In May the regiment moved to Perth, and in September to Aberdeen, where its numbers were considerably increased. In April 1810 they were sent to Ireland, and after visiting Newry, were at Dublin in July. At this time the establishment was increased to 1000 men. In November the regiment embarked for Liverpool 700 strong, and proceeded to Horsham in Sussex. In May 1811 they embarked at Portsmouth for Jersey.

The aggression of the French in Italy, and their threatening attitude towards Sicily, had, in 1806, caused Great Britain to intervene for its defence by occupying that island, which previously formed part of the kingdom of Naples, ruled by a Bourbon dynasty ; but Napoleon having made himself master of all Italy, the King of Naples had taken refuge in his island dominions. The 75th was

---

[1] Regimental Record.

[2] The same sensible decision was at the same time taken with regard to the 72nd, 73rd, 74th, and 91st Regiments.

GENERAL SIR ROBERT ABERCROMBY, K.B., OF AIRTHREY

From a painting by Raeburn in possession of Broderick Chinnery-Haldane, Esq. of Gleneagles

now ordered to form part of the Sicilian garrison, and they sailed from Jersey on the 8th October in two vessels of war, and landed at Messina on the 10th of November.

Although the regiment had lost more than half its numbers in action, and shown undeviating steadiness of character throughout constant detached and harassing duties, which are the greatest trial of discipline, yet, with the exception of Seringapatam, they had not the good fortune to take part in the more brilliant victories of the Eastern wars ; and the corps was deeply disappointed at being thus removed from all hope of joining the army in Spain, and sharing in the glories of the Peninsular Campaigns.[1]

Early in 1812 they were stationed on the heights of Curcurrace, near Messina, and at Melazzo, a small fortified town on the neighbouring north-east coast, with a strength of 680 rank and file under Colonel Swinton.   They were at Messina from June till November, when they moved to the Faro at the narrowest part of the Straits, opposite the famous rock of Scylla, where the French had a small force, which it was determined to attack.   The Naval Commander having reconnoitred the enemy's defences, four companies of the 75th were embarked under the command of Major Stuart on the night of the 14th February 1813, and soon reached the station of Pietro Nero on the opposite shore.   Here they landed, and along with the sailors executed the service committed to them in the handsomest manner, with the loss of a few of their number, among whom was Major Stuart, who was shot after the detachment had reembarked and the object of the descent had been fully accomplished.   The following extract refers to the foregoing :—

District Order.—Major-General Montressor congratulates the troops on the successful attack made on a large collection of the enemy's boats at Pietro Nero, defended by a regiment of the line, two troops of cavalry, and three batteries ; but the enemy found it impossible to resist the enterprising spirit of the flotilla, seconded by the gallantry of four companies of the 75th Regiment under Major Stuart ; the loss of this experienced officer will be long felt by his corps and by the service.[2]

The danger of an invasion of Sicily having subsided, the British Government turned their attention to the disordered state of that country.   Though its preservation from French invasion entirely depended on the English alliance, its rulers resented interference and persevered in such a course of extravagance and oppression that Lord William Bentinck, who was Envoy at Palermo as well as Commander of the Forces, suspended the payment of the English subsidy, and threatened further measures unless the system of government was materially altered.   A new constitution

---

[1] Regimental Record.   [2] *Ibid.*

on British lines was organised for the Sicilians, and to enable him to enforce this beneficial design, a body of troops was ordered to Palermo, including the 75th, who arrived there early in March. In the end of that month the regiment marched with a brigade under General Hinuber to Ponte Margarette and Partana, and in June they were at Castello Vetrano. Having marched back to Palermo in the end of June, and the political atmosphere being quiet, the regiment returned to the district of Messina. Their service in this fruitful and beautiful island was brought to an end on the 1st of July 1814 by an order to embark for the Ionian Islands, which had been taken by Britain from the French in 1809. The regiment arrived at Corfu, July 14th, and formed part of the garrison. In the adjustment of the territories of the different Powers at the Treaty of Paris, 1815, it was agreed " that the Ionian Islands should form a single free and independent state under the exclusive protection of Great Britain."

In 1815 a detachment of 100 men joined from England, when the strength was 725, commanded by Colonel Sir Patrick Ross.

In August 1817 the regiment was moved to Santa Maura, with detachments at Pargo, Ithaca, Cerigo, Paxo, and Corfu. A party of thirty-nine men left Leith in October in the *Elles* transport, which was wrecked on the coast of Spain, and ten of the number were drowned.

In 1818 the Royal authority was received for the 75th Regiment to bear on its colours and appointments the word " Seringapatam," " in commemoration of the distinguished gallantry displayed by the regiment in the storming and capture of Seringapatam in May 1799."

In 1819 the establishment was reduced to 620 privates, and in 1820 the detachment at Pargo, on the coast of Albania, was withdrawn, that place having been ceded to the Turks. In the end of the year the regiment was concentrated at Corfu, and in August 1821 it embarked for Gibraltar, where the establishment was again reduced, and the officers of the two junior companies were placed on half-pay. On leaving Corfu, Lieut.-General Sir Frederick Adam issued an order which was highly complimentary to the regiment, and to Colonel Gubbins, who was in temporary command of it.

The corps was stationed at Gibraltar for two years, commanded by Colonel Gubbins and Sir John Campbell, and in the end of 1823 it returned to England, after an absence of twelve years. Previous to their departure, Lord Chatham, Governor of Gibraltar, expressed in General Orders his high sense of the merits of the corps, and of its excellent conduct while under his command. In March 1824 the 75th left Gosport for Windsor, where they were stationed four months, then returning to Gosport they embarked for Dublin in July, and proceeded to Birr and afterwards to Fermoy. At this period the south of Ireland being in a very disturbed state, the regiment was broken up into detachments in the different villages for the prevention of crime, and employed in patrolling the country by night for the protection of the loyal inhabitants. At the same time, two additional companies were being raised, and a new system of drill had been recently published, which, owing to present circumstances, it was difficult to carry out. The regiment also laboured under the disadvantage of having had for some time a constant change of commanding officers.

In July 1825 the 75th moved to Dublin, with an effective strength of 658 rank and file, commanded by Lieut.-Colonel Viscount Barnard.

Here the regiment had the advantage of being together, and of being brigaded with other good corps, and taking part in the instructive field-days under Major-General Sir C. Grant ; though these advantages were rendered somewhat nugatory owing to so many of the soldiers being too young to profit by them, and by the onerous public duties of the station. After four months in the capital they were moved to Newry, where they were again scattered in detachments, preserving the peace and preventing illicit distillation. In April 1826 they moved to Enniskillen, and to Castlebar in September, being commanded by Lieut.-Colonel England. The detached duties at these places continued ; at Castlebar recruits arrived in great numbers, and several of the remaining old soldiers were discharged, but notwithstanding these untoward circumstances, the regiment received much approbation from the inspecting officer.

In November 1827, General Sir Robert Abercromby, K.C.B., who had been colonel of the regiment since its formation (forty years), died in Scotland, and was succeeded by Lieut.-General Dunlop, the same officer who led the left column at the storming of Seringapatam.

In April 1828 the 75th marched to Mullingar, where, only one company being detached, hopes were entertained that time and opportunity might be afforded to perfect the system of the corps ; and every effort was made for this purpose. The greatest success attended these efforts, and universal commendation was the consequence ; but in two months a sudden order was received to march to Limerick on account of expected riots at the Clare election, three companies being sent to Clare Castle, which was already crowded with troops. After the election the regiment was reviewed at Limerick and marched to Birr. Here, the public duties being light, they had time to perfect the work which had been interrupted at Mullingar. Lieut.-General Sir John Byng, commanding the forces in Ireland, visited the regiment in the autumn, and Major-General Sir T. Arbuthnot was for some days occupied in inspecting the records of the men's service, and examining into the financial system of the corps.

In May 1829 the headquarters were at Galway, and the regiment was again broken up in detachments all over that district. Here the headquarters were inspected by the Commander-in-Chief, and a few recruits were added to the ranks. In September they moved to Fermoy, having two detachments.

The 75th was concentrated at Cork in March 1830, and embarked for Bristol ; thence they marched by Bath across England to Canterbury, where they arrived on 22nd April. On the 4th of May, Lord Hill, Commanding-in-Chief, inspected the corps, which now consisted of a remarkably efficient body of men. The service and reserve companies having been formed, the latter marched, under Major Burney, to Sheerness ; the former took leave of their excellent quarters at Canterbury and embarked on the 21st of May for the Cape of Good Hope, where they arrived after a voyage of three months.

Forty-three years had elapsed since its formation, of which the 75th had served thirty-one years abroad, and twelve in the United Kingdom.

The service companies were now quartered at Cape Castle ; in 1831 the reserve companies were moved from Sheerness to Plymouth, and subsequently to Bristol, enlisting recruits at all these places. Lieut.-Colonel England being employed on separate service in 1832, the service companies were commanded by Major Hammond, and afterwards by Captain Hallifax. In September they embarked for Algoa Bay, and on arrival at Grahamstown they were distributed there and at Fort-Beaufort, Fort-William, Port Elizabeth, Hermann's Kraal, and Double Drift.

On the 9th of April 1833, Lieut.-General Sir Joseph Fuller was appointed Colonel of the 75th, *vice* Lieut.-General Dunlop, deceased.

For two years the service companies remained on the eastern or Kaffir frontier of our possessions.

Towards the end of 1834 and early in 1835 the aggressions of the Kaffir tribes assumed a formidable character. A chief named Macomo had been allowed to reside within British territory, but, owing to some outrages committed by him and his followers, he was deprived of the lands he held on sufferance, and this greatly incensed him against the Government ; while the lenity extended towards predatory Kaffirs emboldened them in these depredations. Multitudes, under various chiefs, invaded the colony, carrying rapine and devastation among the settlers. Grahamstown was hastily barricaded, every house was fortified, and troops were ordered to the frontier. The Governor, Sir Benjamin D'Urban, took command of the forces, consisting of the 72nd Highlanders, 75th Regiment, the Cape Mounted Rifles, the First Battalion Provisional Infantry, the Second Battalion Colonial Infantry ; the Burgher forces from Swellendam, George, Uitenhage, Albany, Beaufort, Kat River, Cradock, and Somerset ; with six guns.[1] On the 1st April he advanced into Kaffraria at the head of over 3000 men, leaving the remainder on an inner line of defence under Lieut.-Colonel England of the 75th. On the 8th of April Sir Benjamin made a concentrating movement on the mountains in which the Keiskama, Kaboosi, and Buffalo Rivers take their rise ; the Third Division, under Major Cox of the 75th, being at the head of the Keiskama Hoek. The Kaffirs, about 7000 in number, finding themselves attacked on all sides, fled with great loss ; several thousand head of cattle were taken, while on our side only one man was killed and 4 wounded, among whom was the Boer Field Commandant Van Wyk, who commanded the Fourth Division.

In General Orders the Commander-in-Chief returned his thanks to the officers commanding divisions as well as the other officers, n.c. officers, and soldiers, for their conduct in this affair. He mentioned the names of Lieutenants Moultrie and Bingham of the 75th, and praised the cool and soldier-like conduct of Private Thomas Quin of that regiment. D'Urban now entered into fruitless negotiations with the powerful chief Hintza, and at length hostile measures were taken against him, resulting in his capture. He was afterwards killed while trying to escape. After various abortive negotiations and unimportant skirmishes, the 75th garrisoned Fort Cox, newly established and named after their Major. Patrolling was actively continued, the enemy attacking various parties of British troops, and on one occasion killing the whole patrol (thirty men) of the First Provisional Battalion. In August they were successful in other affairs, watching from their fastnesses the movement of troops, harassing them and cutting off stragglers, while they made frequent forays within the Colony. D'Urban recalled the Dutch Burghers, who had been dismissed to their homes, and ordered that they should receive a fixed rate of pay ; he sent Brigade-Major Warden to treat with the frontier Kaffirs on condition of their becoming British subjects. Major Cox formed the troops concentrated at his post into three divisions, which, sallying from the fort, were everywhere successful and caused considerable loss to the enemy. Next day he, with Major Warden, proceeded unarmed to meet Macomo and other chiefs, who had

---

[1] Fifty men of the 75th were trained and acted as artillerymen.

assembled with a guard of 800 men, of whom 300 had firearms. These officers were personally known to Macomo, and their conference came to a happy conclusion, each chief sending an assegai in token of submission ; but it was only in September that a treaty of peace was concluded.

During this contest the regiment had little opportunity of distinction, but it maintained its high character by its conduct and endurance.

I find no list of loss in killed and wounded, which the Regimental Record says " was comparatively trifling."

The approbation of His Majesty King William IV was conveyed to the troops in the following words :—" It affords His Majesty high gratification to observe that in this new form of warfare His Majesty's forces have exhibited their characteristic courage, discipline, and cheerful endurance of fatigue and privation."

During the operations Sir Benjamin D'Urban annexed certain territory, which was named the " Province of Queen Adelaide," giving as his reason " the absolute necessity of providing for the future security of the Colony against unprovoked aggression, which could only be done by removing these treacherous and unreclaimable savages to a safer distance " ; and the 75th now occupied King William's Town, the newly founded capital of the province. Here they suffered from scurvy owing to the want of vegetable diet during the campaign. In the end of 1836 the new province was given up by order of the Home Government, and the 75th moved to Fort Willshire and afterwards to the Beaufort district, with a strength of only 416 privates, distributed in no less than thirteen different places.

In July 1837, Lieut.-Colonel England was appointed to the 41st Regiment, and Major Grieve became lieut.-colonel of the 75th.

Since January 1835, fifty men of the regiment had been mounted, and they served as cavalry till October 1839, when, on their return to their regiment, in " Frontier Orders " of the 9th October, the commanding officer was desired to assemble them and thank " this body of well-conducted and good soldiers " for their " very active and useful service " ; and in an order by the Commander-in-Chief at Cape Town he describes their faithful and zealous service to have been such as not only to gain the " admiration of their commanders, but the grateful respect of the inhabitants on the frontier." [1]

[1] The above account of the campaign is taken from " Medals of the British Army and how they were Won," by Thomas Carter ; " History of the 72nd Highlanders," " Autobiography of Sir Harry Smith," and the Regimental Record of the 75th.

In October 1840, Lieut.-General Sir William Hutchinson, K.C.B., was appointed colonel of the regiment, *vice* Sir W. Fuller, deceased.

In April 1842, the regiment was held in readiness to embark for England. Various circumstances, however, postponed their relief, which was still further delayed by the wreck of the transport *Abercrombie Robinson* on the 28th August in Table Bay, with the reserve battalion of the 91st Regiment on board ; and the 75th was again ordered on outpost duty, entailing great expense on the officers, who had just parted with everything necessary for that service. At length the various detachments were ordered to march for Port Elizabeth, where the headquarters arrived on May 20th, 1843 ; but the transport not having sufficient accommodation, only a part of the regiment sailed on June 8th, the remainder proceeding by steamer to Cape Town. The transport experienced a series of westerly gales, and after being driven back to Port Elizabeth, was so much damaged in her second attempt that she had to refit in Simon's Bay. Fortunately H.M. Troopship *Belleisle* touched there on her passage from China; she had ample room for all the service companies, who embarked, and she sailed on July 12th.

During its service in South Africa, several drafts had been received from the depôt to replace those invalided home ; but fifty men desirous of settling in the Colony had been discharged in 1841, and fifty-nine were discharged for the same purpose in 1843. Several men also volunteered to the Cape Mounted Rifles. When the 75th were under orders for home, to be relieved by the reserve battalion 91st, 146 rank and file volunteered for the latter corps. The option was not given to sergeants, " but the officers in command of respective corps may be allowed the privilege of appointing one sergeant to every twenty volunteers to be selected from the corporals, and one corporal to be selected from the privates."

The following extracts show the high estimate in which the 75th was held :—

Frontier Orders, Grahamstown, 13*th May* 1843.—The Colonel Commanding on the frontier cannot part with a corps that has been so distinguished for long and valuable service in this Colony without requesting Major Hall, the officers, n.c. officers and soldiers of that excellent regiment to accept his acknowledgments for conduct which has been as honourable to the corps as it has been of advantage to the Colony.

General Orders, Headquarters, Cape Town, 6*th July* 1843.—His Excellency the Commander-in-Chief cannot allow the 75th Regiment to leave his command without expressing to Major Hall, the officers, n.c. officers and soldiers of that corps his highest approbation of the good conduct and good services rendered by the regiment during the long period of their duty in this Colony.

After a favourable passage of two months, touching at St Helena and Ascension, the *Belleisle* made Plymouth Sound on the 12th September. The service companies, much reduced in numbers from the before-mentioned causes, the same evening occupied the Citadel Barracks,[1] where they were joined by the depôt companies under Major Hallifax, numbering 17 sergeants, 16 corporals, 4 drummers, and 456 privates, nearly all young soldiers.

Part of the depôt companies were employed in suppressing the " Rebecca Riots " in South Wales, and had furnished the guard of honour to H.R.H. Prince Albert at Bristol on the occasion of the launch of the *Great Britain*, the largest steamship then known. The general conduct and appearance of the depôt companies had elicited the approval of every General Officer who inspected them.

In December 1843, Lieut.-Colonel Grieve retired on full pay, and was succeeded by Lieut.-Colonel Hallifax.

On the 27th May 1844, the regiment, now at its full establishment, was inspected by Major-General the Hon. H. Murray, whose opinion was published in a complimentary Order. In July the regiment moved to South Wales, headquarters at Newport, where they were but indifferently lodged in temporary barracks. In September 1845 they embarked for Waterford, *en route* to Birr, having been favourably reported on after every inspection during their stay in Wales. At Birr, Major-General Sir Guy Campbell expressed his satisfaction with the regiment, which, in June 1846, moved to Athlone, and here, as at the previous station, it was broken up into many detachments. In March the regiment received the thanks of the Magistrates and inhabitants of Athlone for their services on the occasion of a destructive fire. During these two years a large number of headquarter recruits had been enlisted. In July 1847 the 75th marched to the Royal Barracks, Dublin, where they were again consolidated, and were inspected by H.R.H. Prince George of Cambridge. At Dublin, in 1848, the establishment was augmented to 1000 rank and file, and recruits were rapidly obtained.

In consequence of the agitation in Tipperary known as the Smith O'Brien Rebellion, the 75th moved by rail, on the 31st July, to Bagnalstown, and marched to Kilkenny, where they encamped in the barrack square. Four companies were pushed on to Callan, and afterwards to Ballingarry and Tertulla, where they encamped, and were joined, August 7th, by the headquarters, and the regiment formed part of the field force under Major-General John MacDonald, C.B. On the 14th the force was inspected by Lieut.-General Viscount Hardinge, who had arrived in Ireland to take

---

[1] There is no disembarkation state of the service companies.

chief command, and on this occasion his Lordship expressed the greatest satisfaction at the appearance of the troops. The field force was broken up on the 10th September, and Major-General MacDonald conveyed his warmest thanks to the officers and men for their zeal and good conduct during the harassing service on which they had been employed. The 75th now occupied barracks at Kilkenny, where they remained till early in March 1849, when they received orders to prepare for immediate service in India, leaving only a skeleton depôt, under 1 captain, 1 lieutenant, and 1 ensign. On the 29th the regiment marched to Fermoy, where they received 2 sergeants and 105 rank and file, volunteers from the depôts of the 73rd and 79th.

CHAPTER XX

1849–1857

THE regiment was embarked on five ships, the first division on May 2nd, and the headquarters on the 7th. They landed at Calcutta from August 8th to September 1st, proceeded by water to Allahabad, and marched to Umballa, where they arrived on December 21st, under Lieut.-Colonel Hallifax. There was a good deal of sickness, and the casualties since leaving Ireland amounted to 103. The regiment was stationed at Umballa, a wing being latterly at Agra, till November 1853, when they marched by wings to Peshawar. While at Umballa, in 1852, the regiment lost Ensign Hardy and ninety-three n.c. officers and men from epidemic cholera and fever. They were moved into camp, when the mortality ceased.

In February 1854, a detachment proceeded to protect the erection of a fort at the entrance to the Kohat Pass. In 1855 they marched in two divisions to Rawal Pindi under Lieut.-Colonel Herbert. On October 1st, 1856, the clothing was changed from the coatee and epaulettes to the tunic. In December the regiment, under Colonel Alexander Jardine, marched to Kasauli, and in March 1857 was inspected by His Excellency General Anson, Commander-in-Chief, who was pleased to express his entire satisfaction with the soldier-like bearing of the corps, an opinion soon to be verified in the arduous campaign which ensued.

On the first intelligence of the mutiny of the Bengal Army, which broke out at Meerut on the 10th of May 1857, the headquarters of the 75th was ordered to proceed, on the 12th, by forced marches to Umballa, a distance of forty-eight miles, which was accomplished in thirty-eight hours. Colonel Jardine having been taken ill, the command devolved upon Lieut.-Colonel Herbert. In consequence of a panic among the European residents at Simla, caused by the conduct of the Nusseree Battalion quartered at Jutogh, the Light Company, made up to 115 men under Captain Brookes, was despatched on elephants to Kalka in order to afford protection to the European families, who were flying for refuge.

On the 16th of May orders were issued for the formation of a field force in two brigades to advance towards Delhi, where the garrison of native troops had thrown in their lot with the revolted soldiery who thronged thither. The Europeans, civil and military, male and female, were murdered, and the city became the focus of the rebellion. The First Brigade, commanded by Colonel Hallifax of the 75th, marched from Umballa on the 23rd of May, and reached Kurnaul on the night of the 25th. Here the force was attacked by cholera. Among its first victims was the Commander-in-Chief, General the Hon. George Anson, and during the continuation of the outbreak the 75th lost Colonel Hallifax (Brigadier) and 29 men.

On May 30th, the troops resumed their march under Major-General Sir Henry Barnard, K.C.B., and on June 3rd reached Alipur, one march from Delhi. Here the force was placed in position for the attack of the advanced entrenchments of the enemy, who were strongly posted at Badli-ki-Sarai for the purpose of preventing the British from advancing on the city by the Grand Trunk Road. On the morning of the 8th of June Barnard advanced ; and when his troops got within range of the guns, which the enemy had placed with great skill so as to sweep the road by which the British must of necessity approach, a most destructive fire, first of round shot, then shell and grape, told with deadly effect on our ranks. The First Brigade was ordered to take ground to the right and deploy into line, when it fell to the lot of the 75th to be immediately in front of the enemy's principal heavy armed battery, from which it was about 1200 yards distant.

Before daylight that morning Brigadier Grant, C.B., with two troops of Horse Artillery and the 9th Lancers, had been despatched to pass round between Delhi and Badli-ki-Sarai with a view to attack the enemy's left rear, and thus effectually aid in dislodging him. Meanwhile the regiment remained in the shelter of some high ground, in order to allow time to carry out this intention. It soon appeared, however, that our light guns could make little impression on the enemy's heavy artillery, which was inflicting severe loss upon our troops. Sir Henry therefore determined to close with the enemy, and called upon the 75th to advance and carry the battery. How the regiment justified the confidence reposed in it is best told by the following honourable testimony borne by Major-General Reed at the time, by the Commander-in-Chief in India after the war was over, and in a letter from a member of the Indian Civil Service :—

Camp before Delhi,
11th June 1857.

Field Force Orders.—The Commander of the Forces congratulates Major-General Sir H. Barnard, K.C.B., the officers and troops under his command upon the brilliant and successful result of the operations so ably designed and conducted by him, and admirably executed by them on the morning of the 8th instant, in the course of which the insurgent enemy were driven from two strong posts defended by numerous cavalry and artillery, served with the greatest precision, most if not the whole have been taken and captured in the most gallant and determined manner by the troops employed ; the whole resulting, in about four hours, in the force being firmly established on the heights in front of and commanding Delhi.

Major-General Reed only awaits the report from Sir H. Barnard to publish the names of officers and men who had the opportunity afforded them of being particularly distinguished. He has, however, in the meantime, brought to the notice of the Major-General Commanding the Forces the admirable gallantry of H.M. 75th Regiment in the attack and capture of the guns in the first strong position of the mutineers, and the distinguished manner in which they were led to the attack by Lieut.-Colonel Herbert and their officers.

This movement, the success of which was completed by the well-planned flank attack of Brigadier Grant, C.B., with two troops of Horse Artillery and H.M. 9th Lancers, was succeeded by the successful advance in two columns on the heights which we at present occupy, and from which the mutineers were driven within the walls of Delhi . . .

The following extract from General Orders, Calcutta, 14th April 1862, is very descriptive :—

The action of Badli-ki-Serai, 1857, was one of the first occasions on which the enemy in position offered serious resistance to the British troops. Advantageously placed in very difficult ground, the rebels in force prevented, with the fire of an entrenched battery of heavy guns, the advance to Delhi of the force under the late gallant Sir H. Barnard, K.C.B. The only means of effecting a passage was the capture of the battery. Resolutely led by Brigadier Showers, C.B., the 75th Regiment, exposed for 1200 yards to a destructive fire of round shot and grape, which caused a very heavy loss to the regiment in killed and wounded, took the battery by storm, and enabled the British force to take up that same day their position before Delhi. Nothing more useful, nothing more brilliant was done during the late campaign than the opening at Badli-ki-Sarai of the road to Delhi by the 75th Regiment.

In a letter to General Chapman, commanding the Scottish District, dated 4th August 1899, from George Ricketts, Esq., C.B., who in 1857 was Deputy-Commissioner of Loodianah, he says, with regard to the 75th on this occasion—

They were first in action at Badli-ki-Sarai, and they had the whole of the hardest fighting, for they had to take the entrenchment and *sarai* in the fort by storm. It was splendidly done at a rush up the glacis with the bayonet, and I daresay no one of them thought any more about it ! It was acknowledged by all as a very good piece of work, but the political effect of that successful rush was enormous, and certainly influenced the whole campaign. It was witnessed by the Raja of Jheend. Jheend was the second in importance of the protected Cis-Sutlej Sikh States—Patiala, Jheend, and Nabha—all related to each other. At the beginning of the row, Patiala was little more than a boy, Nabha was a mere boy of about eighteen. Jheend was an old white-bearded man, who had seen plenty of fighting in his day. . . . He (Jheend) wrote a letter to Patiala saying, " He knew the difficulties the British were in, but he saw the rush of the white soldiers at Badli-ki-Sarai, that in the face of a heavy fire there was no hesitation or halting or seeking cover, but they went *straight* ; and he saw the men who were killed lying across their rifles in the same position on the glacis, and the nation that could produce such men were sure to succeed in the end, whatever the adverse odds might be at the commencement."

A copy of Jheend's letter was placed at the time before Mr Ricketts in Court, and the above is an accurate translation. He considered that there was practically no limit to the importance of the impression produced on the Raja, as it went far to settle which side these states, who dominate the whole trunk road from Ferozepur to Kurnaul, would take.

Although driven from their position, the retreating enemy availed themselves of the numerous houses and enclosures with which the intervening space of about three miles was thickly studded, to offer a determined resistance, and it was only after ten hours' hard fighting that they were forced to take shelter within the city. Piquets were placed along the ridge between the city walls and the cantonment, and the men being much exhausted by their exertions and the tremendous heat of the sun, added to want of food, the force encamped on the parade ground of the latter.

On this occasion the regiment lost Lieutenant A. Harrison and 21 rank and file killed in action ; and Lieut.-Colonel Herbert, Captain R. Dawson, Lieutenant and Adjutant Barker, Lieutenants Fitzgerald, Rivers, Pym, Crozier, and Faithful, Paymaster Chambers and Assistant Surgeon Lithgow, 2 sergeants, and 43 rank and file were wounded. Sir H. Barnard personally thanked the regiment after the engagement.

From the 8th June for three months the overworked handful of Europeans, Sikhs and Gurkhas were rather the besieged than the besiegers. All they could do against the garrison of from 50,000 to 70,000 disciplined men was to hold the ridge and repulse the sallies, often turned into pitched battles, which were made almost daily by the mutineers.

On the 12th the Flagstaff piquet, furnished by the 75th, under Captains Dunbar and Knox, was attacked by large numbers of the enemy, whom they drove back with great loss. In performing this gallant service, Captain Knox and 3 privates were killed, and 17 rank and file were wounded. Again, on the 15th, the piquet at Metcalfe's Grounds, furnished by the 75th, was engaged with the enemy from early morning till noon, when their assailants were compelled to retire, the loss to the regiment this day being 5 men killed and 12 wounded.

The Regimental Orders of 16th June brought to notice the gallant conduct in the actions of June 8th, 12th, and 15th, of Sergeant-major R. Wadeson, Quartermaster-sergeant E. Courtney, Colour-sergeant C. Coughlan, Colour-sergeant M. Welsh, Colour-sergeant J. Bowan, Sergeant T. Colloran, Sergeant T. Exton, Privates J. Fullalove and J. Woods.

On the evening of the 19th the rear of the British position was strongly attacked, and after a sharp engagement darkness set in, leaving the enemy on the ground they had taken till the following morning, when they were driven back to the city, many of them being killed. The 75th, having the advanced outpost duties, suffered no loss on this occasion.

On June 23rd, part of the regiment under Captain Chancellor was again engaged in a severe conflict at the Subzee Mundee, and the Light Company under Captain Brookes, who were escorting a convoy of siege stores from Umballa, successfully resisted an attack from the rear by a large force of cavalry.

On the 27th two of the regiment were wounded at Hindoo Rao's Battery, and one of them afterwards died of his wounds. On the 9th of July a body of about 100 of the enemy's cavalry effected an entrance into the lines, creating great confusion and some loss, but they were quickly driven out, leaving several dead men and horses. To prevent a recurrence of this, the 75th shifted camp to the extreme right, where the regiment, which had throughout the siege been healthy, now suffered great loss in officers and men from cholera and dysentery. Sir H. Barnard died, and was succeeded by General Archdale Wilson.

On July 14th, Captain Chancellor, with a portion of the regiment, was engaged in driving the enemy out of the gardens adjoining Metcalfe's Grounds, and in accomplishing this duty 6 men were wounded—one mortally. On the same day Lieutenants Rivers and Faithful were also wounded at Hindoo Rao's Battery.

On the 18th, Captain Brookes, with 200 men of the regiment, dislodged a force of cavalry and infantry from the Subzee Mundee village after severe fighting, in which Lieutenant Crozier and 3 men were killed, 16 wounded, and 1 was missing. For his conduct on this day Ensign Wadeson, who had lately been promoted from sergeant-major, afterwards received the Victoria Cross.[1] A great struggle took place on the 23rd at Metcalfe's Grounds, in which a part of the regiment, under Captain Drew, was successfully engaged. They had 1 man killed and 8 wounded—2 mortally.

The rains had now set in with all the attendant discomforts. Wilson's army was of the finest mettle, fighting on an average three battles a week for six weeks without making any apparent progress towards their object, a state of affairs in which the discipline of the best troops is apt to deteriorate. The general organised the system of reliefs so as to give his men the greatest possible amount of rest. At the same time he protected the camp followers from the thought-

[1] Granted to Ensign Richard Wadeson " for conspicuous bravery at Delhi on the 18th July 1857, when the regiment was engaged at Subzee Mundee, in having saved the life of Private Michael Farrell when attacked by a Sowar ; also on the same day for rescuing Private John Barry of the same regiment, when wounded and helpless he was attacked by a Sowar whom Ensign Wadeson killed." Ensign Wadeson afterwards commanded the regiment, and became Colonel, and Lieut.-Colonel of Chelsea Hospital.

less ill-treatment of some of the Europeans, and recognising that though attention to personal appearance under such circumstances may seem trivial, it has a powerful effect on the self-respect and discipline of an army, he insisted on the soldiers wearing their uniforms instead of turning out in their shirt sleeves as they had fallen into the habit of doing.

In the constant service of this trying time the 75th bore a distinguished part, notably on August 12th, when a piquet of the regiment, under Captain Freer (of the 27th, attached to the 75th), assisted in the capture of some guns near Ludlow Castle, which had given great annoyance on the previous night. This service was performed with the greatest gallantry : the enemy were surprised, four guns were taken, and the mutineers pursued up to the gates of Delhi. On this occasion the 75th had 2 privates killed and 10 wounded—1 mortally.

About this time the British received considerable reinforcements, both of Europeans and Indians, from the Punjab, which to some extent lightened the piquet duty. On the 4th September a siege train arrived, and the construction of breaching batteries was at once commenced, entailing much labour as well as considerable loss to the troops in their conflicts with the enemy, who constantly attempted to impede the work. During these operations the greater part of the 75th remained in the trenches, acting as covering parties to the batteries, and exposed to direct and flanking fire from the enemy, by which 1 man was killed and 2 officers and 13 men were wounded—3 of them mortally. There was, besides, little or no shelter from the sun, and they were indifferently supplied with water and provisions. Still officers and men kept up their spirits by riding pony races, playing cricket or quoits ; while the bands played, and a tone of cheerfulness pervaded the camp.[1]

The British troops were still too few for systematic attack,[2] but our Indian Empire trembled in the balance ; the critical state of the Punjab demanded immediate success, and, without further delay, the heavy batteries opened on the 8th September. After a bombardment at distances varying from 700 to 200 yards, a breach was reported on the 13th, but it was by no means perfect ; the "berm," invisible from our batteries, remained intact, preventing the debris of the "escarp" from falling into the ditch, while its masonry

---

[1] Holmes' "History of Indian Mutiny."

	European.	Native.
[2] Artillery and Engineers	750	1350
Cavalry	500	1000
Infantry	2600	3800

In addition to these 10,000 regulars, the Raja of Jheend had, since his experiences at Badli-ki-Sarai, joined the British, and was followed on September 7th by a contingent from the Raja of Kashmir, bringing the total strength to about 12,500, about one-fourth of the rebel garrison.

revetment, being unimpaired, necessitated escalade. The front to be assailed comprised about a mile of the enceinte, and included the Moré, Kashmir, and Water Bastions. On the afternoon of Sunday the 13th September, Brigadier John Nicholson, C.B., clearly explained the plan of attack to the officers commanding battalions, their seconds in command, and adjutants ; he then took the adjutants to the trenches, when he showed them the position to be occupied by each battalion before the assault, which was ordered to be made at daybreak on the 14th, and, in view of the scarcely practicable breaches, it was decided to blow in the Kashmir Gate. This daring exploit was performed by Lieutenants Salkeld and Home of the Bengal Engineers, assisted by Sergeants Carmichael, Burgess, and Smith, with Bugler Hawthorne of the 52nd,[1] covered by the First Battalion 60th Rifles. The assault was delivered in four columns ; this narrative is, however, chiefly concerned with the First, of which the 75th, 300 strong, formed the advance, 100 of them carrying scaling ladders to mount the escarp of the berm. The troops fell in quietly after midnight, and the orders were read to the men. Wounded officers and soldiers were to be left where they fell—no man could be spared from the ranks to help them ; no prisoners were to be made, as there were not men to guard them ; care to be taken that no women or children were injured. To this the men answered, " No fear, sir." Just then the Rev. Father Bertrand came up in his vestments, and asked the colonel's permission to give the regiment his blessing, saying—" We may differ, some of us, in matters of religion, but the blessing of an old man and a clergyman can do nothing but good," then lifting his hand towards heaven, he blessed them in a most impressive manner, and as he ceased, the order was given to march to the rendezvous, from which the regiment, led by Lieut.-Colonel Herbert, moved to the attack about 2 a.m. On reaching the Koodree Bagh, a low-toned order was given to halt, for the enemy had during the night filled the face of the breach with fascines and gabions. Our batteries again opened fire, to which the mutineers replied. After half an hour of anxious waiting, the guns on our side ceased, and the signal being given, the regiment advanced in column of fours at the double. The 60th were lining the banks and keeping up a rifle fire on the walls and breach, and just as the sun rose like a red ball, the Green-Jackets cheered the regiment as it passed through a rose garden to the foot of the glacis. Straight before them was the huge gap in the wall, the heads of the defenders showing just over it, while on either side they swarmed like bees, the sun shining on their white turbans, dark faces, and sparkling bayonets, as the

1 Four of this party were gazetted for the Victoria Cross, but only Smith and Hawthorne lived to wear it.

stormers rushed, madly cheering, to the assault. The Colonel fell wounded at the glacis, when Captain Brookes took command. The ditch was the first difficulty ; three times the ladders were snatched from the shoulders of the dead or wounded bearers.[1] Lieutenant I. R. S. Fitzgerald fell in the breach while gallantly leading the stormers, who, notwithstanding the steepness, and the fire of the enemy so close above them that they felt the flash hot on their faces, quickly effected a lodgment within the Kashmir Bastion. The column, led by Brigadier Nicholson, and headed by the 75th, moved to its right along and in rear of the ramparts, capturing successively the Moré Bastion and the Kabul Gate under a galling fire from the streets and houses. They pursued the rebels for more than a mile, till the latter made a determined stand between the Burn Bastion and the Lahore Gate, enfilading with their artillery and musketry the narrow " terreplein " of the curtain and the lane to its rear. The arched recesses of the ramparts afforded a scanty shelter on the right of the column, but their commander, though of indomitable courage and unsurpassed as a leader of men, lacked, perhaps, on this occasion the judgment which would have availed itself of the buildings on his left that offered protection from the fire which decimated the ranks ; and here, bravest where all were brave, the gallant Nicholson fell mortally wounded.[2]

Repeated assaults had failed to dislodge the enemy, and the Fourth Column had been unable to co-operate ; accordingly, Captains Brookes and Drew, on whom had devolved the command of the First Column and the 75th Regiment respectively, perceiving that further attempts only involved loss of life, retired on the Kabul Gate and Canal, the 75th occupying the Moré Bastion and the mansion of Bahadur Jang. The Second and Third Columns had been successful on the left, and the northern part of the city was in our possession.

On the 15th September, Brevet Major C. E. P. Gordon joined from sick leave, and took command of the regiment, its effective strength being about 360 of all ranks, of whom two-thirds were within the city. The left and centre columns stormed the Magazine on the 16th, and took the Bank next day ; but only desultory fighting and reconnaissances took place on the right, where the 75th, under Major Gordon, with fifty Sikh infantry, still held the advanced post. Early on the 18th, Lieut.-Colonel Greathed, of H.M. 8th Regiment, with a mixed force, including a party of the 75th and one gun, advanced on the Habshi-Ka-Phātak[3] in order to capture the

---

[1] Diary of Lieut.-General R. Barter, C.B., Adjutant of the 75th at Delhi, published in *The Tiger and Sphinx*, November 15th, 1896.

[2] Regimental Records.   [3] Gate of the Abyssinians.

Lahore Gate, and so gain the line of the Chandni Chouk, a principal street; but though the Abyssinian Gate was forced, Greathed was compelled to withdraw with loss, the 75th, which led in this unfortunate affair, having Ensign E. Villiers Briscol and 10 men killed. Major Gordon and 10 men were wounded. Gordon, whose wound did not prevent his retaining his command, now proposed that two mortars should be placed on the roof of Bahadur Jang's mansion, which, with General Archdale Wilson's approval, was done. During the 18th and 19th, under cover of the fire of the mortars, Gordon advanced by breaking through the intervening premises, then posting pickets so as to command the interior of the adjacent

works, the enemy was taken in reverse with fatal effect. By the evening of the 19th, having arrived opposite the Burn Bastion, Gordon took 2 officers, 2 sergeants, and 39 rank and file, European and native (1 officer and 10 rank and file from the 75th), and with this small party he entered by the loopholed gorge, and surprised and captured the work after slight opposition. Reinforcements arriving, two guns of the captured bastion were turned on the Lahore Gate, which was taken early next morning ; and so skilfully were these hazardous operations conducted that only 3 men were wounded. Simultaneously with this success the left and centre columns gained the Palace and the Jama Masjid, and by the afternoon of the 20th September the reconquest of Delhi was complete.

To form a true estimate of the magnitude of this achievement, one must bear in mind that the strength of the defenders of Delhi did not lie merely in their fortifications, but in the disparity in numbers of the opposing forces, aided by the effect of the excessive heat at that season on the European troops.

Upwards of 200 pieces of ordnance, immense stores of shot and shell fell into our hands, besides vast wealth, which was, however, seriously diminished by the misconduct of some who preferred booty to duty, and the prize-money of the captors was proportionately reduced.

During the siege the British forces (European and native) sustained a loss of 1012 officers and men killed and 3837 wounded.[1]

The following is an extract from a General Order detailing the services of the 75th during the Mutiny, dated Calcutta, 14th April 1862. After alluding to the conduct of the 75th on June 8th, as given above, it continues—" In noticing the good conduct of the regiment at Badli-ki-Sarai and Delhi, the names of two officers and a n.c. officer of the regiment, whose gallantry was as continued and devoted as it was productive of important results, ought not to be omitted. They are those of Brevet Major Brookes, Captain L. Kelly, and Colour-sergeant Coughlan."

---

[1] The loss of the 75th on the 14th September is not given in its Record, though it evidently was considerable.

CHAPTER XXI

1857–1862

ON the capture of Delhi, the rebel garrison dispersed, some making for Gwalior, while another large body entered the Doab at Mathra and crossed the Ganges into Oude. Troops had been sent from England and China, but these could not reach the North-West Provinces for weeks, and the pursuit and destruction of the flying host was now the task before the victors of Delhi. Two flying columns were formed, the principal one to enter and clear the Gangetic Doab, the other to move down the right bank of the Jumna. The 61st Regiment, detailed for the former, having been reported unfit for present service, the 75th, under Major Gordon, was ordered to take its place. This column, commanded by Lieut.-Colonel Greathed, consisted of eighteen guns Horse and Field Artillery, the 9th Lancers, three regiments of Punjab Cavalry and a squadron of Hodson's Horse, H.M. 8th and 75th Regiments, and two regiments of Punjab Infantry, with two companies of sappers.

At 3 a.m. on the 24th September the column crossed the Jumna. The village of Dadra, where dreadful atrocities had been committed, was taken and burnt on the 26th; on the 28th, a force of 7000 men and eight guns was overtaken, posted in front of and within Buland-shahr, where a sharp action ensued. Greathed directed H.M. 8th and 75th and the 2nd Punjab Infantry to clear the strong position held by the enemy. This duty was well performed, and, seeing his flanks were now protected, the Brigadier ordered Captain Bouchier to advance his field battery; at the same time the 75th charged with a cheer, and the rebels deserted their entrenchments, leaving a 9-pounder in our hands. The rebels were driven through the town, and the infantry halted, while the cavalry and Horse Artillery continued the pursuit. In this combat the 75th lost one man killed and one wounded. The Brigadier, in orders of the 29th, expressed his thanks to every officer and soldier under his command for the manner in which they " forgot fatigue in chasing the rebels who ventured to hold their ground against them." [1]

Next day the stronghold of Malagarh was taken and afterwards blown up, in which operation Lieutenant Home, R.E., one of the gallant band who blew in the Kashmir Gate of Delhi, lost his life. The sick and wounded were sent to Meerut, and on October 3rd the column moved to Kurjah and continued the pursuit till the 5th, when, having passed Aligarh, they overtook part of the rebel Gwalior contingent in position at Koel, but these gave way before the rapid advance of our skirmishers and artillery, and after a brief resistance abandoned their guns, and were pursued and cut up by

---

[1] Greathed's Despatch.

our cavalry. This affair and the march occupied eleven hours. That night they marched fifteen miles, and by dawn on the 6th reached Akbarabad, a locality conspicuous in atrocity, and occupied by a force under the notorious brothers Mangal and Mehtab Sain. Our cavalry and artillery in advance killed about 100, and the infantry entered the town, when the brothers, with many more of their followers, were slain. The place was given up to pillage and burnt.

Now the news arrived that the Rana of Jodhpur had declared against the British, and was moving on Agra with 15,000 men. The column, therefore, changed direction to the south-west, and on the 8th October marched twenty-four miles to Hatras, where they were met by urgent demands for aid, 5000 of the enemy, with eighteen guns, being already at Dholpur, thirty-three miles south-west of Agra, and pushing on to besiege the fort. Greathed sent on his Horse Artillery and 500 cavalry on the morning of the 9th, and they reached Agra, a distance of thirty-one miles, that evening. His infantry, by a night march, during which the Europeans were carried by alternate parties on carts and elephants, neared the left bank of the Jumna at dawn on the 10th, and were defiling over the bridge of boats when the baggage train, three miles long (which had probably been despatched at the same time as the cavalry), came up, and would have blocked the way and divided the column, had not the officer commanding the 75th taken the responsibility of stopping it until the troops had passed. This, as events proved, saved the baggage and commissariat, and probably prevented a disaster. To protect it, the regiment became the rear corps, and only reached the cantonment parade ground at 9 a.m., when, it being reported that the enemy had retired, the troops sought rest. Their position was bad ; it was flanked by houses and trees, and in front were tall crops of maize and millet, while it turned out that the rebels were actually concealed in the city and cantonments. A surprise resulted. The enemy, seeing only a few tents (owing to the delay of the baggage), supposed the force to be weaker than it was, and determined to destroy it ; in which, had the column been divided, they might have succeeded. As it was, though they attacked our right flank and front covered by the fire of their artillery, the rally was as rapid as the surprise had been complete. Within five minutes our cavalry charged, a gun which had fallen into the enemy's hands was retaken, and the 75th with the Punjab Infantry, formed under the direction of Major Gordon, withstood the insurgent cavalry. In fifteen minutes the attack was repulsed, and Greathed assumed the offensive, bringing forward the Punjab Cavalry, H.M. 8th and the 4th Punjab Infantry on the right, while the 75th, with the 2nd Punjab Infantry and the rest of the cavalry and artillery, advanced on the left, and captured four guns. Meanwhile Lieut.-Colonel Cotton (H.E.I. Company's service) reinforced the right with troops from the Fort of Agra and took the supreme command. The enemy, closely pressed, broke and fled, their camp was taken, and they were chased by the Horse Artillery and cavalry for five miles to the Khare River, on the opposite bank of which was posted the rebel reserve ; but before this could act, it was decimated by the rapid fire of our Horse Artillery, and a surprise, which but for the discipline and courage of our troops might have been a disaster, was turned into a complete victory. The enemy's loss was over 1500 in killed and wounded ; fourteen guns, several elephants, and a large quantity of jewels and treasure, including about 170,000 rupees belonging to the Government, were captured. The British loss was 1 officer and 11 men killed, and 4 officers and 51 men wounded, including 1 private of the 75th.

The safety of Agra being thus assured, attention was turned to Oude, where the beleaguered British garrison of Lucknow was in great peril. Outram and Havelock's gallant efforts of the 25th September had added their troops to the number of the besieged, and their critical position required immediate and effectual relief. Accordingly the column, 2400 strong, left Agra on October 13th for Cawnpore, being reinforced next day by 300 men and three heavy guns from Delhi, the 75th receiving 92 men, but no officer. On the 18th the cavalry patrols of the rebel Raja of Mynpuri were driven in, and next day his stronghold was reached by a forced march of twenty-three miles, where 230,000 rupees Government treasure, with artillery and 14,000 lbs. of powder, were taken. Brigadier-General Hope Grant now took command of the column, and having intelligence that the rebels in great numbers were in position at Kanauj and Farakabad, he moved to Bihar, and reaching the neighbourhood of Kanauj on the 23rd by a march of forty-one miles, overtook the retreating enemy, who, after slight resistance, fled towards the Ganges, losing five guns and suffering severely from our cavalry and Horse Artillery.

The column reached Cawnpore on the 26th October, having traversed 340 miles in thirty-three days, and accomplished the first portion of its task by clearing the Gangetic Doab and reopening communication with Delhi and Agra. By orders from Sir Colin Campbell, who had lately arrived in India as Commander-in-Chief, the column was reinforced, and leaving the weakly men at Cawnpore, crossed the Ganges on the 29th and 30th, convoying 2500 camels and 500 carts with supplies. The enemy, though in great force, did not molest them till the 2nd November, when part of the 75th, under Captain Brookes, forming the infantry of the advanced guard, was attacked at Mahagang ; but after a brief struggle the enemy were defeated, though a running fight of a desultory nature was kept up during the pursuit to within five miles of Lucknow. The loss of the enemy was about 200 men and six guns, that of the British three men killed and 23 wounded, none of whom seem to have belonged to the 75th.

The column halted about ten miles from Lucknow, the sound of the firing there being clearly audible. On the 11th November, being joined by several detachments, they moved to Buntheera, where Sir Colin reviewed the force, about 4500 combatants. Next day they advanced to within two miles of the city south of the Alambagh, a large strongly-walled enclosure containing our stores. The enemy, with 2000 infantry and two guns, attacked our advanced guard, but were dispersed, and the guns taken. On the 13th the 75th, under Gordon, after assisting in an operation against Fort Jalalabad, entered the Alambagh, and the effectives of its garrison (20 officers and 642 men, of whom one-third were sick or wounded) joined the camp. On the 14th the Commander-in-Chief, with 6000 of all arms, including arrivals on that date, captured the Dilkusha and Martinière, establishing his field hospital at the former position, which was reinforced on the 16th by the left wing of the 75th and fifty Sikhs, under Captain Brookes. On that day the sanguinary struggle, which lasted till the 20th, began with the capture of the Sikandra Bagh, where over 2000 of the enemy were slain, and by the 21st the women and children (450), the sick and wounded (600), the guns, stores and Government treasure had been safely withdrawn ; and during the following night the relief of the Residency garrison and Outram and Havelock's troops was effected.

But though Sir Colin's plans had been so far successful, the enemy had not been idle. The Alambagh, where was the right wing of the 75th, was daily harassed by the fire of artillery, the Dilkusha was attacked, and our communications with Cawnpore threatened. On the 24th, Sir Colin retired on the Alambagh, leaving Outram's Division at Dilkusha. Here the good and gallant Havelock died, and early on the 26th his remains were silently interred [1] within the Alambagh, the 75th forming the funeral party, but, as in the case of Sir John Moore—

> Not a soldier discharged his farewell shot
> O'er the grave where our hero we buried.

The whole force being now rearranged, the 75th was placed in the First Division, under Sir James Outram, which was posted

[1] A veteran who fought throughout the Indian Mutiny with the 75th and was twice wounded at Delhi, by name of Joseph Davidson, died at Brough, Westmorland, in April 1913, aged 89 years. He is stated to have been one of the party who dug Havelock's grave.

in rear of the Alambagh to hold the enemy in check.   On the 27th November, Sir Colin with the main body moved towards Cawnpore, escorting a train of non-effectives and baggage seven or eight miles long.   Meanwhile the Gwalior contingent crossed the Jumna, and on the 26th and 27th attacked the imperfectly entrenched British position at Cawnpore.   Sir Colin's rapid march and defeat of the insurgents are well known, and need only to be mentioned here to record the conduct of Lance-sergeant John M'Carthy of the 75th, who had been left at Cawnpore when the regiment advanced to Lucknow.   On the second day of the attack he was commanding a guard in the centre of the city, and effected a retreat to the entrenchment, distant a mile and a half, with but one man wounded ;   subsequently, with Sergeant Sellars, he saved and brought in the Regimental Records left in his charge.

Outram's Division, under 4000 combatants (exclusive of a detachment posted at Banni), had its advanced posts at the Alambagh, Fort Jalālabad, and the village of Dungapur, presenting a front of four miles within gunshot of the enemy's works, and had to defend a circuit of nearly eleven miles, this large area being rendered necessary by the nature of the locality and for grazing purposes.   For three months this position was held by our troops against fifteen times their number, who were well provided with artillery and cavalry, and commanded the resources of the entire province.   During the first three weeks of December the division, reinforced by 350 men, was occupied in strengthening its position, their opponents doing likewise, and advancing by open sap.   On the 20th and 21st, however, the enemy began their first attack by cannonading our left, and massing 4500 cavalry and infantry with four guns on our right front, near the village of Gaili.   Outram defeated them with 1550 men of European and native troops (including 103 of the 75th) and six guns, capturing guns, elephants and baggage, and inflicting great loss on the enemy ; while on our side only three privates were killed, and one officer and five privates wounded.   After this lesson the enemy confined their efforts to harassing the outposts, but these were now well sheltered, so that by the 31st only two casualties had occurred, and notwithstanding the uncongenial surroundings, neither the religious services nor the sports appropriate to Christmas Day were forgotten.   On the 30th, Brevet Major Mollan joined, bringing part of a draft from England, and took over the command of the regiment from Brevet Major Gordon.   New Year's Day, 1858, opened with athletic sports, to which Sir James Outram and the officers contributed 1500 rupees (£150).

The rebel host in Oude had received large accessions from the fugitives who had been defeated elsewhere, and the armed force in its capital was now about 85,000 ; but dissension was rife among them, and except an attack on the Alambagh on the 8th January, little occurred till the 12th, when 30,000 of all arms, supported by a heavy artillery fire, attacked the left rear and left front of the division, gradually extending for six miles along its front to the right. The left brigade, in which was the 75th, bore the brunt from 8 a.m. till noon ; the action was continued on the right till 2 p.m., when the enemy was finally repulsed. In this affair the 75th had 1 officer and 5 men wounded. The spies having reported that another attack might be expected, the left advanced post, Dungapur, was reinforced, and Outram selected Major Gordon, 75th, to command at this important point. Early on the 16th January the enemy threatened our position, and after a bold attack, by 3 p.m. they were repulsed along the whole line ; but after sunset five Sepoy battalions and numerous " Najib " (volunteer) corps advanced on Gordon's post. After enfilading their columns with his artillery, he suddenly ceased firing, and kept his men under cover. It was nearly 8 p.m., and not a shot was fired by the hidden garrison ; the enemy, thinking the post abandoned, came on with loud cries of victory. They were allowed to extend and commence their final rush till within eighty yards, then the wily Scot gave the signal—a withering fire of grape and musketry decimated the assailants, and in ten minutes nothing was heard but the groans of the dying, while Gordon had only four men wounded. Sir James Outram visited the post next morning and highly complimented him on his able defence, and in his despatch, after describing the action, he says—" The judgment and coolness with which Major Gordon defended his post deserves much praise."

The remainder of the draft from England joined on this day, and other reinforcements to the division made the duty less severe, though the frequent demonstrations made by the enemy were sufficiently harassing. On the 10th February, Colonel Alexander Jardine joined from sick leave and took command of the regiment, which, on the 14th, proceeded to form part of the reserve at Cawnpore, when Sir James Outram issued the following memorandum :—

CAMP ALAMBAGH,
13th February 1858.

The Major-General, in publishing in General Orders the removal of H.M. 75th Regiment from his command, has to express his regret at losing the valuable services of that regiment, as from what he has seen of their cool and steady conduct while in this camp, he placed every reliance in them. Sir James Outram wishes to record in Division Orders his sense of the merit of the 75th Regiment and his best wishes for their future welfare.

In March the rebel forces in Lucknow were finally defeated

and the city taken, and by the end of May Sir Colin Campbell's victories, together with the successful campaigns of Sir Hugh Rose and General Whitlock, had quenched the flames of the great rebellion, and nothing remained but to stamp out the dying embers. Our Indian Empire, with all its far-reaching advantages, was saved by the self-sacrificing bravery and unstinted exertions of an army which indeed deserved well of its countrymen, who, though they admire and glory in the deeds of their soldiers as a body, often show little gratitude to the individuals who compose it.[1] This ungenerous neglect is said to have been satirised by a soldier in the following lines written on the wall at Cawnpore :—

> When wars are rife and danger 's nigh,
> God and the soldier 's all the cry ;
> When wars are o'er and wrongs are righted,
> God is forgotten, and the soldier slighted.

From February 14th, 1858, there is a blank in the records, but from other sources it would appear that the war-worn survivors of the 75th were sent to seek well-earned rest in the hills.[2] There is an undated order published by " direction of His Excellency Lord Clyde," expressing the satisfaction he experienced at the review of the regiment :—" His Excellency was particularly struck by the clean and soldier-like appearance of the men, their steadiness under arms and the admirable way in which the regiment manœuvred . . . and the report he has heard of their unexceptional good conduct in quarters has been most gratifying."

On the 4th and 5th October 1859 the regiment, under Colonel Radcliff, was inspected at Meerut, with a strength of 955 privates, when Major-General Bradford fully concurred with " the high opinion lately expressed by His Excellency Lord Clyde," and " his report will be that he considers the 75th Regiment in a very high state of order and discipline."

R.O., October 5th.—All the men undergoing punishment by regimental court-martial or by Commanding Officer's order will be released.

On December 27th the regiment marched from Meerut for Cawnpore, and from thence proceeded by rail to Allahabad,[3] where the headquarters, under Lieut.-Colonel Radcliff, arrived on January 25th, 1860. During the year it remained at Allahabad the regiment was most favourably reported on for its efficiency and for the

---

[1] This does not apply with the same force to the present day.   [2] Holmes.

[3] A remarkable circumstance which happened at Allahabad was told me by the Rev. C. M. Pym, rector of Cherry Burton, Yorkshire, who was then a captain in the 75th. One night as he was lying wakeful, he distinctly saw, standing in the room, the figure of his father, who seemed to bid him farewell. In the morning he told his brother officers his experience, and that he felt sure his father was dead. When the mail arrived he found that his father had really died the very night on which he had seen the vision.

good conduct of the men. January 26th, 1861, the 75th moved by Benares and Ranegunge (where Major and Brevet Lieut.-Colonel E. Knollys died of cholera) to Calcutta, and occupied Fort-William on the 9th of March.

April 1st, 1861.—The establishment was reduced to 1079, total of all ranks.

January 1862.—The service companies being held in readiness for England, men wishing to remain in India were allowed to volunteer, and 204 took advantage of the offer.

On the 22nd February was published the farewell order of His Excellency the Viceroy and Governor-General, which, after recapitulating the gallant services of the 75th during their service of more than twelve years in India, continues—" The Viceroy and Governor-General in Council has pleasure in placing on record the valuable services of this regiment, and cordially wishes it a prosperous journey to England and every success hereafter." The Commander-in-Chief's order of March 19th, already quoted as to Badli-ki-Sarai, was published at this time.

75TH FOOT, 1840.

CHAPTER XXII

1862–1881

ON February 24th, 1862, the headquarters, under Colonel Radcliff, embarked on the freight ship *Malabar*, and after touching at St Helena, landed at Plymouth on the 20th of June. The second detachment embarked, February 25th, on the *Salamanca*, touched at the Cape of Good Hope, and disembarked at Plymouth the 28th of June. The third detachment embarked, March 1st, on the *Dartmouth*, and after touching at the Cape, landed on June 19th. The regiment occupied Raglan Barracks, Devonport.

A letter, dated Horse Guards, 6th November 1862, was received, acquainting the officer commanding that, at the recommendation of H.R.H. the Commander-in-Chief, Her Majesty had been graciously pleased to approve the 75th Regiment "being in future distinguished as the 'Stirlingshire,' it having been raised in that county." [1]

On May 15th, 1863, new colours were presented to the regiment by Mrs Hutchinson, the wife of the Major-General commanding the district, and in September the royal authority was received for the words " Delhi " and " Lucknow " to be borne on the colours and appointments, in commemoration of the distinguished conduct of the regiment at Delhi and the relief of Lucknow.

Colonel Radcliff having applied, in August 1863, for permission to change the regimental forage caps, he received a letter, dated October 15th, 1863, informing him that Her Majesty had been pleased to authorise the 75th Stirlingshire Regiment to wear in future the round Kilmarnock forage cap with diced border, similar to that worn by the non-kilted Highland regiments, as a mark of its national origin.

The regiment having decided to erect a monument to the memory of the officers, n.c. officers and private soldiers who fell during the Mutiny, and having chosen the royal burgh of Stirling, the birthplace of the regiment, as the most suitable place for it, and also to hang up the old colours in the church or Town Hall, Colonel Radcliff applied to the Provost for a site, and offered the colours for the acceptance of the town. In a letter, dated Stirling, 23rd October 1863, he received the assurance—

That the civic authorities here consider it an honour to grant a site for the monument, and every assistance will be given to the officer of the regiment when he comes to select a suitable one. The fine feeling that prompted the officers to place the monument in Stirling for the purpose of establishing a connection between the regiment and the county, the name of which it bears,

---

[1] The regiment was *embodied* at Stirling, but any existing evidence is against its having been *raised* in Stirlingshire.

is highly appreciated.   Both the county and the town are proud of the gallant 75th being named the "Stirlingshire Regiment."   On behalf of the Magistrates and Town Council and the whole community, I accept with feelings of pride and gratitude the good old colours of the regiment, which were so triumphantly borne throughout the Indian Mutiny. . . . They will be looked upon as sacred, and will often recall the gallant and distinguished part which the regiment bore in the suppression of the Indian Mutiny.

The monument was erected in the cemetery in 1864, and consisted of an obelisk of polished red granite, terminating in a trefoil cross-crosslet, whose centre bears on one side the number and designation of the regiment, and on the other its "device."   The corresponding faces of the shaft and pedestal contain the names of the officers, with the number of the men who fell in the campaign 1857-58, and a record of the principal campaigns in which the regiment took part.

In December 1863 the regiment, under Colonel Radcliff, moved to Aldershot, having been most favourably reported on during their stay at Devonport.

On the 9th December 1864, Colonel Radcliff retired, and was succeeded by Lieut.-Colonel C. E. P. Gordon, who had served in the 75th since December 1833.   In closing the regimental history for 1864, the record pays a tribute to the memory of Brevet Lieut.-Colonel William Brookes, whose name so often appears with honour in the late campaign.   He had been promoted from the ranks to a commission as ensign and adjutant, and after serving thirty years with great distinction in the regiment, had lately left it on appointment as Town-Major of Dublin, but died in London. The entire regiment attended his funeral at Farnborough Cemetery.

The number of depôt battalions being reduced, No. 11 and 12 Companies, hitherto forming part of the Third Depôt Battalion at Chatham, rejoined headquarters on the 31st January 1865.[1]

While at Aldershot a canteen on the "regimental system" was established, and before the battalion left the camp for the south-western district on the 10th April 1865, Lieut.-General Sir J. L. Pennefather, K.C.B., expressed himself as much satisfied with its progress, general conduct and efficiency, during the sixteen months it had formed part of the division.   Headquarters, under Lieut.-Colonel Gordon, were quartered at Forts Grange and Rouncer, advanced works west of Gosport, and five companies at Weymouth and Portland, where they were employed in the construction of defensive works ; a detachment was at Tipnor.

During this year Falkirk and Battle (Sussex) were added to the recruiting stations of the regiment, but without much success, and

[1] Captains, 2 ; lieutenants, 3 ; ensigns, 1 ; sergeants, 10 ; corporals, 10 ; drummers, 4 ; privates, 85.

the supply of recruits was very far from meeting the year's decrease by discharge.

On the 10th June a memo. was received from the Adjutant-General ordering all companies of infantry to be designated by letters from A to M (omitting J), instead of by numbers as heretofore.

On the occasion of the visit of the French fleet in the autumn, the regiment (headquarters) took part in the reception given to the Minister of Marine and the officers of the Imperial Navy.

In 1866, in consequence of the Fenian conspiracy, the military force in Ireland was increased, and on March 2nd the 75th, under Lieut.-Colonel Gordon, embarked on H.M. troopship *Tamar*. The transport ran foul of the ironclad *Minotaur*, but after repairing damages at Plymouth she reached Kingstown on the 6th, and they proceeded to Richmond and Royal Barracks till the arrival of the 92nd (Gordon Highlanders) in April, when the 75th was concentrated at Richmond Barracks. At this time the regiment was reduced to ten companies, with a total establishment of 750 of all ranks. During the year the emissaries of Fenianism, many from the United States, were daily entering the kingdom, and even tampering with the loyalty of the troops. In some instances these attempts were successful, but the victims were discovered and tried by a general court-martial. Considering that three-fifths of the 75th were at this time Irish, it is creditable to the corps that only two young soldiers were arrested " on suspicion of Fenianism." After being confined from the 15th April till the 5th September, they were liberated with a caution by the Brigadier-General, in accordance with confidential instructions.[1]

While in Dublin the several General Officers expressed themselves satisfied with the state of the regiment, which in September moved, under Lieut.-Colonel Gordon, to Kilkenny with four detachments in the neighbouring disturbed districts. The barracks were rendered capable of defence, and the troops were constantly employed in the prevention of outrage ; on one of these occasions Captain Cliffe was so severely injured as to be incapacitated from further service.

During the last two years large numbers of soldiers had become non-effective under two years' and many under one year's service, but in the latter part of 1866 recruits of a " better physique " were attested.[2]

In 1867 the regiment was released from its disagreeable though necessary duties in Ireland by being ordered to Gibraltar. In March the establishment was increased to ten service and two depôt companies—total of all ranks, 929.

---

[1] Regimental Record.   [2] *Ibid.*

The breech-loading system having been adopted for the army, Snider rifles were issued to the regiment in place of the muzzle-loading Enfield.

On the 20th April 1867 the service companies embarked at Cork, and on the 27th arrived at Gibraltar, and encamped on the North Front ; they afterwards occupied Buena Vista Barracks. H.R.H. the Duke of Cambridge, in his remarks on the first inspection at Gibraltar, was pleased to convey his approbation, and to record that " the state of the 75th Regiment reflected great credit on the Commanding Officer." The musketry practice " was greatly in advance of the performance of the corps during last year."

In July 1868 the 75th was held in readiness for Singapore and Hong Kong. Every effort was made to reinforce the service companies, but recruiting at the depôt was very unsuccessful, and it became evident that the battalion would embark short of its establishment.

Lieut.-Colonel Gordon, after thirty-five years' service in the regiment, was succeeded by Lieut.-Colonel Milles, and the vacant ensigncy was filled by the promotion of Sergeant August Frederick M'Garry, under his proper name of Davies.

The troopship *Himalaya*, with the 75th, sailed on the 8th October, and after touching at the Island of St Vincent, Simon's Bay, Singapore and Manila, arrived at Hong Kong on the 21st December. In February 1869, a wing of the regiment, under Major Grant Suttie, proceeded to Singapore.

The 28th January 1870, Major-General David Russell, C.B., was appointed Colonel of the regiment *vice* Lieut.-General St John Clerke, deceased.

By War Office instructions of 19th May 1870, E and I Companies were broken up, and the service companies reduced to eight.

In 1871 notification was received that the service companies would shortly be moved to Mauritius and Cape Colony, and the right wing, having suffered from intermittent fever at Hong Kong, was detailed for the latter station, while the headquarters and left wing were to go to the former, where they arrived in the *Tamar* on the 25th September (having picked up the right wing at Singapore), but on the regiment being inspected by Major-General Smyth, he considered its state of health so unsatisfactory that he directed that the headquarters should not remain at Mauritius, but should proceed to Natal ; accordingly, the right wing, under Major Malan, disembarked at East London in British Kaffraria on the 10th October 1871, and marched to King William's Town ; the headquarters were landed at Port Natal on the 13th, and marched to Pietermaritzburg, with a company at Durban.

At these stations the regiment remained undisturbed till October 1873, when information was received by the Lieutenant-Governor of Natal that Langalibalele, a Kaffir chief, was setting the Government at defiance ; and an expedition was organised, consisting of a half-battery Royal Artillery, 200 men of the 75th, and a considerable number of Colonial Volunteers, all under Colonel Milles of the 75th.   The troops left Fort Napier on the 30th, and by forced marches succeeded in throwing a cordon round the disaffected tribe ; but on the 4th November the Kaffirs broke through a troop of Volunteers who guarded a pass of the Drakensberg Mountains, killing five of their number, and severely wounding Major Durnford, R.E., who was in command.   The rebels were, however, dispersed, and a neighbouring disaffected tribe being disarmed, the expedition returned to Maritzburg, with the exception of the half-battery and a company of the 75th, under Captain Boyes, who remained near the Drakensberg to protect the settlers and assure the peace of the district.

During 1874 the 75th adopted the Glengarry forage cap instead of the Kilmarnock, and in January 1875 the headquarters bade adieu to Natal and embarked on H.M.S. *Simoom* for Cape Town, where four companies were transhipped to the *Himalaya* for conveyance to England; headquarters, with the band and drummers, encamped while the *Simoom* returned to East London and brought away the remaining four companies, when, picking up the head-quarters at Cape Town, she sailed for England ; but their departure was saddened by the loss of Major Grant Suttie, who died ten days before his detachment left the frontier.   The *Simoom* arrived, March 26th, at Queenstown, where orders were received to proceed to Belfast ; the headquarters landed there on the 31st and went at once to Newry.   The engines of the *Himalaya*, with the other wing of the regiment, had broken down, but with the help of H.M.S. *Sultan* she arrived at Gibraltar.   One company was taken home in H.M.S. *Tamar*, the others being encamped for three weeks, when, after a tempestuous voyage of fourteen days in a hired vessel, they joined the regiment, which had detachments at Armagh, Newtownards, and Drogheda.

In June, Martini Henry rifles replaced the Snider, and the old knapsacks were exchanged for the new valise equipment.   On the 18th December, Colonel Thomas Milles retired with the rank of Major-General, and was succeeded by Lieut.-Colonel Wadeson, V.C.

In April 1876 the regiment went by rail to the Curragh, where it remained till May 28th, 1877, when it embarked on H.M.S. *Assistance* to be stationed at Guernsey and Alderney, picking up seventy men at Weymouth from the 39th Brigade Depôt ; and in November the 75th sent a draft to the 39th Regiment (its linked battalion) in India.

In February 1878 an apprehension of war with Russia caused the Army and Militia Reserve to be called out, and the 75th received 350 men from the First-Class Army Reserve and 177 from the Dorset and Somerset Militia Reserve, the establishment being raised to 1000 rank and file.

After passing a most satisfactory annual inspection in May, the 75th embarked on H.M.S. *Orontes* for Portsmouth, and proceeded to Aldershot ; and in July, the reserves being no longer required, they were dismissed to their homes, and the regiment had only 419 privates, its establishment being fixed at 600 rank and file. In October the 75th were placed in the Army Corps first for foreign service, and in January 1879 its establishment was raised to 740, but again reduced in April to 640 rank and file. In August the regiment underwent a searching annual inspection by Major-General Gordon Cameron, C.B., which proved highly satisfactory to the corps.

In July 1880 the troops at Aldershot marched to Windsor, to be reviewed by H.M. Queen Victoria. The 75th was encamped opposite Ascot Grand Stand. H.R.H. the Field-Marshal Commanding-in-Chief afterwards conveyed to the officers, n.c. officers and men of all arms Her Majesty's approval, and he himself thanked all ranks for their exemplary conduct and cheerful spirit, notwithstanding the wet and inclement weather. In September the regiment took part in the manœuvres on an extended scale, which had been first introduced in 1871, to imitate as far as possible the operations of war. The principles of tactics remain the same, but their application varies of necessity with the invention of new weapons, and with the country in which they are used. The courage and discipline of the British army enabled it to fight in line and thus to develop its fire to the full extent, giving its soldiers a marked superiority over opponents whose training and *moral* accustomed them only to fight in column. The improvement in arms was by now gradually causing an extension and looser formation of the line.

During the year the 75th received several drafts from the 39th Depôt Battalion at Dorchester, and sent reinforcements to the 39th Regiment in India. On October 30th the regiment moved from Aldershot to Chatham. In December, Lieut.-Colonel Richard Wadeson, V.C., retired on completion of five years in command,[1]

---

[1] According to a rule lately introduced. In 1881 the term of command was reduced to four years. As a further preventive to the stagnation in promotion produced by the abolition of purchase, all captains were obliged to retire if not promoted before the age of forty. In 1881 an immense number of captains came under this regulation. This wholesale ejection of men still in the prime of life seems to have alarmed the Secretary of State, and they were promoted to the rank of major, each battalion having two additional majors, who were not, however, mounted, but performed captain's duty, under the sobriquet of " mud majors."

after serving in all ranks from private to lieut.-colonel. He was succeeded by Lieut.-Colonel Hammill.

On the 11th March 1881 the 75th left Chatham for Portsmouth, where they embarked in the hired transport *Egypt*, having been previously inspected by H.R.H. the Field-Marshal Commanding-in-Chief. The *Egypt* arrived at Malta on the 20th March, and the regiment occupied the Floriana Barracks.

Under the system of " linked " battalions, the 39th (Dorsetshire) Regiment and the 75th (Stirlingshire) Regiment had been thus semi-attached. It had, however, been borne in upon the authorities that, though two regiments remaining separate in interests and traditions could never work cordially together for the common good, it might be possible so to unite two regiments that they should become battalions of one corps, with the united honours, traditions and character as its pride and its care. The constant exchange of officers and men, it was expected, would gradually produce a *regimental* feeling, with merely that legitimate desire of each battalion to excel, which has always existed in regiments so composed. Instead of men being drafted to a totally different corps, as had been the case under the " linked " arrangement, they would now find themselves merely transferred to another part of their own, and battalion commanders would have the satisfaction of knowing that in losing the officers and men they had trained, these would not be lost to their regiment. Thus the territorial scheme was introduced, and in carrying this out it was decided that the 75th (Stirlingshire) Regiment should be amalgamated with the 92nd (the Gordon Highlanders), of which it should take the name and uniform and become the First Battalion, the numbers " 75 " and " 92 " being no longer used.[1]

The regiments were not, I believe, consulted, but as in the case of many *mariages de convenance*, the union has been a happy one.

The order for this redistribution was issued on the 11th April 1881, to come into force on the 1st July. On that day the following epitaph was found in Sa Maison Gardens near Floriana Barracks :—

EPITAPH ON THE 75TH, 30TH JUNE 1881.

Here lies the poor old Seventy-Fifth,
But, under God's protection,
They 'll rise again in kilt and hose
A glorious resurrection !
For by the transformation power
Of Parliamentary laws,
We go to bed the Seventy-Fifth
And rise the Ninety-Twa's !

---

[1] Some slight alterations in buttons and badges were made to suit.

The lines are copied (1902) from a stone monument which replaces the more temporary original, " Erected by Letter B or Major J. O. M. Vandeleur's Company, 75th (Stirlingshire) Regiment, Malta, 1881." The author was Sergeant (or Private) Sharpe.

240

1   2   3   4   5   6   7   8

1855.   1890.

R SIMKIN

See List of Illustrations.

CHAPTER XXIII

1882–1884

THE First Battalion paraded in the Highland dress, for the first time since 1809, on the 18th June 1882.[1] During the interval no connection with the Highlands seems to have been kept up, and since about 1820 very little with Scotland. No return of nationality in 1881 is to be found either at the War Office or at the Public Record Office ; but Colonel Mathias, C.B., who was then in the 75th, writes that from his personal recollection he would put the Irishmen in 1880 at " say four-tenths, and Scots and English, say three-tenths each. . . . The figures of 1881 would be much the same, except that South of England men were coming in instead of Irish."

At the request of Major-General Hon. Percy Feilding, commanding the brigade, a party from the Second Battalion had been sent to show how the Highland uniform should be worn ; large drafts followed from it and from the depôt at Aberdeen, among them Piper-corporal M'Lean as Pipe-major, while several young Scottish officers, intended for the Gordon Highlanders, were posted to the First Battalion, so that the national element was quickly introduced. Nor was it long before the battalion had an opportunity of doing credit to the tartan.

In 1875, when the British Government relieved the necessities of Ismail Pasha, who ruled Egypt under the suzerainty of Turkey, by the purchase of shares in the Suez Canal to the amount of four million sterling, it was foreseen that the British policy of non-intervention must be modified by circumstances. England had to see that the interest on the purchase money was secured to her, and jointly with France she had guaranteed the interest of the Ottoman Loan.

In 1878 the extravagance and misgovernment of Ismail had brought the country to the verge of bankruptcy, and its finances were entrusted to the joint control of an Englishman and a Frenchman. Economy had to be introduced, and in order to that economy, many officers of the army and other officials were dismissed, which caused great discontent. In 1879 a revolt broke out at Cairo, and the cry of " Egypt for the Egyptians " was raised. Ismail restored order by his presence, but everything tended to show that he had arranged the affair to make it appear that he was the only real power in the country. His duplicity cost him his throne, for the Sultan was induced, by the strong representations of England and France, to depose him, and his son Tewfik Pasha became Khedive in his stead. Tewfik was regarded as the tool of foreign influence ; the Egyptian or " fellah " officers objected to the

---

[1] In 1882 mounted officers of infantry discontinued the use of the saddle-cloth.

number of Turks and Circassians who occupied high places in the Government and the army ; and the discontent culminated during 1881 in a military rebellion led by Ahmed Arabi (afterwards Arabi Pasha), colonel of the 4th Regiment.   The Khedive was overawed, Arabi became Minister of War, and after a time the greatest power in the country.

In December 1881 the then head of the French Government, M. Gambetta, had suggested that England and France should take joint action to strengthen the authority of the Khedive, and to prevent undue interference on the part of Turkey ; this was agreed to by the British, and on the 19th May 1882, H.M.S. *Invincible*, bearing the flag of Vice-Admiral Sir Beauchamp Seymour, and *La Gallisonière*, with the French Admiral Conrad, each accompanied by two gunboats, arrived at Alexandria.   Here the excitement and tumult continued to increase till, on Sunday the 11th June, crowds of Arabs were swarming up the streets crying " Death to the Christians ! "   The soldiers and police aided in the butchery, a British officer and several seamen were murdered, with numbers of other Christians, European and native.   Thousands of all nationalities took refuge on the British ships in harbour, the town was pillaged, and similar scenes were enacted in other parts of the country, which was in a state of collapse and ruin.

Millions of capital were at stake in Egypt, which had just been saved from bankruptcy by the European Powers, but Great Britain, with its enormous trade and vast Eastern possessions, was most deeply interested in this highway of nations.   A profound sensation was produced in Europe, and indignation meetings were held throughout the United Kingdom denouncing the non-intervention policy of the Government, who now intimated their intention to demand reparation.

The hostile preparations of Arabi in fortifying Alexandria induced the British Admiral, whose squadron now consisted of eight ironclads and seven smaller vessels of war, to write to Toulba Pasha, the Commandant, that unless certain batteries were surrendered, for the purpose of disarming them, by sunrise on the 11th of July, he would open fire on the works.

Meanwhile the Government had been changed in France, and their fleet was ordered to take no part in the bombardment which followed, and which resulted in possession being taken of the city, where German, American, and Greek ships of war, and the P. & O. ship *Tanjore*, landed men to assist our marines and bluejackets in restoring order.[1]   Arabi entrenched himself at Kafr Dawar; British reinforcements arrived, and General Sir Archibald Alison took command of the land forces.

---

[1] Casualties on fleet—5 killed, 28 wounded.

On July 20th, Mr Gladstone's Cabinet had so far realised the gravity of the situation as to decide on the despatch of an expedition to Egypt, with or without the consent of the Powers. Money was voted by Parliament, and a portion of the Reserve was called out.[1]

This was the situation, so important in its after results, when, on the 2nd August, the First Battalion of the Gordon Highlanders embarked at Malta on H.M.S. *Euphrates*, landed at Alexandria on the 7th, and were quartered in Gabari Railway Station, with a strength of 690 of all ranks.

The British General occupied himself with the defences of the town ; reconnaissances were made, for Arabi's forces were increasing, and he had advanced his outposts towards Alexandria. Various skirmishes took place, the most serious of these being two days before the Gordons arrived, when the British loss was 1 officer and 3 men killed and 27 wounded, while that of the enemy was reported to be 3 officers and 76 men killed, and a large number wounded. The battalion was employed on outpost duty at Fort Mex, Moharrem Bey Station, Ramleh Station, and Rosetta Gate.

Meanwhile Sir Garnet J. Wolseley, G.C.B., K.C.M.G., had been appointed to command the expedition, and on the 15th August he arrived at Alexandria and inspected the position at Ramleh ; he made such dispositions as would lead the enemy to suppose he intended to attack from the north, while his real intention was to operate from the Suez Canal.

On the 18th the greater part of the troops re-embarked on seventeen transports, which, convoyed by eight ironclads, sailed on the 19th, and anchored at Aboukir as if with the intention of landing, but after dark the ships steamed off to Port Said, and when they arrived there the next morning they found the whole Canal in the hands of the British navy. At the time of the bombardment of Alexandria, the Egyptian corvette *Sakha*, commanded by an Arabist captain, arrived at Port Said, and information was received that she had dynamite on board to be used against vessels entering the Canal. Captain Seymour of the British despatch vessel *Iris*, at Port Said, moved his ship opposite the *Sakha*, called on the Arabist captain, and politely but firmly informed him that if he did not keep quiet, he, Captain Seymour, would be under the painful necessity of seizing or sinking his ship. The naval force was immediately strengthened by the arrival of Admiral Hoskins with four ironclads. .

M. de Lesseps, President of the Canal Company, claimed that

---

[1] The above is taken from Royle's " Egyptian Campaigns and the Events leading to Them," Lieut.-Colonel Herman Vogt's " Egyptian War of 1882," M'Coan's " Egypt under Ismail," and Sir Alfred Milner's " England in Egypt."

the neutrality of the Canal was secured by a clause in the concession, though by its terms the Khedive's authority over the Canal was expressly reserved. The British were acting under the direct authority of the Khedive, who, on the 15th August, issued a proclamation declaring that the British Commander-in-Chief was authorised to occupy all points on the Isthmus necessary for operations against the rebels. Meanwhile the English ironclad *Orion,* after being delayed under various pretexts by the Canal Company, had anchored opposite Ismailia on the 27th July. On the night of the 19th August the bluejackets and marines of H.M.S. *Monarch* and *Iris* were landed at Port Said, where they surprised the Egyptian sentries sleeping on their posts, and disarmed the garrison ; the Canal Company's office was secured to prevent information being conveyed through it, and Admiral Hoskins gave orders that no trading vessel should be allowed to enter the Canal, which he kept clear for the transports. Ships of war were stationed at various points, and Arabi's intention, expressed in a telegram to M. de Lesseps, of immediately blocking the Canal by its temporary destruction, was prevented only by a few hours. The Paris Press commented in angry tones on the high-handed action of England, though allowing its efficiency as a strategic move, and some journals even regretted that France had, at the last moment, declined to take part in carrying out the policy which Gambetta had initiated.[1]

We will now return to the First Battalion Gordon Highlanders, which moved, on the 19th August, to Ramleh, where it was joined by the rest of the Highland Brigade, viz. 1st Royal Highlanders, 2nd Highland Light Infantry, 1st Cameron Highlanders, the whole commanded by Major-General Sir Archibald Alison. They were employed, with the Second Division, under Sir E. Hamley, in watching Arabi's position at Kafr Dawar, Kinje Osman, and Mandora, and thus impressed on the enemy the idea of being attacked from the north. The only casualty the battalion had to

---

[1] Though England owned the largest number of shares in the undertaking, and her traffic was enormously greater than that of any other nation, the Canal was entirely managed by Frenchmen, under the presidency of M. de Lesseps, the able engineer who constructed it. It had indeed been the dream of many French generals and statesmen at a time when the interests of their country in the East were greater than now. D'Argenson had proposed the cutting of the Suez Canal in 1738, and it had been considered by Louis XIV. Choiseul had again recommended it to Louis XV, and in a decree by the Directory, published April 12th, 1798, when the expedition to take possession of Malta was about to sail, after appointing Bonaparte General-in-Chief of the army in the East, is the following article—" He will have the Isthmus of Suez cut through, and will take all necessary measures to insure the free and exclusive possession of the Red Sea for the French Republic."—Pamphlet by Sir F. W. Grenfell, " Malta in 1798, and its Capture by Napoleon."

In this connection it is interesting to find that on June 18, 1798, six days after Bonaparte's arrival, the French language was ordered to be taught in Primary Schools in Malta and Gozo ; well-paid teachers were appointed for that purpose, and soon French was proclaimed the official language. The British Government is blamed for proposing to do the same after 100 years' possession !

regret was the death of Captain Baynes from disease resulting from exposure.

On the 30th August the First (Highland) Brigade embarked at Alexandria, and, passing through the Canal, arrived in Lake Timsah on the 3rd September, when three officers joined with 155 n.c. officers and men of the Army Reserve. The troops landed daily, and were employed in conveying stores from the Maritime to the Sweet Water Canal at Ismailia, a duty rendered extremely arduous by the yielding sand and hot sun.

The Army Corps, under Sir G. Wolseley, was now composed of a cavalry division, two infantry divisions, corps troops, and an Indian contingent. Each division was formed of two brigades and divisional troops. The Cavalry Division, twenty-three squadrons, mounted infantry and six guns R.H.A., under Major-General Drury Lowe, C.B. The First Division, under Lieut.-General Willis, C.B., consisted of eight battalions, two squadrons, and two batteries R.A. The Second Division, under Lieut.-General Sir E. Hamley, K.C.M.G., C.B., First Brigade (Major-General Sir A. Alison, Bart., K.C.B.) ; Second Brigade [1] (Major-General Sir E. Wood, V.C., G.C.M.G., K.C.B.). The Indian contingent was under Major-General Sir H. T. MacPherson, V.C., K.C.B. The Reserve at Aden consisted of two native regiments. This force amounted to 1180 officers and 28,300 men.[2]

Meanwhile Nefiche was occupied for the protection of the water supply and the railway, and on August 24th, Sir Garnet, with a small force of all arms, which he placed under the immediate orders of Lieut.-General Willis, advanced to a point near El-Magfar on the Sweet Water Canal, where the enemy had constructed a dam, which was taken possession of after a charge by the Household Cavalry. The enemy were found to be in great strength at the village of Tel-el-Mahuta, where they were constructing another dam across the Canal and obstructing the railway. Sir Garnet held his ground, and next morning the enemy attacked him with great determination. Reinforcements arrived in the afternoon, and the force bivouacked at night on the ground they had tenaciously held all day, while the enemy withdrew to Tel-el-Mahuta. On the 25th the enemy was completely driven from his entrenched position there, the water supply was secured, and the railway for more than twenty miles was in possession of the British.[3] They had, however, outrun their commissariat, and on the 27th a foraging party brought in a welcome supply of cattle, sheep, and turkeys, which the General ordered to be paid for. The enemy made a

---

[1] Left at Alexandria.
[2] " History of the Coldstream Guards," by Lieut.-Colonel Ross of Bladensburg, C.B.
[3] Sir G. Wolseley's despatches of 26th and 27th August.

serious effort to regain his lost ground by an attack on General Graham, who with an advanced brigade held the position of Kassassin; an important engagement took place, in which Graham's force, though outnumbered, stood their ground and drove back the enemy, and with the aid of the cavalry under Sir Drury Lowe, who charged by moonlight, inflicted severe chastisement upon them.   The British loss was 3 men killed and 2 officers and 78 men wounded.

Arabi had done his best to render the Canal and railway useless, but though he impeded the advance, he was unable to arrest it. The line was repaired and the dams on the Canal were removed. There was now a pause in the operations ; baggage animals were as yet scarce, and there were no locomotives ; but the navy did yeoman service in bringing stores by the Canal, though barely sufficient for the troops in front.   A supply of mules arrived during the first days of September, and provisions were quickly accumulated at Kassassin ; on the 9th September the First Battalion Gordons, with the Highland Brigade, disembarked, and with the Second Division marched from Ismailia to El-Magfar ; the distance was short, but the soft sand of that part of the desert made it very fatiguing, and the heat was so intense that one man of the battalion fell dead from sunstroke.

Next day they halted at Tel-el-Mahuta, and on the 11th they reached Kassassin, where the whole available British forces were encamped about eight miles from Tel-el-Kebir (the Great Mound). This Arab village is situated to the south of the railway from Ismailia to Cairo, on the bank of the Canal, which here divides the desert from the cultivation produced by its waters.   On the opposite side of the Canal and railway stands the " Mound," near which Arabi had been for some weeks entrenching himself.   The place had been for many years used as a military camp, and is the strongest position in that part of the country.   A range of low hills stretches northwards from the railway at a point a mile and a half east of the station for about two miles, when it is intersected by a second series of rounded slopes.   The crest of the hills was entrenched for about two miles beyond the intersection, making a total frontage to the eastward of about three and a half miles.   There was a dry ditch from eight to twelve feet wide and from five to nine feet deep, in front of a breastwork from four to six feet high, with a banquette in rear.   There were shelter trenches in rear ; passages were provided for field-pieces and were guarded by traverses and breastworks.

The open nature of the country prevented a direct attack by daylight without enormous loss ; to have turned the enemy's position, though it might have forced him to retreat, might also have

MEDITERRANEAN SEA Syria

Rosetta
Mths of the Nile
Aboukir Damietta Port Said
Alexandria Levant Jerusalem
I. Marsa Dead Sea
Tanta El Arish Petra (Rs.)
Desert of Maan
Benha Tuh
Gizeh CAIRO Suez Akaba
Memphis r. Atfeh Penin. of El Hadj
Sinai
Birket el Kayum Benisuef
Medinet el Fayum
Garah Feshn
Behnesa Aboo Girgeh El Harra
Wah el Bahrieh Samalud Minieh Moilah
Kasr Bawiti Roda Ras Mohammed
or Lesser Oasis Mellawi el Wijh W. Hamd
Manfalut
Kasr Farafrah Siut Kheiber
Gow el Kebir
Ekhta Abutum Kossir Hauia
Girgeh Keneh
Wah el Gharbi Dendera Koft
El Kasr Dakhel Thebes Rs. Karnak
Wah el Khargeh Astun Luxor Umbo
El Khargeh Esneh El Kab
or Greater Oasis Edfu
Beris Kum Ombo Wadi Jemal
Kubnieh
1st Cataract Aswan Ras Benass
Tropic of Cancer (Syene) Berenice Rsi.
Shellal G. or Berenice
Kalabshi Mersa Shab

Sahara Derr Korosko C. Elba
Ibrim
2nd Cataract Ibsambol Toska M. Elba
Wadi Halfa Arab Ras Rowaii
Sarras Semna Murat Macowa I.
Selima Akasheh Desert
Saii Ferket Shikr
Ammara Absa
Sedinga Amareh Suakin
Gurgeh Delligo
Hannek 3rd Cataract El Ordeh Mora Abu Hammed
Maraka or New Dongola Argo I. Huela Tamai Suakin
Harnak Kortot Berti Merawan El Teb
Dongola Haialak Merawe Kerbekan El Bagara Tokar
Old Dongola Korti Cataract Solimanieh
Abu Hel Berber El Mekheir Wold Kan
Bir Malha Atbara El Damer Haiai
Abu Klea Atbara R.
Ain Hamed Metemmeh Keren Massowah
El ag Shendi Adua
es Safih Gos Rejeb Filik Kassala
Kailub Halfaia Meroe Is. Axum
Omdurman Khartum
1260 Amtin
el Getena

EGYPT
English Miles
0 100 200

Longitude E of Greenwich

W. & A. K. Johnston Limited Edinburgh

lost the opportunity of grappling with him, and Wolseley wished to make the battle a final one ; he therefore determined to attack by night, and having by frequent reconnaissances ascertained that the enemy kept a very bad lookout, he hoped to surprise him.   Owing to detachments along the lines of communication Wolseley could only place in line about 11,000 bayonets, 2000 sabres, and 60 field-guns.[1]   Arabi's position was defended by about 20,000 infantry, armed with Remington rifles, and three regiments of cavalry, with about 6000 Bedouins and Irregulars and 59 guns.[2]   The British battalions had been largely composed of young soldiers, but they were stiffened by the introduction of reservists, and by their courage and discipline more than made up for the numerical superiority of Arabi's army ; for, though the Egyptians are individually of fine physique, they were badly led, and (except the Soudanese, who showed determined bravery) had no stomach for the fight, being without the military spirit and discipline which, under British commanders, has made the Egyptian army what it now is.

On the 12th September the baggage and men's valises were stacked alongside the railway.   After dark the tents were struck and the troops moved to near " Ninth Hill," where they bivouacked in order of battle ; no fires were allowed, even smoking was pro-hibited.   This part of the desert is comparatively hard and good for marching, but it is no easy matter to bring an army six or eight miles through the darkness, guided only by the stars, to a given point at a given time, and such an operation could only be carried out by the attention to orders of all ranks.   The advance was to be in absolute silence, not a shot was to be fired, but the position carried at the point of the bayonet.   At 1.30 a.m. on the 13th the First and Second Divisions advanced simultaneously ; it was not easy in the dark to maintain the desired formation, but by the exertions of the generals and staff, and by means of connecting poles, all difficulties were overcome.   The Highlanders were in line of half-battalions, in columns of double companies ; and though it was impossible to prevent some confusion arising, it was quickly rectified by the intelligence and discipline of officers and men.   So quiet indeed was the march that the troops passed an advanced redoubt without being discovered by its garrison.

As the columns moved silently along, almost invisible to each other, a sense of suppressed excitement pervaded the whole, and it was probably with a feeling of relief that, as the first streak of dawn was appearing, the troops heard the Egyptian bugle and the shots which announced that the moment for decisive action had arrived ; " then the whole extent of entrenchment in our front,

---

[1] Wolseley's despatch of September 16th.
[2] *Ibid.*

hitherto unseen and unknown, poured forth a stream of rifle fire." [1]
The Highlanders were the leading brigade of the Second Division,
and reached the works a few minutes before the First Division.
They at once fixed bayonets, and to the sound of the bagpipes and
with a tremendous cheer, but without firing a shot, they went
forward at a steady run through a hail of bullets from the troops
who lined the ramparts ; they jumped into the ditch and climbed
over the parapet, where a short but desperate struggle took place.
Many of the Egyptian soldiers showed real courage, but their resistance was speedily overcome ; they were bayoneted where they
stood, or shot as they fled to the inner line of entrenchments ; no
shelter availed them, they were taken in front and in reverse, and
soon the Gordons stood on the crest overlooking Arabi's camp and
the station of Tel-el-Kebir.   Only about twenty minutes had
elapsed between the time when the enemy had opened fire and his
being in full retreat ; a deal of hard fighting was, however, crowded
into that short time, as is shown by the loss on both sides.   It was
now light, and the battalion advanced on the railway station and
formed up with the brigade to wait for further orders.

The First Division had been equally successful, and the Indian
contingent on the left of the Canal had taken an advanced battery,
while their horsemen on the left, and Russell's cavalry on the right,
swept round the enemy's works and thoroughly dispersed the
defeated Egyptians, who threw down their arms, scattered themselves all over the country, and Arabi's army ceased to exist. Their
general and his second in command were the first to escape ; he
rode to Belbeis, where he caught a train, and reaching Cairo the
same evening, prepared to destroy the city.

The loss of the enemy at Tel-el-Kebir was nearly 2000 killed,
besides a large number wounded, for whom the British surgeons
did all they could.   The British loss amounted to 9 officers
and 48 n.c. officers and men killed, and 27 officers and 353 n.c.
officers and men wounded ; 22 n.c. officers and men missing—
total of all ranks, 459.   Of the 1st Battalion Gordon Highlanders,
Lieutenant H. G. Brooks, Corporal P. Fitzgerald, Privates W.
Munro, Thos. Smith, and W. Wilson were killed in action, and
Lieutenant A. G. Pirie and 29 n.c. officers and men were wounded,
of whom Lieutenant Pirie and Private T. Bartlett died of their
wounds.   Private W. Martin missing.[2]

Sir Archibald Alison, in an order of later date, referring to his
brigade says :—

The Major-General does not think that he will be accused of partiality
when he says that the steady discipline of the brigade throughout the night
march, and the determined courage shown in the storming of the works at

[1] Sir E. Hamley.   [2] Public Record Office.

Tel-el-Kebir, constitute it the not unworthy descendant of that historic brigade which Sir Colin Campbell led up the slopes of Alma.[1]

On the 14th the battalion marched to Zagazig and occupied that important railway junction. On the 15th they proceeded by train to Benha and occupied Tantah on the 17th, where they received the surrender of the garrison of Salahieh, consisting of 3000 infantry, a regiment of cavalry, and twenty-four guns.

Meanwhile Sir Garnet had lost no time in reaping the fruits of victory. Macpherson,[2] with an Indian detachment, reached Zagazig at 4 p.m. on the day of the battle, where five trains full of troops were ready to start. The engine-drivers surrendered, except one who tried to start his train, when he was shot by Lieutenant Burn-Murdoch, and the soldiers left the cars and ran away, our men not troubling to make them prisoners. Drury Lowe's cavalry pursued to Belbeis, where they bivouacked, and early next morning pushed on to save Cairo from the fate which befel Alexandria in July. Lowe reached Abbassieh, just outside the city, at 4.45 p.m. on the 14th, his cavalry having marched sixty-five miles in the two days, besides fighting. The garrison of about 10,000 men were summoned to surrender ; they laid down their arms, the British took possession of the citadel, and Arabi surrendered unconditionally. The Guards, under H.R.H. the Duke of Connaught, reached Cairo by rail early on the 15th ; Kafr Dawar, a position more strongly fortified than Tel-el-Kebir, was given up to Sir Evelyn Wood on the 16th without resistance. The rebellion had entirely collapsed, and Wolseley was able to report the war at an end, and the object for which it was undertaken fully accomplished. " Let it be remembered that Great Britain did save Egypt from anarchy, and all European nations from incalculable loss in blood and treasure." [3]

" A British force remained in Egypt for the protection of public tranquillity." [4] Circumstances unforeseen by the Government of the day made it absolutely necessary that this force should be continued, and had a British protectorate been established in Egypt immediately after the war, it would, apparently, at that time have given the greatest satisfaction to the European inhabitants of every

[1] Tel-el-Kebir was the first battle in which colours were not carried. A Horse Guards circular of March 1882 conveyed Her Majesty's command that, in consequence of the altered formation of attack and the extended range of firing, in the event of a battalion being ordered on active service, the colours " will be left at the base of operations, unless the General Officer Commanding should be of opinion that the nature of the service is such as to render the possession of colours with the battalion undoubtedly expedient." Both colours, however, were retained " as affording a record of the services of the regiment, and furnishing to young soldiers a history of its gallant deeds."

[2] The Gordons' Brigadier in Afghanistan.

[3] M'Coan's " Egypt under Ismail."

[4] Lord Granville's Despatch to the Great Powers, January 3rd, 1883.

nation.   When the intention to withdraw the army of occupation was understood, a petition in English, French, Italian, and Greek, signed by thousands of influential persons, was presented, begging that it might be retained.

Arabi and his chief supporters were tried for rebellion against the Khedive, and sentenced to death, which was commuted to exile for life, Arabi being sent to Ceylon.[1]   Correspondence produced in evidence at the trial showed that Arabi had at one period been acting under instructions from Constantinople, though the Sultan pretended to support the Khedive.[2]

The Gordons remained at Tantah till the 28th September, when they moved to Ghezireh on the Nile opposite Cairo, and encamped.   Here they were reviewed by the Khedive, and then went into quarters at the Citadel, forming part of the army of occupation.

In commemoration of the distinguished and gallant conduct of their First Battalion, the Gordon Highlanders afterwards received the royal authority to bear on their colours and appointments the words " Egypt, 1882," " Tel-el-Kebir."   Sir Garnet Wolseley was raised to the peerage, and among the honours to officers and soldiers of the army, Lieut.-Colonel D. Hammill, who commanded the battalion throughout the campaign, was made a Companion of the Bath, while he was also permitted to receive from the Khedive the Third Class of the decoration of the Medjidieh.   Major J. E. Boyes received the Fourth Class of the Osmanieh, and was promoted to Brevet Lieut.-Colonel ; Lieutenant and Adjutant H. H. Burney and Lieutenant A. G. Pirie [3] the Fifth Class of the Medjidieh.   Medals were awarded to all ranks by Her Majesty Queen Victoria, and bronze stars were afterwards presented to the battalion, along with other troops, by the Khedive at the Abdin Palace, Cairo.

January 31*st*, 1883.—Two sergeants, 2 corporals, and 73 privates joined from the depôt at Aberdeen, and in February all the men of the Army Reserve who had not already gone, left for home under Lieutenant H. Wright of the Second Battalion.   In May they were replaced by a draft of 3 sergeants, 2 corporals, and 109 privates.   In June, Lieutenant Payne, 1 sergeant, 1 corporal, 1 drummer, and 26 privates were detached to join the mounted infantry corps at Abbassieh.   In August, cholera broke out, and 13 n.c. officers and men fell victims to the disease.   F Company was encamped at Helouan, and in September a Field Officer's detachment relieved a similar party of the 1st Royal Highlanders at Port Said.   In December, three officers and 124 n.c. officers and men, chiefly recruits, joined the battalion.

---

[1] He was allowed to return to Egypt in 1901.   [2] Royle.
[3] Lieutenant Pirie died of his wounds at Malta in January 1883.

At this time Her Majesty was graciously pleased to approve of the words " South Africa, 1835 " being borne on the colours and appointments of the Gordon Highlanders in commemoration of the services of the First Battalion (then the 75th Regiment).

January 27*th*, 1884.—The detachment from Port Said rejoined, and on February 15th the battalion was held in readiness to proceed on active service.

In 1882 a rebellion had broken out in the Soudan against the Government of the Khedive ; it was led by Mohammed Ahmad, whose reputation for piety and learning had secured him great popularity.   He wandered about preaching a holy war against the Christians, and declared himself to be the " Mahdi " (the being whose advent at about this period had been foretold by Mohammedan writers) and that he was deputed by God to restore the religion of the Arabs to its former purity.   In January 1883, Colonel Hicks, known as Hicks Pasha, a retired Indian officer, was appointed head of the Egyptian Army of the Soudan, and reached Khartum in March.   On the 7th of October, with 10,000 of his men, he was cut to pieces at Lake Rahad, and the " Mahdi " became master of the Soudan.   General Charles George Gordon, R.E., celebrated as the successful leader of the Chinese army in 1860, and as remarkable for his unassuming piety as for his fearless sense of duty, had, in 1874, been appointed by the Khedive Governor-General of the Soudan, where he worked to break up the slave trade, and by his just and merciful rule did much to conciliate the people, over whom he gained great influence.   He had resigned his appointment, but in January 1884, at the urgent request of the British Government, he agreed to return to Khartum to arrange for the evacuation of the interior of the Soudan, which had been decided on, for the safety of the seaports and the prevention of the slave trade.

Meanwhile, Osman Digna, an adventurous slave merchant of Turkish origin, had raised the standard of revolt in the Eastern Soudan, and gained several successes over the Egyptians.   Baker Pasha, formerly lieut.-colonel of H.M. 10th Hussars and latterly a general in the Turkish service, was appointed by the Khedive to command an expedition for the purpose of pacifying the region between Berber and Suakin, and relieving the threatened garrisons of Tokar and Sinkat.   Baker's force was very inferior in quality, and was overwhelmed at El-Teb, February 4th, 1884.   The garrison of Sinkat was massacred after a brave defence.

Britain was now the real and therefore the responsible Power in Egypt, and it was felt that an effort should be made to save the garrison of Tokar.   For this purpose it was decided that a British force, chiefly drawn from the army of occupation, should be sent to Suakin.   The command was given to Major-General Sir Gerald Graham, V.C., K.C.B.

The First Battalion Gordon Highlanders, having been selected to take part in the expedition, left Cairo, under Colonel Hammill, on the evening of Saturday the 16th February, being played from the Citadel to the railway by the band and pipers of the Camerons.[1] After spending Sunday at Suez, they embarked in the evening on the P. & O. s.s. *Thibet*, and after a pleasant passage the *Thibet* slowed down off Suakin on the 22nd.   The men-of-war in the harbour were firing shells at a party of the enemy outside the town, but the Gordons were ordered to proceed to Trinkitat, where they landed in boats with a strength of 720 men.

The force consisted of the 10th Hussars (250 men) and the 19th Hussars (430 men), under Brigadier-General Herbert Stewart, with 150 mounted infantrymen.   There were a party of the Royal Garrison Artillery, under Major Lloyd, equipped with six Egyptian camel guns ; 125 sailors, under Commander Rolfe, R.N., equipped with Gatling guns ; and a party of Royal Engineers.   The First Infantry Brigade, Brigadier-General Redvers Buller, V.C., con- sisted of the 3rd King's Royal Rifles (630 men), 1st Gordon Highlanders (720 men), 1st Royal Irish Fusiliers (350 men). Second Brigade, Brigadier-General Davis—1st Royal Highlanders (730 men), 1st York and Lancaster Regiment (450 men), and 300 Royal Marines.   There were twenty-eight guns, including six machine guns.   For transport and ambulance work there were 700 camels and 350 mules.   The artillery, 10th Hussars, and York and Lancasters, had been stopped on the voyage home from India.

On the 24th news was received that Tokar had already fallen, but it was decided that a blow should still be struck at Osman Digna for the protection of Suakin.   A reconnaissance made by the mounted troops to Fort Baker, three miles inland, showed the enemy to be in force beyond that place ; accordingly the battalion, along with the Irish Fusiliers and two guns, marched in the morning of the 25th, covered by a squadron of the 19th Hussars, and after wading for a mile through the mud and water of a lagoon, took possession of the fort.   There were no casualties, though the enemy fired at long range on the Hussars.   The engineers put up a wire entanglement, and the troops bivouacked in and around the earthwork.   During three days they were employed in making a small redoubt for stores, and in hauling a Krupp gun across the marsh.   A wet night caused some discomfort, and an unpleasant interest was excited by the bullets fired by the enemy, who were, however, kept by our artillery at a respectful distance, and the only

---

[1] Each officer was allowed 40 lbs. of kit as far as Suakin, after that 10 lbs.

damage received was to a Highlander's greatcoat. The rest of the force having arrived, the whole advanced in square formation, about 8 a.m. on the 29th, to attack the enemy at El-Teb, four miles distant, the Gordons forming the front face. The front and rear faces moved in company columns of fours at company intervals, and the flank faces in open columns of companies. The Naval Brigade with their Gatlings occupied the angles in front, and the Royal Artillery the rear angles of the square. In the centre were transport animals with ammunition and surgical appliances. The men carried one day's rations and water-bottles.

A heavy rain had made the ground difficult for the artillerymen and sailors, who dragged their guns by hand, so that frequent halts were necessary. The cavalry was in rear, except those who covered the advance, which was made over low sandhills covered with bush; about ten o'clock the enemy were reported to be strongly entrenched on our left, and Graham inclined the square to the right. About 11.15 he found himself opposite a work armed with two Krupp guns, and he moved still more to the right, when the enemy opened with case and shell, and also with rifle fire. Fortunately they fired high and comparatively few casualties occurred,[1] but it was a trying march past the guns without returning their fire.

After getting to the left of the work, which was on the proper left rear of the enemy's line, the square was halted and the men lay down while the artillery came into action at 900 yards, and silenced the two Krupp guns. Then the square, with bagpipes playing, advanced by its left face, which by the flank movement was now opposite to the work attacked. Strict orders had been given that up to 300 yards only volley firing was to be allowed, and independent firing after 100 yards. As the works were neared, the Soudanese rose from their entrenchments and rifle pits, and boldly charged the York and Lancasters and the Marines, who formed the present front. At headlong speed, brandishing their spears and two-handed swords, they attacked with the same fearless impetuosity which had demoralised and routed Baker's Egyptians, but they now met more steadfast opponents. With bayonets fixed, Graham's soldiers received the onset ; right and left the enemy dropped under their fire, but the survivors rushed on. At one moment the York and Lancasters, borne back by numbers, recoiled a few yards and some Soudanese got inside the square, but only to be bayoneted ; the Marines advanced and the square was closed. As the action developed, the formation became more irregular, but "the Gordon Highlanders speedily rectified this, moving one half-battalion into the fighting line, the other half being

---

[1] Baker Pasha, attached to the Intelligence Department ; Lieutenant Royds, R.N. (mortally), and about twenty men were hit at this time.

thrown back to guard against flank attacks."[1] For over half an hour the Soudanese had struggled to break the square, but they now began to hang back and concentrate behind the hillocks. Fresh ammunition was served out, and the columns re-formed and were ready for the rush of the still undefeated foe, who, availing themselves of every bit of cover to get near, started up and attacked on all sides, but only to be killed or driven back. At length, having partially cleared their front, the troops advanced till within a short distance of the works ; then with a cheer the York and Lancasters, assisted by the bluejackets, made a rush, the work was carried and the guns taken.

Stewart had orders to keep well away from the square with his cavalry, ready to charge the enemy when broken by the infantry. At about 12.30, when the battery was taken, numbers of the enemy were visible in the plain beyond, and Stewart, apparently under the impression that they were defeated, moved round the right of the infantry, formed his horsemen in three lines, and, after a rapid ride of three miles, charged and scattered the Soudanese in his front. They were not, however, broken troops, but part of masses who had not been engaged, and when the two first lines halted, an orderly brought information that the third line (100 Hussars) had been attacked by a large body of Arabs, mounted and on foot, who appeared from the brushwood on their right flank.   Lieut.-Colonel Webster, who commanded, wheeled his squadron and was at once engaged, while the front lines returned to his assistance. The Arab horsemen rode boldly against the Hussars, and fought desperately with their two-handed swords; but the most dangerous foes were the spearmen, who lay concealed and hamstrung the passing horses, or threw heavy clubs at their legs, bringing many to their knees.   So active were they that one sprang panther-like on to the hind-quarters of Major Brabazon's charger, and with his long knife proceeded to carve at the back of its rider, who had some difficulty in ridding himself of the unpleasant incubus with his revolver.   The 10th and 19th charged again and again through the Arab groups, and then dismounted and poured volleys into them, but when they rode back to El-Teb they had lost heavily in men and officers.

While the Hussars were thus occupied, the infantry were engaged in what turned out to be their hardest task—the capture of another battery and the village.   The guns already taken were turned on the former, and the infantry fought its way across the entrenchments.   The battery, taken in reverse, was silenced, but the enemy clung with desperate tenacity to their rifle-pits, and fired from the loopholes of a brick building and from behind a boiler,

[1] Graham's Despatch.

the remains of an old sugar mill ; shells were fired to dislodge them without success, till the sailors with Gatlings and revolvers fired through the windows, while the Highlanders shot those who rushed out.   The Arabs hid in the bushes round the boiler, from which they would rush on the advancing line ; their spearmen would lie pretending to be dead till the soldiers had passed, and then springing up, do much mischief till killed—they neither gave nor asked for quarter.   " By 2 p.m. the enemy had given up all idea of further fighting, and the last work on the right of their line was occupied by the Gordon Highlanders without opposition, as they streamed away in the direction of Tokar or Suakin." [1]

The reckless charge of the Soudanese was of no avail against breechloaders in the hands of steady soldiers, and, except for one moment, they never got near enough in sufficient numbers to be really dangerous.   Their loss was terrible ; that of the British was 4 officers and 26 n.c. officers and men killed ; 17 officers and 142 n.c. officers and men were wounded—of the latter 10 privates belonged to the Gordons.   Among the many narrow escapes, Private Turnbull was struck on the union locket of his waist-belt. His officer thought he was done for, but he soon rejoined, having only had his wind taken by the grape-shot.   Some men were wounded while giving water to their wounded enemies ; among them Piper Macdonald was nearly scalped while thus charitably employed.

The battalion bivouacked that night in line.

On the 1st of March the whole force, except half of the Royal Highlanders, advanced on Tokar, from which the enemy fled after firing a few shots, and only the surrendered Egyptian soldiers, whose lives had been spared, were found in the place.   After burying the remains of those who had been killed in Baker's disaster, the troops returned to Trinkitat on the 3rd.   On the 8th the battalion embarked on the s.s. *Utopia*, and the same evening landed at Suakin.   During the absence of the force at Trinkitat, Major Holley, R.A., had equipped the detachment of M Battery, First Brigade R.A., with four naval 9-pounders, and these now joined as a reinforcement.   On the evening of the 11th the battalion moved with the other troops about eight miles to a zareba made by Baker some weeks before, where, after a hot march by moonlight, they bivouacked at 11.30 p.m.   After dinner next day the advance was continued in square formation.   About 4.30 the enemy opened a desultory rifle fire from about 1000 yards, which was soon silenced by a few rounds of shrapnel, and the force halted and formed a zareba of prickly mimosa bushes round the bivouac, the enemy's position being about one and a half miles distant.   After midnight

[1] Graham's Despatch.

there was an alarm, and the enemy continued a distant dropping fire during the night, causing a few casualties, Lieutenant F. Gordon and a private of the battalion being wounded. The bright moon made the front visible, but the *ping* and occasional *thud* of bullets was not conducive to repose. On the morning of Thursday the 13th, at 7.30, the force left the bivouac in charge of two companies of Gordons, under Major Smail, and this time the General did not put all his eggs in one basket, but moved in direct echelon of brigade squares from the left, Major Lloyd, with his six camel guns, being attached to the First Brigade, and Major Holley, with four naval 9-pounders, to the Second Brigade. The battalion furnished three companies to the front face, two to the right face of the First Brigade square, and one as escort to the guns, which were in the centre between the Gordons and the Fusiliers, who formed the left front and left face, while the King's Royal Rifles closed the rear. The Second Brigade led, accompanied by General Graham, who, being informed that the enemy were strongly posted in a dry watercourse, directed the advance towards the left of this position, hoping to sweep the ravine with his artillery ; and he desired Major Holley to come into action outside and slightly to the rear of the right face of the square. The enemy at once opened a heavy but ill-directed fire, the mounted skirmishers were withdrawn, and the brigades advanced ; when the Second Brigade (Brigadier Davis) was about 200 yards from the ravine, a series of rushes was made by the enemy, but the fire of the square prevented them from reaching it.

Then Graham ordered the Royal Highlanders, who formed the front face, to charge, which they gallantly did, accompanied by a few of the York and Lancasters on their right, who, seeing the Highlanders go forward, also rushed on. The smoke of the Gatlings and rifles hung thick, and under its cover hundreds of Arabs crept up the side of the ravine among the bushes, and getting into the gap in the square between it and those who had charged, did fearful execution, stabbing and slashing with dagger and sword. The rear rank of the Royal Highlanders turned about, and the regiment maintained its formation, fighting back to back, but nearly all their supernumerary rank were either killed or wounded. So close were the combatants that the soldiers had hardly room to use their bayonets, and officers fought not only with the point but with the fist in the hilt of their claymores. The brigade lost some ground and was driven back, and the machine guns had to be abandoned, but there was no panic. The troops retreated facing their foes, and firing when not engaged in meeting the attacks with the bayonet. Soldiers, sailors, and marines vied with each other in examples of individual heroism, and though at one moment the scene was described as resembling the scramble at a football match, the steadiness of the retiring groups enabled them soon to rally when covered by the fire of the First Brigade. This brigade was heavily attacked on its front and right, but Buller was able to advance far enough to cover Holley's guns and get them into his square before the Arabs reached them. Not content with attacking the square in front and flanks, the Arabs, with extraordinary determination, passed round through the scrub and threw themselves on the riflemen in rear, so that all four sides were engaged at once ; but so well was the brigade handled, and so steady were the men, that Buller was able not only to hold his own ground, but seeing that something was wrong, he moved forward and poured a heavy cross fire on the enemy, who were assailing the other brigade. A small depression in the ground clothed with scrubby bushes ran almost up to the feet of the Gordons in the centre of the right face of the square, and before Buller could move he had to clear the enemy from this. Two of Lloyd's guns were accordingly run up by hand so that their muzzles just cleared the front rank of the Gordons, and the attacking Arabs were literally blown away by rounds of inverted shrapnel. At the same time, Stewart moved the cavalry to the left, dismounted his men, and fired a volley into the right flank of the enemy, who were driven back. After a short halt, when fresh ammunition was served out, Buller advanced closer to the ravine, and was thus able by his fire to cover the Second Brigade, as Davis again led them forward. In ten minutes the lost ground was regained, the guns were recaptured, and at once turned on the enemy.

The First Brigade was now sent forward to take possession of a ridge about 800 yards off, on which the enemy were gathered. Down they went and across the ravine. With a cheer they took the ridge and then advanced, firing at the Arabs on a second hill, but these were disheartened, feebly returned the fire, and sullenly retreated. From the second ridge the village of Tamai could be seen 180 feet below, with the tents of Osman Digna's camp, and before noon these were in possession of the British. Parties were sent to search for and bring in the dead and wounded—a dangerous task, as the wounded Arabs would seize the opportunity to attack or fire at a passing soldier. The killed numbered 5 officers and 86 n.c. officers and men ; 7 officers and 103 n.c. officers and men were wounded, and 19 men missing. The casualties of the battalion were 4 privates killed, viz. John Lebreth, John Payne, Chas. Ryder, and Jas. M'Leod ; and 9 n.c. officers and men wounded, of whom a corporal died of his wounds.

After resting near the wells to refresh till 4 p.m., the troops returned to the zareba ; where Major Smail and his two companies had also been engaged, and had repulsed the attack.   In the evening the melancholy duty of burying the dead was performed.   After a quiet night the battalion took part in the destruction of Osman Digna's magazine and camp at Tamai ; then, halting for dinner by a stream, marched back to Baker's zareba, passing yesterday's battlefield—a ghastly scene.   On the 15th they arrived at Suakin, where they enjoyed a bathe, for washing was a luxury in which they had not for some days been able to indulge.

On the 18th March the Gordons struck camp, and along with the 19th Hussars and mounted infantry made a fairly easy march of about thirteen miles to the wells of Handoub, and formed a zareba at the base of a hill held by a company of the Highlanders. Here newspapers were received, showing that their conduct at El-Teb had been appreciated at home—always a great encouragement to soldiers on service.   They were joined by two batteries and the 10th Hussars, and on the 23rd the battalion was sent to form a zareba at a point near the entrance of the valley of Tamanieb, where it was reported Osman's forces were increasing and he intended to fight.   The remainder of Graham's force having come up, the advance was continued at 5 a.m. on the 27th, the First Brigade in square leading ; the morning was cool and the men in the best of spirits, but the ground was both sandy and rocky, and the great heat of the sun was severely felt before they reached Tamanieb at noon.   Bodies of the enemy could be seen, and the guns of the First Brigade opened fire ; the mounted troops also skirmished, but little resistance was offered and the enemy retreated.   The troops halted at the wells—men and horses drank— and those who have passed through a dry and thirsty land where no water is, know what that means.   There were no casualties, and after burning Osman Digna's village and magazine the force returned to the last night's bivouac, having been on the move about thirteen hours.[1]

On the 1st April the battalion sailed from Suakin on board the *Utopia*, and landing at Suez early on the 5th, had time while the train stopped at Tel-el-Kebir to see that their comrades' graves there were well kept.   On reaching Cairo an enthusiastic reception awaited them at the station, and the tourists at Shepheard's Hotel cheered tremendously as they passed to their quarters in the Citadel, where the Camerons, with true Highland hospitality, had provided entertainment for their friends.

In commemoration of the distinguished and gallant behaviour

---

[1] The above account of the campaign is taken from Royle's "Egyptian Campaigns," General Graham's Despatches, the Regimental Record, Notes by General Sir Redvers Buller, V.C., G.C.B., and the Journal of Lieutenant F. Neish.   The names of those killed in action are taken from War Office Pay Lists, Public Record Office.

of their First Battalion, the Gordon Highlanders were afterwards granted permission to add the date " 1884 " to the words " Egypt, 1882," already on their colours, and the following officers were granted the Order of the Medjidieh :—Third Class, Colonel F. F. Daniell ; Fourth Class, Captain Kevill-Davies ; Fifth Class, Lieutenant Payne.[1]

[1] Lieutenant Payne, with thirty-four n.c. officers and men, had served in the corps of mounted infantry during the campaign.

CHAPTER XXIV

1884-1894

MEANWHILE, though Osman Digna's forces had been broken, they were not destroyed. When the Government withdrew Graham's army, they lost the opportunity of opening the route by Berber to Khartum. Gordon's people were daily expecting aid, and could not bring themselves to believe that they were to be abandoned, but the British Government refused till too late the assistance asked for. In June, Gordon heard of the fall of Berber ; in July, he was shut up in Khartum. It was only on the 5th August that Mr Gladstone moved a vote of credit to enable operations to be undertaken for the relief of Gordon. There were two ways by which Khartum could be approached ; the Suakin-Berber route involved a march of 280 miles through a country badly supplied with water, in addition to the journey by river of only 200 miles. The Nile route meant a distance of 1650 miles against the stream. General Stephenson, commanding the army of occupation at Cairo, after conferring with the naval officers who had been for weeks examining the difficulties of the river navigation, came to the conclusion that there was not time to relieve Gordon by the latter route and, as time was of vital importance, he recommended the former ; but Lord Wolseley had formed an opposite opinion, which was adopted by the Government, and they informed General Stephenson that as he considered their plan impracticable, they would not ask him to carry it out, and that Lord Wolseley was appointed " to take temporarily the chief command in Egypt." [1]

Lord Wolseley selected a force of 7000 men for the expedition. Among them was the First Battalion Gordon Highlanders,[2] and on the evening of the 5th November they started, under Colonel Hammill, C.B., in two trains from the Boulac Dacrour Station, where many distinguished officers were assembled to wish them God-speed ; among others, General Baker Pasha, who was loudly cheered by the men. Arriving at Assiout next morning, the battalion embarked on two steamers and four barges. The air was bracing : by day they enjoyed the scenery, and noticed the strange customs and agriculture of the people ; they saw, as they passed along, the wonderful temples and monuments of former ages at Carnac, Luxor, and Thebes. At sunset the vessels anchored near the bank of the river, which varies in width from a mile and a half to 400 yards ; music, vocal and instrumental, was not wanting to cheer the evening hour, and except mosquitoes at night there was nothing to interrupt the pleasure of the voyage, till on the 19th

---

[1] The event proved that General Stephenson was right.
[2] Marching out strength, 24 officers and 757 n.c. officers and men.

they reached Assouan, when four companies at once proceeded by train to Shellal, above the Island of Philae and the First Cataract, and the other four followed next day. Lieutenant F. Neish and fifty men were left in charge of the hospital, rejoining in a fortnight.

From Shellal the companies worked up independently in boats to Wady Halfa, and proceeded by train to the bend of the Second Cataract, where they received " whalers," boats specially built for the passage up the river.[1] Provisions were stowed in each boat, and the first company sailed from Sarras on the 4th December, the others following at intervals of a few days. The work was new to the men, but soldiers can turn their hand to anything ; the Gordons soon became expert boatmen, and " the splendid manner in which they behaved and their eagerness to push on, was marked throughout the whole expedition." [2]

For about six weeks the troops were engaged in this difficult and dangerous navigation, rowing or sailing as wind and open water permitted, sleeping in tents and sometimes in the open, hauling the boats for hours up rapids when, to lighten them, the stores were carried by natives, or, if the portage was long, by camels. Sometimes the boats were wrecked on sunken rocks, or swamped, as in the Semneh Cataract, where Corporal Taylor was drowned. The boats' crews vied with those of other companies and of other regiments in rowing and hauling and general dexterity, being often assisted by the Canadian Voyageurs. They landed for meals, when milk and eggs could be bought to add to their rations, and men compared notes and exchanged remarks more or less complimentary with other competitors in the dangerous race ; broken boats and tackle had to be repaired, clothes mended, and many odd jobs done by the handy soldiers, to whom nothing came amiss.[3]

After passing Ambigul and the cataracts of Sangin, Okneh, Okasheh and Dal, in which several boats came to grief, they had open water to Kaibar Cataract, which took four hours' hard work to cross. A long and difficult passage brought them from Shaban to Hanneck Cataract, where Lieutenant Burney's boat struck on a rock and was capsized under full sail ; the crew were thrown into the river, several being unable to swim, but the officer swam from one to another, bringing them oars, etc., and otherwise helping them till all were safe, when, greatly exhausted, having been three-quarters of an hour in the water, he was himself picked up by

---

[1] Eight hundred of these had been ordered from England, fitted with twelve oars and two masts with lugsails. Steam pinnaces were also equipped. T. Cook & Son contracted for the transport of the expedition to above the Second Cataract. A number of Canadian boatmen had also been engaged to assist.

[2] Regimental Record.

[3] No drink stronger than tea was carried, except for the sick.

a boat belonging to the Black Watch. Several boats were wrecked in the Shaban Rapids, but with no fatal result. The Nile now became more open, sandbanks taking the place of rocks ; palm trees and cultivation skirted each bank of the river, crocodiles and occasionally hippopotamuses were seen. There was no cessation from toil on Christmas Day, and they were too tired to bring in the New Year with any festivity beyond a longer chat round the camp fire ; for the troops were pushing on, trying, as the army has often done, to redeem by their exertions the results entailed by the costly economy of vacillating and pusillanimous politicians.

In the smoother parts, when the wind was fair, twenty or thirty boats might be seen within a mile, their white sails showing against the dark waters or high banks of the Nile, while the sky was lit up by the orange and crimson hues of an African sunset. Passing Dongola and many other places they arrived, about the 14th January 1885, at Korti, from which Lord Wolseley directed the operations.

He despatched two columns. The first (the Desert Column), under Major-General Sir Herbert Stewart, went across the Bayuda Desert to secure the shortest route to Khartum, and hold the wells at Gakdul and Abu-Klea, and to hold Metemmeh while communications were maintained with Gordon. The second (the River Column), under General Earle, was to proceed along the Nile to disperse the rebels around Hamdab, fifty-two miles distant ; to punish the Monassir tribes who had treacherously murdered Colonel Stewart while he was bringing despatches from General Gordon ; to rid Abu Hamed of the enemy, and open up the desert route from there to Korosko ; and covering a great bend of the Nile, this column would dislodge the rebels from Berber and join hands with General Stewart at Metemmeh. The Gordons formed part of Earle's Column, which was already assembling at Hamdab, and was composed of two squadrons 19th Hussars, an Egyptian Camel Battery, some Egyptian Mounted Infantry, the 1st South Staffordshire, 1st Royal Highlanders, and 2nd Duke of Cornwall's Light Infantry, with a proportion of Royal Engineers, commissariat and transport. After a thorough repair of the boats, the battalion pushed up the river by companies, taking five days to make Hamdab, which the headquarters reached on the 21st January. On that day news was received of Sir Herbert Stewart's engagement at Abu-Klea.

On the 24th, General Earle moved forward, but the Gordons were left at Hamdab to await the arrival of G Company with boats to complete the battalion. General Earle, however, took D Company,[1] which formed his escort, and afterwards that of General

---

[1] Under Captain Ian Hamilton, made up to one subaltern and 129 n.c. officers and men.

Brackenbury, throughout the expedition. On the 29th, reports arrived from the front that the column was in touch with the enemy, and that a fight was imminent ; Colonel Hammill immediately sent off a messenger to General Earle asking permission to join him at once without waiting for the expected company. The same night he received orders to close up, and on the morning of the 30th January the battalion (16 officers and 383 n.c. officers and men) sailed in thirty-eight whalers. The ascent was difficult. On the 1st of February two boats were swamped at the Fourth Cataract and one totally wrecked ; on the 4th a boat was caught by the main current, but, though tossed like a straw on the seething waters and dashed against the rocks, she reached the foot of the cataract, where the men managed to land without loss of life. Though all hands worked from sunrise to sunset the progress was necessarily slow.

Earle with the column was at Berti on the 6th, when he received orders to await further instructions. The fall of Khartum on the 26th of January, and the death of Gordon, was now known, and Lord Wolseley was communicating with the Government as to further operations.

The battalion halted at " Palm Tree Camp," five miles below Berti, where a zareba was formed and every precaution taken to meet an attack. On the 8th the general was desired to advance to Abu Hamed. He ordered the battalion to push on and join him ; they started at noon, but the difficulties of the Berti Cataract were such that they only reached that place on the afternoon of the 10th, when they received orders to halt for the night. At daybreak next morning they proceeded, having scouts thrown out on each side, who sighted parties of the enemy, and a few shots at long range were fired at the boats as they anchored. Whilst steps were being taken to guard against surprise during the night, a messenger from the front arrived with the news that a successful engagement had been fought on the 10th at Kirbekan, about five miles further on, when the enemy, strongly posted in the rocks commanding the river, had been totally defeated and dispersed ; but the victory was dearly purchased. General Earle and Lieut.-Colonel Eyre of the South Staffordshire, Lieut.-Colonel Coveney of the Royal Highlanders, and 9 n.c. officers and men were killed, and 4 officers and 39 n.c. officers and men were wounded and 1 missing.

Early on the 12th the battalion arrived at Kirbekan, where the troops were halted. General Brackenbury, who now commanded the column, was instructed that the expedition was to stay in the country till the Mahdi's power at Khartum was destroyed, and arrangements were to be made for co-operation with General Buller in an attack on Berber. Accordingly the column continued its progress, and on the morning of the 13th February the battalion left Kirbekan and, passing the razor-backed heights from which the enemy had been driven on the 10th, reached the Shakook Pass, through which, for more than six miles, the river is narrowed by massive rocks 300 feet high on each side. Here the enemy had prepared to offer opposition, but their late defeat had altered their intention, and the troops passed unmolested. At Salamat on the 17th the house and property of Sheik Suliman Wad Gamr, the chief instigator of Colonel Stewart's murder, were destroyed. As they advanced the Gordons were the leading battalion. Officers and men slept in their clothes ready to turn out, no lights were allowed at night, and they stood to their arms before daybreak. At Hebbeh, Colonel Stewart's steamer lay opposite the village, and the house to which he had been treacherously enticed, and in which he was afterwards murdered, was burned. Here the force crossed the Nile, the 800 horses and camels swimming across towed by the boats. The Duke of Cornwall's took up a position on the right bank, and the Gordons on the left to cover this movement, and the force advanced, the mounted troops being on the right bank, till on the morning of the 24th at Ellemeh, a village about fifteen miles from Abu Hamed,[1] just as the boats were starting, they were stopped and the order to dress and accoutre was given. Armed men had been seen in the distance, and all supposed this order meant fighting, for they worked the boats in fatigue clothing, but marched and fought in the Highland dress ; but it turned out that a messenger from Korti had just swum across the river and delivered despatches from Lord Wolseley to the effect that, having punished the Monassir tribe and as the hot weather was beginning, the column was to return and take up summer quarters between Abu Dom and Dongola.

In March an expedition had been sent from England to Suakin, where it was joined by 500 Australian infantry and a force of native troops from India. To crush Osman Digna and open up the Suakin-Berber route to Khartum were the ostensible objects, and circumstances appear to have decided Lord Wolseley to hold the line of the river from Merawi to Dongola during the summer, and prepare for an autumn campaign.

Within an hour of the receipt of the order the descent of the river was commenced, the Gordons forming the rear guard. The passage down the river was far more difficult and dangerous than the ascent, and the Regimental Record bears witness to the admirable manner in which the Canadian Voyageurs steered and worked the boats throughout this part of the expedition. At Hebbeh the cavalry and transport took the shortest route to Berti, where they

---

[1] Royle. The Regimental Record says twelve miles.

again united with the infantry, who had even more exciting adventures than on the way up ; and on the 6th of March the force was at Abu Dom, having had several boats wrecked and three men drowned.

The Desert Column had also arrived at Korti.   They had had much more fighting than the River Column, and had also lost their General, Sir Herbert Stewart, but their exploits do not come within the scope of this history, except to record that the Gordons were represented by Lieutenant Payne, Lieutenant Stewart, and thirty-one n.c. officers and men, who, as mounted infantry, took part in the actions of Abu-Klea and Gubat and the reconnaissance before Metemmeh, their casualties being five men wounded.

At Korti the battalion was inspected by Lord Wolseley, who expressed his approbation of the officers, n.c. officers and men whilst employed on the late active duties.   Here they heard of the death of Brevet Lieut.-Colonel Cross, who died at Cairo, deeply regretted by all ranks, of disease contracted in the performance of his duties on the river.   The Gordons were brigaded with the 2nd Royal Irish and the Duke of Cornwall's Light Infantry, under Brigadier-General Brackenbury, at Kurot.   The men were employed in erecting straw huts for themselves, which gave great protection from the sun and the dreadful dust-storms ; but the reaction from the active life on the river told on the men, there were several deaths from enteric fever, and a number were invalided to Cairo.   They were not, however, without amusements, and the Gordons won a well-contested boat race between the battalions of the brigade ; there were also foot races and other manly games to beguile the time.

The British Government having decided to evacuate the Soudan, the Gordons left Kurot on the 1st of June and descended the river in forty-four whalers to Akasheh, where they left their boats ; and on the 14th the battalion marched twenty-six miles across the desert to the railway near Ambigul, whence they were conveyed next day by train to Halfa, where they embarked on dahabeyahs, towed by steamers to Assouan ; and thence, with the Guards Camel Corps, in barges to Assiout, which they reached on the 29th.

Meanwhile a new Government had come into office, but the measures taken by Mr Gladstone's Cabinet were practically accomplished, and though Wolseley had emphasised his opinion that Britain could not get out of Egypt for many years, and that " the Mahdi sooner or later must be smashed, or he will smash you," Her Majesty's Government were not prepared to reverse the orders given by their predecessors by countermanding the retreat of the force from Dongola.   But Lord Salisbury (the new Premier) recognised that Britain had a mission in Egypt, and that till it was accomplished it was idle to talk of withdrawal.   Accordingly, orders were received for the battalion to proceed to Alexandria and to be camped at Fort Mex, four miles from that city, where it arrived on 1st July.

The officers, n.c. officers, and soldiers of the Gordon Relief Expedition received a vote of thanks from both Houses of Parliament, and in referring to their services and labours, it was acknowledged that the failure to fulfil the main purpose for which they were sent was through no fault of their own.   Lord Wolseley was created a Viscount.

Major W. A. Smail of the Gordons was promoted to Brevet Lieut.-Colonel, and Lieutenant (afterwards Captain) C. H. Payne to Brevet Major.   All who had served at or south of Korosko received the Egyptian medal, and those who already possessed it had a clasp added, inscribed " Nile, 1884-5." 'Those who had served with the Desert Column also received a clasp for " Abu-Klea," and those who had been present at " Kirbekan " were awarded a clasp for that action.[1]   A gratuity was issued to all who had served at or south of Assiout, of which a private's share was £5.

On the 8th September 1885, the battalion embarked at Alexandria, and landed at Malta on the 12th.[2]

On the 19th December, Colonel F. F. Daniell took the command of the battalion in succession to Colonel D. Hammill, C.B., who retired with the honorary rank of Major-General.

On the 1st of July 1887, Colonel J. E. Boyes succeeded Colonel Daniell in the command of the battalion, which occupied various quarters in Malta and Gozo till November 1888.   During their stay at that pleasant station, where there was agreeable society for all ranks, and the presence of the fleet contributed to make life cheerful, the battalion had received 620 n.c. officers and men from the Second Battalion to replace those who had served their time.

The First Battalion was now ordered to Ceylon.   The officers were entertained at a dinner given in their honour by H.R.H. the Duke of Edinburgh, Naval Commander-in-Chief, and on the 14th of November 1888 the battalion embarked on H.M.S. *Himalaya*,[3] which left Valetta amid the cheers of the sailors, and was convoyed from the harbour by the officers of the flagship— H.M.S. *Alexandria*.

---

[1] D Company was present at Kirbekan.

[2] At about this period n.c. officers of the Foot Guards, Highlanders, Fusiliers, and Light Infantry were ordered to wear chevrons only on the right arm as in other corps, and no longer on both arms as heretofore.

[3] The *Himalaya* was a famous old troopship, having carried troops to and from the Crimea.   Her accommodation, and the general conditions of a voyage in her, could hardly be credited by soldiers who have only experienced a post-war troopship voyage.—*Ed.*

They reached Colombo on the 6th December, when head-quarters, under Colonel Boyes, occupied barracks. Detachments were sent to the old Dutch fort of Trincomalee, under Captain R. D. Jennings Bramly, and to Kandy, under Major H. H. Mathias.[1]

On the 23rd, 24th, and 25th September 1889, the headquarters were inspected by Major-General Dunham Massy, C.B., who also inspected the detachments in October. In an order which he desired to be recorded, the General expressed himself

" much pleased with the manner in which the manœuvres were carried out, the spirit and zeal displayed, and the evident desire of all ranks to do their best . . . It will be his pleasing duty to report to H.R.H. the Commander-in-Chief that the First Battalion of the Gordon Highlanders is in a thoroughly satisfactory condition."

The Inspector of Army Signalling in his report, published in General Orders, referring to the proficiency of the signallers of the battalion at this time, says—" The figure of merit, 351·79, is the best ever obtained by any regiment or corps."

On the 8th April 1890, General I. I. Hill, C.B., was transferred to the Duke of Cornwall's Light Infantry.[2]

In the end of 1891 the battalion was destined for Mauritius and the Cape of Good Hope, but this was countermanded, and it was ordered for India. During their service in Ceylon, the Gordons had been remarked upon at all inspections for smartness, intelligence, and general efficiency, and the General " was particularly pleased with the behaviour of the battalion, which is remarkably

[1] Strength on disembarkation :—Officers, 25 ; warrant officers, 2 ; sergeants, 47 ; corporals, 40 ; drummers, 21 ; privates, 760.

[2] Since the amalgamation of the 75th and 92nd, the Colonel of each had been continued, but now General J. A. Ewart, C.B., of the Second Battalion, became colonel of the whole regiment.

NATIONALITY AND SIZE OF FIRST BATTALION GORDON HIGHLANDERS,
JANUARY 1ST, 1890.

N.C. Officers and Men.		Height N.C. Officers and Men.		
		Feet.	Inches.	No. of Men.
English	143	6	0 and upwards	9
Scots	650	5	11	19
Irish	23	5	10	46
Born in India or the Colonies *	25	5	9	87
	—	5	8	116
	841	5	7	166
* Probably soldiers' sons.		5	6	180
		5	5	157
		5	4 ⎫	61
		5	3½ ⎭	
				841

good." Officers and men enjoyed their visit to this lovely island. At Colombo there were many Scots among the tradesmen of the town, who exchanged hospitalities with the members of the sergeants' mess ; matches at cricket and football were played with the planters from the interior ; the officers played polo, and all ranks made excursions along the palm-shaded roads, and bathed in the breakers on the beach at Mount Lavinia. Kandy, one of the most beautiful spots in creation, and much frequented by tourists, was a pleasant quarter, cooler than Colombo, and within reach by rail of Newera Éliya, famous for its climate and its tea-gardens. From Trincomalee the men made excursions in the neighbouring forests as far as Kantalai, shooting wild pig, deer, and jungle fowl, while officers penetrated still further into the wonderful jungles, camping out, and enjoying a sport which is in itself the best military training, and which included every sort of game from a snipe to an elephant. But for war training the conditions of the Ceylon countryside were extremely ill adapted.

The battalion kept New Year's Day, 1892, at Colombo, where they bade farewell to two officers and 136 n.c. officers and men who were going home. On the 4th of January it embarked, under Lieut.-Colonel F. S. Gildea,[1] on board H.M.I.M.S. *Canning*, and having picked up the company at Trincomalee, landed at Kurrachi on the 17th of January,[2] and proceeded in two divisions by rail to Umballa, where General Pretyman expressed himself highly pleased with the appearance of the battalion. It marched on March 15th to the hill station of Subathu, where the families of the married men had proceeded on first arrival in India. Two companies were detached at Jutogh, near Simla, the centre of Government and the fashionable resort at that season, and in April, one colour-sergeant, two sergeants, and 150 rank and file arrived from the home battalion.

In Malta a small newspaper, *Sociability*, had been started in the battalion by the n.c. officers, Corporal Thomson being the leading spirit. It was succeeded about this time by a monthly magazine, *The Tiger and Sphinx, or Gordon Highlanders' Chronicle*, with Lieutenant F. Neish as the first editor ; and it continued its useful career till the battalion came home. It gave much interesting information of the two regular battalions, and also of the Militia and Volunteers, and to its columns I am indebted for many details of the Life of the Regiment.

After inspecting in April, the General congratulated Colonel

---

[1] Lieut.-Colonel Gildea had been promoted from the Seaforth Highlanders, in 1891, to succeed Colonel Boyes on his completion of four years in command.

[2] Embarkation strength :—Officers, 20 ; warrant officers, 2 ; sergeants, 36 ; drummers, 21 ; rank and file, 668.

At Ceylon, over 100 n.c. officers and men had been received from the home battalion.

Gildea and all ranks on their soldier-like appearance and steadiness, their dash and appreciation of ground when skirmishing on the hillside ; and remarked on the excellent interior economy of the battalion, which was now fitted out with mobilisation equipment and transport.   In September a sergeant and corporal in charge of the regimental transport (96 mules and attendants) were sent on service with the Black Mountain Expedition.

Military life at an Indian hill station has been described in the account of the 92nd, and need not be repeated.   On the 1st November the First Battalion marched down to Umballa for the cold weather, and went into camp on the 5th.   On March 8th, 1893, a draft of two officers and 257 n.c. officers and men arrived from the Second Battalion, and on the 23rd the battalion, with a total strength of 1067, returned to Subathu, Kasauli, and Jutogh. In June, General Pretyman's report contained the following remarks—" The First Battalion Gordon Highlanders is in excellent order, courts-martial and minor offences are much below the average of other regiments, all ranks turn out smartly, drill efficiently, and are well trained in musketry."

The Commander-in-Chief, in noticing the improvement in signalling throughout the army in India, says, " Special credit is due to the First Battalion Gordon Highlanders," who were first with a figure of merit 607·73.

The battalion returned to Umballa in November, and on the 6th January 1894, one officer, one sergeant, and 102 rank and file arrived from the Second Battalion to replace those sent to the Reserve.   The battalion was now ordered to Rawal Pindi, and after being thanked by the General for their conduct while under his command, they marched on the 15th January, arriving on February 21st—a distance of 367 miles—and were joined by a sergeant and 117 rank and file from the Second Battalion.   General Sir W. Ellis soon after inspected, and formed the same high opinion of the battalion as had been expressed by Brigadier-General Pretyman.   In April the headquarters marched to spend the hot weather at Thobba, a hill station seven miles from Murree, and encamped. Major Mathias with seven officers and 500 men were left, however, for duty at Rawal Pindi, and a detachment under Lieutenant S. L. Murray was at Campbellpore.   In October the battalion returned to Rawal Pindi, and in November marched (170 miles—seventeen days) to Lahore in order to take part in the great Viceregal Durbar.

Nothing can be more agreeable than such excursions at that season.   Starting before daybreak, a halt is called to refresh at " coffee shop," which is sent forward to a convenient distance, and the camping ground is reached by 10 or 11 a.m., guards are mounted, the native cooks produce an excellent dinner, and after cleaning their things the men bathe, or sleep in the shade, or amuse themselves according to their inclination. Often there is game to shoot, or a stream in which anglers can exercise their craft. After tea, sing-song or music, and so early to bed.

Lahore was gay with the picturesque retinues of native grandees, who, in gorgeous garments of silk and satin—light green, saffron, or orange, wonderfully embroidered coats, and often, especially the frontier folk, immense parti-coloured turbans—gave brilliancy to the scene. There, with a gold ornament on his head, was a descendant of the Great Mogul ; here the Maharajas of Kashmir, Patiala, Kapurthala, and many Rajas, resplendent in diamond aigrettes and strings of pearls ; Sikhs with their high, white head-dress ; Mirs of Scinde in long, black robes ; noble-looking old frontier chiefs with aquiline noses and flowing white beards, their keen eyes peering from beneath their shaggy eyebrows—all come to pay homage, through her Viceroy, to the great Queen-Empress. British officials, civil and military ; globe-trotting M.P.'s, qualifying for future debates on India—a varied and motley gathering, but all subjects of Queen Victoria. The Royal army, European and Indian, was represented by two batteries of Horse Artillery, five of Field Artillery, eight regiments of cavalry and twelve battalions of infantry ; among the latter were the 2nd Seaforths and the 2nd Argyll and Sutherland Highlanders (late 93rd). Before the " thin red line " had earned its fame in war, their Sergeant M'Gillivray was the champion athlete in Scotland, and the battalion was well known for its prowess in such contests. They had defeated the Gordons last year in the tug-of-war, and Mr Forbes Mitchell of Calcutta, an enthusiastic veteran of the 93rd, who had served as sergeant in the Mutiny war and was now owner of the greatest rope works in India, had presented a splendid rope to be pulled for by the European regiments. He came to see the victory of his old corps, whose team of heavy muscular men looked, to the assembled spectators, all over like winning ; but the Gordons had been well trained—and training and discipline go for more than half the battle. They beat the Seaforths ; the East Kent (the Buffs) were pulled by the Argyll and Sutherland, and the great event of the day rested between them and the Gordons, whose perfection of training and condition was soon apparent ; their opponents gradually gave way—a final effort for a minute delayed the end—and amidst the tremendous excitement of the crowd, the Gordons were victorious in the mimic war, a happy presage for the success of their arms in the more serious strife in which they were soon to take part. The team were cheered again and again as they marched off the ground to the tune of the " Cock o' the North." " Geordie, man, that itsel' was worth coming 170 miles to see ! " was the remark of a Gordon to his comrade.

There was a great dinner on St Andrew's Day, at which the Viceroy (Lord Elgin), the Commander-in-Chief (Sir George White),[1] the officers of the Highland battalions, and most of the Scotsmen then at Lahore, among them Mr Forbes Mitchell, were present (for Scotsmen pay far more respect to their patron saint abroad than at home), and a most successful national gathering it was. When the ceremonies and reviews incident to the Durbar were over, the battalion marched on the 6th December and returned to Rawal Pindi.

---

[1] Whom we last heard of as Major of the " 2nd Battalion " in the Afghan War.

CHAPTER XXV

1895

EARLY in February 1895, at Rawal Pindi, the battalion bade farewell to Lieut.-Colonel Gildea, who was succeeded in the command by Lieut.-Colonel Mathias.

On the 12th, 13th, and 14th, a district assault-at-arms took place, when wild and wonderful feats of horsemanship were performed by the Bengal Lancers, and soldiers of the 4th Dragoon Guards emulated the chivalrous exercises of the knights of old. The Gordons won the tug-of-war, defeating the supposed invincible gunners of the Mountain Batteries ; they also were first in physical drill, marching order race, dancing, etc., gaining the cup for the battalion winning most events.

Musketry, drill, and field-days ensured professional fitness, while shooting, fishing, and polo matches between the various regiments kept officers in training for the ensuing warfare.

On March 15th the battalion was warned for active service.

The events which led to this order were briefly as follows:—

Umra Khan of Jandol had at this time become one of the most powerful chiefs on the north-western frontier of India. He had ousted the Khan of Dir, and extended his rule over most of the neighbouring tribes, and had further cemented his authority by marrying the daughter of the Mehtar of Chitral. On the 1st of January 1895, the Mehtar, Nizām-ul-Mulk, was murdered at the instigation of Umra Khan and Sher Afzul. At this time the Government of India had a small detachment as guard to their Political Agent at Chitral, where Surgeon-Major Robertson arrived on February 1st to report on the situation. He had come from Gilgit, where was a considerable British force of native troops, and soon after his arrival the garrison of Chitral was augmented.

During February Umra Khan, having captured the important stronghold of Kila Drosh, was joined by Sher Afzul and threatened Chitral Fort. On March 3rd, in consequence of the invaders' arrival on Chitral plain, a force of 200 men under Captain Campbell moved out from the fort, when an engagement took place, in which the native troops behaved with the greatest gallantry, losing twenty-three officers and men killed and thirty-three wounded before they regained the fort. Captain J. M. Baird died of his wounds. The British force was now shut up within the walls of the fort, and nothing was heard of them for many weeks, the last message being dated March 1st. Information of the serious turn of affairs began to reach Gilgit on the 6th, and was received by the Government of India on the following day, but they were not yet aware that war had actually been waged upon our troops. A final warning was sent to Umra Khan against interfering with Chitral, and he was told that if by the 1st of April he had not withdrawn, the Government of India would compel him to do so. At the same time a proclamation was issued to the people of Swat and other border tribes, promising friendly treatment to those who did not oppose the march of our troops. Simultaneously with this proclamation orders were issued for the mobilisation of the First Division of the Field Army, with certain modifications with regard to cavalry and artillery.

On March 21st news reached Gilgit of an attack made early in the month on our troops between Mastuj and Chitral, in which Captain Ross and about fifty men were reported to have been killed, while another detachment under Lieutenant Edwardes was said to be surrounded. It was now known to the Government that before it had taken the action described above, war had actually been waged by Umra Khan and Sher Afzul. The necessity for relieving the garrison in Chitral was more imminent than had been supposed, while the reason for giving Umra Khan a period of grace had disappeared. It was felt that to relieve Chitral from Gilgit, a distance of 221 miles of snow-covered mountains, was, at this season, probably impracticable, while the road from Peshawar to Chitral was only 190 miles in length, and though it led through a country rendered difficult by high mountains and rapid rivers, there was only the Laorai Pass which might still have snow on it.

Orders were therefore issued for the immediate despatch of the Chitral Relief Force, and Major-General Sir R. C. Low, K.C.B., was appointed to the command, with Brigadier-General B. Blood, C.B., R.E., as Chief of the Staff. The division was composed of three infantry brigades of two European and two native battalions each. The First Brigade was commanded by Brigadier-General A. A. Kinloch, C.B., the Second by Brigadier-General H. G. Waterfield, and the Third by Brigadier-General W. F. Gatacre, D.S.O. The divisional troops consisted of two regiments of native cavalry, two battalions of native infantry, three companies Bengal sappers and miners, with a Field Battery and two Mountain Batteries Royal Artillery, a native Mountain Battery, and a Maxim gun and detachment of the 1st Devonshire Regiment ; British and native field hospitals being attached to each brigade. The lines of communication troops were under Brigadier-General A. G. Hammond, V.C., C.B., D.S.O., A.D.C. A reserve brigade at Rawal Pindi and a movable column at Abbottabad were also formed.

Numerous offers were received by the Government from states which maintain Imperial troops, as well as from other states and chiefs. The Jeypore and Gwalior transport corps were accepted, and quickly reached the frontier.

Within seventeen days of the order to mobilise, 15,000 troops, rather more than that number of followers, and over 20,000 transport animals, had been concentrated at Hoti Mardan and Nowshera, while forty days' supplies had been collected at and beyond the base.[1]

Leaving a depôt with the women and children under Captain Haldane (who was afterwards relieved by Captain Henderson), the battalion entrained on the evening of March 26th, arrived at Nowshera next morning, and encamped at the " Marble Rocks " on the road to Hoti Mardan. On the 30th the battalion, with that part of the Second Brigade [2] already formed, marched fourteen miles through a country green with corn to Hoti Mardan, with its charming rose gardens, handsome trees and smooth lawns, and bivouacked a mile beyond. The place swarmed with people, and the fields were covered with hundreds of camels, cattle, carts, and transport of every sort. Here they were joined by the Third Brigade and halted for the Sunday. They had waterproof sheets and *tentes d'abri* to sleep under, and there was a stream to bathe in.

There are three passes leading into the Swat Valley—the Mora, the Shahkot, and the Malakand. All are equally difficult, and they were known to be strongly held, especially the Shahkot. The General decided to threaten the Shahkot and Mora Passes, while his real attack was made on the Malakand ; [3] accordingly the First Brigade bivouacked in sight of the Shahkot, and a cavalry reconnaissance towards Mora attracted the enemy's attention, and prevented their concentrating at the Malakand. All the troops having arrived, they advanced towards the frontier on the 1st of April.

The Gordons, with the Second Brigade, marched to Jallala, where a wet night turned the bivouac into a slough of despond ; and next day a tramp of sixteen miles brought them, drenched by a thunderstorm, to Dargai,[4] on the slopes of the hills about two miles from the foot of the Malakand Pass, where groups of men and standards were visible on the mountains above. Every military precaution was now taken, and orders were issued for the Second Brigade, supported by the First, to attack next morning. The Pass is at the head of a valley about four miles long, down which runs a dry watercourse, and the ridge for two miles was strongly held by the enemy, consisting of various tribes, some armed with Martini Henry and Snider rifles, but the greater number with

---

[1] Official Account of the Chitral Expedition.

[2] The Second Brigade consisted of the Second Battalion King's Own Scottish Borderers, First Battalion Gordon Highlanders, Guides Infantry, and 4th Sikh Infantry. On April 1st the strength of the battalion was twenty-three officers and 798 of other ranks. The K.O.S.B.'s and Gordons had each a maxim gun.

[3] It is worthy of remark that General Low's tactics on this occasion were the same as those used by the Yusafzai invaders of Pagan Swat in the Mahomedan conquest some 800 years before.—Ferdausi's (Persian) " History of Mahomed of Ghuzni."

[4] Not the Dargai which afterwards became famous.

smooth-bore muzzle-loaders, jezails, swords, and even slings. The evening was fine, the men busied themselves in drying and cleaning their arms,[1] and then all sank into a sound and well-earned sleep.

The morning of Wednesday, April 3rd, dawned clear and fresh after the rain. All had an excellent breakfast, and the Gordons fell in at 7.30. The baggage was left at Dargai, the soldier carrying only his greatcoat, arms and ammunition, while the officers assured themselves that each man had also a cooked half-ration in his haversack, and that his water-bottle was filled. At 8.45 a.m. the first shots were fired by the enemy at the cavalry in advance, and at 9.10 our artillery opened fire from a spur on the east side of the valley on the enemy's sangars on the western side. The range, however, was found to be too great, and the general advance was continued at ten o'clock. The artillery moved along the foot of the hills on the east side, and the infantry up the centre of the valley. The advanced guard meanwhile drove off small parties of the enemy higher up the valley, and behind them the sappers cleared a way for the guns through the bushes and fenced fields.

The Guides Infantry was now directed up the steep hills to the west, on a peak some 1500 feet above the valley, where the enemy were in considerable strength. As they climbed, it was seen that the enemy also occupied high ground on the left of the Guides' advance, and the 4th Sikhs were sent to strengthen the exposed flank. Two companies of the King's Own Scottish Borderers now went forward as an advanced guard, and the guns again came into action at a range of about 2400 yards from the enemy's main position, but soon advanced to within 1200 yards. Here their fire was more effective, and some of the lower sangars were evacuated, while the Devonshires' maxims fired across the ravine from a position nearer the enemy and north of the guns. The Guides and Sikhs had completed more than half the ascent, and, by taking several sangars, made a decided impression on the enemy on that flank. Meanwhile the Gordons had been merely spectators, but at noon they advanced, under cover of artillery and maxim fire, to make a direct attack upon the centre of the position, having the Scottish Borderers on their left ; the objective being the village on the crest of the ridge, which consisted only of a few huts.

" It was a fine and stirring sight to see the splendid dash with which the two Scottish regiments took the hill."[2] The crest was about 1000 feet above the little stream at the foot of the ascent, which was broken by intermediate ravines, in many places quite

---

[1] Some years previously, musicians had been deprived of their swords, but to prevent their going into action unarmed, drummers and pipers were supplied with them on this occasion. Bandsmen had rifles, and were partly employed to carry stretchers.

[2] Younghusband, " The Relief of Chitral."

precipitous. It was necessary to advance on a very narrow front, even in single file, and often to climb as much with the hands as with the feet, the difficulties being increased by bushes, trees and rocks, while the ascent was commanded by fire from the sangars, each of which was obstinately held, and when carried, came at once under the fire of the one above it. The King's Own Scottish Borderers attacked by two spurs, part of the regiment being held in reserve. The Gordons, moving up the ravine to attack on their right, came, on rounding a projecting rock, under fire from the enemy's sangars on both sides of the precipitous gorge, which at this point is little wider than the rocky bed of the nearly dry watercourse.

A and B Companies, under Captain H. H. Burney, were sent up a spur leading directly to the village, accompanied by the maxim gun of the battalion. F Company, under Lieutenant W. E. Gordon, was sent to stop a galling fire from a large sangar on the left of the main advance, and afterwards joined Captain Burney. The difficult advance was continued up the watercourse, C and D Companies being sent, under Major Downman, to drive the enemy from some sangars from which a hot fire was being poured on the watercourse, and these companies, having established themselves on the north side, materially assisted the advance by well-directed volleys. Meanwhile Lieut.-Colonel Mathias, with G, H, and K Companies, worked his way up the narrow glen, the crags over which they clambered sheltering them from the bullets, which struck the rocks around and splashed the water in the burn, as men and officers helped each other up.

A young officer's journal relates how, as he was trying to pull Corporal Gilchrist up a rock, the latter's foot slipped, and their hands parted—it was a forty-foot drop. The corporal rolled over as he fell, but managed to grip a bush and stop himself, when he at once climbed up again, none the worse. In this manner the men overcame the difficulties of the ground, keeping down the enemy's fire by using their rifles when opportunity offered, running across open and exposed bits, or sheltering to take breath behind the boulders. The crags on each side echoed and re-echoed the roar of artillery and the sharp volleys of the infantry, while the deafening din was swelled by the more spasmodic fire from the enemy above. Under a great cliff the leading men waited till others arrived, safe from fire and from the rocks thrown down by the defenders, which bounded harmlessly over their heads ; then, climbing a narrow ledge one by one, they got up, just as a burst of cheering from the village announced its capture.

The attack had been strengthened by the King's Royal Rifles from the First Brigade, acting between the Guides and the Borderers; as the crest was neared and the guns could no longer safely fire, the

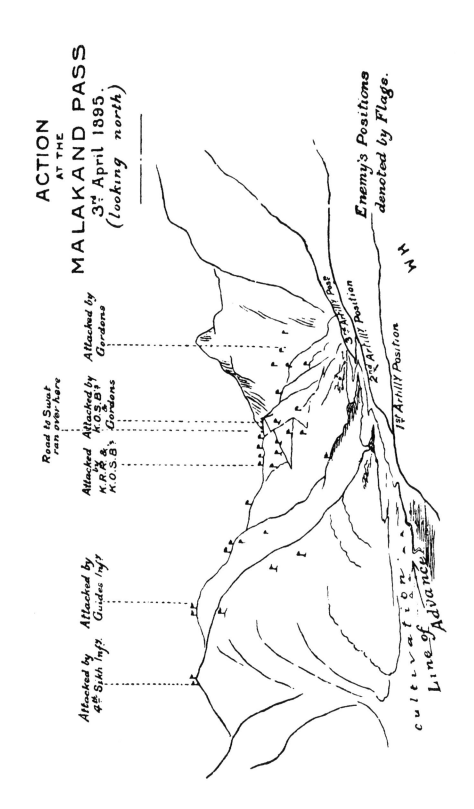

ACTION
AT THE
MALAKAND PASS
3rd April 1895.
(looking north)

Enemy's Positions
denoted by Flags.

Attacked by
Gordons

Road to Swat
ran over here

Attacked by
K.O.S.B's &
Gordons

Attacked
by K.R.R. &
K.O.S.B's

Attacked by
Guides Inft.

Attacked by
4th Sikh Inft.

3rd Artilly Post

2nd Artilly Position

1st Artilly Position

cultivation

Line of Advance.

energy of the remaining defenders was renewed.   Incited by their mullahs (priests), they fought with great individual bravery at close quarters, firing at a few yards' distance and charging, sword in hand, on a few officers and men of the Borderers and Gordons who had together gained a footing on the crest, when a hand-to-hand struggle ensued, with bayonet, pistol and sword.   Several attacked Lieutenant and Adjutant Kerr ; his revolver missed fire and he was fighting with his sword—too blunt to penetrate the *poshteen* [1]— when Lieutenant Craufurd with his revolver rid him of his oppo-nent.   Those few brave men who disdained to fly were shot down, the village was in flames from the shells, and by 2 p.m. the fight was won.   Almost simultaneously the Borderers, the Rifles, and the main body of the Gordons reached the crest ; the Guides and Sikhs had gained the heights they attacked at about 1.15, and co-operated with the other troops in driving the enemy from his whole position, which, had it been held by a disciplined and well-armed foe, would have been impregnable.

Immediately after the crest was gained, volleys were fired at the enemy as they retired down the opposite side, and the pursuit was taken up by the Bedfords and 37th Dogras, who had followed the Gordons up the ravine.

The British loss, which fell principally on the Second Brigade, was comparatively small, the very difficulties of the ascent giving cover to the assailants.   The casualties amounted to a total of eleven killed and fifty wounded.[2]   The Gordons had three killed, viz. Privates Francis, Pardoe, and Couborough.   Captain H. H. Burney, Lieutenant D. M. Watt, Second Lieutenant W. Hesketh (attached), and nine n.c. officers and men were wounded ; several others were hurt, though not returned as wounded.

The loss of the enemy was computed at about 500.   " The fire discipline in the attack was without doubt excellent : from the comparatively small amount of ammunition expended, it is evident how well the fire was under control." [3]

Among the officers brought to the notice of the Commander-in-Chief in India by General Low in connection with this action were Lieut.-Colonel H. H. Mathias and Lieutenant and Adjutant F. W. Kerr, who had come under his personal notice ; and among those recommended by the general officers commanding brigades was Major G. F. F. Downman.   In his report called for by the general officer commanding the Second Brigade, Lieut.-Colonel Mathias mentioned the following officers, n.c. officers and men, viz. Major Downman, Captain Burney, Lieutenant and Adjutant

---

[1] Sheepskin coat.   [2] Official Account.
[3] Major W. G. Hamilton, D.S.O. (D.A.A.G. and Q.M.G., Second Brigade).   The Gordons fired an average of 11·61 rounds per man.

Kerr, Second Lieutenants Watt, Craufurd, Younger, and Hesketh (attached), Colour-sergeant Mackie, Sergeants Ewan (maxim gun), F. Martin, Mathers, and Priest, Lance-corporal Edmonstone, Privates Kerr and Smith.

The Gordons rested, discussing the contents of their haversacks and talking over what was to most of them their first fight, till they were relieved by the First Brigade, and the Second returned to their bivouac at Dargai.   On their way they could see how cleverly the sangars were constructed and loopholed to command the native path, which, fortunately, had not been much used in the ascent ; round these sangars lay many dead.   The path was choked by mules carrying guns and the baggage of the First Brigade ; and as darkness set in, the glen was crammed with transport animals, some slipping and falling over rocks, with field hospitals, troops, and followers—a fire here and there lighting up the absolute confusion of the whole.   At length the battalion struggled through, and about 9.30 p.m. reached their bivouac, very tired and ready for the hot tea and supper which awaited them.   The officers, having seen their men served, fully appreciated an excellent meal at 10.30.

Next morning the battalion, with the Second Brigade, marched back to the Malakand, leaving a party under Lieutenant Gardyne to give respectful burial to the remains of their comrades killed in action.   The native path was so difficult as to be almost impassable for the transport of the force, but by a remarkable stroke of good fortune, the officer commanding the King's Royal Rifles had noticed and reported an old pathway, which turned out to be a Buddhist road, disused for hundreds of years, but so well made originally that it took our engineers but two days to make it into a camel road.   The sappers were busy at this useful work and at laying a field telegraph, as the Gordons arrived at the foot of the pass, which was blocked by the Guides cavalry and transport animals pressing on to join the First Brigade ; so they had to climb the face of the hill clear of the path, leaving their mules with their kits and rations to follow when the way was open.   The brigade bivouacked half a mile north of the Pass, where a neighbouring eminence commanded a bird's-eye view of the action near Khar fought by the First Brigade in the afternoon.   As their transport did not arrive till morning, the brigade spent rather a hungry night, and a cold one too.   "Any inconvenience, however, which though felt was not expressed, vanished with the rising sun." [1]

Leaving the Gordons in bivouac, the rest of the brigade moved on the 5th to join the First Brigade near Khar.   On the 7th the battalion marched down into the hot but fertile valley, well watered, green with corn, and interspersed with fruit trees and wild flowers,

[1] Major W. G. Hamilton.

contrasting with the barren and snow-capped mountains which towered beyond. In the afternoon they arrived at the camp in front of Aladand, just as the troops were returning from the affair at the Swat River, in which they had twelve casualties. As the Borderers were marching back, they were amused at meeting a party of the newly arrived Gordons quietly, though not without arms, going to fish in the river which had been the scene of the fight !

On the 8th the battalion, with other troops at Aladand, crossed the river to Chakdarra. The stream was swollen, and crossing with baggage and transport over a somewhat dangerous ford, three and a half feet deep, was a work of time. The Gordons slung their kilts round their necks, each section of fours linked their arms together, and double distance was left between sections to minimise the deepening of the water by the blocking of the stream.

On the 9th April the Brigade remained at Chakdarra, while the cavalry reconnoitred to the Panjkora River, meeting with no opposition. On the 10th,[1] Sir Robert Low's headquarters, with the Second Brigade, moved by Uch through a cultivated strath and over the Katgola Pass to Gambat, where they bivouacked on a pretty terrace in a grove of wild olive trees. The distance was only about sixteen miles, but the narrow path was interrupted by deep ravines, causing constant delays to the column, which took from 8 a.m. to 2.30 p.m. to accomplish the march ; and the transport with its 4000 mules and 300 camels, which started at 10 a.m., did not finally arrive till 8.30 p.m.

At 6 a.m. on the 11th, the march was continued down the strath by the Shigukhas defile to the Panjkora River, then along the shore by a narrow track, which in places overhung the rushing torrent below. Constant halts, while sappers and pioneers made the path passable for the battery mules and baggage, though tiresome to the troops, gave time to admire the splendid scenery, enlivened by long drawn lines of men, the sun flashing bright on rifle and sporran. It was nine in the evening before the rear guard reached Sado, a distance of ten miles, where they found the advanced guard of cavalry, Guides and Sikh infantry encamped among villages and cornfields. The transport had been fired on, which had caused confusion and delay. At night shots were fired across the river at the camp, but from a safe distance.

On the 12th the Brigade signallers were fired on while establishing communication with the Third Brigade in rear ; a company of Sikhs was sent to support them, and engaged some 200 of the enemy across the river at a range of 300 to 500 yards, obliging

---

[1] This day the Third Brigade crossed the Swat to Chakdarra, the First Brigade being left to guard the Swat Valley and the communications.

them to retire with loss. The sappers were engaged all day in making a raft bridge where the river narrowed to about sixty yards. By the evening it was reported fit to bear men, and the Guides infantry were ordered across just before sunset, and bivouacked on the far side close to the bridge-head. As they left the bivouac of the brigade, the pipers of the two Scottish regiments played at their head, while the soldiers lined the path cheering their gallant Indian comrades. Lieut.-Colonel Battye, who commanded the Guides, had orders to burn certain villages from which there had been persistent firing on our transport ; he was to have been supported, but a flood in the night rendered the bridge useless. Colonel Battye, however, proceeded on the morning of the 13th to carry out his instructions, which he did with success till about noon, when large bodies of the enemy were noticed advancing towards his party. This information was heliographed to headquarters at Sado, and he was ordered to return to his entrenched post at the bridge, while the Gordons, with the Second Brigade, were sent to cover the retirement with long-range rifle fire and artillery. Meanwhile, Captain Burney's company had been sent to cover the erection of a suspension bridge about a mile down stream, where they piled arms, preparatory to assisting in the work. No sooner had they done this than the enemy opened so hot a fire from across the river that Burney ordered his men to rush to cover, whence they returned singly to regain their arms. From their position on the left bank they admired the deliberate retreat of the various companies of the Guides. Fiercely assailed on all sides they fired with the greatest coolness by word of command, quietly relinquishing one position to take up another a few yards back. In the open fields below the hills, the enemy pressed on them still more vigorously, and for the second time the Guides fixed bayonets, but the enemy did not charge home. Here Lieut.-Colonel Battye, conspicuous among the last at each retirement, fell mortally wounded. Part of the Afridi company of his regiment, who had already retired a short distance, at once turned and charged, drove the enemy some way up the hill, and brought off the body of their loved commander.

The enemy were now exposed to the steady volleys of the Borderers and Gordons ; numbers were killed, and their banners, waving as the standard-bearers ran forward, were seen one by one to fall. The Guides reached the bridge-head at 5.30 p.m., but a strong force of the enemy, occupying a ridge overlooking the entrenchment, now opened a rifle fire at 800 yards on them and on the covering troops. This lasted till dark, and a few men were hit ; then a company of Sikhs, and the Devonshire maxims under Captain Peebles, crossed the river on rafts to join the Guides, while

CAMP AT JANBATAI

five companies of the Gordons and a mountain battery covered their entrenchment from the high southern bank. Firing was continued till 11 p.m., and by daybreak on the 14th most of the enemy had dispersed, but a few remained for a time, by whose fire Captain Peebles was killed. They were put to flight by the Guides, and soon not a man of them was in sight.

In this affair the battalion had two men wounded, also a signaller attached to it. The total loss of the force amounted to two officers and three men killed, and twenty n.c. officers and men wounded.

On the 14th and 15th a deluge of rain caused great discomfort to the troops, who bore it, British and native alike, with soldierly cheerfulness. The rise in the river threatened to carry away the suspension bridge in course of construction, but the waters subsiding, it was completed, and the troops crossed on the 17th. The Third Brigade were engaged at Mamugai, with a loss of eight men wounded, but the enemy declined to stand. The Second Brigade remained near the river, and marching at daylight on the 18th, joined the Third, when both brigades, preceded by cavalry, advanced on Mundah and Miankili, the chief fort and town of Umra Khan. Both places were found unoccupied. Part of the Third Brigade continued to advance towards Chitral, while the Second bivouacked near Mundah, and occupied that important strategical point and other posts in the Jandol valley. On the 2nd of April, Chitral was relieved by Colonel Kelly with his force from Gilgit, but the battalion, with the Second Brigade, remained in the country till its final settlement and the restoration of peace.

At Mundah shots were fired into the camp by night, without, however, any serious attack, though a sentry was wounded by a Ghazi swordsman.

In his despatch of 1st May 1895, Lieut.-General Low, in praising all ranks, both British and native, says—" When not fighting or marching every man has laboured with the greatest cheerfulness all day on road-making, and altogether the month has been one of continued exertion, and cheerful self-denial and devotion under circumstances of unusual difficulty and hardship."

May 7th.—Headquarters moved to Janbatai Kotal, a range of hills with an elevation of 7500 feet.

In June, Sergeant-major Skelly bade a sorrowful farewell to the battalion, in which he had served as man and boy twenty-two years. The pipers played him out of camp to the tune of " Happy we 've been a' thegither," officers and men lining the sangars to see the last of him.

Here, and at Mundah, they suffered from dysentery and enteric fever, losing twenty-one of their comrades. The tents and kits, which had been left behind, had now arrived, so they were comparatively comfortable.

August 9th.—The brigade moved to Kambat, and on the following day to Mundah, where they halted, and on the 14th retired over the Panjkora River. Sarai was reached on the 16th, and the mountain ridge of Barchanrai next day. In this high and healthy situation the battalion was encamped with the King's Own Scottish Borderers and No. 5 Mountain Battery, R.A. Here, as at their late stations, their stay was enlivened by concerts, athletic games, and dancing classes in the evening. The author has had descriptions of the evening "sing-songs," held in a natural amphitheatre of the mountainside dug out by fatigue parties into terraced seats, before a central bonfire; and further lit with torches of resinous pinewood held by bearded pioneers, the flames lighting up the hundreds of faces, the rifle barrels—for all would be ready to turn out if the alarm went—the tents and pine trunks in the background: the whole forming scenes worthy of a Meissonnier or a Sargent. Fishing and shooting helped to pass the sportsmen's time, while the magnificent scenery and the picturesque costumes of the natives offered varied subjects for the artist's pencil.

On the 13th September the even tenour of their life was agreeably broken by a visit from the Commander-in-Chief (Sir George White), and on the 20th the march back to India was begun. On the 23rd they halted for breakfast on the Malakand, where General Waterfield now commanded, and came to wish them God-speed as they passed, the battalion cheering their late Brigadier. By easy stages they reached Nowshera, where they entrained, arriving at Rawal Pindi early on the 28th.[1]

In recognition of the services rendered by the First Battalion in the operations connected with the relief of Chitral, Her Majesty was graciously pleased to approve of the word " Chitral " being borne on the colours and appointments of the Gordon Highlanders. Lieut.-Colonel Mathias was made a Companion of the Bath, Lieutenant and Adjutant Kerr received the Distinguished Service Order; while the Indian Medal, and Clasp inscribed " Relief of Chitral," was (in 1898) granted to all who had served in the expedition.[2]

The following officers went with the battalion to the campaign, viz. :—

Lieut.-Colonel H. H. Mathias.	Captain J. S. Henderson.
Major G. T. F. Downman.	,, S. Thomson.
Captain H. H. Burney.	Lieutenant S. L. Murray.
,, C. C. Miller Wallnutt.	,, E. B. B. Towse.

---

[1] Marching-in strength—19 officers and 599 n.c. officers and men.

[2] The sum of Rs. 10,200 was afterwards granted to the battalion for distribution among the next of kin of men killed or died of wounds or disease during the expedition.

Lieutenant A. D. G. Gardyne.

    ,,   W. E. Gordon.

    ,,   G. R. Macnab.

    ,,   A. S. Wingate.

    ,,   M. F. M. Meiklejohn.

    ,,   G. D. MacKenzie.

    ,,   K. Dingwall.

2nd Lientenant D. M. Watt.

    ,,   G. S. G. Craufurd.

    ,,   D. R. Younger.

    ,,   W. Hesketh (at-
          tached).

Lieutenant and Adjutant F. W. Kerr.

Captain and Quartermaster H. Carlaw.

Captain J. A. L. Haldane joined the 3rd May, while Captain R. D. J. Bramly, Lieutenant A. F. Gordon and 2nd Lieutenant G. E. E. G. Cameron joined 18th April.

The account of the expedition is taken from an official account compiled by Captain Robertson, D.S.O. ; "The Relief of Chitral," by Captain F. Younghusband ; "The Second Brigade in the Chitral Relief Expedition, 1895," by Major W. G. Hamilton, in *Journal of U.S. Institutions* ; The Regimental Record ; the Journal of Lieutenant A. D. G. Gardyne ; and Notes by Lieutenant G. S. G. Craufurd.

AT THE VILLAGE OF MALAKAND

CHAPTER XXVI

1896–1897

IN the last week of April 1896, the battalion proceeded by detachments to spend the hot season in the Murree Hills, where musketry was practised, field-days took place, n.c. officers were instructed in military sketching; there was a regimental theatre, the soldiers had gardens; athletic contests took place between the companies of the battalion and between the various regiments— notably a hill race between ten of the Gordons and ten of the 3rd Rifle Brigade, which was well contested, and was won by the Gordons. The distance was just over five and three-quarter miles, which Private Kerr, the first man in, did in $37\frac{1}{2}$ minutes. Lady Lockhart presented him with the gold medal and his nine comrades with silver ones. The Rifle Brigade entertained the Gordon team at a banquet, their commanding officer presiding. In congratulating the winners, he remarked on the good feeling between regiments engendered by such friendly contests ; Sergeant Bennett replied for the Gordons, and hoped that when next it was a question of medals, the two battalions would be shoulder to shoulder against a common foe.

The following remarks on the annual inspection, 1895-6, were made by the Lieut.-General Commanding in the Punjab. " This report is very satisfactory, and the First Battalion Gordon Highlanders is a particularly fine one. The officers as a body are an exceptionally nice set ; the warrant and n.c. officers seem to be very efficient, and the privates have an admirable physique."

A communication was received from the Rev. Mr Scott, being an extract from Deliverances on the Report of the Committee on Indian Churches to the General Assembly of the Church of Scotland, and Mr Scott was requested to convey to the Scottish regiments of the Chitral Expeditionary Force the Assembly's high appreciation of their conduct in the campaign.

July 5th.—The Commanding Officer (Lieut.-Colonel Mathias) presented the Indian medal with Waziristan clasp to Lieutenant and Adjutant W. Campbell and five n.c. officers and men (employed there as signallers in the campaign of 1894-5).[1]

His Excellency the Commander-in-Chief remarked on the very satisfactory advance made by the infantry in signalling during the past year, and in Division Orders, " The Major-General desires to add his congratulations to the officers, n.c. officers and men of the Gordon Highlanders in being first on the roll of British regiments in India in army signalling in 1895-96, and his appreciation

---

[1] Lieutenant J. D. S. Lockhart, Second Battalion Gordon Highlanders, A.D.C. to Sir W. Lockhart, was accidentally shot during this campaign. He was the son of Captain L. Lockhart of the 92nd, whose uncle, General A. I. Lockhart, commanded that regiment.

of the work done that has led to so honourable a result." The Gordons excelled equally in shooting, and the battalion won the " Queen's Cup " of the Army Rifle Association in 1896.

In October the battalion returned by detachments from Gharial (Murree Hills) to Rawal Pindi.

In April 1897, the battalion made its annual migration to the Murree Hills, reaching Kuldana on the 12th, where in May they won the Murree Brewery Football Challenge Cup, open to the Punjab Army.

But while by work and sport the Gordons were kept in training for active service, the political horizon of India, which seemed so cloudless, was suddenly disturbed on the 10th May by a treacherous attack on the escort of Mr Gee, a political officer, at Maizar in the Tochi Valley, when three British officers and twenty-three native officers and soldiers were killed. A punitive expedition started under Major-General Bird, which destroyed the village of Maizar, and the Madda Khel tribe submitted.

The Third Battalion Rifle Brigade formed part of the Tochi Field Force, and four companies of the Gordons marched, June 23rd and 26th, to replace them at Rawal Pindi.[1] On the 26th July an entirely unexpected attack was made on the British garrisons at the Malakand and Chakdarra, followed by several other attempts which, though unsuccessful, resulted in considerable loss to the British, and much greater loss to their assailants. A strong force, under Sir Bindon Blood, was formed to operate in the nighbourhood of the Malakand. In consequence of these disturbances the headquarters of the battalion left Kuldana at noon on the 2nd of August and, marching straight through, reached Rawal Pindi at 9.30 a.m. on the 3rd, having accomplished thirty-seven miles in twenty-one and a half hours in the middle of the hot weather. On the afternoon of the 3rd they received orders to mobilise and form part of the Reserve Brigade of the Malakand Field Force.

Meanwhile the warlike spirit of the whole frontier was roused, and the news arrived that the Mohmands, a tribe living near Peshawar, had attacked Shabkadr Fort, in British territory, on the 8th. Its police garrison held the fort, but the neighbouring village was burnt and many of its inhabitants murdered. That night the Gordons were ordered to Peshawar, where they arrived on the morning of the 9th, on which day Brigadier-General Ellis defeated the invaders at Shabkadr. The aspect of affairs on the frontier being so serious, and the Afridis and other warlike clans showing

---

[1] Lieutenant Wingate was attached to the Rifles ; Major Burney was appointed Railway Transport Officer and afterwards A.A.G. of the Malakand Field Force ; Lieutenant Tytler was employed as Transport Officer with the Mohmand Column. A few n.c. officers and men also went with the Tochi Force.

such a spirit of unrest, columns were sent in different directions to overawe them.[1]

August 18th.—The left half-battalion, under Major Downman, proceeded to Jamrud, followed on the 22nd by headquarters and the right half-battalion, under Lieut.-Colonel Mathias, C.B.

The Jamrud Movable Column, under Brigadier-General West-macott, consisted of K Battery R.H.A., No. 3 Mountain Battery R.A., the 4th Dragoon Guards, 1st Gordon Highlanders, 1st Gurkhas, half-battalion Pioneers, with details of native infantry and cavalry.

Any doubt as to the intentions of the Afridis was settled on the 23rd August by their attack in overwhelming numbers on Ali Musjid and Fort Maude ; the news reached Jamrud in the after-noon, and the Horse Artillery, with an escort of cavalry and in-fantry, including the Gordons, at once started for the scene of action, when Fort Maude was seen to be in flames. The Gordons lined a ridge of low hills and lay watching the artillery. " It was splendid," writes an officer, " to see the way they got the range (3200 yards) and dropped shell after shell into the enemy's posi-tion, while the noise made by the reverberation of the roar of the guns in the pass was magnificent." This accurate fire caused the tribesmen to retire for the time, and the garrison escaped, but next day the enemy took the fort of Landi Kotal, and the important trade route of the Khyber Pass was in their hands.

The battalion remained inactive at Jamrud, where Lieut.-Colonel Mathias was in command of the column from September 9th till October 7th. The monotony of the life was broken, however, by occasional reconnaissances. Sports were held, in which the tug-of-war, open to batteries, squadrons, and companies of the garrison, was won by F Company of the battalion. The enemy often fired

---

[1] Strength of battalion on leaving Rawal Pindi, 801 warrant officers, n.c. officers and rank and file, with the following officers in addition :—

Lieut.-Colonel H. H. Mathias, C.B. (Commanding).	Lieutenant G. D. MacKenzie.
Major G. T. F. Downman (Second in Command).	„ G S. G. Craufurd.
	„ A. Lamont.
Major F. Macbean.	2nd Lieutenant P. S. Allan.
„ Jennings Bramly.	„ Dalrymple Hay.
Captain C. C. Miller Wallnutt.	Captain and Adjutant W. Campbell.
„ S. Thomson.	Captain and Quartermaster H. Carlaw.
„ H. P. Uniacke.	2nd Lieutenant Lyall ⎫
„ F. W. Kerr, D.S.O.	„ Young ⎪ Attached.
Lieutenant R. A. N. Tytler (Transport).	„ Gunning ⎬
„ A. F. Gordon (Signaller).	„ Campbell ⎭
„ M. F. M. Meiklejohn.	Surgeon-Captain Gerard, A.M.S.

Later in the campaign Lieutenants R. Gordon, Queensland Mounted Infantry ; F. G. Thoyts, Somerset Light Infantry ; Elliot, Royal Sussex ; and Hutchinson, Staff Corps, were attached to the battalion.

into the fort at night and on the cavalry patrols, sometimes with effect.

In the meantime the Afridis realised the gravity of the situation in which they had placed themselves, and they appealed to the Amir at Kabul for help, which was refused. The Government of India felt that the unprovoked aggression of the Afridi and Orakzai tribes in attacking our frontier posts demanded immediate punishment, and the invasion of Tirah, their summer home, was considered the best way of inflicting it. It was decided to organise a force strong enough to cope with all opposition, even from the 40,000 to 50,000 fighting men whom the mountaineers could muster if the various clans combined.

Sir William Lockhart was appointed to the command, and at once hastened from England.

The force was called the " Tirah Expeditionary Force," [1] and was distributed as follows :—

A main column of two divisions, each consisting of two infantry brigades and certain divisional troops, to start from Kohat and advance on Tirah from the neighbourhood of the Samana range.

A strong force of all arms to hold the lines of communication.

A mixed brigade, styled the Peshawar Column, to operate from Peshawar.

The Kurram Movable Column, to be employed according to circumstances.

A reserve brigade was formed at Rawal Pindi. The loyal native princes of India offered their Imperial Service troops, of which a large contingent was accepted.

The First Division was commanded by Brigadier-General W. P. Symons, C.B. The Second Division by Major-General Yeatman-Biggs, C.B. The First Battalion Gordon Highlanders, 1st Dorsets, First Battalion 2nd Gurkhas, the 15th Sikhs, with British and native field hospitals, formed the First Brigade, Second Division, which marched on the 7th October, under Brigadier-General Ian Hamilton, D.S.O., *via* the Kohat Pass, for Shinauri. The stages were easy, and the road led through fertile valleys and wooded hills towards the Samana Mountains. From Kai they could see the ruins of the Fort of Saragarhi, just made famous for the gallant stand made by its garrison of twenty-one soldiers of the 36th Sikhs, who all fell in its defence. On the 15th they arrived at Shinauri, where (Hamilton having met with an accident) Brigadier-General

---

[1] The approximate strength of the force was 32,882 officers and soldiers (European and native), with 19,558 followers ; 8000 horses, 1440 hospital riding ponies, 18,384 mules, and an enormous number of camels, carts, and baggage ponies.—Colonel H. D. Hutchinson's " Campaign in Tirah."

F. J. Kempster, D.S.O., A.D.C., assumed command of the brigade, which was now styled the " Third Brigade, Tirah Field Force." It was intended to advance on the 20th, but the enemy had skilfully occupied the village of Dargai, situated on a rocky spur, which forms the western boundary of the Chagru Valley, and dominates the road by which the British must march.   Sir William Lockhart, therefore, ordered the Second Division to dislodge him.   Westma-cott's Brigade was to engage the enemy in front, supported by two Mountain batteries, while Kempster's Brigade, led by the scouts of the 3rd Gurkhas, with one Mountain battery and some Madras sappers, was to make a wide detour to the west, get round his right flank, and threaten his rear.   General Yeatman-Biggs being ill, General Sir Power Palmer was entrusted with the command.

The Gordons, with Kempster's Brigade (accompanied by Sir Power Palmer), marched off before 5 a.m. on the 18th October. The way was up a dry watercourse "like the Holm Burn " (near Inverness), says an officer, but getting rougher and rougher as they advanced, till after five miles the narrow path became so steep that the Gurkhas in front looked like flies crawling on a wall.   The precipitous track being found impossible even for such sure-footed animals as mules, the General decided to send back his guns and the field hospital, under escort of the Dorset Regiment, with part of the 15th Sikhs, and the battalion had to wait till these all passed through.   About 11 a.m. heliograph communication was established with General Westmacott's column, and after a long and stiff climb of two hours, latterly under fire, the Gordons reached the top, where they had been preceded by their signal party, and by two native regiments of their brigade who had not been delayed, and who by long-range volleys accelerated the flight, though they were too late to cut off the retreat, of the enemy, who had been driven back by Westma-cott.   That officer had reached the Chagru Kotal about 9 a.m., and his batteries at once came into action against Dargai.   His infantry toiled up the ascent, often in single file, sometimes under fire, till by noon a point was reached where a rush had to be made across an open space exposed to a hail of bullets from the rocks and walled terraces above.   Bravely the Gurkhas, supported by the Scottish Borderers, streamed across, carried the crest of the hill, and the enemy were in full retreat.   It was gallantly done, but at the cost to the Gurkhas of thirteen killed and wounded, and to the Borderers of six.   " It is quite marvellous that this was all the loss, but the fact is that Kempster's Brigade was beginning to make the pressure of its advance felt, and the tribesmen, ever anxious when their rear is threatened, gave way probably with greater readiness than they otherwise would have done." [1]

[1] Hutchinson ; also Lockhart's Despatch of December 9th.

It was late in the afternoon before Kempster's Brigade had joined hands with Westmacott, and General Palmer, finding that the water supply of Dargai was at a distance, and that the adjacent heights would have to be held to obtain it, did not consider himself justified, taking all circumstances into consideration, in retaining possession of Dargai, which it was not expected the enemy would reoccupy. The retirement was begun by Westmacott's Brigade, which reached the camp in safety, and between 4 p.m. and 5 p.m. as the sun was sinking in the west, Kempster prepared to follow, retaining, however, from Westmacott's troops, two companies of Scottish Borderers ; for at this time a force of about 4000 men was observed advancing from the Khanki Valley, where they had evidently been encamped, while another body of the enemy began to ascend to Dargai Heights from the same direction. It was clear that the tribesmen, having heard the sound of the guns early in the day, had resolved to reinforce the Alikhels, who had just been driven out of Dargai ; and now, seeing the withdrawal had begun, they pressed closely on the rear of Kempster's troops.

The retirement was covered by the 15th Sikhs, they in turn being covered by the Gordons and the two companies of the Borderers. Whilst five companies of the Gordons were thus engaged (on the ridge destined to be the " zone of fire " on the 20th) Major Bramly was killed, and several men of his company were hit. When the Sikhs and Gurkhas had passed through, three of the Gordon companies and the Scottish Borderers were withdrawn, two companies of the former being left to hold the enemy in check till their friends had taken up a fresh position. The enemy were now firing at these two companies from all sides, but Captain Miller Wallnutt, whose company was one of the three retiring, took up a position to cover them when they should also retire. One of the two companies (Bramly's) was now ordered to withdraw, and finally the other (Captain Kerr's). Two sections of the latter were complying, and only half the company remained, when suddenly the enemy appeared over the hill from behind, and gave them a volley at about thirty yards, throwing them into momentary confusion. Fortunately for themselves they promptly formed up within six yards, for the enemy fired and rushed on them, thinking them defeated ; but Kerr's men stood steady, and shot six within a few yards of their bayonets, when the others turned and ran. Captain Miller Wallnutt's timely support was, however, gratefully acknowledged. During this scrimmage Lieutenant Young (Indian Staff Corps), attached to the Gordons, with the help of Surgeon-Captain Gerrard and Colour-sergeant Craib, gallantly saved the life of a soldier who was lying wounded close to the enemy, who would have killed him.

The enemy had suffered so severely that they gave no further trouble, but as it now became dark it was terrible work getting the wounded down the two miles of steep and rugged path to where the road began. The men had to carry the stretchers, for there were no native bearers ; the wounded bore the suffering which this entailed with the greatest pluck. " I walked beside one poor fellow who was badly hit," says an officer's letter ; " he grasped my hand as firmly as he could, but never complained, though the jolting of the stretcher must have been agony." Officers and men assisted in carrying them and the bodies of their dead comrades along the six miles of road to camp, where they arrived at 11 p.m., after marching and climbing up and down hill since 5 a.m. A fine instance of good comradeship was shown by the men of the K.O.S.B.'s, who carried water a mile out from camp to meet the thirsty Gordons.

In this rear guard action, of which the Gordons bore the brunt, they lost Major R. D. Jennings Bramly and Private Hagan killed, Lieutenant M. L. Pears (Scottish Rifles, attached), one sergeant and six privates wounded.[1] Among the many narrow escapes a bullet grazed Lieutenant Dalrymple Hay's cheek ; Lieutenant Young's helmet was shot off, and many men had bullets through their clothes.

Lieut.-General Sir A. P. Palmer commented most favourably in his report as to the steadiness and gallantry of the troops, and brought to the notice of Sir W. Lockhart, Lieut.-Colonel H. H. Mathias, C.B. Private W. Rennie, " who shot down four of the enemy at very close quarters," is also specially mentioned.

It had been intended by Sir William Lockhart that the work of improving the road should be carried on by the Second Division, and it was thought that the presence of the working parties with their strong covering-parties would deter the enemy from re-occupying the Dargai Heights. The officer commanding the division, however, decided to give his troops a rest on the 19th, and on the evening of that day Lockhart received information that the enemy in force again held the heights.

On October 20th the advanced guard of the Second Division left camp at Shinauri at 4.30 a.m. and reached the Chagru Kotal at 8 a.m., at which time the 1st Northamptonshire and a Mountain Battery R.A. were in position on the Samana Suk. The 2nd Derbyshires, 3rd Sikhs and a Mountain Battery from the First Division assisted in the advance of the Second Division. The Third (Kempster's) Brigade began its attack on the Dargai Heights

---

[1] Regimental Record.
  Colonel Abbot of the 15th Sikhs afterwards wrote to Colonel Mathias and thanked the Gordons for saving his regiment from being cut off and suffering heavy loss.

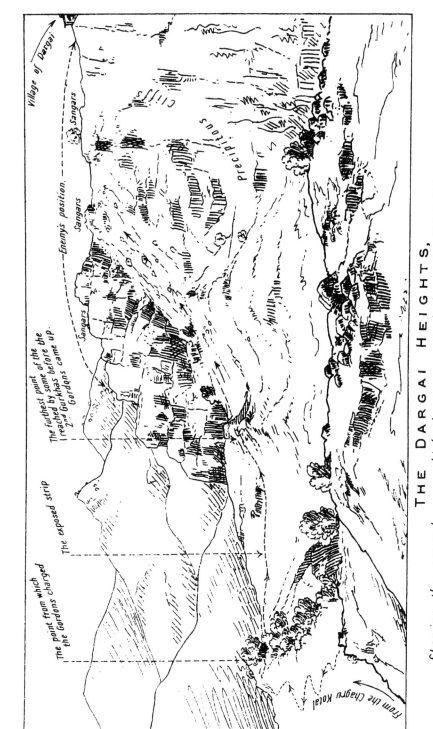

THE DARGAI HEIGHTS,

Shewing the ground over which the troops attacked on the 18th & 20th October 1897.

Village of Dargai

Sangars

Enemy's position.

Sangars

Sangars

CLIFFS

precipitous

Sangars

The furthest point of the
I reached by some of the
2d Gordons came up.
Gurkhas before the

The exposed strip

The point from which
the Gordons charged

From the Chagru Kotal

at 10 a.m. by a concentrated artillery fire ; but a series of peculiar clefts in the rock at the crest of the position, mostly three or four feet deep and five or six feet wide, gave the enemy complete shelter from the shells. The assault was led by the First Battalion 2nd Gurkhas, supported by the First Battalion Dorsetshire Regiment. The Second Battalion Derbyshire was in reserve, followed by the First Battalion Gordon Highlanders, who covered the advance by long-range volleys from a village half-way between the Kotal and the heights.

By 11.30 a.m. the above force was in formation under cover, in readiness to capture the heights, but when the 2nd Gurkhas, accompanied by the Gurkha scouts of the First Battalion 3rd Gurkhas, made their first rush across the open, they were met by such a hot and well-aimed fire that all they could do was to hold on to the position they had reached without being able to advance further.

At 2 p.m. the Dorsetshire Regiment was ordered to storm the enemy's entrenchments, but though a few men were able to get across the fire-swept zone, an advance beyond the line held by the 2nd Gurkhas was reported by the commanding officer to be impossible, owing to the large numbers of tribesmen lining the edge of the Dargai plateau and the steepness of the slope leading up to it. The General Officer commanding the Second Division accordingly ordered Brigadier-General Kempster to move up the Gordon Highlanders and the 3rd Sikhs, the former regiment being replaced on the lower spur which it had hitherto occupied, by the Jhind Imperial Service Infantry. The Gordon Highlanders went straight up the hill without check or hesitation. Headed by their pipers, and led by Lieut.-Colonel Mathias, C.B., with Major Macbean on his right and Lieutenant A. F. Gordon on his left, this splendid battalion marched across the open. It dashed through a murderous fire, and in forty minutes had won the heights, leaving three officers and thirty men killed or wounded on its way. The first rush of the Gordons was deserving of the highest praise, for they had just undergone a very severe climb, and had reached a point beyond which other troops had been unable to advance for over three hours. The first rush was followed at short intervals by a second and a third, each led by officers, and as the leading companies went up the path for the final assault, the remainder of the troops, among whom the 3rd Sikhs were conspicuous, streamed on in support. But few of the enemy waited for the bayonet, many of them being shot down as they fled in confusion.[1]

In amplification of the above despatch, it must be remembered that after the first party of Gurkhas had rushed across to their place of shelter, the vigilance of the enemy was fully roused. There was no turning movement to distract them as on the 18th, and from the crest of the precipice, at a distance of 200 yards, they poured down such a fatal fire that though parties of the Dorsets, Derbys, and Gurkhas again and again tried to follow, they suffered so terribly that few could succeed in crossing. The constant stream

[1] Sir W. Lockhart's Despatch to the Adjutant-General in India, dated 9th December 1897.

of their dead and wounded as they were carried past was not an encouraging sight to the Gordons ; while the enemy, full of confidence in the impregnability of their position, were waving their standards, beating their drums, and shouting defiance.   On reaching the spot where the Derbys and Dorsets were, the Highlanders lay under cover while the guns concentrated their fire for three minutes on the summit.   When the moment for action came, Colonel Mathias addressed them in these simple and soldier-like words, which sent a thrill not only through his own men, but through the whole British Empire—" The General says this hill must be taken at all costs—the Gordon Highlanders will take it." [1]

There was a momentary hush—then the answering cheer assured him that his confidence was not misplaced.   The bugle sounds the " Advance," the pipers play, the officers cry " Come," and a wave of kilted soldiers bursts into the fire-swept open.   Almost at once Major Macbean fell shot through the thigh.   Dragging himself to the shelter of a boulder-stone, he continued to cheer his comrades as they passed, their figures dimly seen through the mist of dust raised by the pelting hail of bullets.   The gallant young Lamont was killed instantaneously ; Lieutenant Dingwall, wounded in four places, was carried out of further danger by Private Lawson. The first division reach the sheltering rocks panting for breath ; they shout, the officers waving their swords to those behind ; while Piper Findlater, though wounded and unable to move, still inspires them with his war-like strains.   Quickly their numbers increase to about 400 men, and more are coming ; they start again, " the men cheering like mad," up the precipitous path leading to the crest, where they look for a warm reception.   But the top is reached—it forms a succession of ridges along which the Highlanders rush unopposed, and great is the cheering as they realise that the enemy are in flight.   Seeing that our men would not be denied, they dared not stand against such determined courage, and the position in which, for several hours, they had defied a whole brigade, was abandoned.[2]   The Gordons gave three cheers for their gallant Colonel ; then Gurkhas, Sikhs, Derbys, and Dorsets —for some of all these had come forward—joined with them in hearty handshaking and congratulation.   " Nothing," says the letter of an officer of the Gordons, " can describe the way the men behaved.   It was simply splendid." [3]

" Stiff climb, eh, Mackie ? " said the Colonel, somewhat

---

[1] Regimental Record.   [2] The position was won at 3.15 p.m.

[3] " Their (First Gordons) conduct at Dargai helped Yeatman-Biggs out of a great difficulty, and one that was, as hour by hour passed without driving the Pathans off, rapidly passing into an actual danger."—Letter from Sir G. S. White, V.C., G.C.B., then Commander-in-Chief in India.

AFTER DARGAI

THE GORDON HIGHLANDERS CARRYING DOWN THE WOUNDED GURKHAS

blown, to a colour-sergeant as they breasted the last ascent ; " Not quite—so young—as I was—you know."

" Never mind, sir," answered the gallant sergeant, giving his commanding officer a slap of genuine admiration on the back, " Never mind, sir ! ye 're ga'un vara strong for an auld man ! " Among the many narrow escapes, Major Downman got a bullet through his helmet, Lieutenant MacKenzie one through his kilt ; when Major Macbean, lying wounded on the ground, tried to drink from his water-bottle, he found nothing in it but the bullet which had let out the contents ! Numbers of the men had similar escapes. Many were the instances of personal bravery and self-sacrifice in trying to save wounded comrades, " and many a Cross was earned that day though not won, either because he who did the deed was not observed or died in doing it."

The General determined to hold the heights, and the Dorsets, with the 1st and 2nd Gurkhas, bivouacked on the summit. The Gordons volunteered to carry down the wounded men of the Dorsets and Gurkhas, a kindly act much appreciated by their comrades, and as they moved down to their comfortless bivouac on the Chagru Kotal, each regiment broke into cheers as they passed, officers and men pressing forward to offer their water-bottles, though they well knew the precious liquid would be unattainable during the night.

The total casualties of the troops engaged were 3 officers and 33 n.c. officers and men killed, and 12 officers and 147 n.c. officers and men wounded, mostly in a space of about 150 yards across. The determined rapidity of their advance rendered the loss sustained by the Gordons less than might have been expected, but their success was dearly purchased by the death of Lieutenant Alexr. Lamont,[1] Corporal A. Bell, and Private Quinn, killed in action. Lieut.-Colonel Mathias, C.B., Major Forbes Macbean, Captain H. P. Uniacke, Lieutenants M. F. M. Meiklejohn, Kenneth Dingwall, and G. S. G. Craufurd, and 35 n.c. officers and men were wounded, of whom 4 died of their wounds, viz. Colour-sergeant E. Pickersgill, and Privates A. Civil, J. Davie, and John M'Kinnon.

The General Officer commanding the Second Division brought to the special notice of Sir W. Lockhart " the gallant conduct of Lieut.-Colonel Mathias, C.B., in leading his battalion to the assault of a most difficult position at a critical period of the fight when previous attempts had failed. . . . I recommend this officer for the Victoria Cross." [2] Major-General Yeatman-Biggs " also

[1] Son of Lamont of Knockdow, Argyllshire.

[2] Lockhart's Despatch. It having been decided by the War Office that neither general officers nor officers commanding battalions are eligible for the Cross, Colonel Mathias did not receive it.

reported most favourably " of the following Gordons, among others of the various regiments engaged : " Major F. Macbean, who was the first to spring out of cover and lead his company to the attack, and who, being immediately afterwards wounded, continued to cheer his men on while lying on the ground. . . . Piper Findlater, who, after being shot through both feet and unable to stand, sat up under a heavy fire playing the regimental march to encourage the charge. . . . Private E. Lawson, who carried Lieutenant Dingwall, when wounded and unable to move, out of a heavy fire, and subsequently returned and brought in Private Macmillan, being himself wounded in two places in so doing. . . . I recommend Piper Findlater and Private Lawson for the Victoria Cross. . . . The General Officer commanding the Second Division has also brought to notice the services of the following officers, n.c. officers and men as deserving of recognition " :—

Major G. T. F. Downman.	Colour-sergeant T Craib.
Captain C. C. Miller Wallnutt.	Sergeant F. Ritchie.
Captain and Adjutant W. Camp- bell.	,, D. Mathers.
	,, J. Donaldson.
Lieutenant G. D. Mackenzie.	,, J. Mackay.
,, G. E. E. G. Cameron.	Lance-corporal (Piper) G. Milne.
Colour-sergeant J. Mackie.	

Many congratulations were telegraphed to the battalion—from the Queen enquiring for Lance-corporal Milne, who had been shot through the chest while leading the pipers ; from the Commander-in-Chief, Lord Wolseley, " Well done, Gordon Highlanders " ; from the Second Battalion, from the Royal Highlanders (Black Watch), and from Scottish and Highland Societies in all parts of the world, including the United States.

Piper Findlater [1] and Private Lawson afterwards received the Victoria Cross. The above named n.c. officers were awarded the medal for distinguished service in the field, and the Queen personally presented that honourable decoration to Lance-corporal Milne, who had been invalided home.

---

[1] The incident of the wounded piper continuing to play, being telegraphed home, took the British public by storm, and when Findlater arrived in England he found himself famous. Reporters rushed to interview him ; managers offered him fabulous sums to play at their theatres ; the streets of London and all the country towns were placarded with his portrait ; when, after his discharge, he was brought to play at the Military Tournament, Royal personages and distinguished generals shook him by the hand ; his photograph was sold by thousands ; the Scotsmen in London would have let him swim in champagne, and the daily cheers of the multitude were enough to turn an older head than that of this young soldier. A handsome pension enables Findlater to rest on his laurels and turn his sword into a ploughshare on a farm near Turriff. He re-enlisted for the Great War, though not fit for foreign service.

CHAPTER XXVII

1897–1898

A T daybreak on the 21st October the Second Division marched to Khorappa where they spent a few days, and though every military precaution was taken, the camp was fired into at night by large bodies of the enemy, and the foraging parties were pertinaciously opposed. The losses from this cause were considerable, but the Gordons escaped with two men wounded. On the 22nd, Sir William Lockhart had the battalion paraded, and addressed them with reference to their conduct on the 20th. " Your records," he said, " testify to many a gallant action, and you have now added to them another which may worthily rank beside those that have gone before. There is more hard work ahead for us all, and I am confident you will do your share of it well."

On the 28th the battalion marched to Gundaki, and next day both divisions took part in the attack on the Sampagha Pass. The Gordons, however, with the Third Brigade, were held in reserve, and did not come under fire. That afternoon they halted for a day to get up supplies, and on the 31st the enemy were driven with little resistance from the Arhanga Pass, from which our troops looked down on the fertile Tirah Maidan, the summer quarters of the Afridis. The battalion remained in Maidan, and was daily employed in covering foraging parties and in destroying the fortified villages from which our troops had been repeatedly fired upon. In fulfilling these very adventurous duties, skirmishes often took place which brought out the soldier-like qualities of individual officers and men. On the 9th November the Northamptonshire Regiment, while returning in the evening to camp through a ravine without sufficient flankers, were attacked from above on both sides, and a combat took place in which, after fighting with great gallantry, they lost 2 officers and 19 men killed and 1 officer and 29 men wounded ; 1 officer and 6 men of the Dorsets were wounded, 2 Sikhs were killed and 4 wounded. On November 10th, Lieutenant G. E. E. G. Cameron and 2 rank and file of the Gordons were wounded, of whom Private J. Stott died of his wounds. The return of one of these foraging parties was less dignified than dangerous. Finding themselves obliged to go, they went quickly, and on their arrival in camp the general, who had been anxiously watching their retreat, remarked to the abashed subaltern in charge—"There is one good thing you possess, at all events, young man—you can show a clean pair of heels ! "

On the 12th, representatives of the Orakzai clans were received in state by Sir William Lockhart and his political advisers, when a guard of honour of 100 rank and file was furnished by the Gordons

Terms of submission were offered, and the representatives retired to report these to their clansmen.

On the 13th, Kempster's Brigade, with the addition of the 36th Sikhs, was sent into the Waran Valley by the Tseri Kandao Pass, partly to carry out survey operations and partly to punish the Zakka-Khels and destroy the stronghold of the Mullah Sayid Akbar, the principal leader of the revolt. Though the distance was short, the difficult nature of the country and the care of the baggage made the march a trying one, and it was long after dark before they reached their camping ground. On the 14th, Sayid Akbar's house was blown up. On the 15th the Gordons remained in camp, but a reconnaissance in force was made by other troops who, while retiring, were fired at and followed by the enemy to the outlying piquets. They attacked one of these held by a corporal and eight of the Gordons, obliging them to withdraw, but two companies coming to their aid the post was immediately reoccupied, and B Company remained on the hill. The enemy fired from a distance on the piquet as long as it was light, and after dark fired volleys into the camp. Three men of the Gordons were wounded on piquet duty.

On the 16th the brigade returned to rejoin the main column at Maidan. The baggage being sent early ahead, the main body was started by 9 a.m.; and the rear guard, under Colonel Eaton Travers, began its movement shortly after. It consisted of five guns R.A., the 2nd Gurkhas and 3rd Gurkha Scouts, a company of the Dorsets and a company of the Gordons who, under Captain Kerr and Lieutenant Dalrymple Hay, had relieved B Company at daylight on the high piquet, with orders to hold it till told by Colonel Travers to withdraw. As the other piquets retired, the enemy advanced and fired on Kerr's men, but they kept well under cover and waited for the signal to follow the retirement. Colonel Travers held on to his position till past noon, to enable the main body to increase its distance. His guns opened fire on the enemy who threatened to cut off the Gordon piquet, which was at last signalled to retire on the guns ; the men were then withdrawn singly from the sangars, and having passed the exposed part of the hill, retired by alternate half companies at a run, and finally succeeded in joining the Gurkhas. So well was the matter managed and so fortunate were they that, beyond clothing torn by bullets, they suffered no loss. When the retirement was continued, the Gordon company was sent back with the Gurkhas to hold a burning village till the rest of the rear guard had passed. There was good cover, but Lieutenant Wylie of the Gurkhas was killed and several of his men were killed and wounded. Of the Gordons, only one corporal was slightly wounded.[1]

[1] Corporal Walker, not mentioned in casualty list.

Owing to the extraordinary difficulties of the ground, and having continually to occupy commanding heights on each side of the route, Travers' force was a good deal exhausted when it arrived, after dark, at the top of the Tseri Kandao Pass, and the 15th Sikhs now took the place of the Gordon company and the Gurkhas, who arrived safely in camp at Maidan. The Sikhs were soon hard pressed ; their countrymen of the 36th and two companies of the Dorsets who had not been engaged were sent to their assistance, but the enemy now showed in such force that had it not been for the admirable dispositions made by Colonel Abbot (who was wounded), and by Colonel Haughton, their troops might have been overwhelmed. They defended themselves till the early morning, when Gaselee's brigade went out to aid the belated rear guard. They came in safely, but their killed and wounded were many. The loss of the brigade on the 16th November amounted to 4 British officers and 25 n.c. officers and men (British and native) killed, 3 British and 3 native officers, with 37 n.c. officers and men (British and native) wounded. This was one of the few occasions on which the enemy suffered severely ; they acknowledged a loss of 290.

While at Maidan the battalion was employed on outpost and convoy duties, which sometimes gave rise to exciting adventures— as when, on the 20th, the enemy were cleverly caught while trying to intercept a convoy. A company of sappers working near drove the tribesmen towards the head of the pass, and two companies of the Gordons hurried down, one on each side of the ravine, caught them between two fires and accounted for twenty or thirty of them. Occasional shots were fired into the camp at night, one bullet going into the fire while the officers were at dinner, and another pierced Lieutenant Hay's pillow while he was sleeping ; indeed, several officers and men of the force were killed in this manner.

A story is told apropos of firing into camp at night—" sniping," as it is called—and burning villages. A number of Afridi headmen came in to see Sir William Lockhart to talk over the terms of submission, and during the meeting they complained of the burning of their villages. Lockhart on his part complained of the " sniping " by the villagers. " We are very sorry," they said, " but we have a lot of young bloods who *will* go out shooting at night, and how can *we* stop them ? " To which Sir William replied, " Well, you see what a lot of young bloods I have, and when they hear shooting at night they *will* go out burning villages in the morning, and how am *I* to stop them ? "

On the 21st the battalion, with the brigade, moved a short distance to Bagh, a sacred spot, where the Afridi rebellion and the Khyber raid were planned. The 15th Sikhs, who had suffered so severely, were sent back to Shinauri for well-deserved rest, their place in the Third Brigade being taken by the 2nd Punjab Infantry.

At Bagh life was comparatively peaceful. The officers celebrated St Andrew's Day (the 30th) by a grand dinner, Generals Yeatman-Biggs and Kempster, with their staffs, being among the guests. A native house had been cleared out, partitions taken down, a fireplace built, and lanterns hung on the rafters, so that it was warm and well lighted ; plaids were hung on the walls and trophies of arms arranged on them. A plentiful dinner, including such luxuries as haggis and ham, graced the board ; afterwards the pipers marched round the table and the party adjourned to the open air where the men had a bonfire and torches, and by their light danced reels, the Highland fling, and the sword dance. Then a sing-song, in which Mr Gillan, the respected " padre," distinguished himself by his admirable rendering of Scotch comic songs. A glass of toddy finished the evening, and all felt the better for the unusual if modest dissipation. The troops not more seriously engaged had sports on December 3rd and an inter-regimental tug-of-war, in which the Gordons were victorious. Lieutenant R. Gordon, of the Australian Horse (attached to the battalion), gave a wonderful exhibition of the use of the boomerang.

On December 5th the brigade started before dawn to forage and burn villages and towers, whose destruction was a necessity, as they were a standing danger to the force ; during the return a man of the Gordons was severely wounded. These houses and villages are all fortified, and the inhabitants won the respect of our troops for their marksmanship, their skill in taking advantage of ground, their patience in waiting for the favourable moment, and the dash and boldness with which they attacked. They have plenty of practice, for when not united against a common foe they are generally fighting with each other.

The weather was now cold, with hard frost at night. The baggage and tents having been sent to the base, the troops were in bivouac. The following is the description of an officer's bedroom in a letter written at Bagh :—

It is a hole dug in the ground about three feet deep and walled up on one side by bags filled with earth ; over them my bivouac tent forms a roof, and under my waterproof sheet I have six inches deep of straw. Of course one cannot stand upright, but one can move about a bit, which is a great thing.[1]

Several of the tribes had promised submission, but the Khani Khel Chamkanis showed no signs of coming in, and Lockhart

---

[1] The troops had warm khaki coats lined with flannel, Balaclava caps, and worsted gloves.

determined to look them up. The Gordons did not take part in this expedition. After having effectually punished the Chamkanis, Sir William returned on the 6th of December to Bagh, where preparations had been completed for evacuating Tirah. The cold was already intense (20 degrees of frost), and directly the snow fell it would be impossible to remain in these mountains, which the Afridis themselves abandon during the depth of winter. The heavy baggage had already been sent off, with all weakly men and the staff and departmental officers not absolutely required on the march. The remaining troops were to move with the lowest possible scale of baggage and without tents. The base of operations was changed from Kohat to Peshawar ; Sir William Lockhart, with the Second Division under Yeatman-Biggs, was to march by the Dwatoi Pass down the Bara Valley to Barkai ; General Symons, with Gaselee's and Hart's brigades, was to move down the Mastura, destroying the defences in the Waran Valley, thence across the Sapri Pass to join the Second Division near Barkai. Here the whole force would join hands with Hammond's Peshawar column, and the heavy baggage would be picked up at Bara. Thus the whole of the Afridi-Orakzai Highlands would have been explored, and the force would be in a position to operate against the Afridi settlements in the lower valleys and to reoccupy the Khyber.

Lockhart, in carrying out his plan of proving to the Afridis that their country was not impregnable, visited every part of it, and had in November made a reconnaissance in force through the Dwatoi defile, which had been then surveyed, so that its difficulties were now known. The road is a mere rocky track, sometimes on the right, sometimes on the left of the river, and as often as not in midstream of ice-cold water. The gorge is in places scarcely thirty yards across. On each flank were high cliffs, affording positions from which a few men could prevent the passage of an army, but the tribes in the immediate neighbourhood had been influenced by Colonel Warburton, a political officer well acquainted with the Afridis, and they promised not to obstruct the march on condition that their houses should be respected.

The thermometer registered 21 degrees of frost when, long before daybreak on the 7th of December, Lockhart marched for Dwatoi with the Fourth Brigade. The Third Brigade followed next morning, the Gordons being rear guard ; the transport animals could hardly be got through the difficulties of the defile, increased as they were by the rising of the river, and the baggage constantly blocked the way, causing long halts, whilst sleet and rain increased the discomfort ; till after having advanced only five miles darkness overtook them, and at 6 p.m. it was decided to bivouac and make themselves as comfortable as the keen frost permitted.   In the morning they moved slowly on, constantly wading in the river and halting while the baggage overcame the difficulties of the way.   They joined the brigade at Dwatoi, having taken from 8 a.m. on the 8th till 4 p.m. on the 9th to accomplish about seven or eight miles.   Next day the Fourth Brigade led the march, followed by the Third, the Gordons being flank guard and the Gurkhas rear guard.   They had now left the friendly territory and commenced the descent of the narrow Bara Valley ; soon the enemy were firing upon them from points of vantage from which they had to be dislodged.   The mist which hung over the river to some extent spoiled their aim, though the Gurkhas and Punjab Infantry had several casualties ; the Gordons had a good deal of skirmishing in the hills, but arrived at Karanna without loss.   The enemy fired at long range into camp, wounding several of the Dorsets, but the guns opened on them and they were dislodged ; after which the troops spent a quiet night in the swampy fields, the Fourth Brigade being about three miles in advance.   On the 11th the Third Brigade was ordered to catch up the Fourth at Sher Khel, a distance of fourteen miles of very difficult ground ; the battalion had again the honourable but harassing position of rear guard, and the expectation of fighting by the way was at once unpleasantly realised.   The troops breakfasted in a pouring rain which had rendered the ground so deep and slippery that there was great delay in getting the baggage animals along.   Firing began on the piquets with daylight; and the guns, under escort of a company of the battalion, came into action before leaving the camping ground ; but the piquets, when recalled, ran down from their sangars on the hills and, though fired at, safely joined the rear guard ; the enemy followed closely, shouting and yelling and firing from the heights vacated by our flankers as they moved on.   The troops had to cross the snow-swollen river nearly up to their waists, and though the mist and rain lessened the accuracy of the enemy's fire, three of the Gordons were wounded, one of them mortally ; the enemy kept increasing in numbers, and half the escort of the guns joined the firing line.   As the animals became tired the baggage moved slower and slower, the companies taking up successive positions for its protection, their difficulties being in places increased by the smoke from villages fired by the leading brigade, which, mingling with the mist, prevented a clear view ; the river had to be continually crossed and recrossed, while fighting continued more or less the whole way.   They were now hampered by the care of their own wounded as well as some of the Fourth Brigade ; an officer was found by the river, where he had been lying for some hours, deserted by his doolie bearers.   The Indian mule-drivers, benumbed by the cold and terrified by the bullets which occasionally knocked over men and beasts, had to be helped and driven by the soldiers ; many exhausted animals with their loads had to be abandoned. Some Highlanders, tired as they were, volunteered to carry ammunition-boxes till spare mules could be got for them, and the Gurkhas under Norie behaved equally well. About 5 p.m. the enemy became still bolder and tried to cut off the tail of the rear guard ; the transport and wounded were moved down to a plain bounded on each side by hills on which the companies took up a succession of positions, passing and repassing each other as they fell back, thus keeping the enemy at bay. Many of the hospital doolies got stuck in a difficult spot, their bearers completely demoralised and done up, when a number of the Highlanders carried the wounded, and though bullets whistled over and around, surprisingly few men were hit.

When darkness set in the guns were sent on, and, keeping to the river, the main body of the brigade (including Colonel Mathias and the leading companies of his battalion) reached Sher Khel. The rearmost companies, however, had often to wait to bring away wounded men, British or native, and Major Downman, who could see the lights of the camp looking nearer than they really were, took what seemed a more direct, though as it turned out a more difficult road, when the enemy, finding he had quitted the river way, came down into it cutting off communication. The Major with a fixed force of Dorsets, Gordons, Gurkhas, and Punjabis, fixed bayonets and formed a sort of square, with the wounded in the centre, and though the enemy were firing from surrounding heights, even Afridis, good marksmen as they are, shoot badly on a wet night with shots coming in return, and the bullets mostly passed over. Meanwhile Captains Miller Wall-nutt and Kerr, who with Captain Uniacke were further forward, remembering the disasters which had happened to the Dorsets and Northamptons by being surrounded at night, came to the conclusion that it would be dangerous to proceed under present circumstances, and seeing a fortified house on an elevation nearly 500 yards off, determined to occupy it. Captain Uniacke with fifteen men at once started for this purpose. After going a short way, a volley was fired at them ; they dropped for a moment, then Uniacke ran hard for the house, but when near it he found that only three Gordons and a Gurkha they had picked up by the way had kept up with him. It was pretty dark, but they could see a line of the enemy taking up a position between the house and the hill to cut off the rear guard. The captain told his men not to fire, but to rush straight at them, and " Shout like hell." The enemy, apparently thinking them really denizens of the lower regions, and uncertain of their numbers, fired one wild volley, rose up, and went as if the devil had kicked them. Uniacke and his men got into the house, shouting orders to imaginary legions from the roof, with the result that those surrounding Downman's party thought a force from camp had arrived, and made themselves scarce. While this was enacting, Miller Wallnutt and Kerr had tried to communicate with Downman, but found it impossible owing to the enemy closing in ; they then moved after Uniacke, the enemy firing from a short distance, only the flash of the rifles being seen. Two of their men were wounded, and as they approached the house they saw through the gloom dark figures entering it ; thinking them the enemy they were just ordering a charge with fixed bayonets, when they were greatly relieved to hear Uniacke's whistle, and they gladly reached the welcome shelter. Whistles were blown and answered by Downman's party who were not far off, and in ten minutes all were safe within the building, which was of stone and, as is usual, loopholed for defence. Sentries were posted on the roof, the tower and rooms were divided among the various corps, amounting to about 450 men ; in the centre were the British and native hospitals (they had 21 dead and wounded with them). Among the wounded was the gallant Norie, who lay uncomplainingly all night on the floor in his wet clothes, with a torniquet made with a bayonet on his shattered arm. Fortunately two doctors were present, who spared no pains to alleviate the sufferings of their patients. The Gurkhas had dragged a goat with them, which they killed for supper, but the others had scarcely a mouthful of food. Soaked as they were, sleep was practically out of the question, and they passed the night in trying to dry their clothes and in talking round the fire, not of military glory, but of imaginary good dinners. At last day dawned on the 12th December, the sun rose brightly, and some went to the door to enjoy it, but the house was commanded from the hills near and they were soon driven in by a volley ; the men on the roof replied, but Corporal Harding was killed and four privates wounded. About 9 a.m. a party of the 2nd Punjab Infantry came from the camp and reached some neighbouring houses, whence a few men ran across, but several were hit in doing so, even when entering the door. Soon after, the Scottish Borderers, with a native battalion and a battery, came to their relief, in which operation they lost 2 killed and several wounded, and by 1 p.m. the weary rear guard were in camp. Thirty-six hours wet through, with little food or sleep and plenty of fighting, is hard and hungry work. " However," says an officer's letter, " we were none of us the worse for it, but we were well out of ' Fort Downman.' "

In this affair the rear guard had over 40 officers and soldiers killed or wounded,[1] of whom the Gordons lost 5 rank and file killed in action,[2] viz. Corporal B. Harding, Privates G. Morley, Jas. Langham, J. Neale, and H. Furniss, and eleven wounded. About 100 followers were killed, wounded, or missing, besides 150 animals. The difficulties of this march may be better imagined when it is observed that it took from the morning of the 8th till the afternoon of the 12th to accomplish the distance, only about forty miles, from Bagh to Sher Khel.

On the 13th the retirement was continued, but this time the Fourth Brigade formed the rear guard, and were constantly and heavily engaged, having 70 casualties. The Third Brigade was in front, and the Gordons being advanced guard, had a comparatively easy time, till after about eleven miles' march they joined hands with General Hammond's column near Swaikot (Barkai), and bivouacked on the Lakrai Kotal ; there was no water, and though the men had been warned to fill their bottles at a river, that barely gave enough for one drink of tea. It was only at nightfall that Westmacott's brigade (the Fourth) had fought its way to within a mile of Kempster's troops, where, owing to the darkness, they bivouacked. At dawn the enemy tried to get between the brigades, and when these moved they continued to harass the rear guard (which had a few casualties) for two miles, when they disappeared. The Third Brigade again led the division and protected the flanks, and all the available men of the battalion helped to carry the wounded to the camp at Mamani, where, no arrangements having been made, the poor sufferers had no shelter for some time till the hospital arrived.

On the 17th the brigade marched to Ilam Gudar, and on the 18th the battalion under Colonel Mathias, war-worn and dishevelled but hard and healthy, reached Bara in the immediate neighbourhood of Peshawar, glad to be once more in British India. Here tents and comforts awaited them, while the wounded went into hospital at Peshawar. The Duke of Cornwall's Light Infantry now replaced the Dorsets, but the Gordons remained and were joined on the 23rd by 161 n.c. officers and men from Pindi under Captain Towse, Lieutenants Cameron, Ingilby, and Anderson (Staff Corps, attached).[3] Over 100 of this draft had lately arrived from the Second Battalion and, says an officer's letter, were almost without exception Scotsmen, though only a few of them were Highlanders.

Christmas Day was the first time they had been in a church since they left Kuldunnah, but they were accompanied throughout the expedition by the Rev. D. H. Gillan, Presbyterian chaplain,

---

[1] Shadwell.   [2] Regimental Record.
[3] Second-Lieutenants Ogston and Maclaren followed in February, 1898.

who by word and deed did much to cheer and comfort his military congregation. By New Year, 1898, they were ready to enjoy the rest and relaxation of that festive season.

Lockhart, however, was not idle. The First Division explored the Bazar Valley, and Hammond's troops, who had not taken part in the previous campaign, continued to destroy the defences of the Zakka Khels along the line of the Khyber, having daily encounters with that determined and well-armed race. The battalion, with the Second Division, remained quietly at or near Bara till January 29th, 1898, when the Third and Fourth Brigades made a combined movement with the intention of surrounding and capturing the Afridi flocks and herds which, it was reported, were brought down daily to graze on the Kajurai plain to the west of Bara. Four columns were employed, but though the utmost secrecy was observed, the news had evidently reached the Afridis, and the Bara column returned without seeing either the enemy or their cattle ; the Mamani column, however, though its advance was unopposed, was vigorously attacked in the Shin Kamar Pass directly the retirement began, and suffered severely, especially the King's Own Yorkshire Light Infantry, who, fighting at close quarters, kept their foes at bay till all the wounded had been sent to the rear, but they had to abandon the dead. Next day the Gordons, with the Scottish Borderers and Gurkhas, were sent to recover the bodies, which they effected on the 31st without difficulty, but in the retirement the brigade had eight casualties ; none, however, in the battalion, which with the Gurkhas returned to Bara, February 1st.

Owing to the tardy compliance of the Afridis with the terms offered by the Indian Government, the Third Brigade (now commanded by Brigadier-General Ian Hamilton) marched on the 11th to Swaikot and reached Barkai next day, meeting with no opposition. On the 16th the brigade headquarters and the troops, except the Duke of Cornwall's Light Infantry and the Gordons, moved to Ghuli Kadar (thieves' den), near Guli Khel. The battalion was employed at Barkai in making roads and escorting convoys. During this, as on all occasions of comparative rest, officers and men kept themselves fit by athletic exercises and games, which were not always played without a spice of danger. While a party who had been to play a shinty match against the Fourth Brigade were returning from Mamani, armed though they were, they were attacked and two of their number wounded. Some of the clansmen, however, would enter into friendly conversation ; a Gordon officer, talking to some of them at Barkai, showed them his helmet with a bullet hole in it, saying in joke, " Look what you scoundrels did to me." When one of their number, not to be outdone, replied,

" Look what you did to me," at the same time taking off his turban, which had also been pierced by a bullet.

At last even the most truculent of the tribes tendered their submission and paid in the fines and rifles demanded of them, and peace being declared, several hundreds of his late enemies assembled at Peshawar when Sir William Lockhart was about to depart ; they wanted to drag his carriage to the station, they shouted and cheered him as the train steamed off, and vowed that in future they would be the friends of the British and fight on their side ! They had learned not only to respect the British, but to confide in their General.

Under these happy circumstances the battalion marched from Barkai on the 5th of April, entrained at Peshawar on the 7th, and reached Rawal Pindi the following day, with a strength of 22 officers and 591 n.c. officers and men. During the expedition 2 officers and 6 n.c. officers and men of the battalion had been killed in action ; 71 officers, n.c. officers, and men had been wounded, of whom 6 n.c. officers and men died of their wounds. The loss of the various columns of Lockhart's army amounted, up to January 26th, to 1050 killed and wounded.[1]

Hardly a day or night has been passed without casualties, and whether we advanced or retired, every soldier had to be constantly on the alert against enemies who made no stand in the open, but were unrivalled as skirmishers and marksmen. . . . I am glad to say the troops responded nobly to the call made upon them. Cheerful and soldier-like under exceptionally trying circumstances, officers and men have upheld to the utmost the traditions of their corps and the honour of Her Majesty's army.[2]

The following testimony to the character of the battalion was borne in a memo. dated July 17th, 1899, by Captain (now Major-General) Cookson, late of the Bengal Cavalry, who was in charge of the Jeypur Imperial Service Transport during the Tirah Campaign. He says that the Gordon Highlanders were remarkable for their readiness to help under all circumstances, that he never asked a n.c. officer or private of that regiment to lend a hand

---

[1] That the sufferings of many were lessened and their limbs saved was due to the enterprise of Surgeon-Major Beevor, of the Guards, who obtained leave to join the expedition, and took with him his own Röntgen Rays apparatus.—Shadwell.

[2] Lockhart's farewell order.

AUTHOR'S NOTE.—The Afridis were well armed mostly with Martini Henry rifles ; some had Sniders and a few Lee-Metfords.—Hutchinson. Some jezails were taken by the Gordons which were rifled.

The above account of the Gordons' share in the campaign is taken from " The Risings on the Tirah Frontier," published at the *Pioneer Press*, India ; " Lockhart's Advance through Tirah," by Captain Shadwell ; " Campaign in Tirah," by Colonel Hutchinson ; the Regimental Record ; Notes by Colonel Mathias, C.B., A.D.C., and Captain Craufurd, D.S.O. ; the letters of Lieutenant A. F. Gordon, the letters and journal of another officer of the battalion, and the *Tiger and Sphinx*.

with fallen kits, etc., without a cheerful answer and ready help. He was not with them (their brigade), but they never asked if the fallen baggage belonged to their own battalion or to others. " It 's not the baggage of my regiment " or " my company " was an answer he never got from any of the Gordons, and he remarked their extraordinary *esprit de corps* and good discipline.

Another testimony is narrated by Lieut.-Colonel A. D. Greenhill Gardyne. When staying in 1912 with Sir Pertab Singh,[1] Maharaja Regent of the Jodhpore State in Rajputana, the

To Camp
←———⇒
two miles.

FORT DOWNMAN

a Ruined outhouse occupied by 2nd Gurkhas.
b Place where Corporal Harding was killed and five men wounded.
c Door of British Hospital seen at back of courtyard.
d Tower occupied by Dorsets.
e Ambush of enemy on night of 11th, cleared by Uniacke charging them.

latter, on hearing that Colonel Gardyne belonged to the Gordon Highlanders, kept repeating " Very fine regiment, very grand regiment, I saw it often in Tirah, very fine regiment, all Sahibs " ; and related the following incident :—" During an action in Tirah, Sir William Lockhart, on whose staff I was serving, went to observe from a signalling post of the Gordon Highlanders, but as the hostile fire became severe we made Sir William move ; but I stayed and talked to the men and offered

[1] Sir Pertab Singh was an outstanding figure in India for half a century, and the best example of recent years of the ancient and splendid Rajput chivalry. He fought for the Empire in Tirah, in China, and in France and Palestine in the Great War, and his feats in sport and horsemanship have not been surpassed by any Briton. His description " Quite like Rajput " was the highest praise he could give.

them cigarettes.   One man reached out to take a cigarette when a bullet struck his hand aside ; he smiled, stretched out the other hand for the cigarette, lit it, and then looked at his wound.   A very cool man, a very good man, quite like Rajput."

The following officers were mentioned in despatches for their conduct during the Tirah expedition :—Lieut.-Colonel Mathias, C.B. ; Majors Downman and Forbes Macbean ; Captains Miller Wallnutt, Uniacke, and W. Campbell; Lieutenants A. F. Gordon, G. D. Mackenzie, G. Cameron, and 2nd Lieutenant Young (Staff Corps, attached) ; and the services of the following were recognised by promotion or decoration.   Lieut.-Colonel Mathias, C.B., was appointed A.D.C. to the Queen, with the rank of Colonel in the army ; Majors Downman, Macbean, and Burney were made Brevet Lieut.-Colonels ; Captain and Adjutant W. Campbell was promoted Brevet Major ; Captain Miller Wallnutt and Lieutenant Mackenzie were created Companions of the Distinguished Service Order.

CHAPTER XXVIII

1898

ON the 26th and 27th April the battalion moved to the Murree Hills, and arrived at Gharial on the 29th and 30th. Here a letter, dated at Netley Hospital, March 31st, and signed by " The wounded men of the Gordon Highlanders," was received by Sergeant-major M'Lennan, asking him, on their behalf, to thank the officers and n.c. officers for their " extreme kindness at Rawal Pindi, and for the splendid farewell they gave us. . . . Though we may be away from the battalion, *esprit de corps* is still our motto."

An important event in the Life of the Regiment at this time was the appointment of H.R.H. the Prince of Wales to be Colonel-in-Chief.

London Gazette of 11th June 1898

THE GORDON HIGHLANDERS

Field-Marshal His Royal Highness Albert Edward Prince of Wales and Duke of Cornwall, K.G., K.T., K.P., G.C.B., G.C.S.I., G.C.M.G., G.C.I.E., G.C.V.O., Colonel 10th Hussars, Colonel-in-Chief 1st Life Guards, 2nd Life Guards, and Royal Horse Guards, Personal Aide-de-Camp to the Queen, to be Colonel-in-Chief.

At Gharial a letter was received from Colonel Eaton Travers, commanding the First Battalion 2nd Gurkhas, on behalf of the officers, n.c. officers and men of his battalion, who had agreed to present the Gordons with a memento of their service together in Tirah, in the shape of two specimens of the Gurkha national weapon —the Kukri—made in the private workshops of Sir Bir Shamshere Jung Rana Bahadur, Prime Minister of Nepal. The blades had been specially manufactured for his Excellency's own use, and he presented the horns of rhinoceros shot by himself, for the handles. That for the officers' mess was beautifully mounted in gold, and that for the sergeants' mess in silver. The gifts and the good wishes which accompanied them are an interesting expression of good feeling between native and European troops, which will ever be gratefully remembered by the Gordons.[1]

September 8th.—The following remarks by the Commander-in-Chief in India on the inspection report by Brigadier-General Kempster were received :—" This battalion increased its high

---

[1] Another instance of *camaraderie* between different branches of the service was exhibited by the London Scottish Volunteers, between which regiment and the Gordon Highlanders a friendship of very old standing existed. They held a concert in their Drill Hall, and forwarded the proceeds, £25, to Colonel Dick-Cunyngham for the benefit of the relatives of Gordons who had fallen in battle or died from sickness during the late campaign.

AUTHOR'S NOTE.—A fund was started by the subscribers to the *Englishman* newspaper, Calcutta, called " The Gordon and Gurkha Fund." It amounted to between 4000 and 5000 rupees, and was divided between the 1st Gordons and 1st and 2nd Gurkhas for the widows and children of men who had died in the campaign.

reputation by its conduct in Tirah. The spirit of the battalion is high, its discipline is excellent, and its efficiency marked."

All officers, n.c. officers and men received the Frontier Medal with clasps " Punjab Frontier, 1897-98 " and " Tirah, 1897-98 " ; all those already in possession of the Indian Medal, 1895, were entitled to these clasps.

The battalion, being now under orders for home, left 514 n.c. officers and men at Gharial for transfer to the Second Battalion, and marched in two divisions on the 19th and 20th September for Rawal Pindi, where they encamped. On the 26th they entrained for Deolali, which they reached October 3rd ; as the train steamed into the station the Second Battalion, which had arrived from England on the 1st, was seen drawn up in quarter-distance column, under Lieut.-Colonel Dick-Cunyngham, V.C., who called for three cheers for their comrades of the First Battalion, their pipers playing " The Cock o' the North " as the battalion detrained, when the regiment, united for the first time, marched to camp. The First Battalion was in khaki and the Second in white. In the afternoon photographs were taken of the whole regiment on parade, and after spending eight hours agreeably together, the Second Battalion entrained, the band of the First playing the appropriate air, " O ye 'll tak' the high road and I 'll tak' the low road, and I 'll be in Scotland afore ye."

October 7th.—The First Battalion, under Colonel H. H. Mathias, embarked on the hired transport *Nubia* at Bombay for England,[1] but, owing to the strained relations between Britain and France caused by the Fashoda incident, at Suez they received orders by telegraph to land at Alexandria, which they did on the 19th September, and occupied Ras-el-Tin Barracks. Two officers, however, and forty men for discharge, with all the women and children, proceeded to England.

The battalion stayed in the land of the Pharaohs till the 24th November, when they embarked on the s.s. *Menes*, and, after touching at Malta and Gibraltar, arrived on the evening of the 8th December in Liverpool Docks, where many old comrades and friends had journeyed to meet them. Here they bade farewell to 100 time-expired men.

On the morning of the 9th the Gordons were cordially greeted and loudly cheered as they marched through the city to the station *en route* for Edinburgh. At Carlisle, Hawick, and other places these friendly demonstrations were renewed, till at 5 p.m. the train reached Waverley Station, to which only a few friends of the regiment were admitted, among them the members of the Gordon

---

[1] Embarked—22 officers, 2 warrant officers, 527 n.c. officers and men, 2 officers' wives, 21 women and 39 children.

Highlanders' Association.   The bands of the Scots Greys and the
Q.R.V.B., with the boy pipers of Dr Guthrie's School, led the way
as they marched out of the terminus, but as at Dargai it was only
as they got into the open that they realised the difficulties of the
situation.   The scene they now encountered baffles description.
All Scotland seemed to be there to do them honour, the cheering
was deafening, and so close did the crowds press in trying to shake
the soldiers by the hand, that at times they were fairly borne off their
feet, and could only make their way in single file, the Gordons
finding it more difficult to get through the friendly press of their
admirers than ever they did to break the ranks of their enemies.
The story of Dargai had been taken as an honour to Scotland, and
caused a display of patriotic enthusiasm which has seldom been
equalled.   It took all the exertions of the police and a squadron of
the Greys to enable the battalion to proceed along Princes Street,
where the houses were decorated with flags and the windows were
filled with ladies waving their kerchiefs.   At the Lothian Road one
might almost have walked on the people's heads, so closely were
they packed.   " D—n it, this is waur than Dargai ! " was the
exclamation of a struggling Highlander.   The scene was the same
all the way by Castle Terrace and the Lawnmarket till they reached
the Castle.   Here the old friendship of the Greys and Gordons was
pleasantly renewed, for the former had prepared a dinner for the
Gordons, and entertained them right royally.

On the following day the battalion received its official welcome
to the city, when all ranks were the guests of the Lord Provost
and the municipal authorities at a banquet in the Corn Exchange.
Flowers, flags, and festoons of evergreens ornamented the walls,
conspicuous among the decorations being the legends " Scotland for
Ever ! " "Dargai," and "Welcome to the Gay Gordons."   General
Chapman, commanding in Scotland, with a large number of distinguished noblemen and gentlemen, were present, while representatives from each squadron of the Greys had also been invited.   The
Chairman, in proposing the toast of " The Gordon Highlanders,"
said that the enthusiastic reception they had received from the
citizens on their arrival in Edinburgh the previous evening was
only an indication of the esteem and admiration in which their
gallant regiment was held by all Scotsmen, and, indeed, by every
British subject.   Colonel Mathias, in returning thanks, said the
battalion had only done its duty, but they were proud to find that
the manner in which they had done it was appreciated at home ;
from the time they set foot in the docks at Liverpool their journey
had simply been one royal progress.   He was only sorry that the
exigencies of the service required so many of his gallant men to
be left behind, but the report of the welcome their battalion had

received would warm their hearts. The Colonel gracefully alluded to the gallant services of the other regiments, European and native, who had served in the late campaign, and particularly to Major Norie, who was present, and the Gurkhas, who had so often fought side by side with the Gordons, notably in the Bara Valley just a year before.

The Lord Provost said that on his own part and on the part of his colleagues of the Corporation, he could assure the battalion that they would do all they could to make things pleasant for them during their stay in Edinburgh—that he had no doubt whatever that they would get on well with the civil authorities, and would show to the country that they were not only brave soldiers, but good citizens.

A great crowd had gathered outside the Corn Exchange, and as the battalion marched back to quarters, they were again enthusiastically received by the spectators.

Nothing had been spared to make the entertainment a success, and nothing could better show the improved habits of the time as compared with the reception of the troops after Waterloo (when the one idea of the entertainers was to fill their guests with strong drink [1]), than the cheery sobriety which characterised the present occasion.

On the Sunday there was a special service at St Giles' Cathedral, when the Rev. Mr Robertson, Garrison Chaplain, and the Rev. Mr Gillan, Chaplain with the Gordons in Tirah, officiated, the departure of the soldiers being witnessed by a large crowd who had waited patiently to see them.

The Corporation also entertained the women and children of the battalion. The sergeants were invited by the Management to the Pavilion Theatre, and they were also entertained by the Queen's Edinburgh Rifle Volunteers. The officers were the guests of the Caledonian Club, London—the Earl of March in the chair—when H.R.H. the Prince of Wales, Colonel-in-Chief, honoured the Club by his presence.

In deference to a wish expressed by the inhabitants of Aberdeen, a party numbering about 120, under Captain Tytler, was detached to the Granite City, where they were officially received at the station by the Lord Provost and members of the Town Council. On the way to barracks they experienced the same enthusiastic demonstrations of goodwill as in Edinburgh, and in the evening they were entertained by the civic authorities to an excellent repast in the Town and County Hall.

After the *fêtes* by which their countrymen and countrywomen did them honour, furloughs were granted, so that all could in turn

[1] "Anton's Memoirs."

visit their friends, and few had not some curious and valuable present from the East for mother and sisters at home, where, free for a time from the alarms of military life, each man could live at ease and whistle his own *réveillé*.

We may now leave the First Battalion to rest on its laurels in the capital of Scotland, while we follow the fortunes of the Second to the same period.

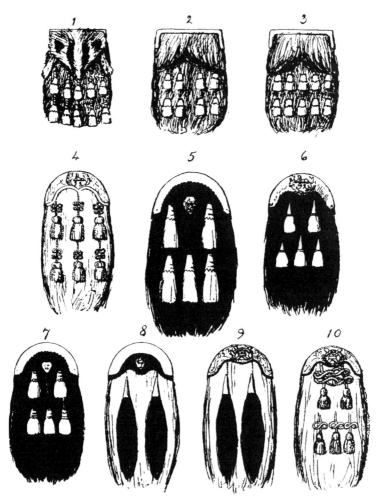

VARIOUS REGIMENTAL SPORRANS. *(See List of Illustrations)*
The tassels of Nos. 1, 2, and 3 have red tops

CHAPTER XXIX

1882–1898

IN January 1882, the establishment of the Second Battalion was reduced to 440 privates. The Commander-in-Chief was pleased to notify that Sir Evelyn Wood's report of the battalion before it left South Africa had been very satisfactory, as was His Royal Highness' own inspection on the occasion of its return from active service. In March the battalion received the new valise equipment, and the first draft to the First Battalion embarked for Malta on the 16th, consisting of 1 sergeant, 2 corporals, and 100 privates. They were followed by other large drafts in August and September. In May, Sergeant-major Ross was promoted quartermaster, Third Battalion, twenty-two years after he had enlisted as a drummer boy at Inverness.[1]

While at Portsmouth the n.c. officers and their families were entertained at Goodwood by the Duke of Richmond and Gordon.

During August and September men were received from, and sent to, the First Battalion, and men joined from the First Class Army Reserve of the 1st and 75th Regimental districts. On the 5th October the battalion, under Lieut.-Colonel White, V.C., embarked[2] on H.M.S. *Assistance*, landed at Granton on the 9th, and marched to Edinburgh Castle, being very cordially greeted by the assembled inhabitants as they marched through the city. In January 1883, Captain I. S. M. Hamilton and Lieutenant Gilpin Brown were seconded for service on the staff of the army in Egypt. Sergeant Alexander M'Gill was transferred to the Royal Scots as bandmaster. In March 1883 the battalion was completed with new white sporrans with two long black tassels, which replaced those of black goat-skin with five white tassels hitherto worn by n.c. officers and men,[3] the officers having a similar one for undress, and five gold tassels instead of six for full dress. Other minor changes had been made on the amalgamation with the 75th, the *Tiger* becoming the badge on the coat collars, which would have been appropriately matched had the *Sphinx* been retained on the bonnets.

[1] The late Major-General Forbes Macbean had a good story of this n.c. officer during the winter 1879-80 at Kabul. At church parade one Sunday the Adjutant had just finished telling off the parties for the different services. He was in the act of reporting to the C.O. "All ready to march off," when the Sergeant-major interrupted :—"Halt a minute, please, sir, there's a Roman Catholic fallen in with the Christians."

[2] Field officers, 3 ; captains, 3 ; subalterns, 7 ; staff, 2 ; sergeants, 38 ; corporals, 38 ; drummers, 19 ; privates, 345 ; women, 34 ; children, 34.

[3] Goats, which in old times formed part of a Highland farmer's wealth, are no longer kept, and their skins, once the cheapest for sporrans, are now imitated by other materials.

AUTHOR'S NOTE.—*June 1st,* 1883, the establishment of the regiment was altered to :—

	Officers.	Warrant Officers.	Sergeants.	Corporals.	Drummers and Pipers.	Privates.	TOTAL.
First Battalion	28	2	48	44	21	760	903
Second ,,	24	2	40	40	21	480	607
Depôt ,,	5	1	10	10	2	40	68

In August a Guard of Honour to H.M. Queen Victoria proceeded to Ballater under Captain Bayley and Lieutenants Boyd and A. D. Fraser.

Meanwhile numbers of the old soldiers had been discharged, and drafts sent to the First Battalion in Egypt, whose places were filled by young lads ; the minimum height for recruits had been reduced in 1881 to 5 feet 4 inches, and the battalion no longer presented the martial appearance which attracted so much attention on its arrival in England.

On the 31st May 1884, General John Alexander Ewart, C.B., was appointed Colonel of the Second Battalion, *vice* General Mark Kerr Atherley, deceased.

On the 30th June the battalion left Edinburgh by rail, embarked at Greenock on H.M.S. *Assistance*, disembarked at Devonport on the 3rd July, and occupied Raglan Barracks. They had been favourably reported on by Major-General A. M'Ian Mac-Donald (an old 92nd officer), who commanded in Scotland ; and in December 1884, H.R.H. the Commander-in-Chief was much gratified by the excellent order in which the battalion had been found, " notwithstanding the large influx of recruits."

An incident occurred at Devonport which is well worth recording. An officer of the 60th, quartered in the same barracks, related that, hearing loud cheering from the mess-room of the Gordon sergeants, he remarked to a passing Highlander, " You seem very happy at your mess to-day." " We are that, sir," replied the sergeant, " General Roberts is there ! "

At their dinner hour on that day, the sergeants had been equally astonished and gratified by a visit from Sir Frederick, who told them that having just been made Commander-in-Chief in India, he had come down from London on purpose to thank them, as representatives of his Afghan army, for their conduct which had enabled him to overcome all the difficulties of the campaign, and had thus led to his present appointment.[1]   He then paid a similar compliment to the sergeants of the 60th, and having lunched with the officers, he drove to the station, followed by numbers of Highlanders and riflemen, whose cheers expressed their appreciation of such a generous recognition of their services.

During the years 1884-85, large drafts were sent to the First Battalion. At Plymouth, Corporal K. Beresford was promoted to a commission in the Royal Irish Rifles.

Lieut.-Colonel G. S. White, V.C., C.B., having been appointed to the staff of the army in Egypt, was succeeded in the command of the battalion by Lieut.-Colonel J. C. Hay, under whose command they embarked on H.M.S. *Assistance* on the 11th December 1885

---

[1] This incident was corroborated by the late Field-Marshal Earl Roberts.

for Guernsey, with a detachment at Alderney ; at the latter place
the sound of the bagpipes brought a number of Highlanders
to meet them, who, it appeared, had lately settled in that fertile
island.

Lieut.-Colonel White crowned his military career by his
Defence of Ladysmith as commander of the garrison during the
South African War of 1899-1902. He died in 1912 as Field-
Marshal, whilst Governor of the Royal Hospital, Chelsea, the 1st
Battalion being present at his funeral in London. He had a fund
of old regimental anecdotes, of which the following is an example.
Talking of some of the old characters he had known in the Regiment, he told of one of the old incorrigibles with scores of
" drunks " against him, such as no longer exist in the sober
army of to-day. One day he came across this man as a prisoner
awaiting disposal at the Orderly Room and said, " Hallo, what 's
brought you here again ? " " Jist twa o' the polis, sir." " Um !
drunk again I suppose ? " " Yes, sir," shaking his head
sorrowfully, " baith o' them."

Another story is recorded by the late Colonel C. Greenhill
Gardyne who stayed with White when he was Governor of Gibraltar. Kaiser Wilhelm II had lately visited Gibraltar ; and when
driving with White, having asked permission to smoke, he turned
to the latter's aide-de-camp to ask for a light, which the aide could
not supply ; on which the Kaiser turned to his host :—" How is it
that a British Staff Officer cannot produce a match ? " to which
White replied, " Because, sir, the British Staff is matchless."

In 1886 drafts were sent to the First Battalion, and reservists
and recruits joined from the depôt. On the 1st of June the establishment was raised to 700 privates. At Guernsey, Sergeant M. F.
Fenwick was promoted Second Lieutenant in the Royal Lancaster
Regiment.

In May, Lieut.-Colonel J. C. Hay was appointed a Companion
of the Most Honourable Order of the Bath, and on the 30th of
June 1887, he bade farewell to the battalion in which he had served
thirty-two years. All ranks, including the families of the n.c.
officers and men, united in showing their respect and their regret
at parting. He was succeeded in the command by Lieut.-Colonel
Edward Essex from the First Battalion.

The battalion remained at Guernsey till the 26th August 1887,
when they embarked under Lieut.-Colonel Essex on board their
old friend the *Assistance*, and on the 30th landed at Belfast.

The reports of the battalion had hitherto generally been good,
but on the 21st January 1888, H.R.H. the Commander-in-Chief
" regrets to have to observe that the number of Courts-martial is
high."

In April 1889, Sergeant F. H. Gordon Cunliffe was promoted Second Lieutenant in the Seaforth Highlanders.

Detachments were at Willowbank, Downpatrick, and Carrickfergus. On the 21st of May 1889, H.R.H. Prince Albert Victor visited Belfast and honoured the officers' mess with his company at dinner.

In 1890 the size of the men and the proportion of Scots in the battalion were both much less than formerly.[1]

On the 26th June 1891, Lieut.-Colonel and Brevet Colonel Essex was placed on half-pay on completion of four years' service in command of a battalion, according to the rule lately established, and was succeeded by Lieut.-Colonel Oxley.

At this period a number of recruits had been sent from the London district. The officers of the depôt brought the matter to the notice of Lieut.-General Lyon Fremantle, then commanding in Scotland, who at once wrote to the Inspector-General of Recruiting on the subject.[2] A Londoner makes a good soldier in his proper place, but it is putting a square man in a round hole to send him to a Highland regiment, and the effect is to deter the real article. A gentleman in Skye mentioned that at this time a young shepherd of excellent character and the finest hillman in the district, having been fired with military ardour by the tales of a Gordon pensioner, went to Aberdeen and enlisted, expecting the society of his countrymen. He was put in a room with these London recruits, whose manners and slang were so entirely uncongenial that he bought his discharge, his disappointment discouraging his friends from following his example.

The battalion was inspected at the Curragh Camp by Major-General Lord R. D. Kerr, C.B., on the 6th July 1891, and in

---

[1] NATIONALITY AND HEIGHT OF SECOND BATTALION GORDON HIGHLANDERS, JANUARY 1ST, 1890

N.C. Officers and Men.		Height N.C. Officers and Men.		
		Feet.	Inches.	No. of Men.
English	130			
Scots	470	6	0 and upwards	8
Irish	15	5	11	10
Born in India or the Colonies	7	5	10	18
Foreigners	0	5	9	38
		5	8	76
Total	622	5	7	107
		5	6	138
		5	5	144
		5	4 }	83
		5	3½ }	
		Total		622

[2] Mentioned to the Author at the time by General Fremantle.

In 1893 the mess waistcoat of the officers of both battalions, which had been laced as in the original uniform of the Gordon Highlanders, was changed to plain red.

August 1893 by Major-General Moncrieff in Dublin, but the Record does not mention when they moved to these places.

At the Curragh, Sergeant Martin Turner was promoted Second Lieutenant in the Duke of Cornwall's Light Infantry, and Sergeant C. E. Birch, Second Lieutenant in the Royal Berkshire Regiment.

On the 9th June 1894, the battalion embarked at Dublin on H.M.S. *Tyne*, landed at Glasgow on the 12th, and occupied Maryhill Barracks.

.   .   .   .

It will be remembered by those interested in this History, that the Gordon Highlanders were raised by the Fourth Duke of Gordon in 1794. The year 1894 therefore marked their centenary, and since the return of the regiment to Scotland, arrangements had been in progress for celebrating this interesting event in the Life of the Regiment. On the 8th of August, all the officers serving, a large proportion of surviving retired officers, with Lieut.-Colonel Welby and two other officers of the Scots Greys, being a deputation from their regiment at Aldershot, assembled in Glasgow, and dined together, upwards of fifty in number, in Maryhill Barracks.

On the 9th the battalion paraded at 11 a.m., in review order, under Lieut.-Colonel Oxley, for the purpose of receiving new colours from His Grace the Duke of Richmond and Gordon, great-grandson of Alexander, Fourth Duke of Gordon. On the plateau which overlooks the parade ground, upwards of 5000 spectators stood closely packed, whilst special arrangements were made for the friends of officers and men, and for upwards of 300 old soldiers of the battalion, most of them wearing the Afghan Medal and Kandahar Star, who had gathered from various parts of Scotland.

The ceremony of trooping the old colours having been performed, the hymn " Brightly gleams our banner " was sung by the whole battalion, after which the prescribed prayers were read by the Chaplain. His Grace then presented the new colours, and addressed the battalion as follows :—

I esteem it a great honour to have been entrusted with the duty of presenting the new colours to the regiment which has so nobly illustrated the name of Gordon in every quarter of the globe. It is just 100 years since my great-grandfather raised this regiment, and the very names of the various battles blazoned on your colours bear testimony to the distinguished services of the regiment during the century that has elapsed. " Egypt," " India," " The Peninsula," " Waterloo," and " South Africa " make up the history of Great Britain during that period, and justify me in addressing to you the eloquent words of the Speaker of the House of Commons to the Great Duke of Wellington : " You have written your names with your conquering swords in the annals of the world, and we shall hand them down with exultation to our children's children."

I have presented to you the new colours in place of those which you received thirty years ago, at the hands of Lady MacDonald, the wife of a distinguished Colonel of the regiment, with full assurance that if this country should unfortunately be engaged in war, the Gordon Highlanders will be found, as of old, in the forefront of the battle, and will maintain the honour and glory of Scotland, as their predecessors have done, on many a well-fought field.

Lieut.-Colonel Oxley in reply, after thanking the Duke for presenting the colours, continued :—

The grand history of this battalion has been built up at the cost of 109 officers and upwards of 1600 men, who have fallen killed or wounded from its ranks. I trust that all now serving, and all who come after them, will bear in mind this record of bravery and devotion, be jealous of the reputation of their regiment, and true to their Queen and the colours which your Grace has presented to us.

As the battalion formed column, the veterans in four companies crossed the parade ground and joined it amidst great enthusiasm, and the column marched past ; after which Lieut.-Colonel Oxley turned the battalion about so that it faced the old soldiers, and spoke some words of welcome to them. The proceedings throughout elicited the greatest enthusiasm, and the smart appearance, perfect drill, and steadiness of the battalion called forth the warmest praise.

After the parade, a party of upwards of 300 ladies and gentlemen were entertained to luncheon in a large marquee. Lieut.-Colonel Oxley, in proposing the health of the Duke of Richmond and Gordon, alluded to the fact that it was through the energy and powerful influence of his Grace's father [1] that the army was granted the Peninsula Medal.

The former sergeants of the Gordon Highlanders were entertained in the Gymnasium by the warrant officers and sergeants of the battalion during their stay in Glasgow, and each of the companies and the band entertained the remainder of the veterans. Many of their wives and children were present, and upwards of 100 women and children were provided with a sumptuous meal. The day ended with Highland games, which were continued on the 10th, when the centenary rejoicings were brought to a close. It was much to the credit of the battalion that throughout this period of rejoicing there was no sign of intemperance.

September 11th.—A detachment—1 captain, 2 lieutenants, 3 sergeants, 47 rank and file—formed the guard of honour to Her Majesty at Ballater, and by Her Majesty's command the band of the battalion played at a bazaar held at Balmoral for the restoration of the Parish Church of Crathie.

On its return journey it was detained at Aberdeen to take part

[1] Who had at one time been a captain in the 92nd.

in the ceremony of handing over the old colours to the County of Aberdeen. The colours and escort were loudly cheered as they passed through the streets to the Municipal and County Buildings, where they were met by Lord Provost Stewart and the Town Council in their robes. Lieut.-Colonel Oxley then addressed the Lord Provost, alluding to the regiment having been embodied at Aberdeen, and more particularly to the fact that in 1881, when the 92nd went from India to South Africa, while the women and children returned to Great Britain in the middle of a very severe winter, lightly clad from a hot climate, a fund was raised in Aberdeenshire to help them on their arrival.

We now wish to mark our appreciation of the kindness shown to the regiment on that occasion by presenting to Aberdeenshire the old colours with which we now part. I would remind you, my Lord Provost, that these colours are very dear to us. They have been an emblem of our duty to our Queen and to our country, and we have endeavoured to do our duty consistently and well. We now place them in your keeping, sure that you and those who succeed you in the high office of Lord Provost of Aberdeen will watch over and protect and guard them.

He alluded to the neighbouring statue of George, the Fifth Duke of Gordon, first Colonel of the Gordon Highlanders ; he " did not know if all who passed the statue knew how much had been done for Scotland and for Europe by raising the Gordon Highlanders. If not, they should read the History of the Regiment."

Sergeant-major Hart, formerly of the 92nd, on behalf of a large body of men who had served in the battalion and who accompanied him, presented a beautiful wreath as a memorial of their comrades who had fallen in battle, expressing the hope that it would be allowed to remain with the colours.

In accepting the gift on behalf of the community, the Lord Provost in an eloquent speech assured Colonel Oxley, the officers, non-commissioned officers, and men that the history of their regiment was so intermixed with the history of the nation that it would be impossible to separate the two ; that the services of the Gordon Highlanders are well known to the people of Aberdeen, who, although fully aware that the regiment was never altogether recruited from that district, consider Aberdeen as now the home of the regiment. " We hope that in leaving these colours with us, you leave a record that will inspire our young men to prize the regiment more and more, to look with pride upon its noble history, and be always willing to serve under its colours."

July 1st, 1895.[1]—Lieut.-Colonel Oxley having completed four

---

[1] *June 30th*, 1895.—Lieut.-General C. E. P. Gordon, C.B., was appointed Colonel of the regiment, *vice* General Sir John Ewart, K.C.B., transferred to the Argyll and Sutherland Highlanders.

years' command, was placed on half-pay with the rank of Brevet Colonel, and the command devolved on Lieut.-Colonel the Hon. John Scott Napier.

July 24th, 1895.—Field-Marshal H.R.H. the Duke of Cambridge, who had so long been Commander-in-Chief of the British Army, and who was about to retire, visited Glasgow with the object of taking farewell of the troops in garrison, and honoured the officers of the Second Battalion with his presence at a ball in St Andrew's Hall. On the 25th he inspected the troops, consisting of the 66th Field Battery and the 2nd Gordon Highlanders under Lieut.-Colonel Napier. There were also present about thirty old soldiers, who paraded on the left of the saluting base, and to whom H.R.H. addressed a few gracious remarks ; he then personally directed the battalion in a number of manœuvres, after which a hollow square was formed, when H.R.H. said that the first time he had inspected this battalion was fifty years ago. It was then mainly composed of old soldiers, and their steadiness in drill could not be excelled in those days, but from what he had seen to-day, and taking into consideration the large proportion of young soldiers in the ranks, they compared well even with the veterans of the old 92nd. "Solid drill was the groundwork of discipline which always went hand in hand with *esprit de corps*, which is the backbone of an army."

When the veteran Commander-in-Chief left the barracks after luncheon, the whole battalion turned out of their own accord, the band playing "Auld Lang Syne," and the soldiers cheering heartily.

According to the new system recruiting was no longer carried on by parties from the regiment, but by recruiters for the army at large. They received a higher fee for men tall enough for the Household Troops than for those for the cavalry and infantry of the line, and the size of the men of the regiment having deteriorated, at this time the officers of both battalions, with their usual *esprit de corps*, formed a fund to be used for the purpose of encouraging the enlistment of the best class of men.

In the spring of 1896 a detachment of 1 sergeant, 29 rank and file, under Lieutenant the Hon. R. F. Carnegie, proceeded to Aldershot to be trained, and formed part of a force of Mounted Infantry which embarked on the 25th April for South Africa, owing to the disturbed state of the territory of Rhodesia.

August 25th.—The battalion, under Lieut.-Colonel Napier, left Glasgow by rail for Aldershot, there to take part in the autumn manœuvres, and were encamped at Watts' Common.

Military manœuvres gave country people the opportunity of seeing and observing soldiers *en masse*, and they found them not the idle dissolute set they are conventionally represented to be, but a quiet, orderly body of men who work hard and play hard.[1]

On the 21st September the battalion marched from its camp, and occupied Malplaquet Barracks.

On the 11th February 1897, Lieut.-Colonel the Hon. J. S. Napier relinquished the command on being removed to an appointment on the Staff. He was succeeded by Lieut.-Colonel W. H. Dick-Cunyngham, V.C., from Major, Argyll and Sutherland Highlanders, to which regiment he had been previously promoted from the Gordons.

Many of the Mounted Infantry detachment in South Africa had volunteered for the Mashonaland Police Force, and on May 31st, 1897, a letter was received by the commanding officer from the G.O.C. Natal and Zululand, quoting a telegram from Earl Grey, Administrator of Rhodesia, with reference to these Mounted Infantry—"Please accept my best thanks for sending us such good men."

On the 22nd of June the battalion, under Lieut.-Colonel Dick-Cunyngham, proceeded to London, and formed part of the force, 46,943 in number, under command of H.R.H. the Duke of Connaught, K.G., etc., which was on duty on the occasion of the Jubilee celebration of the sixtieth year of the reign of Her Majesty Queen Victoria. During the procession of Her Majesty through the streets of London, the battalion was on duty at Hyde Park Corner.

The last time the battalion (then the 1st 92nd) had taken part in a great ceremonial in London was on the occasion of Nelson's funeral in 1806.

On the 25th the detachment of Mounted Infantry rejoined from South Africa.

At this time a number of sergeants of the army were employed with the Egyptian army, and one of them, Sergeant J. Scott-Barbour of the battalion, was afterwards promoted lieutenant in the Highland Light Infantry " in recognition of his services in the Soudan."

July 13*th*.—The battalion was inspected by Major-General

---

[1] *Spectator*, January 1899.

It has been repeatedly asserted that numbers of discharged soldiers seek refuge in the poorhouse, and become a burden on the rates. This is absolutely disproved by a Parliamentary paper issued in 1898, by which it appears that in December 1897 there were, of the industrial male population of the United Kingdom over twenty years of age (excluding soldiers and ex-soldiers), 1 in 37 in receipt of relief from the rates. Of the whole male population, including all classes, rich and poor, except soldiers and ex-soldiers, 1 in 45 were in receipt of relief, while of reservists or discharged soldiers, with or without pensions, there was only 1 in 176 receiving relief from the rates.—*Times*, August 19th, 1898. There are, however, many pretended soldiers who try to excite commiseration and charity by claiming to have served in the army, sometimes showing false certificates.

In 1896, Regimental Savings Banks were done away with.

Osborne Barnard, commanding the Second Infantry Brigade.   He considered it to be in a highly efficient condition, and complimented the Lieut.-Colonel " on the magnificent marching powers of the men, which, in his opinion, left nothing to be desired."

On August 20th, 1897, Lieut.-General (local General) Sir George White, V.C., G.C.B., G.C.I.E., Commander-in-Chief in India, was gazetted Colonel of the Gordon Highlanders *vice* Major-General and Honorary Lieut.-General C. E. P. Gordon, C.B., deceased.

On the 10th of June 1898, as already mentioned, Field-Marshal H.R.H. Albert Edward, Prince of Wales (who had been Colonel of the Third Battalion), was gazetted Colonel-in-Chief of the Gordon Highlanders, and in that capacity His Royal Highness honoured the regiment by marching past Her Majesty Queen Victoria at the head of the Second Battalion at Aldershot.   He was also graciously pleased to preside at the Regimental Dinner at the Hôtel Metropole on the 20th June 1898 and 17th June 1899.

There had been regimental dinners of the 92nd occasionally, both in Edinburgh and in London, from about 1863.   On the 26th May 1882, at a dinner in the Albion Tavern, Field-Marshal Lord Strathnairn in the chair, Colonel D. M. Crichton Maitland, Grenadier Guards (formerly of the 92nd), was deputed to arrange with the First Battalion (late 75th) for a joint annual regimental dinner club, which began in 1883.   On the 17th June 1890 the present club, embracing the two regular and the third (reserve) battalions, held its first meeting at the Albion.

At this period, associations of old Gordons had been inaugurated in the great centres of industry to which men from all parts of Scotland flock for employment.   They are formed on the lines of the Clan societies, for the social meeting of the members and the aid of those who require it.   The Gordon Highlanders' Associations admit to membership n.c. officers and soldiers who have served in the first or second battalions ; and as honorary members, officers who have so served.   They keep up the connection with old comrades, assist men of good character to obtain employment when they leave the regiment, and encourage young men of good character to join it.

The first to be instituted was in Glasgow, at a meeting in the Waterloo Rooms, on the 26th September 1888, Major A. R. A. Boyd in the chair.   The first President was Mr John Gilmour.

On the 16th February 1889, a meeting of old Gordons was held in Edinburgh, Colonel A. Forbes Mackay in the chair, when a Gordon Highlanders' Edinburgh Association was formed, with Sir George Warrender, Bart. of Lochend, as Hon. President, and Mr Thomas Fife, President.

OFFICERS, 2ND BATTALION, ALDERSHOT, 1897

SHOWING VARIATIONS OF UNIFORM IN USE FOR DIFFERENT OCCASIONS JUST BEFORE THE INTRODUCTION OF KHAKI INTO THE ARMY AT HOME

1. Orderly officer.
2. Review order.
3. Drill order.
4. Court-martial order (sitting).
5. Mess dress (trews).
6. Review order.
7. Captain of the day.
8. Transport duties (sitting).
9. Levée dress.
10. Signalling duties.
11. Court-martial order.
12. Marching order.
13. Marching order (cloaked).
14. Drill order.
15. Adjutant, drill order.
16. Commanding officer, review order (Lieut.-Colonel W. H. Dick-Cunyngham, V.C.).
17. Field officer of the day (marching order).
18. Marching order (field-day order).
19. Musketry duties.
20. Mess dress (ball dress).
21. Levée order.
22. Barrack duties.

On January 12th, 1895, a similar Association was formed at Aberdeen at a meeting held in Holburn Parish Church Hall, Mr A. M. Cumming (late quartermaster-sergeant, Gordon Highlanders) in the chair. He was elected President ; Hon. President, His Grace the Duke of Richmond and Gordon ; Hon. Vice-Presidents, the Marquis of Huntly and the Lord Provost of Aberdeen. This Association was amalgamated with the County Association [1] in 1897, and all subscribers to the funds were admitted as honorary members, Captain H. V. Brooke being elected President. It is now joined to the Gordon Highlanders' Memorial Institute.

Each Association has its quarterly or other meetings, besides a great annual gathering, where old comrades of all ranks renew their youth by talking of old times, while they are kept in touch with the regiment by the presence of officers and soldiers still serving. These associations have had the happiest effect on the life of the regiment.

The Second Battalion remained at Aldershot till the 6th September 1898, when it embarked at Southampton on the P. & O. transport *Nubia*, sailed on the 7th, receiving in the Solent a "goodbye" from H.R.H. the Prince of Wales, and landed at Bombay on the 30th. After the picturesque meeting with the First Battalion at Deolali, as described above, the Second proceeded to Umballa, where I will leave them till some abler pen than mine recounts the gallant services so soon to be performed in South Africa, not only by the First and Second, but by the Reserves of the Third Battalion, and not least by the Volunteer Companies. These latter, already thoroughly trained and efficient, most patriotically came forward, without the inducement of high pay or the *éclat* of serving in a special corps, satisfied with the honour of doing yeoman service in the ranks of their territorial regiment.

---

[1] An Association of county gentlemen interested in the regiment, though not necessarily belonging to it.

CHAPTER XXX

IN the beginning of this book I gave a sketch of life in the Highlands at the end of the 18th century, and its relation to recruiting. In this connection it may be interesting to consider the
effect of the social and economic changes which have taken place
throughout Great Britain during the hundred years of the Life of the
Regiment. In the districts where the Gordons were raised, these
changes were, in the first instance, principally felt by the introduction of sheep-farming, which replaced the cultivation necessary for
rearing cattle. The same process had taken place on the Borders
and in parts of England at an earlier period, and its tendency was
to lessen the numbers employed on the land. In the Highlands
the immediate result was a redistribution of the people rather than
a decrease in the population, which, in fact, steadily increased till
the great famine of 1846-7, after which it gradually fell to its present
level ; [1] but the clearance of the glens produced a change in the life
and spirit of the Highlanders, which, along with other causes hereafter noticed, affected recruiting.

It was shown in the opening chapters how the ranks of the
Gordons were filled by the influence of the lairds and tacksmen, of
whom many had served in the army, in whom the people had confidence ; and whose sons, familiar with the recruits and with their
parents, formed the majority of the officers.

A touching instance of the feeling between officer and soldier is
told by the Rev. Charles Macdonald, priest of Moidart. Many
years after the death of Simon MacDonald of Morar, Major in the
Gordon Highlanders, a veteran who had served under him, having
been threatened with eviction, went to the grave of his old officer,
and, kneeling down, conjured him to intervene and prevent this
injustice to his follower, emphasising his entreaty by striking vigorously with his stick on the green sod of the grave, and exclaiming in
Gaelic, " Simon, Simon, you were ever good to me ; come once
more to the help of an old comrade and save him from being driven
from hearth and home ! " It is satisfactory to know that his trust
was rewarded. His action being reported to some of the neighbouring gentry, their representations prevailed with the estate
agents, and he was allowed to remain.

The old race of resident gentlemen-tacksmen [2] and their small
tenants was gradually replaced in the glens by graziers from the
Borders and their shepherds, but though the Highlanders soon

---

[1] The population of the Highland counties, except Argyll and Sutherland, is slightly
greater than in 1801. The greatest decrease in the last ten years is not in the Highlands, but in
the lowland County of Selkirk.—Census of Scotland, 1801 to 1901. See Appendix VIII.

[2] A list made by Alexander M'Lean, Esq. of Pennycross, gives about 100 officers of the
army and navy connected with the Mull and Morven districts who served during the French
wars. There are not nearly 100 gentlemen altogether now in the same districts, of whom,
however, about nineteen have served or are serving in the army, four of them in the Gordons.

learned the management of sheep stock, sheep-farming in its turn is likely to disappear owing to foreign competition in wool ; and thus what had become another home industry will follow the failure, from similar causes, of the kelp manufacture, charcoal burning, and the once important trade in birchwood. In the corn-growing districts of the north, the light iron plough, worked by one man with two horses, replaced the heavy wooden plough with ten oxen and two men which was in use a hundred years ago.[1] The reaping machine instead of the sickle, the threshing machine instead of the flail ; all these are improvements in agriculture, but have helped to reduce the numbers employed.

Meanwhile various causes, chiefly the effects, direct or in-direct, of railways and steamboats, have given an abnormal value to Highland scenery and sport. The embarrassed native landlords are to a great extent replaced by richer proprietors, and the great sheep farmers by sporting tenants. Both classes are generous, and do much for the material well-being of the people, who are, as a rule, better housed and in every way better off than at any former period.[2] Still these gentlemen for the most part are only resident for a few months of the year, and with some exceptions are not in touch with the inner life and ideas of the Highlanders as were the old chiefs and gentry so long as they lived constantly among them, ruling them, but entering into their joys and their sorrows. " Co ris a theid mi g'am ghearan, 's gun Mac-Mhic Ailean 'am Muideart ? "[3]

So many of their natural leaders being gone, and the influence of the remainder greatly decreased, the people are left to follow the teaching of the popular Press[4] and the political agitator, who are apt to re-echo complaint and intensify discontent, and in general do not encourage enlistment in the army. A certain section of the clergy, with a perverted idea of Christianity, confused harmless pleasures with vice, and did their best to stop such innocent and intellectual amusements as music and the recitation of the poems and legends which did so much to foster the martial spirit ; while manly games and the graceful exercise of dancing were for some years rigorously tabooed. Though the severity of this unreal and repellent religious teaching has been relaxed, it had a chilling effect on military ardour, and it became the young Highlander's ambition to imitate the townsman, whose habits his ancestors despised. It

[1] " Northern Rural Life," by W. Alexander, LL.D.

[2] According to the report on the social condition of Lewis by the Crofter Commission, 1902, the increased comforts in food and clothing have not been accompanied by an improve-ment in health and strength. On the contrary, they are, with excessive tea-drinking, held responsible for a marked increase in dyspepsia, rheumatism, and nervous diseases.

[3] " To whom shall I carry my complaint when there is no Clanranald in Moidart ? " Said when the Chief of that name was killed at Sheriffmuir.

[4] A newspaper which now costs 1d. cost 7d. in 1830 for a much smaller sheet.

has often been repeated, and probably with some truth, that military service was unpopular in England, where the ancient jealousy of a standing army was the origin of the dislike. There was, however, no such prejudice in the Highlands, where the best youth of the country formed the bulk of the old Highland regiments. English opinion has, however, been reflected in the north, and particularly among Highlanders who are resident in the cities of the south. But for their kilted representatives in the army, Highlanders, as apart from other Scotsmen, would be practically unknown to the outside world, and Celtic gatherings constantly claim credit for the deeds of the Highland regiments ; yet so lately as 1898, at a meeting of the Highland Societies in Glasgow, the question whether Highlanders should be encouraged to join the army was advisedly and seriously debated, when the contrary was carried by a majority.

Notwithstanding the decline of native industries, the wealth brought into the country of late years and the employment it gives has enormously raised the wages of labour, while education and the easier means of communication have opened many careers besides soldiering. The police force, offering as it does something of the military life, though without the same opportunities of distinction as the army—the police of the world—attracts, by its high pay and pension, the very same class who used to form the Grenadier Company of the Gordons ; and the fact remains that comparatively few, though they are probably the most high-spirited of the Highland youth, at present enlist in the regular army.[1]

These general changes to some extent affect also the nationality of the officers, of which, however, the official returns hardly give a fair impression, the basis being the place of birth ; for in the present day a Highland gentleman is as likely to have been born in London as in Lochaber. Yet it is evident from their names that the officers of the Gordons are, like their men, mostly of Scottish and many of Highland blood, and it is equally evident from the late history of the regiment that the traditional good feeling between all ranks is still strong, though it may not date, as in former times, from a period anterior to their joining the regiment. There was a time when commissions in the army were bestowed upon infants, who were " on leave " till old enough to assume their unearned rank. The nurse of one of these embryo soldiers, passing through the poultry-

---

[1] In the 72nd and 79th Regimental Districts, which embrace the counties of Inverness, Ross and Cromarty, Sutherland, Caithness, Nairn, and Moray, there were enlisted for the various branches of the regular army in 1901 :—72nd, 70 ; 79th, 47—total, 117 men. 1902—72nd, 104 ; 79th, 44—total, 148 men.—Return from Regimental District. This is, however, a great increase on the numbers in 1893-5. For comparison we give the figures for the Regimental District (counties of Kincardine, Aberdeen, and Banff) for recruiting years 1926-7-8. They are : Total 208, of which 138 joined the Gordons ; 169 and 100 (emigration and a decrease of pay adversely affected recruiting) ; and 224 and 145.

yard, being asked by the hen-wife after her charge, who was clinging for protection from a warlike turkey, replied—" Oh, the Captain's a fine wee mannie, but he's sair hadden doun wi' the Bubbly-jock ! " Even after the Gordons were raised, young officers occasionally joined the army, as till recently did midshipmen in the navy, at twelve or fourteen years of age.[1]

This is all changed for the better, and only highly instructed young men of riper years are admitted, who are socially equal and educationally superior to their predecessors, though possibly the often recurring courses of special instruction they are required to attend, and the duties performed apart from their battalion may prevent their being so constantly with the same company, which was formerly considered to be of the greatest importance. In the early days of the regiment the habits of all classes were more homely, and less money was required to support the position of an officer. Except in the hunting field, uniform was always worn, and thus the great expense consequent on plain clothes was avoided. The first army dress regulations were published in 1822, and even then a good deal of latitude was allowed to Highland regiments, especially in things pertaining to the Highland garb.

The social circumstances already mentioned have almost entirely done away with the use of the Highland dress among the peasantry. In the winter of 1852 I took part in a week's shooting at Castle Menzies, where the Chief and the neighbouring gentry joined in the festivals and encouraged the native customs of the country. On this occasion there were, including the guns, about 110 men present, and of these over seventy wore the kilt. Some years later knicker-bockers were introduced by the sporting tenants and became the fashion with all.[2] To wear the kilt came to be (wrongly) considered " fast " for any but gentlemen and soldiers. While this is the case in civil life, however, the Highland uniform has become more general in the army. It has been adopted of late years by the Cameron and Gordon Militia, and by many of the Volunteer corps. The quality and comfort of the soldiers' clothing is greatly im-proved : formerly, whatever the weather, he never wore his great-coat except on duty ; now he goes to the other extreme, and may be seen wearing it when civilians, three times his age, are more lightly clad. The soldier no longer carries the immense weight

---

[1] When John Malcolm (afterwards G.C.B. and Governor of Bombay), then not quite twelve years old, was taken to be seen by the directors with a view to a commission in the East India Company's service, he was about to be rejected on account of his youth, when a director asked, " Why, my little man, what would you do if you were to meet Hyder Ali ? " " Cut aff his heid," was the laconic reply of the little Scotsman. " You'll do," said the director, and he was passed.—" Sidelights on the Georgian Period," by G. Paston.

[2] This change is very noticeable in Landseer's pictures and " Scrope on Deer-stalking," as compared with later illustrations of that sport by Crealocke and Millais.

under which he formerly marched and generally fought—a decided advantage, though it may sometimes result in his being separated from his kit. Tattoo formerly recalled men to their barracks at 9 p.m., a rule which is now relaxed to an extent that would not be permitted at a university or in a private family. Among the ameliorations of military life none is more marked than the separate quarters for married men, which formerly did not exist. An institution now long and rightly abolished was the barrack-room court-martial. If by being slovenly or careless a man brought discredit on his company he was tried by his comrades, whose award was more dreaded than that of the orderly room.

The Gordons have generally been a well-educated class of men, and the regimental school has often been noticed for excellence. Indeed, the admirable schools which for 300 years had existed in every parish in Scotland gave Scottish soldiers a marked superiority, till the introduction of Board schools south of the Tweed put their English comrades on a footing of educational equality. In former times a valuable library was carried about with the regiment for the use of the soldiers. The books, I understand, were ordered to be disposed of about twenty years ago on account of causing an undue quantity of baggage.

For many years after the Gordons were raised Gaelic was the language of the majority of the men, while most of the officers could also speak it. The late MacDonald of Glenaladale used to tell how, as a young man on a visit to Edinburgh, he dined at the Castle with the 92nd soon after they returned from Waterloo, when the commanding officer said—"Here is a young Highland laird, let Gaelic be the language to-night"; and with a few exceptions the officers present continued to converse in the Celtic tongue. In the present day the Highland lairds or Highland officers who can do so are the exceptions, and it is seldom a recruit joins who cannot express himself in English, for the Highlanders are now generally bilingual, and though Gaelic is the language commonly used and best understood, many speak English more correctly than a Yorkshireman. The number who can speak Gaelic is yearly diminishing, and in a few places, such as the Highland districts of Banff and Aberdeen, the language is gradually dying out. Apropos of the mother tongue is the story of a Gaelic-speaking Scottish nobleman who, on making the acquaintance of a distinguished officer, late of the Gordons, asked him if he had the Gaelic; "D—— it, man, I say my prayers in Gaelic!" was the reply.

The practice of rifle shooting, lectures, and various courses of instruction, with a less mechanical drill, give the modern soldier more interest in his profession. The rules of the service are more elastic and its advantages increased by the abolition of many charges which formerly were made on his pay ; and if the recruit is not always a hardy hill-man, his strength and activity are developed by an admirable system of physical drill.

Though some of the reasons which formerly made the Highlanders take freely to soldiering have not now the same force, there can be little doubt that if the life and emoluments of the soldier improve in the future as they have done in the immediate past, the natives of the north will again take their place in the ranks to their own advantage and the credit of their country.

AUTHOR's NOTE.—Since the above was written, I find that a new rate of pay will come into force April 1904, so that the soldier's position and prospects financially are now better, winter and summer, than those of the majority of his countrymen, even without taking into account the chance of rising to commissioned rank. See Appendix VIII.

APPENDICES

I

COLOURS

Lord Hopetoun (now Marquis of Linlithgow) informs me that he has at Hopetoun a colour inscribed—

MANDORA

BERGEN   2ND BATT.   OP ZEE
XCIIND REGT.

EGYPT

and also a colour very much tattered and torn, which is kept in a glass case. He does not know its history, but it is probably the Waterloo colour referred to by Mr Milne, as noticed in note, p. 22.

Lord March describes those at Gordon Castle thus :—

" 92nd—Buff colour, small union next pole, embroidered crown and thistle within garter and embroidered wreath round. Scrolls—' Gordon Highlanders ' and ' 92 ' below. Sphinx in bottom corner. Size, 5 ft. 6 ins. by 4 ft. 8 ins."

" Large union colour, ' 92 ' ; also a shield in centre, wreath round, no crown. Sphinx in corner. Size, 5 ft. 8 ins. by 4 ft. 6 ins."

These may be the earliest colours with the number changed from " 100 " to " 92 " and " Sphinx " added. The " buff " colour may be yellow faded, but till about 1856 the facings worn by the officers were very pale yellow or buff, and the colours may have been the same.

II

This song, made by the sweetheart of a Gordon Highlander, was taken down from the recitation of an aged native of Badenoch, by the Rev. Thomas Sinton, minister of Dores, who describes it as delightfully characteristic of the feeling in that district in the early part of the 19th century :

Tha Nollaig a' tighinn,
'S cha bhi mi cridheil gu ceòl,
Cha 'n eisd mi ceòl fìdhle,
'S cha 'n fhaighear mi 's an tigh-òsd ;
Cha'n eisd mi ceòl fìdhle,
No ni 's am bi spòrs,
'S mi fo chumhadh an fhleasgaich so,
Ghreas mi gu 'n fhòd.

Tha mo chion air a' ghille
Dh' fhàg fo iomadan mi,
'S chaodh cha ghabh mi fear eile,
Gus an tig thu 'mi rìs ;

Gus an tig thu 'mi dhachaidh
Le do *phass* agad sgriòbht',
B' annsa pòg bho d' bheul daithte
Na n' bheil aca do ni.

Tha no chion air a' ghaisgeach
Is maisich tha beò,
Dha 'm math an tig breacan,
Feile preasach is còt ;
Ite 'n eoin an deadh-chleachdadh
Air an fheasach is bòidhch'—
'S thug mi gaol dhuit gun teagamh
A ghreas mi gu'n fhòd.

Tha mo ghaol-sa an comhnaidh
Fo chòt' aig an Righ,
'S gur e 'm fleasgach is boidhche
Thug Diuc Gordon bhuam fhìn ;
Ach na 'n tight' thu air fòrlach,
'Smi gu'm pòs' tu gun ni,
'S ged a bhiodh tu a' d' Choirneal,
Ghaoil ! bu leòir dhuit-sa mi.

'S lìonar maighdean òg uasal
Tha 's an uair so gun mhiadh,
'S mur pòs iad ri buachaillean,
Cha 'n eil daoin'-uails' ann dha 'n trian ;
'S ma 's a fiù leo bhi luaidh riu—
Balaich shuarach nach fhiach—
'S ann tha na fiùranan suairce
'S an ruaig fo an Righ !

The following translation, though not absolutely literal, gives very closely the spirit of the original :—

Though Christmas is coming, no joy may be mine,
My true love has left me in sorrow to pine.
No mirth may delight me, nor Music's gay sound ;
Ah, would I were lying beneath the cold ground !

He is dear to my heart, though he causeth my pain :
No lover shall woo me till he come again.
More precious than riches, or holding of land,
Is the kiss from his lips, and the clasp of his hand.

How gallant his presence, my brave soldier lad,
Arrayed all in scarlet, with kilt and with plaid ;
With feathers that wave from his bonnet of blue,
And a heart full of fondness, so constant and true !

My hero delights in the glories of war ;
'Twas the Great Duke of Gordon that led him afar.
But whether as private or Colonel he came,
The troth that we plighted would still be the same !

How many young maidens are sighing in vain
For the lads that are gone from the hillside and plain ;
If they will, let them wed with the herdsman or clown,
But mine be the Soldier that fights for the Crown !

A. A. G. G.

III

NA GORDANAICH [1]

Air fonn—AM FEILE PRESACH

Seisd.—Fair am botul, lion a' chuach,
    Cuir an deoch so làn mu 'n cuairt :
    Slaint' nan gaisgeach choisinn buaidh,
    Luchd bhreacan-guailne 's boineidean.

'S e Morair Hunndaidh thog air tùs,
Feadh nam beann, nan gleann, 's nan stùc,
Na Gordanaich, fir òg mo ruin,
A choisinn cliù 'sna cogaidhean.

B' e colg nan àrmunn, cùl an lann,
A ruag an nàmh 'san Eiphit thall,
Aig Aboukir mu bhruaich na Nile,
Nuair thug na Frangaich coinneamh dhaibh.

La Chorùna chluich na sàir,
'S thuirt Moore an treun 's e'n glaic a' bhàis,
Mu'n dùin mo shùil a chaoidh's gu bràth,
Thoìr dhomh, mar fhàbhar, sealladh dhiubh.

Is lionmhor blàr 'san d' fhuair iad cliù,
Fuentes, Maya, Nive, Toulouse.
Quatre-bràs 'us Bhatarlù,
Almarez, 'us Bhittoria.

Bhoillsg an reul as ùr an dràsd,
Fo chomannd MhicIllebhàin ; [2]
Aig Cabul chaidh dhaibh mar 'b'àbhaist,
Thug an nàmh na bonnaibh di.

---

[1] This song was composed by Mr John MacFadyen, the well-known Bard, during the Afghan War.
[2] Alluding to Major G. Stewart White.

Bha fir-stàit a' cur an cèill,
Mòid 'us connsachaidh gun fheum,
Ged 's geur na pinn, cha d'rinn iad rèit,
Gus'n d'ràinig luchd nam boineidean.

Sud na laoich nach gèill 'san strìth,
Na leoghainn chalm 'san earb an rioghachd,
Co e'n nàmh nach creanaich cridh
Roimh luchd nam pìc 's nam boineidean.

Soraidh bhuam gu sluagh mo ghràidh,
Is balla-dìon do'n tir a dh'fhàg ;
Is tric air chuimhne 'n seirm nam bàrd
    " A' phàirc 'gam fàl na boineidean."

THE GORDON HIGHLANDERS

Chorus—Pass the flagon, fill the cup,
    Charge the brimming glasses high,
    To pledge the lads with kilt and plumes,
    The sons of victory.

From mountain-side and rocky glen,
They hear, they answer Huntly's call—
The gallant Gordons well-beloved—
    Prepared to fight or fall.

Dauntless behind the flashing blades
Our warriors chase the routed foe ;
In Egypt by the banks of Nile
    They laid the Frenchmen low

[1] Upon Corunna's blood-stained field
They steadfast stood, their courage high ;
The dying Moore was fain to turn
    On them his darkening eye.

In many a fight their fame was won—
Almarez and Vittoria too ;
Fuentes, Maya, Nive, Toulouse,
    And fateful Waterloo.

And now the star of their renown
In Afghan wars shines bright once more,
Where Stewart White hath shown the road
    They trod so oft of yore.

[1] This verse applies more properly to the 42nd, Moore being near them when wounded.

When Statesmen urge the hot debate
With argument of warring words,
They raise a storm they cannot quell
    Till speak the keen-edged swords.

O Guardians of your Country's fame,
The foremost found where all are brave—
What foe is he that shrinks not back,
    Where Highland bonnets wave ?

They guard us well, those steadfast hearts,
Their homes' defence and sheltering stay ;
The Bards shall sing their gallant deeds,
    And blessings crown their way !

Fifty years ago, singing on the line of march was, as it probably still is, a decided feature in the Life of the Regiment. On the call, "Singers to the front," the best vocalists came forward, often book in hand, their arms being carried by other men ; all joined in the chorus, and the effect was very picturesque and inspiriting. Indeed, no instrumental music is so good for marching. On these occasions I have heard many of the best of the old songs of Scotland, some of them little known.

IV

Death of Lieutenant Forbes and Colour-Sergeant Drummond

On receipt of Mr Drummond Forbes' letter, as mentioned in note, page 124, I at once wrote to Surgeon-Lieutenant-Colonel J. Duke, from whose account my description was principally taken ; to Major-General Douglas, who was adjutant and present on the occasion ; to the Rev. G. W. Manson, Presbyterian Chaplain, who was with the guns ; and to the Secretary of the Gordon Highlanders' Association in Glasgow. Colonel Duke wrote in answer from Srinagar, Kashmir : "The incident of Forbes' death I saw with my glasses quite clearly. . . . Forbes dropped backwards and fell over, leaning partly on his elbow. He was *alone*, and the first man I saw hit. . . . As the Afghans then came on I dropped my glasses." Colonel Duke then goes on to say that Surgeon (afterwards Sir George) Robertson continued looking through his glass, and exclaimed as recorded in the text. Colonel Duke's letter continues—"Forbes, a cool and gallant young officer, as proved on this and other occasions, fell while leading on his men ; the colour-sergeant died in trying to defend his officer."

General Douglas (after explaining details of formation to be altered) says, "Otherwise I think your description quite accurate," and he goes on to say that what Dick-Cunyngham wrote was only a rumour ; "No one could be found who could state that they actually saw Forbes defending Colour-sergeant Drummond. White, Cunyngham, and myself were all together going up the hill when Forbes was killed on the top—none of us saw it."

Mr Manson writes :—" I lived always *with* the regiment, and heard naturally a good deal of what was discussed in camp and at mess. My recollection of what I heard about the manner in which Lieutenant Forbes met his death tallies with the account you have put together on the basis of Duke's printed narrative, supplemented by the memory of Lieutenant Grant and Major White. Hensman's account in his book gives the version set forth in Dick-Cunyngham's letter. Hensman was a professional correspondent of the *Pioneer*. He made it his business to verify his facts as far as possible. On that particular day I did not see Hensman on the ground, and I feel as nearly sure as I can venture to be that he is relating, not what he *saw* of this incident, but what he heard. On the other hand, Duke's statement is, as you rightly put it, that of an eye-witness. This I can distinctly corroborate. I was standing with the group behind the guns at that moment ; Duke was surveying the scene through his field-glasses. It was a bright, crisp, frosty day, the air remarkably clear and brilliant, and the naked eye could follow plainly the movements of the little figures on the mountain side and crest. From the exclamations of those who were using glasses I gathered that the officer was ' down,' and *then* that a Highlander who was closely following the officer was also ' down.' " Mr Manson mentions that, not having glasses and his sight being only moderately good, he could not have distinguished the rank of the figures on the ridge ; " but the rapid comments, or rather exclamations, of those who were using glasses, showed that they believed it was the officer who was first. I accept Duke's statement as the authentic one, and I see no improbability in his having been able to see what he says he did see." Mr Manson's letter speaks of Lieutenant Forbes as a delightful companion, of his loveable character, good nature and buoyant spirits, while yet he was serious in the pursuit of his profession.

Mr Maver, Secretary G.H. Glasgow Association, wrote that he had seen a number of members, giving their names, who had been with the regiment in Afghanistan, and that all agreed that the account in the text is correct.

Major D. F. Gordon, to whom the whole account of the campaign was sent for remarks or correction, wrote, " As far as my recollection goes, it is so accurate that I am unable to suggest any corrections."

V.—

THE MACDONALDS OF DALCHOSNIE,

Compiled by S. D. Stewart, Esq.

THE MACDONALDS OF DALCHOSNIE are a branch of THE McDONNELS OF KEPPOCH, which family they now represent.

ALLAN MACDONALD (First of Dalchosnie).
Fought in 1689 under Viscount Dundee, and was present at Killiecrankie.

JOHN MACDONALD, Officer in Atholl Regiment in 1715.

DONALD MACDONALD, Officer in Atholl Regiment in 1715. Executed at Preston.

DONALD MACDONALD, Officer, Old Buffs. Fell in Germany, 1745.

ALEXANDER MACDONALD, Killed at Culloden, 1746.

ALLAN MACDONALD, Out in 1715. Died in prison, Manchester.

ARCHIBALD MACDONALD, Officer in Army.

JOHN MACDONALD, Killed at Culloden, 1746.

ALLAN MACDONALD, Out in 1745. Died of wounds.

JOHN MACDONALD, Out in 1745, and the only member of the family who came through that campaign alive.

WILLIAM MACDONALD, Major 37th.

DONALD MACDONALD, C.B., Commanded **92nd** at Waterloo. Died of effects of wounds after years of suffering.

JULIA MACDONALD, Married Captain Alex. MacDonald of Moy.

ALEXANDER MACDONALD, Major 42nd. Served with great distinction in India. Present at Mangalore.

WILLIAM MACDONALD, Major 37th. Died of effects of wounds.

JAMES MACDONALD, **92nd.** Peninsula.

WILLIAM MACDONALD, MACDONALD, 91st Regt., also **92nd.**

ALLAN MACDONALD, **92nd** Regt.

RANALD MACDONALD, **92nd** Regt.

GENERAL SIR JOHN MACDONALD, K.C.B. **92nd.** Lieut.-Col. 1828-1846; Col. of same, 1855-1866. Peninsula, etc.

ALEXANDER MACDONALD, **92nd.** Died of wounds, Maya.

WILLIAM DONALD MACDONALD, MACDONALD, 68th Regt.

GENERAL ALASTAIR MACIAN MACDONALD, **92nd** Regt. Wounded, Crimea. Commanded the forces in Scotland.

JOHN ALAN MACDONALD, **92nd** Regt.

CHARLES MACDONALD, Crimea. 93rd Regt. Killed, Indian Mutiny.

DONALD MACDONALD, 79th Regt. Crimea and Indian Mutiny. Died on parade.

VI

This letter is interesting as showing that Scottish soldiers kept the character ascribed to them by the Belgians in 1815 : " Mild and amiable in peace, but terrible in war." Mr Wood describes Emam Khan, an old Mahomedan soldier who had served under Lord Roberts in Afghanistan, and who "cherishes a wild idea that some day he may serve again ; and as ' all war is much walking,' he walks long distances at regular intervals that he may be ready when the great Chief, who is the servant of the White Queen, calls. He holds that the Gordon Highlanders are the very best regiment in the world. He says his regiment—the 23rd Pioneers—did not think much of them, because they were quiet and gentle in their talk, so they thought them overpraised, for they came with a great reputation. . . . ' We marched to Kandahar town, and when the battle came the hearts of strong men were melted within them, for those we had called soft-voiced and women in secret, because they were gentle, they were angry in the battle, and *arè bhai* ! they were men ! and they got up to the Pathans with the bayonet, and there many died ! '

" Emam cherishes the memory of a soldier named Hamilton, from a place called Imberwori (Inverurie), who taught him many things, how to speak English amongst others, and who was apparently a paladin of very great might."

VII

This letter has often been quoted to support a statement that the kilt formed no part of the ancient Highland dress, but was introduced in later times by an Englishman, a misapprehension arising from not recognising the various senses in which the word *kilt* was used. The Englishman merely cut the kilted plaid in two and used the lower part separated from the upper, which was apt to fall down and inconvenience a working man. This form of the dress was called the *feile-beg* to distinguish it from the full Highland garb, which continued also to be worn for some time. The *shirts* he refers to were of home-made woollen cloth. General Stewart refers to this kilt without pleats as the *fealdag*.

" In answer to your inquiries I do report according to the best of my knowledge and the intelligence of persons of credit and very advanced years,

Author's Note.—Lieutenant George Ross of Cromarty, who retired from the 92nd, 1851, was one of the last Highland gentlemen who could put on the ancient plaid-kilt properly. He was one of many officers of the regiment who constantly wore the kilt in plain clothes for shooting, etc.

Till well on in the 19th century, a prize was given at the Northern Meeting for the man best turned out in the ancient form of the garb of Old Gaul.

that the piece of Highland dress termed in the Gaelic *felie-beg*, and in our Scots *little kilt*, is rather of late than ancient usage. The upper garment of the Highlanders was the tartan or parti-coloured plaid termed in Gaelic *breacan*. When buckled round by a belt, the lower part pleated and the upper loose about the shoulders, the dress was termed in the Gaelic *felie*, and in the Scots *kilt*. It was a cumbersome, unwieldy habit to men at work, and the lower class could not afford the expense of the belted trousers or breeches. They wore short coats, waistcoats, and shirts of as great length as they could afford, and such parts as were not covered by these remained naked to the tying of the garters on their hose.

" About fifty years ago, one Thomas Rawlinson, an Englishman, conducted an ironwork carried on in the countries of Glengarrie and Lochaber ; he had a throng of Highlanders employed in the service, and became very fond of the Highland dress and wore it in the neatest form, which I can aver, as I became personally acquainted with him above forty years ago. He was a man of genius and quick parts, and thought it no great stretch of invention to abridge the dress and make it handy and convenient for his workmen, and accordingly directed the wearing of the lower part, plaited, of what is called the *felie* or *kilt* as above, and the upper part was set aside ; and this piece of dress so modelled as a diminutive of the former was in the Gaelic termed the *felie-beg* (*beg* in that tongue signifies *little*) and in our Scots termed *little kilt*. And it was found so handy and convenient that in the shortest space the use of it became frequent in all the Highland countries and in many of our northern low countries also. . . . The great *felie* or *kilt* was formed of the plaid double or twofold, the *felie-beg* of it single."

VIII

Wages in the Highlands, 1816-1900

Ross-shire, 1816-40.—Farm hands, £5 to £8 a year, bed and board. Gamekeepers, £6 to £10 ; house, grazing for two cows, an allowance of meal, some salt fish, and two hinds for winter use. Labourers, 1s. a day (rose after 1840 to 1s. 6d.). Estate carpenters and masons, 2s. a day ; house, milk, and potato ground. Ghillies (temporary employment), 6s. a week, bed and board.

Ross-shire, 1890-1900.—Farm hands, £18 to £20 a year, with bed and board. Gamekeepers, £45 to £60 a year ; house, croft, grazing for two cows, and followers. Labourers, 2s. 6d. a day (minimum). Ghillies (temporary employment), £1 a week. (Notes from the Flowerdale Estate Books, by Sir Kenneth Mackenzie, Bart. of Gairloch.)

Skye, Inverness-shire, 1850.—Ploughmen, £6 to £8 a year ; bed and board in house. Young shepherds, £5 to £6 a year ; bed and board in house. Lads for general work, £3 to £5 ; bed and board in house. Day labourers, 6s. and 9s. a week. Masons, joiners, carpenters, 3s. to 3s. 6d. a day. Apprentices to above—first year, no money, board, and a suit of clothes ; second and third year, enough to buy clothes and shoes, and board.

SKYE, INVERNESS-SHIRE, 1900.—Ploughmen, £16 to £28 a year ; bed and board. Shepherds, £12 to £20 a year ; bed and board. Lads for general work, £14 to £20 ; bed and board. Labourers, 15s. to 18s. a week (anything special up to 24s.). Masons, joiners, and carpenters, 6s. to 8s. a day. Apprentices to above—first year, 8s. ; second and third year, 12s. to 16s. a week. (From notes by D. MacDonald, Esq., Tormore, late Factor to Lord MacDonald.)

GLENGARRY.—" Labourers' wages have risen at least 33 per cent. in the last forty years. Under-keepers and stalkers had £30 to £35, now £52 a year."—George Malcolm, Esq., Factor, Invergarry, 5th July 1902.

MULL, ARGYLLSHIRE, 1840.—Labourers, 1s. a day. Best ploughmen, £10 a year ; bed and board. Lads, £6 a year ; bed and board. These rates differed little till 1860.

MULL, ARGYLLSHIRE, 1860-65.—Estate carpenter, 10s. a week ; house, croft, and cow's grass, right to cut peats. Gamekeeper, £35 a year ; house and cow's grass, peat, and potato ground. Under-gamekeeper, 11s. a week and bed. Wages rose gradually till 1886, when they were nearly at present rates.

MULL, ARGYLLSHIRE, 1900.—Labourers, 2s. 6d. to 3s. a day. Farm hands, £14 to £20 a year ; bed and board in house. Gamekeepers, £50 to £52 a year ; house, cow's grass, peat, and potato ground. Under-gamekeepers, 17s. to 18s. a week. (From notes by D. MacKinnon, Esq., Tobermory, and Glenforsa Estate Books.)

Labourers working for a contractor in 1860 were paid 9s. to 12s. a week. In the present day they earn from £1 to £1 2s. 6d. In the same period masons' wages have gradually risen from £1 2s. to £2 2s. 6d. a week. Joiners in like proportion. (These rates are from the pay sheets of Mr Donald Fletcher, contractor, Tobermory, and may be taken as representing accurately the wages prevailing all over the Highlands.)

In Forfarshire and the North Lowlands generally a ploughman's wages have risen from £9 to £10 a year in 1850, to £40 to £42 a year in 1900, in each case with meal, milk, and bed in the bothy ; these are valued for insurance under the Employers' Liability Act at £18 5s. a year, making his pay and allowances equal, at the latter rates, to from £1 2s. to fully £1 3s. a week. Estate labourers from 16s. to 18s. a week.

In comparing daily wages in civil life with soldiers' pay, it must be remembered that the former is for six days, often with broken time, the latter for seven, wet and dry, all the year (extra pay being sometimes earned by special employment) ; and that in the days of long service every man was entitled to a pension, as is still the case with those who serve twenty-one years with the colours.

It would appear that the soldiers' pay and prospects compared most favourably with those of the Highland population during the period from about 1800 to 1840, and at the present time (1903) ; worst between about 1880 to 1890.

The pay and allowances of an infantry soldier aged nineteen years who has completed six months' satisfactory training are, in the opinion of working men whom I have consulted, fully of the value of 19s. a week.   After 1st April 1904, each private who has served five years will have an addition of 3s. 6d., or if of good character and a good shot, 4s. 1d. — in all, £1 3s. 1d. weekly.

The allowances are moderately calculated thus :—

		A Week.	
Ration of bread and meat and messing allowance of 3d. daily, bed, fire, and light,	£0	9	0
He is clothed from head to foot, and all necessary articles, from a greatcoat to a toothbrush, from a Bible to a box of blacking, are given him free.			
His clothing and shoes are renewed at regular periods. With these a civilian could hardly supply himself for £7 16s. a year, or	0	3	0
Cash at 1s. 7d. a day (not including the 3d. messing allowance),	0	11	1
TOTAL	£1	3	1

Besides the messing allowance of 3d. there is also a daily allowance of 2d. for upkeep or repair of clothing.

The allowances to sergeants are really more valuable, but calculating them at only the same rate as for privates—

		A Week.	
A corporal would have the value of	£1	7	9
Sergeant	1	12	5
Colour-sergeant	1	17	1
Quartermaster-sergeant	2	4	1
Sergeant-major	2	11	1
With pension after twenty-one years, rising in proportion to rank and service.			

IX

POPULATION OF THE HIGHLANDS, EXCLUSIVE OF BUTE AND THE COUNTIES WHICH ARE ONLY PARTIALLY HIGHLAND

	1801.	1851.	1901.
Caithness,	22,609	38,709	33,859
Sutherland,	23,117	25,246	21,550
Ross and Cromarty,	56,318	82,707	76,421
Inverness,	72,672	96,500	90,182
Nairn,	8,322	9,217	9,291
Argyll,	81,277	89,298	73,665
	264,315	341,677	304,968

or a net increase of 40,653 since 1801.

X
COLONELS OF THE REGIMENT

75TH REGIMENT

12.10.1787.	Gen. Sir R. Abercromby.
10.11.1827.	Lt.-Gen. J. Dunlop.
9. 4.1832.	„ Sir J. Fuller.
26.10.1841.	Gen. Sir W. Hutchinson.
16. 9.1845.	Maj.-Gen. S. H. Berkeley.
22. 3.1858.	„ Sir J. A. Clerke.
18. 1.1870.	„ D. Russell.
24.10.1872.	Lt.-Gen. J. T. Hill.

92ND REGIMENT

3.5.1796.	George, Marquis of Huntly.
3.1.1806.	Lt.-Gen. Hon. Sir John Hope.
29.1.1820.	Lt.-Gen. John Hope.
6.9.1823.	„ Hon. Alex. Duff.
20.7.1831.	„ Sir J. Hamilton Dalrymple.
31.5.1843.	„ Sir W. Macbean
20.6.1855.	„ Sir John Mac-Donald.
25.6.1866.	F.-M. Rt. Hon. Hugh, Lord Strathnairn.
3.3.1869.	Lt.-Gen. J. Campbell.
29.12.1871.	„ G. Staunton.
16.4.1880.	Gen. M. Kerr Atherley.

THE GORDON HIGHLANDERS

1.7.1881.	Lt.-Gen. J. T. Hill. ⎫ Joint.
12.3.1884.	Gen. J. A. Ewart. ⎭
30.6.1895.	Lt.-Gen. C. E. P. Gordon.
20.8.1897.	Gen. Sir G. S. White.

LIEUTENANT-COLONELS OF THE REGULAR BATTALIONS

1ST BATTALION

24.10.1787.	J. Hartley.
1. 9.1795.	G. V. Hart.
16. 1.1806.	S. Swinton.
12.10.1815.	P. Ross.
23. 4.1824.	Viscount Barnard.
6. 7.1826.	R. England.
7. 7.1837.	P. Grieve.
12.12.1843.	R. D. Hallifax.
1 6.1849.	A. Jardine.
7.12.1858.	W. Radcliff.
9.12.1864.	C. E. P. Gordon.
14.10.1868.	T. Miles.
18.12.1875.	R. Wadeson.
18.12.1880.	D. Hammill.
13. 2.1885.	F. F. Daniell.
1. 7.1887.	J. E. Boyes.
14. 2.1891.	T. S. Gildea.
14. 2.1895.	H. H. Mathias.

2ND BATTALION

10. 2.1794.	George, Marquis of Huntly.
1. 5.1796.	C. Erskine of Cardross.
5. 4.1801.	A. Napier of Blackstone.
23. 6.1808.	J. Cameron of Fassiefern.
18. 6.1815.	J. Mitchell.
2. 9.1819.	Sir F. Stovin.
4.10.1821.	D. Williamson.
21.11.1828.	J. MacDonald of Dalchosnie.
9.11.1846.	J. A. Forbes.
23.11.1849.	M. K. Atherley.
26.12.1857.	A. I. Lockhart.
1. 9.1865.	C. M. Hamilton.
15.12.1869.	F. Macbean.
24.12.1873.	A. W. Cameron of Inverailort.
28.10.1876.	G. H. Parker.
1. 7.1881.	G. S. White.
10.10.1885.	J. C. Hay.
1. 7.1887.	E. Essex.
1. 7.1891.	R. D. Oxley.
1. 7.1895.	Hon. J. S. Napier.
12. 2.1897.	W. H. Dick-Cunyngham.

INDEX

Printed in Great Britain
by Amazon